AN INTRODUCTION TO THE POPULAR RELIGION AND FOLK LORE OF NORTHERN INDIA

An Introduction to the Popular Religion and Folklore of Northern India

W. Crooke

LOW PRICE PUBLICATIONS
Delhi-110052

int. to popular religion and floklore of n india 2nd page

Distributed by
D.K. Publishers Distributors (P) Ltd.
4834/24, Ansari Road, Darya Ganj,
New Delhi-110002
Phones: 23278584, 23278368, 23261465
e-mail: dkpd@del3.vsnl.net.in
url: www.dkpd.com

First Published 1894

Reprinted in LPP 2003

ISBN 81-7536-312-6

Published by
Low Price Publications
A-6, Nimri Commercial Centre,
Near Ashok Vihar Phase-IV,
Delhi-110052
Phones: 27401672, 27452453
e-mail: lpp@nde.vsnl.net.in
url: www.lppindia.com

Printed at
D K Fine Art Press P Ltd.
Delhi-110052

PRINTED IN INDIA

AN INTRODUCTION

TO THE

POPULAR RELIGION AND FOLKLORE

OF

NORTHERN INDIA.

By W. CROOKE, B.A.,

BENGAL CIVIL SERVICE.

HONORARY DIRECTOR OF THE ETHNOGRAPHICAL SURVEY, NORTH-WESTERN PROVINCES AND OUDH.

ALLAHABAD:

Printed at the Government Press, North-Western Provinces and Oudh.

1894.

ERRATA.

Page 5, line 7, *for* "(Súryamahál)" *read* "(Súryamahal)."

" 9, line 11, *for* "moou" *read* "moon."

" 11, bottom line of foot-note, *for* "Brehat" *read* "Brihat."

" 48, line 28, *for* "Linga" *read* "Lingas."

" 50, line 7, *for* "Bhadrináth" *read* "Badrinath."

" 69, line 21, *for* "(Ardhanari)" *read* "(Ardhanári)."

" 69, bottom line of foot-note, *for* "Letournean" *read* "Letourneau."

" 70, first line of foot-note, *for* "Moiner" *read* "Monier."

" 70, third line of foot-note, *omit* the colon after "Náráyaní."

" 71, line 28, *for* "woship" *read* "worship."

" 83, line 7, *for* "persons" *read* "person."

" 83, line 16, *for* "dustis" *read* "dust is."

" 88, line 30, *for* "Kanjávatí" *read* "Kunjávatí."

" 94, fifth line of foot-note, *for* "Lubboch" *read* "Lubbock."

" 97, line 12, *for* "Insense" *read* "Incense."

" 103, line 17, *for* "lessens" *read* "learns."

" 139, first line of foot-note, *for* "Mr. Mírs" *read* "Mrs. Mír."

" 142, line 9, *for* "*tomentosa*" read "*tormentosa*."

" 145, line 13, *for* "Synonomous" *read* "Synonymous."

" 151, line 15, *for* "Enmœus" *read* "Eumœus."

" 174, line 22, *for* "Funcreosque" *read* "Funereosque."

" 187, fourth line, from bottom *for* "hat" *read* "that."

" 187, third " " " *for* "tafflicted" *read* "afflicted."

" 187, bottom line *for* "gilrs" *read* "girls."

" 197, in side note *read* "Incense."

" 204, in side note *read* "tattoo."

" 213, *number* the foot-notes "1" "2" "3" "4" consecutively.

" 222, *number* the foot-note "2" on fifth line.

" 243, line 20, *for* "Khiddo" *read* "Kluddo."

" 272, *number* the bottom foot-note "5."

" 282, line 2, *for* "Smith" *read* "Smith.[1]"

" 282, line 14, *for* "goat[1]" *read* "goat.[2]"

" 283, in side note, *for* "Davidians" *read* "Dravidians."

" 287, line 8, *for* "Dewak" *read* "Devak."

" 350, line 34, *for* "Bhirava" *read* "Bhairava."

" 354, line 14, *for* "atiger" *read* "a tiger."

" 354, line 22, *for* "wherc" *read* "where."

" 373, second in side note, *for* "Javi" *read* "Jayi."

" 387, line 32, *for* "Dundhás" *read* "Dundhá."

round the chief idol, and like his kindred, rules the weather: the Nâg Kuân or dragon well is one of the oldest shrines in the city.[1] Among these serpent gods we have actual deified snakes like Vâsuki and Sesha Nâga, as well as heroes raised to the heaven in connection with snakes. Vâsuki or Bâsuki Nâg has many temples, and in all of them, as in his shrine at Dârâganj near Allahabad, the priest in charge is always a man of low caste,—a fact pointing to the non-Aryan character of his worship. Vâsuki often appears in the folk-tales. We find him resisting Garuda, the destroyer of his subjects. His brother's son, Kirtisena, according to the legend, [illegible] Brahman and weds a devoted maiden by the Gandharva form; his eldest brother Vasunemi presents a benevolent Savara with a magic lute; Vâsuki himself marries the princess Yasodhara, and their son is Priyadarsana. Vâsuki himself has a thousand eyes and a thousand ears. Once he served the gods by becoming the rope with which Mount Mandara was whirled round and the sea was churned and produced Sri or Lakshmi.[2] The foot of the celebrated iron pillar at Delhi was driven so deep that it was supposed to rest on the head of Vâsuki. A Brahman told the king that this would ensure the stability of his kingdom. The Râja doubted this and had the pillar dug up, when the base was found wet with the blood of the serpent king. Owing to this incredulity of the Râja it could never again be firmly fixed, and his want of faith led to the ultimate ruin of his dynasty.

The Sidhas, snake gods.

Next come the Sidhas or snake gods of the Panjab and western part of the North-Western Provinces. They are males, and though they cause fever they are not very malevolent, often taking away pain. They have got great power over cattle, and the milk of the eleventh day after calving is sacred to them, and libations of milk (as in the case of the Bhûmiya) are always acceptable. They are generally distinguished by some colour, the most commonly

[1] Sherring, *Sacred City*, 78, 87 [illegible]

[2] [illegible] *Kathâ Sarit Sâgara*, [illegible]

CONTENTS

PREFACE.

Many books have been written on Bráhmanism, or the official religion of the Hindus; but, as far as I am aware, this is the first attempt to bring together some of the information available on the popular beliefs of the races of Northern India.

My object in writing this book has been threefold. In the first place, I desired to collect, for the use of all officers whose work lies among the rural classes, some information on the beliefs of the poeple which will enable them, in some degree, to understand the mysterious inner life of the races among whom their lot is cast; secondly, it may be hoped that this introductory sketch will stimulate enquiry, particularly among the educated natives of the country, who have as yet done little to enable Europeans to gain a fuller and more sympathetic knowledge of their rural brethern; and lastly, while I have endeavoured more to collect facts than to theorize upon them, I hope that European scholars may find in these pages some fresh examples of familiar principles. My difficulty has arisen not so much from deficiency of material as in the selection and arrangement of the mass of information which lies scattered through a considerable literature, much of which is fugitive.

I believe that the more we explore these popular superstitions and usages, the nearer are we likely to attain to the discovery of the basis on which Hinduism has been founded. The official creed has always been characterised by extreme catholicism and receptivity, and many of its principles and legends have undoubtedly been derived from that stratum of the people which it is convenient to call non-Aryan or Drávidian. The necessity, then, of investigating these beliefs before they become absorbed in Bráhmanism, one of the most active missionary religions of the world, is obvious.

I may say that the materials of this book were practically complete before I was able to use Mr. J. S. Campbell's valuable collection of "*Notes on the spirit basis of belief and custom*:" but in revising the manuscript I have availed myself to some extent of this useful collection, and when I have done so I have been careful to acknowledge my obligations to it. Even at the risk of over-loading the notes with references, I have quoted the authorities which I have used, and I have added a Bibliography which may be of use to students to whom the subject is unfamiliar.

The only excuse I can plead for the obvious imperfections of this hasty survey of a very wide subject is that it has been written in the intervals of the scanty leisure of a District Officer's life in India, and often at a distance from works of reference and libraries.

MIRZAPUR, W. CROOKE.

February 1893.

CHAPTER I.

THE GODLINGS OF NATURE.

Ἐν μὲν γαῖαν ἔτευξ', ἐν δ' οὐρανὸν, ἐν δὲ θάλασσαν,
Ἠέλιόν τ' ἀκάμαντα σελήνην τε πλήθουσαν,
Ἐν δὲ τὰ τείρεα πάντα, τά τ' οὐρανὸς ἐστεφάνωται,
Πληιάδας θ' Ὑάδας τε, τό τε σθένος Ὠρίωνος,
Ἄρκτον θ', ἣν καὶ ἅμαξαν ἐπίκλησιν καλέουσιν,
Ἥ τ' αὐτοῦ στρέφεται καί τ' Ὠρίωνα δοκεύει,
Οἴη δ' ἄμμορός ἐστι λοετρῶν Ὠκεανοῖο.

ILIAD, xviii, 483–88.

The Deva and the Devata.

THE general term for the great gods of Hinduism, the supreme triad—Bráhma, Vishnu and Siva—and other deities of the higher class which collectively constitute the Hindu official pantheon is Deva or "the shining ones." With these supremely powerful deities we have now little concern. They are the deities of the richer or higher classes, and to the ordinary peasant of Northern India these great gods are little more than a name. He will, it is true, occasionally bow at their shrines: he will pour some water or lay some flowers on the images or fetish stones which are the special resting places of these divinities or represent the productive powers of nature. But from time immemorial, when Bráhmanisim had as yet not succeeded in occupying the land, his allegiance was bestowed on a class of deities of a much lower and more primitive kind. Their inferiority in rank to the greater gods is marked in their title. They are called Devata or "godlings," not "gods."

Godlings pure and impure.

These godlings have been conveniently classified by Mr. Ibbetson into "the pure" and "the impure." To the former the offerings are such as are pure food to the Hindu—cakes of wheaten flour, and in particular those which have been still further purified by intermixture with clarified butter (*ghí*), the most valued product of the sacred cow. Such offerings are usually made on a Sunday, and they are taken by Bráhmans. "Of course the line cannot always be drawn with precision, and Bráhmans will often consent to be fed in the name of a deity, while they will not take offerings made at his shrine, or will allow their girls, but not their boys, to accept the offering, as, if the girls die in consequence, it does not much matter.[1]" The deities of this class are usually benevolent, and most of them are, in a somewhat modified form, survivals of the primitive nature gods of the earlier Aryan faith. But, as we shall see, their worship has been to some extent degraded by the influence of association with godlings of the impure description, who will be separately considered.

Súraj Devata, the Sun-god.

The first and greatest of the pure godlings is Súrya or Súraj Devata, the sun-godling.[2] He was one of the great deities of the Vedic pantheon: he is called Prajapati or "lord of creatures;" he was the son of Dyaus, or the bright sky. Ushas, the Dawn, was his wife; and he moves through the heavens drawn by seven ruddy mares. His worship was perhaps originally connected with that of fire, but it is easy to understand how, under a tropical sky, the Indian peasant came to look on him as the lord of life and death; the bringer of plenty or of famine. He is now, however, like Helios in the Homeric mythology, looked on as only a godling, not a god, or even as a hero who had once lived and reigned on earth. As far as the village worship goes, the assertion that no shrine is erected in his honour is correct enough: and there is no doubt that images of Surya and Aditya are comparatively rare in recent epochs. But there are many noted temples in his name at Taxila, Gwalior, Gaya, Multán and Jaypur,[3] and his shrine at Kanárak in Orissa near that of Jagganáth is described as one of the most exquisite memorials of sun-worship in existence.[4] Mr. Bendall recently

---

[1] Ibbetson, *Panjáb Ethnography*, page 113.

[2] For sun-worship generally see Tylor, *Primitive Culture*, II, 285 *sqq.*: Farrer, *Primitive Manners and Customs*, 295 *sq.* The special development of sun and moon-worship among the Rájputs is discussed by Tod, *Annals*, I, 565 *sqq.* 596; *sq.*

[3] Cunningham, *Archæological Reports*, II, 114, 342, 353; III, 110, 112; XIII, 63: *Rájputána Gazetteer*, II, 160.

[4] Hunter, *Orissa*, I, 188: Jarrett, *Aín-i-Akbári*, II, 128.

found in Nepál an image dedicated to him as late as the 11th century.[1] There is a small shrine in his honour close to the Annapurna temple in Benares, where the god is represented seated in a chariot drawn by seven horses, and is worshipped with the fire sacrifice (*homa*) in a building detached from the temple.[2]

Special worship of Súrya.

In the time of Sankara Ácháryá (A. D. 1000) there were six distinct sects of sun-worshippers—one worshipped the rising sun as identified with Bráhma: the second the meridian sun as Siva: the third the setting sun as Vishnu: the fourth the sun in all these places as Trimurti: the fifth class of worshippers of the sun regarded him as a material being in the form of a man with a golden beard and golden hair. Zealous members of this sect refused to eat anything in the morning till they had seen the sun rise: the sixth class worshipped an image of the sun formed in their mind. They were in the habit of branding circular representations of his disc on their forehead, arms and breast.[3] The Saura sect worship Súryapati as their special god. They wear a crystal necklace in his honour, abstain from eating salt on Sundays and on the days when the sun enters a sign of the zodiac.[4] They make the frontal mark with red sandars and now-a-days have their headquarters in Oudh. Another sect of Vaishnavas, the Nimbárak, worship the sun in a modified form: their name means "the sun in a *Ním tree*" (*Azadirachta Indica*). The story runs that the founder of the sect, an ascetic named Bháskárácharya, had invited a Bairági to dine with him and had arranged everything for his reception, but unfortunately delayed to call his guest till after sunset. The holy man was forbidden by the rules of his order to eat except in the day time, and was afraid that he would be compelled to practise an unwilling abstinence, but at the solicitation of his host the Sun-god, Súraj Náráyan, descended on the tree (a *ním*) under which the feast was

---

[1] *Asiatic Quarterly Review*, II, 236

[2] Sherring, *Sacred City of the Hindus*, 59, 127: Bholanáth Chandra, *Travels of a Hindu*, II, 384.

[3] Monier Williams, *Religious Thought and Life*, 343, quoted by Campbell, *Notes*, 319 *sq*.

[4] Wilson, *Essays*, II, 384.

spread and continued beaming on them until dinner was over.[1] In this we observe an approximation to the Jaina rule by which it is forbidden to eat after sunset lest insects may enter the mouth and be destroyed. This overstrained respect for animal life is one of the main features of the creed.[2] The great Akbár endeavoured to introduce a special form of Sun-worship. He ordered that it was to be worshipped four times a day, in the morning, noon, evening and midnight. "His Majesty had also one thousand and one Sanskrit names of the sun collected and read them daily, devoutly turning to the sun. He then used to get hold of both ears, and turning himself quickly round, used to strike the lower ends of his ears with his fists." He ordered his band to play at midnight, and at break of day, and used to be weighed against gold on his solar anniversary.[3]

Village worship of the sun.

The village worship of Súraj Náráyan is quite distinct from this. Many peasants in Upper India do not eat salt on Sundays and do not set their milk for butter but make rice-milk of it and give a portion to Bráhmans. Bráhmans are sometimes fed in his honour at harvests, and the pious householder bows to him as he leaves the house in the morning. His more learned brethren repeat the Gáyatri—"*Tat Savitur varenyam bhargo devasya dhimahi; dhiyo yo nah pracodayát*, May we receive the glorious brightness of this, the generator, the God who shall prosper our works." In the chilly mornings of the cold weather you will hear the sleepy coolies as they wake, yawning and muttering "Súraj Náráyan" as the yellow gleam of dawn spreads over the eastern sky. In fact, even in Vedic times there seems to have been a local worship of Súrya connected with some primitive folklore. Haradatta mentions as one of the customs not sanctioned in the Veda, that when the sun is in Aries the young girls would paint the sun with his retinue on the soil in coloured dust, and worship this in the morning and

[1] Growse, *Mathura*, 180: The story of Joshua (X. 12-14) is an obvious parallel.
[2] On this see Burgess, *Indian Antiquary*, II, 14 *sqq.*: Ibbetson, *Panjáb Ethnography*, 131.
[3] Blochmann, *Aín-i-Akbári*, I, 200, 266.

evening; and in Central India the sun was in the Middle Ages worshipped under the local form of Bháilla or "Lord of life."—a term which appears to have originated the name of Bhilsa, known in more recent times as a famous seat of Buddhism.[1] At Udaypur in Rájputána the sun has universal precedence. His portal (*Súryapul*) is the chief entrance to the city: his name gives dignity to the chief apartment or hall (*Súryamahál*) of the palace, and from the balcony of the sun (*Súryagokhru*), the descendant of Ráma, shows himself in the dark monsoon as the Sun's representative. A huge painted sun of gypsum in high relief with gilded rays adorns the hall of audience, and in front of it is the throne. The sacred standard bears his image, as does the disc (*changi*) of black felt or ostrich feathers with a plate of gold in its centre to represent the sun, borne aloft on a pole. The royal parasol is called *kirariya* in allusion to its shape, like a ray (*kiran*) of the orb.[2]

Sun-worship among non-Aryan races.

In the lower ranges of the Himálayas, sun-worship is conducted in the months of December and January and when eclipses occur. The principal observances are the eating of a meal without salt at each passage of the sun into a new sign of the zodiac, and eating meals on other days only when the sun has risen. Among the Drávidian races along the Vindhyan and Kaimúr ranges sun-worship prevails widely. When in great affliction the Kharwárs appeal to the sun. Any open place on which he shines may be his altar. The Kisáns offer a white cock to him when a sacrifice is needed. He is worshipped by the Bhuiyas and Oráons as Borám or Dharm devata, "the godling of piety," and is propitiated in the sowing season by the sacrifice of a white cock. The Korwas worship him as Bhagwán or "the only God" in an open space with an anthill as an altar. The Kharias adore him under the name of Bero. "Every head of a family should, during his lifetime, make not less than five sacrifices to this deity—the first of fowls, the second of a pig,

[1] Max Müller, *Ancient Sanskrit Literature*, 53, Note: Hall, *Vishnu Purána*, II, 150: *Journal, Asiatic Society, Bengal*, 1862, p. 112.

[2] Tod, *Annals*, I, 597.

the third of a white goat, the fourth of a ram, and the fifth of a buffalo. He is then considered sufficiently propitiated for that generation, and regarded as an ungrateful god if he does not behave handsomely to his votary." He is addressed as Parameswar or "great god," and his sacrifices are always made in front of an anthill which is used as an altar. The Kols worship Sing Bonga, the creator and preserver, as the sun. Prayer and sacrifice are made to him as to a beneficent divinity who has no pleasure in the destruction of any of his subjects, though, as a father, he chastises his erring children, who owe him gratitude for all the blessings they enjoy. He is said to have married Chandu Omal, or the moon: she deceived him on one occasion and he cut her in two; but, repenting of his anger, he allows her to be restored to her original shape once a month when she shines in her full beauty. The Oráons address the sun as Dharmi or the "holy one"[1] and do not regard him as the author of sickness or calamity: but he may be invoked to avert it, and this appeal is often made when the sacrifices to minor deities have been unproductive. He is the tribal god of the Korkus of Hoshangábád: they do not, however, offer libations to him as Hindus do: but once in three years the head of each family, on some Sunday in April or May, offers outside the village a white she-goat and a white fowl, turning his face to the east during the sacrifice. Similarly the Kúrs of the Central Provinces carve rude representations of the sun and moon on wooden pillars, which they worship near their villages.[2]

Sun-worship in the domestic retual.

Traces of sun-worship are common in the current domestic ritual. The bride and bridegroom are made to revolve round the sacred fire or central pole of the marriage shed in the course of the sun: the pilgrim makes his solemn perambulation (*parikrama*), round a temple or shrine in the same way: in this direction the cattle move round the stake as they tread out the grain. This custom prevails all the world over.

---

[1] Dharmarája was the title of the censor appointed by Asoka. It is also a term applied to Yudhishthira and Yama.

[2] Dalton, *Descriptive Ethnology*, 130, 132, 133, 141, 157, 159, 186, 233: Elliott, *Hoshangabad Settlement Report*, 255: Hislop, *Papers*, 26.

Even to this day in the Hebrides animals are led round a sick person following the sun: and in the Highlands it is the custom "to make the deazil," or walk three times in the sun's course round those whom they wish well. We follow the same rule in passing the decanters round our own dinner tables. [1] The mystical emblem of the Swástika, which appears to represent the sun in his journey through the heavens, is of constant occurrence. The trader paints it on the fly-leaf of his ledger: the man who has young children or animals liable to the Evil Eye makes a representation of it on the wall beside his doorpost. It holds the first place among the lucky marks of the Jainas. It is drawn on the shaven heads of children on the marriage day in Gujarát. A red circle with a Swástika in the centre is depicted on the place where the family gods are kept.[2] In the Meerut Division the worshipper of the village god Bhúmiya constructs a rude model of it on the shrine by fixing up two crossed straws with a daub of plaster. It often occurs in folklore. In the drama of "The Toy Cart" the thief hesitates whether he shall make the hole in the wall of Chárudattá's house in the form of a Swástika or of a waterjar.[3]

Moon-worship.

The fate of Chandra or Soma, the moon god, who has also become a godling, is very similar.[4] In Vedic times he was the impersonation of the holy Soma (*asclepias acida*), one of the many plants which, like the *mahua* and the cocoa palm, owe most of their honour to their intoxicating properties. One of the legends current among the Kols to account for the changes of the moon has been already noticed. According to another story, Soma married the twenty-seven asterisms, the daughters of the Rishi Daksha:[5] but his attentions to one of

---

[1] Gordon Cumming, *From the Hebrides to the Himalayas*, II, 164: Henderson, *Folklore of the Northern Counties*, 61. Tawney, *Katha Sarit Ságara*, I, 98, 573.

[2] Campbell, *Notes*, 70.

[3] Manning, *Ancient India*, II,160: for a full discussion of the Swástika see Thomas in *Indian Antiquary*, IX, 65 *sqq.*; 135 *sqq.*

[4] On the worship of the moon by the Rájputs see Tod, *Annals*, I,565 *sqq.*: on moon worship generally, Farrer, *Primitive Manners and Customs*, 74 *sqq.*

[5] For Daksha see the preface to the *Gopatha Bráhmana*—(*Bibliotheca Indica*, Nos. 215, 252; preface, 30, 35.

them, Rohiní, aroused the jealousy of the others and his angry father-in-law cursed the moon god with childlessness and consumption. His wives, in pity, interceded for him, but the curse could not be wholly removed; and all that was possible was to modify it so that the decay should be periodical, not permanent. Hence the wane and increase of the moon. Another explanation is current in Bombay. One evening Ganesa fell off his steed, the mouse, and the moon laughed at his misfortune. To punish him the angry god vowed that no one should ever look at the moon again. The moon prayed for forgiveness, and the god agreed that the moon should be disgraced only on the god's birth-day the *Ganesa Chaturthí*. On this night the wild hogs hide themselves that they may not see the moon, and the Kunbis hunt them down and kill them.[1] There are also many explanations to account for the spots on the moon. According to one account the moon became enamoured of Ahalyá, the wife of the Rishi Gautama, and visited her in the absence of her husband. He returned and, finding the guilty pair together, cursed his wife, who was turned into a stone: then he threw his shoe at the moon, which struck him and left a black mark, which exists even to this day. In Oudh, little children are taught to call the moon *mámú* or maternal uncle, and the dark spots are said to represent an old woman who sits there working her spinning wheel. The halo round the moon is the light shed from the council of the gods who sit there and settle the affairs of the world. If they sit round the sun the halo brings abundant rain. When they sit round the moon it portends a drought and famine. The moon-god now fails to receive the honour of a temple, but the occurrence of his phases largely influences the domestic ritual. The Code of Manu[2] directed that ceremonies were to be performed at the conjunction and opposition of the moon, but now-a-days the observance is generally restricted to bathing at the full moon, which, as Ewald[3] remarks, is suited for national celebrations, while the new moon is prescribed for ceremonies of a domestic character. There seems, indeed, some reason to believe

[1] *Bombay Gazetteer*, XXII., 93.
[2] *Institutes*, VI, 9: Wilson, *Vishnu Purána*, 145, 275, *Note*.
[3] *Antiquities of Israel*, 349, *sq*.

that the observance of the lunar month marks in India, as elsewhere, the nomadic stage when journeys were undertaken at night.[1] Like rustic Phidyle—

Cœlo supinas si tuleris manus,
Nascente Luna rustica Phidyle,[2]

or the Yorkshire maids of whom Aubrey speaks who "doe worship the new moon on their bare knees, kneeling upon an earth-fast stone," or Irish girls who on first seeing the new moon fall on their knees and address her in a loud voice with the prayer "O moon! leave us as well as thou hast found us."[3] Hindus at the first sight of the new moou hold one end of their turbans in their hands, take from it seven threads, present them to the moon with a prayer, and then exchange the compliments of the season. On the full moon of April and May the houses of the pious are freely plastered with a mixture of earth and cowdung, and no animal is yoked. Whoever looks at the new moon of *Bhádon* (August) will be the victim of false accusations during the ensuing year. The only way to avoid this is to perform a sort of penance by getting some one to shy brickbats at your house, which at other times is regarded as an extreme form of insult and degradation. There is a regular festival held for this purpose at Benares on the fourth day of *Bhádon* (August), which is known as the *Dhela chauth mela* or "the clod festival of the fourth."[4] Much of this respect for the moon is due to the belief that it is regarded as the abode of the *pitri* or sainted dead, a theory which is the common property of many primitive races.[5] Moon-worship, again, was popular among the Buddhists.[6] At the new moon the monks bathed and shaved each other; and at a special service the duties of a monk were recited. On full moon days they dined at the houses of laymen. On that night a platform was raised in the preaching hall. The

[1] Goldziher, *Mythology among the Hebrews*, 63.
[2] Horace, *Od.* III, 23,1,2: and compare *Job*, XXXI, 26,27: *Psalms*, LXXXI, 3.
[3] Lady Wilde, *Legends*, 205, *sq.*
[4] Sherring, *Sacred City*, 221: *Panjáb Notes and Queries*, II, 42.
[5] *Folklore*, II, 221: Monier Williams, *Religious Life and Thought*, 343.
[6] Hardy, *Eastern Monachism*, 149.

superior brethren chanted the law and the people greeted the name of Buddha with shouts of *Sádhu* or "the holy one."

Eclipses and the fire-sacrifice.

Hindus, like other primitive races, have their eclipse demons.[1] Ráhu, whose name means "the looser" or "the seizer," was one of the *Asuras* or demons. When the gods produced the *amrita* or nectar from the churned ocean, he disguised himself like one of them and drank a portion of it. The sun and the moon detected his fraud and informed Vishnu, who severed the head and two of the arms of Ráhu from the trunk: the portion of the nectar which he had drunk secured his immortality, the head and tail were transferred to the solar sphere, the head wreaking his vengeance on the sun and moon by occasionally swallowing them, while the tail, under the name of Ketu, gave birth to a numerous progeny of comets and fiery meteors. By another legend Ketu was turned into the demon Sainhikeya and the Arunáh Ketavah or "Red apparitions," which often appear in the older Indian folklore. Ketu now a days is only a vague demon of disease and Ráhu too has suffered a grievous degradation. He is now the special godling of the Dusádhs and Dhángars, two menial tribes found in the eastern districts of the North-Western Provinces. His worship is a kind of fire-sacrifice—a ditch seven cubits long and one and a quarter cubits broad (both numbers of mystical significance) is dug and filled with burning faggots, which are allowed to smoulder into cinders. One of the tribal priests, in a state of religious afflatus, walks through the fire into which some oil or butter is poured to make a sudden blaze. It is said that the sacred fire is harmless; but some admit that a certain preservative ointment is used by the performers. The worshippers insist on the priest coming into actual contact with the flames, and a case occurred some years ago in Gorakhpur when one of the priests was degraded on account of his perfunctory discharge of this sacred duty. The same rule applies to the priest who performs the ritual at the Holí ceremony. In connection with this they have another

[1] Tylor, *Early History*, 163; *Primitive Culture*, I, 328: Lubbock, *Origin of Civilisation*, 229.

function in which a ladder is made of wooden sword blades, up which the priest is compelled to climb, resting the soles of his feet on the edges of the weapons. When he reaches the top he decapitates a white cock which is tied on the summit. This sacrifice is, as we have already seen, one of the means of propitiating the sun-god. Bráhmans so far join in this low-caste worship as to perform the fire-sacrifice (*homa*), near the trench where the ceremony is being performed. In Mirzapur one of the songs recited on this occasion runs—"O Devotee! how many cubits long is the trench which thou hast dug? How many maunds of butter hast thou poured upon it, that the fire billows rise in the air? Seven cubits long is the trench: seven maunds of firewood hast thou placed within it. One and a-quarter maunds of butter hast thou poured into the trench that the fire billows rise to the sky!" All this is based on the idea that fire is a scarer of demons, a theory which widely prevails. The Romans made their flocks and herds pass through fire over which they leaped themselves. In Ireland, when the St. John's Eve fire has burned low "the young men strip to the waist and leap over or through the flames, and he who braves the greatest blaze is considered the victor over the powers of Evil."[1] By a curious process of anthropomorphism, another legend makes Ráh or Ráhu, the Dusádh godling, to have been not an eclipse demon, but the ghost of an ancient leader of the clan who was killed in battle.[2] A still grosser theory of eclipses is found in the belief held by the Ghasiyas of Mirzapur that the sun and moon once borrowed money from some of the Dom tribe and did not pay it back. Now a Dom occasionally devours them and vomits them up again when the eclipse is over.

Eclipse observances.

"Eclipses usually portend or cause grief: but if ruin without unusual symptoms fall within a week after the eclipse, all baneful influences come to nought."[3] Among high-caste Hindus no food which has remained

---

[1] Ovid, *Fasti*, IV, 728: Lady Wilde, *Legends*, 113: *Folklore*, II, 128: Dalton, *Descriptive Ethnology*, 326: *Indian Antiquary*, II, 90; III, 6, 8; VII, 126 *sqq*: Wilson, *Essays*, s.v. *Holi*: *Leviticus*, XVIII, 21; II *Kings*, XXIII, 10: Herklot, *Qánun-i-Islám*, s.v. *Muharram*.

[2] Cunningham, *Archæological Reports*, XVI, 28.

[3] *Brehat Sanhita*: Manning, *Ancient India*, I, 371.

in the house during an eclipse of the sun or moon can be eaten it must be given away, and all earthen vessels in use in the house at the time must be broken. Mr. Conway[1] takes this to mean that "the eclipse was to have his attention called by outcries and prayers to the fact that if it was fire he needed there was plenty on earth: and if food, he might have all in the house, provided he would consent to satisfy his appetite with articles of food less important than the luminaries of heaven." The observance is more probably based on the idea of ceremonial pollution caused by the actual working of demoniacal agency. The bathing in sacred streams and the recital of appropriate formulas (*mantra*) are intended to be a kind of expiation with the object of releasing the planet from the attacks of the demon. Confectioners who are obliged to keep large quantities of cooked food ready, relieve themselves from the taboo by keeping some of the sacred *kusa* or *dúb* grass in their vessels when an eclipse is expected. In Bombay[2] a pregnant woman will do no work during an eclipse, as otherwise she believes that her child would be deformed, and the deformity is supposed to bear some analogy to the work she does. Thus, if she were to sew anything, the baby would have a hole in its flesh, generally near the ear: if she cut anything the child would have a cut on its body usually near the lip. On the same principle in Upper India the horns of pregnant cattle are smeared with red paint during an eclipse, because red is a colour abhorred by demons.[3] No respectable Hindu will sleep, sit or lie on a bedstead during this time, and he will give alms to the poor, because this is supposed to relieve the pain which the sun or moon endures while being swallowed. In Ladakh[4] rams' horns are fixed in the stems of fruit trees as a propitiatory offering at the time of an eclipse, and trees thus honored are believed to bear an unfailing crop of the choicest fruit. Among Muhammadans[5]

1 *Demonology*, I, 45.
2 *Panjáb Notes and Queries*, II, 78.
3 *Ibid*, II, 94: Campbell, *Notes*, 64 *sqq*.
4 *North Indian Notes and Queries*, I, 38. For offerings during an eclipse see *Katha Sarit Ságara*, I, 532.
5 Mrs. Mir Hasan Ali, *Observations*, I, 297 *sq*.

a bride elect sends offerings of intercession (*sadqa*) to her intended husband, accompanied by a goat or kid which must be tied to the leg of his bedstead during the continuance of the eclipse. These offerings are afterwards distributed in charity. Women expecting to be mothers are carefully kept awake, as they declare that the infant's security depends on the mother being kept from sleep: they are not allowed to use a needle, scissors, knife or any other instrument for fear of drawing blood which, at that time, would be injurious both to mother and child. The Hindu custom of bathing on such occasions has been already mentioned. At an eclipse of the moon it is expedient to bathe at Benares, and when the sun is eclipsed at Kurukshetra. Bernier [1] gives a very curious account of the bathing which he witnessed at Delhi during the great eclipse of 1666. In the lower Himalayas the current ritual prescribes an elaborate ceremony, when numerous articles are placed in the sacred water jar: the image of the snake-god stamped on silver is worshipped and the usual gifts are made.[2] Saints, of course, have the same power over eclipses as they have over nature in general. Thus we read that an eclipse of the moon was miraculously terminated by the birth of Chaitanya, the great religious reformer.[3] For all this there are exact parallels in European folklore. Aubrey,[4] for instance, tells us that "according to the rules of astrology it is not good to undertake any business of importance in the new of the moon, or at an eclipse:" and that the wild Irish and Welsh during eclipses "run about beating pans, thinking their clamour and vexation availeable to the assistance of the higher orbes."

The Earth-goddess.

Next in order of reverence comes the earth-goddess Dharitrí or Dhartí Mátá or Dhartí Máí, a name which means "the upholder" or "supporter." She is distinguished from Bhúmi, the soil, which, as we shall see, has a god of its own, and from Prithiví, "the wide, extended world," which

---

[1] *Travels*, II, 2 *sqq.*
[2] Atkinson, *Himalayan Gazetteer*, II, 913 *sq.*
[3] Wilson, *Essays*, I, 133.
[4] *Remaines*, 37, 85; and see Brand, *Observations*, 664 *sq.*

in the Vedas is personified as the mother of all things, an idea common to all folklore.[1] We meet with the same theory in the case of Demeter "the fruitful soil," as contrasted with the earlier, Titanic, formless earth personified as Gœa: unless, indeed, we are to accept the recently-announced theory of Mr. Frazer[2] that Demeter is "the Corn Mother."

Worship of Mother Earth.

The worship of the earth-goddess assumes many varied forms. The pious Hindu does reverence to her as he rises from his bed in the morning, and even the indifferent follows his example when he begins to plough and sow. In the Panjáb[3] "when a cow or buffalo is first bought, or when she first gives milk after calving, the first five streams of milk drawn from her are allowed to fall on the ground in honour of the goddess and at every time of milking the first stream is so treated. So when medicine is taken, a little is sprinkled in her honour." On the same principle the great Kublai Khán used to sprinkle the milk of his mares on the ground. "This is done," says Marco Polo, "on the injunction of the idolators and idol priests, who say that it is an excellent thing to sprinkle milk on the ground every 28th of August, so that the earth and the air and the false gods shall have their share of it, and the spirits likewise that inhabit the air and the earth, and thus those beings will protect and bless the Kaan, and his children, and his wives, and his folk, and his gear, and his cattle, and his horses, and all that is his." It was also probably through respect to mother earth that Kublai Khán ordered his captive Nayan "to be wrapped in a carpet and tossed to and fro so mercilessly that he died: and the Kaan caused him to be put to death in this way because he would not have the blood of His Line Imperial spilt upon the ground, and exposed to the eye of heaven and before the sun."[4] Marco Polo adds that the Tartars have a god called Natigay, the god of the earth "who watches over children, cattle and crops; they show him

[1] Tylor, *Primitive Culture*, I, 326 *sq.*, II, 270.
[2] *The Golden Bough*, I, 331 *sq.*: and see Lang, *Custom and Myth*, II, 262.
[3] Ibbetson, *Panjáb Ethnography*, 114.
[4] Yule's *Marco Polo*, I, 291, with Note, II, 543.

great worship and honour, and every man hath a figure of him in his house made of felt or cloth, and they also make in the same manner images of his wife and children."

Sanctity of earth.

Throughout Northern India the belief in the sanctity of earth is universal. The dying man is laid on the earth and so is the mother at the time of parturition. In the eastern districts of the North-Western Provinces there is a custom universal among the lower castes, that a few days before a marriage the women in procession go to the village clay pit, attended with music and fetch from there the sacred earth (*matmangara*), which is used in making the marriage altar and the fire-place on which the wedding feast is cooked. There are various elements in the ritual which point to a very primitive origin. The drum is always beaten by the Chamár, one of the menial or out-caste tribes: the earth is dug in secret by the Baiga or aboriginal devil-priest, and it consists of five shovels full, which is a lucky number, and it is brought home concealed in the sheet of a virgin. In the same way little village children collect and pat with their hands the dust which has been sanctified by the touch of an elephant's foot. Among the Kunbis in Kolába [1] when the women neighbours come in to see a new-born child, they touch the soles of the mother's feet, as if picking some dust off them, wave it over the child and blow the dust partly into the air and partly over the baby. It is apparently on the same principle that Mother Earth is, by some tribes, regarded as the family deity (*kuladevata*) and worshipped in times of physical danger. The Hindu troopers at the battle of Kampti at the crisis of the engagement took dust from their grooms and threw it over their heads. As in the classical legend of Antœus, wrestlers touch the earth before they engage in combat and sprinkle dust over their bodies. It is possible that from the same connection of thought ascetics smear dust over their bodies in recognition of its purity, as it is always used to clean the cooking-pot which every Hindu regards with particular respect. But in the case of the ascetic there is possibly another theory at work at the same time.

[1] *Bombay Gazetteer*, XI, 55.

The practice was common to the Greek as well as the barbarian mysteries, and, according to Mr. Lang, "the idea clearly was that by cleansing away the filth plastered over the body was symbolised the pure and free condition of the initiate.[1]" It must also not be forgotten that, as shown by numerous examples collected by Mr. Campbell,[2] ashes are generally regarded as a powerful protection (*raksha*) and most efficacious as a stancher of blood, a remedy for sores and a scarer of evil spirits. It is, perhaps, on the same principle that some burial customs common to Muhammadans and Christians have originated. The Muhammadan phrase for burial is "to give earth" (*matti dená*); the unburied mariner asks Horace for the gift of a little earth, and we ourselves, like many Hindu races, consider it a pious duty to throw a little earth on the coffin of a departed friend. The same conception was probably the basis of the universal custom of funeral oblations. Even now a days in Scotland all the milk in the house is poured on the ground at a death, and the same custom is familiar through many Hebrew and Homeric instances.[3]

Earth-worship among Dravidians.

Among the Dravidian races of Central India earth-worship prevails widely. In Chutia Nágpur the Oráons celebrate in spring the marriage of the earth. The Dryad of the *sál* tree (*shorea robusta*), who controls the rain, is propitiated with a sacrifice of fowls. Flowers of the *sál* tree are taken to the village, and carried round from house to house in a basket. The women wash the feet of the priest and do obeisance to him. He dances with them and puts some flowers upon them and upon the house. They first douse him with water as a spell to bring the rain, and then refresh him with beer.[4] In Hoshangábád[5] when the sowing is over, its completion is celebrated by the Machandrí Púja, or worship of Mother Earth, a ceremony intended to invoke fertility. "Every cultivator does

[1] *Custom and Myth*, I, 285; II, 229; *Note.*
[2] *Notes*, 42 *sqq.*
[3] Gregor, *Folklore of North-east Scotland*, 206: Aubrey, *Remaines*, 37: Ewald, *Antiquities of Israel*, 34: Spencer, *Principles of Sociology*, I, 259, 314.
[4] Dalton, *Descriptive Ethnology*, 261.
[5] Elliott, *Settlement Report*, 125.

this worship himself with his family, servants, etc.: no Bráhman need mingle in it. At the edge of one of his fields intended for the spring harvest, he puts up a little semicircular or three-sided wall of clods about a foot high, meant to represent a hut. This is covered over with green *káns* grass (*imperata spontanea*) to represent thatch. At the two ends of the hut two posts of *palása* wood (*butea frondosa*) are erected with leaves round the head to represent those put up at a marriage. They are tied to the thatch with red thread. In the centre of this little house, which represents the temple of Machandrí or "Mother Earth" a little fire is made, and milk placed on it to boil in a tiny earthen pot. It is allowed to boil over as a sign of abundance. While this is going on, the ploughmen who are all collected in a field, drive their ploughs at a trot, striking wildly: it is the end of the year's labour to the bullocks. The cultivator meanwhile offers a little rice, molasses and saffron to Machandrí, and then makes two tiny holes in the ground to represent granaries: he drops a few grains in and covers them over: this is a symbol of prayer that his granary may be filled from the produce of the land. Then he puts a little saffron on the foreheads of the ploughmen and the bullocks and ties a red thread round the bullocks' horns. The bullocks are then let go, and the ploughmen run off at full speed across country scattering wheat boiled whole as a sign of abundance. The ceremony is then over, and every one returns home." All this is an excellent example of what is called "sympathetic magic," of which we shall meet numerous examples.

Earth-worship in Mirzapur.

Many similar usages prevail among the jungle tribes of South Mirzapur. The Korwas consider *Dhartí Mátá* one of their chief godlings. She lives in the village in the general local shrine (*Deokár*) under a *sál* tree. In the month of Aghan (November-December) she is worshipped with flowers and the sacrifice of a goat. When she is worshipped duly the crops prosper and there are no epidemics. The Patáris and Majhwárs also recognise her as a village goddess and worship her in Sáwan (August). The local priest or Baiga offers to her a goat, a cock and rich cakes (*púri*). She is also worshipped in the cold weather before the gram and barley are sown, and again on the threshing floor before winnowing begins. The flesh of the animals offered is consumed by the males and unmarried girls, no grown-up girl or married woman is allowed to touch the flesh. The Ghasiyas also believe in Dhartí Mátá. She is their village goddess, and is presented with a ram or goat and cakes. The offering is made by the Baiga for whom the materials are supplied by a village contribution. The Kharwárs worship her at the village shrine before wood-cutting and ploughing begin. In Sáwan (August) they do a special service in her honour known as the *Haryárí Púja* or "worship of greenery" at the time of transplanting the rice. In Aghan (November) they have the *Khar púja* to her when they begin cutting thatching grass (*khar*); a cock, some *mahua* (*bassia latifolia*) and parched grain are offered to her. All this is done by the Baiga who receives the offerings, and none but males are permitted to attend. Similarly the Pankas worship her before sowing and harvesting the grain. They and the Bhuiyárs offer a pig and some liquor at the more important agricultural seasons. The Kharwárs sometimes call her Deví Dáí or "Nurse Deví," and in times of trouble sprinkle rice and pulse in her name on the ground. When the crops are being sown they release a fowl as a scapegoat and pray—*He Dhartí Mahtárí! kusal mangal rakhiyo! Harwáh, bail, sab bachen rahen* "O, Mother Earth! keep in prosperity and protect the ploughman and the oxen." In much the same spirit is the prayer of the peasant in Karnál to Mother Earth. "*Sáh, bádsháh se surkhrú rakhiye! aur is men achchhá náj de, to bádsháh ko bhí paisa de, aur sáh ká bhí utar jáwe.* "Keep our rulers and bankers contented! and grant a plentiful yield! so shall we pay our revenue and satisfy our money-lender."[1]

Secrecy in earth worship.

We have already met with some instances of the rule by which married women are excluded from ceremonies of this class, and of the enforcement of secrecy in the celebrations. The latter condition prevails almost universally.[2]

[1] *Settlement Report*, 168.
[2] Lang, *Custom and Myth*, II, 262 : Tylor, *Primitive Culture*, II, 273.

Earthquakes.

Earthquakes are naturally an object of terror. As Pythagoras believed that they were caused by dead men fighting beneath the earth and making it shake,[1] so the common explanation of these occurrences in India is that Vishnu in his Varáha or boar incarnation is changing the burden of the world from one tusk to another. By another account this is done by the great bull or elephant which supports the world. Derived from a more advanced theological stage is the theory that the earth shakes because it is overburdened by the sins of mankind in this evil age. Colonel Dalton[2] describes how a rumbling (probably caused by an earthquake) in the cave in which the bloodthirsty divinity of the Korwas was supposed to dwell, caused extreme terror among them.

River-worship.

Next to mother earth among the benevolent local deities of Upper India are the great rivers, especially the Ganges and Jumná, which are known respectively as Gangá Máí or "Mother Ganges" and Jumná Jí or "Lady Jumná." Gangá, of course, in the mythologies has a divine origin. According to one account she flows from the toe of Vishnu, and was brought down from heaven by the incantations of the Saint Bhagíratha to purify the ashes of the sixty thousand sons of King Ságara, who had been burnt up by the angry glance of Kapila the Sage. By another story she descends in seven streams from Siva's brow. The descent of Gangá disturbed the Saint Jahnu at his austerites and in his anger he drank up the stream: but he relented and allowed the river to flow from his ear. By a third account she is the daughter of Himavat, the impersonation of the Himalayan range. Yamuná, again, was a daughter of the Sun and sister of Yama, the lord of death. Balaráma, in a state of inebriety, called upon her to come to him that he might bathe in her waters: and as she did not heed, he in a rage seized his ploughshare weapon, dragged her to him, and compelled her to follow him whithersoever he wandered through the wood. The river then assumed a human

[1] *Folklore*, I, 150.
[2] *Descriptive Ethnology*, 229.

form and besought his forgiveness : but it was some time before she could appease the angry hero. This has been taken to represent the construction of some early canal from the river: but Mr. Growse shows that this idea is incorrect.[1]

Ganges worship.

The worship of Mother Ganges is comparatively modern. She is mentioned only twice in the Rig Veda, and then without any emphasis or complementary epithet. Apparently at this time the so-called Aryan invaders had not reached her banks.[2] She has her special festival on the seventh of the month Baisákh (May-June), which is celebrated by general bathing along the banks of the sacred stream. Ganges water is carried by bearers long distances into the interior, and is highly valued for use in sacrifices, as a remedy, a form of stringent oath, and a viaticum for the dying. The water of certain holy wells enjoys a similar value in Scotland.[3] But it is by bathing in the sacred stream at the full moon, during eclipses, and on special festivals that the greatest efficacy is assured. On these occasions an opportunity is taken of making oblations to the sainted dead whose ashes have been consigned to her waters. Bathing is throughout India regarded as a means of religious advancement. The idea rests on a metaphor—as the body is cleansed from physical pollution, so the soul is purified from sin. The stock case of the merit of this religious bathing is that of King Trisanku or "he who committed the three deadly sins"—killing a cow, displeasing his father, and eating flesh not duly consecrated. Another story is that he killed a Bráhman and married his stepmother. At any rate, he and the wicked Rája Vena were the types of violent sinners in the Hindu mythology. At length the sage Viswámitra took pity on the wicked king, and having collected water from all the sacred places in the world, washed him clean of his offences.[4] Many famous springs are supposed to have underground connection with

[1] *Mathura* 171 *sq*.
[2] Duncker, *History*, IV, 11, *Note*. Romesh Chandra Datt, *History of Civilisation*, I, 94.
[3] Gregor, *Folklore of North-east of Scotland*, 41.
[4] Buchanan, *Eastern India*, I, 399: Wilson, *Works*, VIII, 294.

the Ganges. Such is that at Chángdeo in Khándesh, of which Abul Fazl gives an account[1] and that at Jahánpur in Alwar.[2] When two sacred rivers combine their water the junction (*sangama*) is regarded as of peculiar sanctity. Such is the famous junction of the Ganges and Jumna at Pryág, the modern Allahábád. The same is the case with the junction of the Ganges and Son. In the Himalayas cairns are raised at the junction of three streams, and every passer-by adds a stone. At the confluence of the Gaula and Baliya rivers in the hills there is said to be a house of gold, but unfortunately it is at present invisible on account of some potent enchantment.[3] Bathing in such rivers is not only a propitiation for sin, but is even efficacious for the cure of disease. Even the wicked Rája Vena, who was, as we have seen, a type of old-world impiety, was cured, like Naaman the Syrian, of his leprosy by bathing in the Saraswati, the lost river of the Indian desert.[4]

Sanctity of minor streams.

Even minor streams have their sanctity and their legends. The course of the Sarju was opened by a Rishi, from which time dates the efficacy of a pilgrimage to Bagheswar.[5] The sacred portion of the Phalgu is said occasionally to flow with milk, though Dr. Buchanan was not fortunate enough to meet any one who professed to have witnessed the occurrence.[6] The Narbadá was wooed by the river Sohan, who proved faithless to her, and was beguiled by the Jholá, a rival lady stream, who acted the part of the barber's wife at the wedding. The Narbadá, enraged at her lover's perfidy, tore her way through the marble rocks at Jabalpur, and has worn the willow ever since.[7] She is now the great rival of Mother Ganges. While in the case of the latter only the northern (or as it is called the Kási or Benares) bank is efficacious for bathing, or for the cremation of the dead, the Narbadá is free

---

[1] Jarrett, *Ain-i-Akbári*, II, 224.
[2] *Rájputána Gazetteer*, III, 219.
[3] Buchanan, *loc cit*, I,11 : Madden, *Journal, Asiatic Society, Bengal*, 1847, 228, 400 : Wright, *History of Nepál*, 154, 163.
[4] Cunningham, *Reports*, II, 224.
[5] Madden, *loc cit*, 233.
[6] *Eastern India*, I,14.
[7] Sleeman, *Rambles*, I,18.

from any restriction of the kind. The same is the case with the Son, at least during its course through the district of Mirzapur. By some the sanctity of the Narbadá is regarded as superior even to that of the Ganges. While according to some authorities it is necessary to bathe in the Ganges in order to obtain forgiveness of sins, the same result is attained by mere contemplation of the Narbadá. According to the Bhavishya Purána the sanctity of the Ganges will cease on the expiry of 5,000 years of the Kaliyuga or the fourth age of the world, which occurs in 1895, and the Narbadá will then take its place. The Ganges priests, however, repudiate this calumny, and it may safely be assumed that "Mother" Ganges will not abandon her primacy in the religious world of Hinduism without a determined struggle[1].

Ill-omened streams.

But all rivers are not beneficent. The name of one stream is accursed in the ears of all Hindus—the hateful Karamnása, even to touch which destroys the merits of works of piety, for such is the popular interpretation of its name. No reason for the evil reputation of this particular stream has been suggested, except that it may have been in early times the frontier between the invading Aryans and the aborigines, and possibly the scene of a campaign in which the latter were victorious. The *Karama* tree is, however, the totem of the Dravidian Kharwárs and Mánjhís, who occupy the neighbourhood, and it is perhaps possible that this is the real origin of the name, and that its association with good works (*Karam*) was an afterthought. The legend of this ill-omened river is connected with the wicked King Trisanku, already referred to. When the sage Viswámitra collected water from all the sacred streams of the world, it fell burdened with the monarch's sins into the Karamnása, and has remained defiled ever since. By another account, the sinner was hung between heaven and earth as a punishment, and from his body drips a baneful moisture which still pollutes the water. Even nowadays no good Hindu will touch or drink it, and at its fords many low caste people make their living by conveying on their

[1] *Central Provinces Gazetteer, Narbadá,* 264, *s. v.*

shoulders their more orthodox and scrupulous brethren across the hated river.

Origin of river-worship.

It is perhaps worth considering the possible origin of this river-worship. Far from being peculiar to Hinduism it is common to the whole Aryan world. The prayer of Odysseus to the river[1] may be heard daily in Upper India. We have already noticed the efficacy of bathing as a propitiation for sin. This was no doubt one cause of the respect paid to them. In a thirsty land the mighty stream of the Ganges would naturally arouse feelings of respect and admiration. Rivers, again, are revered from their connection with the great ocean, which is regarded by many races as the home of the sainted dead. Thus the Dravidian tribes of the Vindhyan plateau take the bones of their dead relations to some tributary of the Ganges and there reverently consign them to be carried to the sea, the resting place of their people. The Ganges and the streams connected with it come thus to be associated with the ancestors of successive generations of Hindus.

Water-snakes and demons.

Again, much of the worship of rivers is connected with the propitiation of the water-snakes, demons and goblins with which, in popular belief, many of them are infested. Such were Káliya, the great black serpent of the Jumná, which attacked the infant Krishna; the serpent King of Nepál, Karkotaka, who dwelt in the lake Nágarása, when the divine lotus of Adi Buddha floated on the surface[2]. At the temple of Triyugi Náráyana in Garhwál is a pool said to be full of snakes of a yellow colour which come out at the feast of the Nágpanchamí to be worshipped. The Gardeví or river sprite of Garhwál is very malignant and is the ghost of a person who has met his death by suicide, violence or accident[3]. These malignant water demons naturally infest dangerous rapids and whirlpools, and it is necessary to propitiate them. Thus we learn that on the river Tapti in Berár timber

[1] *Odyssey*, v. 450; and for other instances see Tylor, *Primitive Culture*, II, 213: Campbell, *Notes*, 325 *sqq*.

[2] Growse, *Mathura*, 55: Tod, *Annals*, I, 575: Oldfield, *Sketches from Nepál*, II, 204.

[3] Atkinson, *Himalayan Gazetteer*, II, 788, 832.

floated down sometimes disappears in a subterraneous cavity: so before trying the navigation there the Gonds sacrifice a goat to propitiate the river demon[1]. Another variety of these demons of water is the Nág and his wife the Nágin, of whom we shall hear more in connection with snake worship. In the Sikandar, a tributary of the Kanhar river, which runs into the Son, is a deep water-hole where no one dares to go. The water reaches down as far as the infernal regions (*Pátála*). Here live the Nág and the Nágin. In the middle of the river is a tree of the *kuálo* variety, and when ghosts trouble the neighbourhood an experienced sorcerer or Ojha is called, who bores holes in the bark of the tree and there shuts up the noxious ghosts, which then come under the rule of the Nág and the Nágin, who are supreme. Another Mirzapur river, the Karsa, is infested by a demon (*deo*) known as Jata Rohini or "Rohini of the matted locks." He is worshipped by the Baiga priest to ensure abundant rain and harvests and to keep off disease. The Baiga catches a fish which he presents to the demon, but if any one but a Baiga dares to drink there, the water bubbles up and the demon sweeps him away. There is another famous water-hole known as Barewa. A herdsman was once grazing his buffaloes near the place, when the water suddenly rose and carried off him and his cattle. Three virulent spirits known as Bhainsásura or the buffalo demon and the Nág or Nágin now dwell here, and no one dares to fish there until he has propitiated the demons with an offering of fowls, eggs and a goat. Another kind of water demon attacks fishermen; it appears in the form of a turban which fixes itself to his hook and increases in length as he tries to pull it to land. Many of these demons, like the Nág and Nágin, have kingdoms and palaces stored with treasure under the waters, and there they entice young men and maidens who occasionally come back years after to tell of the wonders they have seen. These water demons are, it is needless to say, the common property of folklore. The water bull of Manxland is a creature of this class[2]. Such,

---

[1] *Berár Gazetteer*, 35.
[2] *Folklore*, II, 284, 509.

again, is the Hydra of Greek mythology and the Teutonic Nikke or Nixy who has originated the legend of the Flying Dutchman, and in the shape of Old Nick is the terror of sailors. Like him is the Kelpie of Scotland, a water-horse who is believed to carry off the unwary by sudden floods and devour them. Of the same kindred is the last of the dragons, which St. Patrick chained up in a lake on the Galtee Mountains in Tipperary [1].

Water gods.

But besides these dragons which infest rivers and lakes, there are special water-gods. Such is Mahisoba in Berár, who is like Bhainsásura already mentioned, and in the form of a buffalo infests great rivers and demands propitiation [2]. The Kols, again, have Nága Era, who presides over tanks, wells, and any stagnant water, and Garha Era, the river goddess. "They," as Colonel Dalton [3] remarks, "are frequently and very truly denounced as the cause of sickness, and propitiated by sacrifices to spare their victims."

Floods and drowning people.

Floods are, as we have already seen, regarded as produced by demoniacal agency. In the Panjáb, when a village is in danger from floods, the headman makes an offering of a cocoanut and a rupee to the flood demon. He holds the offering in his hand and stands in the water. When the water rises high enough to wash the offering from his hand, it is believed that the flood will abate. Some people throw seven handsful of boiled wheat and sugar into the stream and distribute the remainder among the persons present. Some take a male buffalo, a horse or a ram, and, after boring the right ear of the animal, throw it into the stream. If a horse is the victim, it should be saddled before it is offered. In the same connection may be noticed the very common prejudice which prevails in India against rescuing

[1] Conway, *Demonology*, I, 110 *sq.*: Sir W. Scott, *Letters on Demonology*, 85: Spencer, *Principles of Sociology* I, 219: Farrer, *Primitive Manners*, 366: Aubrey, *Remaines*, 30: Gordon Cumming, *From the Hebrides to the Himalayas*, I, 139: Tylor, *Primitive Culture*, I, 109 *sq.*; II, 208: Gregor, *Folklore*, 66 *sq*: Lady Wilde, *Legends*, 216. For these water sprites in Indian folklore see Tawney, *Katha Sarit Ságara*, I, 58.

[2] *Berár Gazetteer*, 190.

[3] *Descriptive Ethnology*, 188.

drowning people. Numerous instances of this from other races have been collected by Messrs. Tylor and Conway[1]. Dr. Tylor considers this to indicate a belief that to snatch a victim from the very clutches of the water spirit is a rash defiance of deity which would hardly pass unavenged. Mr. Black[2] accounts for the belief on the idea that the spirits of people who have died a violent death may return to earth if they can find no substitute : hence the soul of the last dead man is insulted or injured by preventing another from taking his place. This last theory is very common. Thus Lady Wilde[3] writes from Ireland,—"It is believed that the spirit of the dead last buried has to watch in the churchyard until another corpse is laid there, or to perform menial offices in the spirit world, such as carrying wood and water until the next spirit comes from earth. They are also sent on messages to earth, chiefly to announce the coming death of some relative, and at this they are glad, for their own time of peace and rest will come at last." This quite agrees with popular feeling in India and is an adequate explanation of the prejudice against rescuing the drowning.

Khwája Khizr, the god of water.

But besides these water spirits and local river gods, the Hindus have a special god of water, Khwája Khizr, whose Muhammadan title has been Hinduised into Rája Kidár, or as he is called in Bengal, Káwaj, or Pír Bhadr. This is a good instance of a fact, which will be discussed elsewhere, that Hindus are always ready to annex the deities and beliefs of other races. According to the *Sikandarnáma*, Khwája Khizr was a saint of Islám, who presided over the well of immortality, and directed Alexander of Macedon in his vain search for the blessed waters. The fish is his vehicle, and hence its image is painted over the doors of both Hindus and Muhammadans, while it became the family crest of the late royal house of Oudh. Among Muhammadans a prayer is said to Khwája Khizr at the first shaving of a boy. At marriages a little boat is launched on a river or tank in

---

1 *Primitive Culture*, I, 108 *sqq.* : *Demonology*, I, 285 : Sir W. Scott's *The Pirate* is based on the same idea.

2 *Folk-medicine*, 28 *sq.*

3 *Legends*, 82 *sq.*

his honour, and the same rite is performed at the close of the rainy season, when it is supposed to have some connection with the saint Ilisha, that is to say the prophet Elijah. Another legend represents him to be of the family of Noah, and the son of a king. In some Muhammadan books he seems to be confounded with Elias, and in others with St. George, the patron saint of England. He is called the companion of Moses, and the commentator Husain says he was a general in the army of Zú'l Qarnain, "He of the two horns," or Alexander the Great [1]. Out of this jumble of all the mythologies has been evolved the Hindu god of water, the patron deity of boatmen, who is invoked by them to prevent their boats from being broken or submerged, or to show them the way when they have lost it. All through the Eastern Panjáb he is intrusted with the safety of travellers. He is worshipped by burning lamps, feeding Bráhmans, and by setting afloat on a village pond a little raft of grass with a lighted lamp placed on it. Another curious function is allotted to him, of haunting markets in the early morning and fixing the rates of grain, which he also protects from the Evil Eye.[2]

Wells in folklore.

In this connection some of the folklore of wells may be mentioned. The digging of a well is a duty requiring infinite care and caution. The work should begin on a Sunday, and on the previous Saturday night little bowls of water are placed round the proposed site, and the one which dries up least marks the best site for the well. The circumference is then marked, and they commence to dig, leaving the central lump of earth intact. They cut out this clod last and call it *Khwájají* (perhaps after Khwája Khizr, the water-god), worship it, and feed Bráhmans. If it breaks it is a bad omen, and a new site will be selected a week afterwards. After the well is finished the Sálagráma, or spiral ammonite stone sacred to Vishnu, is solemnly wedded to the Tulasí or basil plant representing the garden, with the regular marriage ceremonies. The relations are collected

---

[1] Herklots, *Qánún i-Islám*, 21 ; 66 *sq.* ; 292 : Hughes, *Dictionary of Islám*, s.v.
[2] Ibbetson, *Panjáb Ethnography*, 114 : *Panjáb Notes and Queries*, II, 1 ; III-7; IV, 68.

and the owner of the grove represents the bridegroom, while a kinsman of his wife stands for the bride. Gifts are given to Bráhmans, and a feast is held in the grove, the fruit of which may then be used without danger[1]. In Sírsa they have a legend that long ago in time of drought, a headman went to a *faqír* to beg him to pray for rain and promised him his daughter in marriage if his prayer was successful. The rain came, but the headman would not perform his promise, and the *faqír* cursed the land, so that all the water became brackish; but he so far relented as to permit sweet water to flow on condition that it was given to all men free of cost. In one village the spring at once became brackish when a water rate was levied and turned sweet again when the tax was remitted. In another the water, once sweet, became bitter since a man was drowned in the well. In another the brackish water became sweet at the intercession of a *faqír*. There is a class of persons called "Sniffers" (*súnga*), generally holy *faqírs*, who can smell sweet water below ground. This reminds us of the common use of the divining rod in England for discovering springs[2]. Some well water is efficacious as a remedy. In Ireland the first water drawn from a sacred well after midnight on May eve is considered an effective antidote to witchcraft[3]. In India the water of seven wells is collected on the night of the Diwálí or feast of lamps, and barren women bathe in it as a spell to procure children. In a well in Orissa the priests throw betel nuts into the mud and barren women scramble for them. Those who find one will have their desire for children gratified before long.[4] In the same way, to look down seven wells is a popular cure for hydrophobia. In the Panjáb the sites of deserted wells are discovered by driving about a herd of goats, which are supposed to lie down in the place where search should be made. Some people discover wells by dreams: others, like the Luniyas, a caste of navvies, are said, like the *faqírs* in Sirsa, to be

[1] Ibbetson, *loc., cit.* 119: Crooke, *Rural Glossary*, s.v. *Bágh-ká-byáh*.
[2] *Settlement Report*, 178.
[3] Lady Wilde, *Legends*, 124.
[4] Ball, *Jungle Life in India*, 531: other instances are collected in Campbell, *Notes*, 33: *Panjáb Notes and Queries*, II, 166: Temple, *Legends of the Panjáb*, I, 2: Lady Wilde, *Legends*, 236 *sqq*.

able to discover by smell where water is likely to be found. I was shown a well in the Muzaffarnagar district into which a *faqír* once spat, and for a long time after the visit of the holy man it ran with excellent milk. The supply had ceased, I regret to say, before my visit.

Sacred wells.

Sacred wells, of course, abound all over the country. Many of these are believed to have underground connection with the Ganges or some other holy river. Many wells are connected in legend with the wanderings of Ráma and Sítá after their exile from Ayodhya. One of these is on the Bindáchal hill in Mirzapur and is a famous resort of pilgrims. There is another near Monghyr, and a third in the Sultánpur district in Oudh. The Monghyr well has been provided with a special legend. Sítá was suspected of faithlessness during her captivity in the kingdom of Rávana. So she threw herself into a pit filled with fire where the hot spring now flows and came out purified. When Dr. Buchanan visited the place they had just invented a new legend in connection with it. Shortly before, it was said, the water became so cool as to allow of bathing in it. The Governor prohibited the practice because it made the water so dirty that Europeans could not drink it. "But on the very day when the bricklayers began to build a wall in order to exclude the bathers, the water became so hot that no one could dare to touch it, so that the precaution being unnecessary, the work of the infidels was abandoned [1]." The well at Sihor in Rájputána is sacred to Gautama and is considered efficacious in the cure of various disorders. So with various sacred springs in Kashmír. In one, water rushes out when a sheep or goat is sacrificed: another runs if the ninth of any month happens to fall on Friday: in a third those who have any special needs throw in a nut; if it floats it is considered an omen of success, if it sinks it is considered adverse [2]. Hot springs are naturally regarded as sacred. We have already noticed an example in

---

[1] *Eastern India*, II, 43 *sq*.

[2] Jarrett, *Aín-i-Akbári*, II, 355, *sqq*. For the fountains which have power to restore life see Tawney, *Katha Sarit Ságara*, I, 499.

Sítá's well at Monghyr. The holy tract in the hills known as Vaishnava Kshetra contains several hot springs in which Agni, the fire-god, resides by the permission of Vishnu. At Askot in the Himalaya there is a holy well which, like those in Kashmír noticed by Abul Fazl, is used for divination of the prospects of the harvest. If the spring in a given time fill the brass vessel to the brim into which the water falls, there will be a good season; if only half full scarcity may be expected; if only a little water comes a drought may be looked for[1]

Waterfalls.

Waterfalls, naturally uncommon in the flat country of Upper India, are, as might have been expected, regarded with veneration; and the deity of the fall is carefully propitiated. The visitor to the magnificent waterfall in which the river Chandra Prabha pours its waters over a sheer precipice three hundred feet high in its descent from the Vindhyan plateau to the Gangetic valley will learn that it is visited by women, particularly those who are desirous of offspring. On a rock beside the fall they lay a simple offering consisting of a few glass bangles, ear ornaments made of palm leaves and cotton waist strings.

Sacred lakes.

There are also numerous lakes which are considered sacred and visited by pilgrims. Such is Pushkar or Pokhar, the lake *par excellence* in Rájputána. One theory of the sanctity of this lake was that it was originally a natural depression and enlarged at a subsequent date by human agency. "Every Hindu family of note has its niche for purposes of devotion. Here is the only temple in India sacred to Bráhma, the Creator. While he was creating the world he kindled the sacred fire, but his wife Sawantarí was nowhere to be found, and as without the presence of a woman the rites could not proceed, a Gújar girl took her place. Sawantarí on her return was so enraged at the indignity that she retired to the height close by known as Ratnagiri or "the hill of gems" where she disappeared. On this spot a fountain gushed out, still called by her name, close to which is her

[1] Atkinson, *Himalayan Gazetteer*, II, 793, 798.

shrine, not the least attractive in the precincts of Pokhar." Like many of these lakes such as are known in Great Britain as the Devil's Punchbowls, Pokhar has its dragon legend, and one of the rocks near the lake is known as Nágpábár, or "Dragon Hill[1]." There is a similar legend attached to the Lonár lake in Berár, which was the den of the giant Lonásura, whom Vishnu destroyed.[2]

Mána Sarovar lake.

Most famous of all the lakes is Mána Sarovar in Tibet, about which there are many legends. "The lake of Mána Sarovar was formed from the mind of Bráhma, and thence derived its name. There dwelt also Mahádeva and the gods, thence flow the Sarju and other female rivers, and the Satadru (Satlaj) and other male rivers. When the earth of Mána Sarovar touches any one's body, or when any one bathes therein, he shall go to the Paradise of Bráhma: and he who drinks its waters shall go to the Heaven of Siva; and shall be released from the sins of a hundred births: and even the beast which bears the name of Mána Sarovar shall go to the Paradise of Bráhma." It is said that the sons of Bráhma, Maríchi, Vasistha, and the rest of the sages proceeded to the north of Himalaya and performed austerities on Mount Kailása, where they saw Siva and Párvatí, and remained for twelve years absorbed in meditation and prayer. There was very little rain and water was scanty. In their distress they appealed to Bráhma. He asked them what their wishes might be. The Rishis replied "we are engaged in devotion on Kailása, and must always go thence to bathe in the Mandákini river: make a place for us to bathe in." Then Bráhma by a mental effort formed the holy lake of Mánasa,[3] and the Rishis worshipped the golden *linga* which rose from the midst of the waters of the lake. So the Naini Tál lake is sacred to Kálí in one of her numerous forms. The goddess Sambrá, the tutelary divinity of the Chauhán Rájputs, in return for some religious service on their part, converted a dense forest into

---

[1] Tod, *Annals*, I, 814 *sq*: Conway, *Demonology*, I, 113.
[2] *Berár Gazetteer*, 169.
[3] From the *Mánasa Khanda*: Atkinson, *Himalayan Gazetteer*, II, 308.

a plain of gold and silver. But they, dreading the strife which such a possession would excite, begged of the goddess to retract her gift, and she gave them the present lake of salt.[1]

The lake of the fairy gifts.

In the Chánda district of the Central Provinces is the lake of Taroba or Tadala, which is connected with an interesting series of folklore legends. A marriage procession was once passing the place and, finding no water, a strange-looking old man suggested that the bride and bridegroom should join in digging for a spring. They laughingly consented, and after removing a little earth a clear fountain gushed forth. As they were all drinking with delight the waters rose, and spreading into a wide lake, overwhelmed the married pair. "But fairy hands soon constructed a temple in the depths where the spirits of the drowned are supposed to dwell. Afterwards on the lake side a palm tree grew up, which appeared only during the day, sinking into the earth at twilight. One morning a rash pilgrim seated himself on the tree and was borne into the skies where the flames of the sun consumed him." This part of the story reads like a genuine solar myth. "The palm tree then shrivelled away into dust and in its place appeared an image of the spirit of the lake, which is worshipped under the name of Taroba or "the palm tree deity." "Formerly at the call of pilgrims all necessary vessels rose from the lake, and after being used were washed and returned to the waters. But an evil-minded man at last took those he had received to his house: they quickly vanished, and from that day the mystic provision wholly ceased." This same fairy gift legend which has been admirably illustrated by Mr. Hartland[2] appears in various forms in European folklore. It is also told of the Amner lake in Elichpur.[3] At Taroba on quiet nights the country people hear faint sounds of drum and trumpet passing round the lake, and old men say that in one dry year when the waters sank low, golden pinnacles of a fairy

---

[1] Atkinson, *Himalayan Gazetteer*, II, 309, 798: *Rájputána Gazetteer*, II, 131.
[2] *Science of Fairy Tales, chapter* VI.
[3] *Berár Gazetteer*, 148.

temple were seen glittering in the depths.[1] This is exactly the legend of Lough Neagh immortalised by Thomas Moore.

The Sháhgarh lake.

A lake at Sháhgarh in the Bareilly district is the seat of a legend which also widely prevails. When Rája Vena ruled the land, he, like Buddha, struck by the inequality of human life, retired with his young wife Sundarí to live like a peasant. One day she went to the lake to draw water and she had naught but a jar of unbaked clay and a thread of untwisted cotton. In the innocence of her heart she stepped into the lake, but the gods preserved her. After a time she wearied of this sordid life and one morning she arrayed herself in her queenly robes and jewels and going as usual to the lake walked on the lotus petals. When she plunged in her jar, it melted away, and the untwisted thread broke and she herself sunk in the pool. "But she was saved and thenceforward learned the evil of vanity and pride in riches; and the strength of innocence and a pure mind. And the lotus pool, in honour of the good Queen Sundarí, was called by all men the Ráni Tál or Queen's Tank, and is to be seen to this day just outside the town of Kabár, though the lotus flowers have perished and the castle at Sháhgarh has sunk into dust."[2] The same legend reappears in many forms in Northern India[3].

Other scared tanks.

The number of lakes and tanks associated with some legend or endued with some special sanctity of their own is legion. The tank of Beguthiya in the Sultánpur district was inhabited by the fairy Makrí, an attendant, like most fairies, of the Court of Indra, who was turned into a tadpole by the curse of the god. She was restored to her former shape by touching the foot of the monkey-god, Hanumán, who halted there to drink. In her gratitude she saved her deliverer from the machination of his enemies.[4] Many of these tanks are efficacious

---

[1] *Central Provinces Gazetteer*, 486.
[2] *Bareilly Settlement Report*, 20 sq.
[3] *Bhandara Settlement Report*, 47: Temple, *Legends of the Panjáb*, I, 39.
[4] *Oudh Gazetteer*, I, 39.

for the cure of disease or various bodily infirmities. At Qasúr is the shrine of the Saint Basant Sháh, and near it is a pool in which children are bathed to cure them of boils. Similarly many tanks cure leprosy. In one of the Bengal folktales the old discarded wife bathes in a tank and recovers her beauty.[1] It is a frequent condition imposed on pilgrims to such tanks that they should remove a certain quantity of earth and thus improve it. Many tanks again are supposed to contain treasure, which is usually under the custody of a Yaksha. Hence such places are regarded with much awe. There is a tank of this kind in the Bijaigarh Fort in the Mirzapur district: another forms an incident in Lál Bihári De's tale of Govinda Sámanta.[2]

Mountain-worship; the Himálaya.

"He who thinks of Himáchal (the Himálaya), though he should not behold him, is greater than he who performs all worship at Kasi (Benares); as the dew is dried up by the morning sun, so are the sins of mankind by the sight of Himáchal.[3]" Such was the devotion with which the early Hindus looked on it as the home of the gods. Beyond it their fancy created the elysium of Uttara Kuru, which may be most properly regarded as an ideal picture created by the imagination of a life of tranquil felicity, and not as a reminiscence of any actual residence of the Kurus in the north.[4] From early times the Himálayan valleys were the resort of the sage and the ascetic. Almost every hill and river is consecrated by their legends, and the whole country teems with memories of the early religious life of the Hindu race. As in the mythology of many other peoples,[5] it was regarded as the home of the sainted dead, and the common source or origin of Hinduism. Its caves were believed to be the haunt of witches and fairies. Demons

---

1 For instances see *Berár Gazetteer*, 158, 176: *Panjáb Notes and Queries*, III, 42: Wright, *History of Nepál*, 135: *Bombay Gazetteer*, V, 140: *Rájputána Gazetteer*, II, 220: Lál Behári Dé, *Folktales of Bengal*, 281: Campbell, *Notes*, 29.

2 I, 17.

3 *Mánasa Khanda*.—Atkinson, *Himalayan Gazetteer*, II, 271.

4 See remarks of Lassen quoted by Muir, *Ancient Sanskrit Texts*, II, 337.

5 Spencer, *Principles of Sociology*, I, 200 *sq.*; 210, 336.

lurked in its recesses as at the Blockberg where, as Aubrey tells us, "the devils and witches do dance and feast."[1] But there is reason to suspect that this respect for mountains may be a survival from the beliefs of non-Aryan peoples who were supplanted by the Hindus. At any rate, the belief in the sanctity of mountains survives among existing aboriginal or Drávidian races. They worship mountains in connection with the god of the rain. The Santáls sacrifice to Marang Búra on a flat rock on the top of a mountain, and after fasting, work themselves up into a state of frenzy to charm the rain. The Korwas and Kúrs worship in the same way Mainpát, a plateau in the mountainous country south of the Son. The Nágbansis and the Mundári Kols worship a huge rock as the abode of "the great god" Baradeo.[2] So in Garhwál in the Chhipula Pass is a shrine to the god of the mountains. At Tolma is a temple to the Himálaya and below Dunagiri in the same valley a shrine in honour of the same peak.[3] So in Hoshangábád in the Central Indian plateau, Súryabhán or "Sunrays," is a very common name for isolated round-peaked hills on which the god is supposed to dwell, and among the Kurkus, Dúngardeo, the mountain god, resides on the nearest hill outside the village. He is worshipped every year at the Dasahra festival with a goat, two cocoanuts, five dates, and a ball of vermilion paste. He is regarded as their special village god.[4] As in the Himálayas, one of the main peaks, Nandá Deví, has been identified with Párvatí who, as her name shows, is a special mountain goddess, so the aboriginies of the Central Provinces have in Kattarpár, the Kattipen of the Khándhs, a special god of ravines.[5] So in the Mirzapur hills the aboriginal races have an intense respect for mountains. On the Mátara hill is a demon (*deo*) known as Darrapátdeo. When Rávana abducted Sítá, he kept her on this hill for some time, and her palanquin, turned into stone, is there to this day. No one ascends the mountain through fear

---

[1] *Remaines*, 18 : Sir W. Scott, *Letters on Demonology*, 135.

[2] Dalton, *Descriptive Ethnology*, 188, 210, 223, 230, 135, 186 ; Lubbock, *Origin of Civilisation*, 306.

[3] Atkinson, *Himálayan Gazetteer*, II, 832.

[4] *Settlement Report*, 121, 254.

[5] Atkinson, *Himálayan Gazetteer*, II, 792 ; Hislop, *Papers*, 14.

of the demon, except an Ojha or sorcerer, who sacrifices a goat at the foot of the hill before he makes the attempt. On the Chainpur hill lives Kotí Rání, who is embodied in the locusts which are usually found there. Bansaptí Mátá, who is half a forest and half a mountain goddess, lives on Jhurma hill, and if any one dares to sing in her neighbourhood, he becomes sick or mad. These mountain demons very often take the form of tigers and kill incautious intruders on their domains. On the Aunri hill are two dreaded demons, Deorásan and Birwat, the latter a malignant ghost (*bír*) of some one who died a violent death. They rule the hail, and at harvest time the Baiga offers a goat, and spreading rice on the ground prays "O lord, Mahádeva! may this offering be effectual!" Mangesar, the rugged peak which frowns over the valley of the Son, is a popular local god of the various Kolarian races and a shrine to Bába or Rája Mangesar, "the father and the king," is found in many of their villages.

Respect paid to the Kaimur and Vindhyan ranges.

The Kaimúr and Vindhyan ranges also enjoy a certain degree of sanctity. On the latter the most famous shrines are those of Asthbhuja, or the "eight armed" Deví, Sítákund or "the pool of Sítá," and the temple of the Mahárání Vindhyesvarí, the patron goddess of the range, built where it trends towards the Gangetic valley. She has travelled as far as Cutch, where she is worshipped under the corrupted name of Vinján.[1] Her shrine has evil associations with traditions of human sacrifice derived from the coarser aboriginal cultus which has now been adopted into Bráhmanism.[2] There the Thags used to meet and share their spoils with their patron goddess, and her *Pandas* or priests are so disorderly that a special police guard has to be posted at the shrine to ensure the peaceable division of the offerings among the sharers, who mortgage and sell their rights to participate in the profits like the advowson of a living in the English Church. These two ranges are, says the legend, an offshoot of the Himálaya.

[1] *Bombay Gazetteer*, V, 252.
[2] Human sacrifice to the Durgá of the Vindhyas occurs often in Indian folklore, see Tawney, *Katha Sarit Ságara*, I, 64.

When Rama was building the bridge across the strait to Lanka, he sent his followers to Himálaya to collect materials. They returned with a mighty burden, but meanwhile the hero had completed his task, so he ordered them to throw down their loads, and where the stones fell, these ranges were produced. There is another legend of the Vindhyas told in the story of Nala and Damayantí. They were jealous of the Himálaya, the peaks of which were each morning visited by the earliest rays of the rising sun. The sun, on being appealed to, declared that it was impossible for him to change his course. Immediately the Vindhyas swelled with rage, and rising to the heavens, intercepted the view of the sun, moon and constellations. The gods, alarmed, called on the Saint Agastya to interfere. He went, accompanied by his wife, and requested the Vindhyas to sink and let him pass to the south and not to rise till he returned. They agreed and gave passage to the saint, but as he never came back they have never resumed their former size. The legend possibly goes back to the arrival of the earliest Bráhmanic missionaries in Southern India, and the name, which probably means "the divider," marked the boundary between the Aryan and Drávidian peoples.[1]

Other famous hills.

A mention of two other famous North Indian hills may close this account of mountain worship. At Gaya is the Dharmasila or "rock of piety," which was once the wife of the Saint Maríchi. The lord of the infernal regions, by order of Bráhma, crushed it down on the head of the local demon.[2] Another famous hill is that of Gobardhan near Mathura. This is the hill which Krishna is fabled to have held aloft on the top of his finger for seven days to cover the people of Braj from the tempests poured down upon them by Indra when deprived of his wonted sacrifices. There is a local belief that as the waters of the Jumna are yearly decreasing in volume, so this hill is gradually sinking. Not a particle of stone is allowed to be removed from it, and even the road which crosses it at its lowest point, where

[1] A similar story is told of one of the Nepál ranges: Wright, *History*, 178.
[2] Buchanan, *Eastern India*, I, 51 *sq.* Tawney, *Katha Sarit Ságara*, II, 333.

only a few fragments of the rock crop up over ground, had to be carried over them by a paved causeway.[1]

The spirits of the air.

"Aërial spirits or devils are such as keep quarter in the air, cause many tempests, thunder and lightnings, tear oaks, fire steeples, houses, strike men and beasts, make it rain wool, frogs, &c. They cause whirlwinds on a sudden, and tempestuous storms, which, though our meteorologists refer to natural causes, yet am I of Bodine's mind they are more often caused by those aërial devils in their several quarters." This statement of Burton[2] is a good summary of current Hindu opinion on the subject: and it is just this class of physical phenomena which civilised man admits to be beyond his control that primitive races profess to be able to regulate. The old weather-god was Indra, who wars with Vitra or Ahi, the demon of drought, whom he compels to dispense the rain. He was revered as the causer of fertility and feared as the lord of the lightning and thunder. He has now been deposed from his pre-eminence and is little more than a *roi fainéant*, who lives in a luxurious heaven of his own, solaced by the dances of the fairies who form his court, one of whom he occasionally bestows on some favoured mortal who wins his kindness or forces him to obey his orders. Mr. Wheeler[3] suggests that this degradation of Indra may possibly be due to the fact that he was a tribal god notoriously hostile to Bráhmans; and it is certainly significant from this point of view that he has come to be regarded as the great deity of the Burman Buddhists. It is still further remarkable that at Benares, the headquarters of Bráhmanism, he has been replaced by a special rain-god Dalbhyeswara, who must be worshipped and kept properly dressed if the seasons are not to become unfavourable.[4] Bhímsen, of whom more will be said later on, is regarded by the Gonds as a god of rain, and has a festival of four or five days' duration held in his honour at the end of the rainy

[1] Growse, *Mathura*, 278; where all the local legends are given in detail.
[2] *Anatomy of Melancholy*, 123.
[3] *History of India*, chapter III, 21, 330.
[4] Sherring, *Sacred City*, 129.

season, when two poles about twenty feet high and five feet apart are set up with a rope attached to the top by which the boys of the village climb up and then slide down the poles.[1] This is apparently an instance of rude sympathetic magic representing the descent of the rain.

Demoniacal control of the weather.

The demoniacal control of the weather is well illustrated by Marco Polo. "During the three months of every year that the Lord (Kublai Khán) resides at that place, if it should happen to be bad weather, there are certain crafty enchanters and astrologers in his train, who are such adepts in necromancy and the diabolic arts, that they are able to prevent any cloud or storm passing over the spot on which the Emperor's palace stands. Whatever they do in this way is by the help of the devil: but they make those people believe that it is compassed by dint of their own sanctity and the help of God. They always go in a state of dirt and uncleanness, devoid of respect for themselves or for those who see them, unkempt and sordidly attired." Timur in his memoirs speaks of the Indian Jats using incantations to produce heavy rain which hindered his cavalry from acting against them. A Yadachi was captured, and when his head had been taken off, the storm ceased. Bábar speaks of one of his early friends Khwájaka Mulai who was acquainted with Yadagari or the art of bringing on rain and snow by means of enchantments. In the same way in Nepál the control of the weather is supposed to be vested in the Lamas.[2]

Rain-making and nudity.

One very curious custom of rain-making has a series of remarkable parallels in Europe. In Servia, in time of drought, a girl is stripped and covered with flowers. She dances at each house, and the mistress steps out and pours a jar of water over her, while her companions sing rain songs.[3] In Russia, the women draw a furrow round the village and bury

[1] Hislop, *Papers*, 18.
[2] Yule, *Marco Polo*, I. 292, 301: Oldfield, *Sketches from Nepál*, II, 6.
[3] *Notes and Queries*, V. Ser III, 424: Farrer *Primitive Manners*, 70: Frazer, *Golden Bough*, I, 16.

at the juncture a cock, a cat and a dog. "The dog is a demonic character in Russia: while the cat is sacred. The offering of both seems to represent a desire to conciliate both sides."[1] Mr. Conway thinks that the nudity of the women represents their utter poverty and inability to give more to conciliate the god of the rain: or that we have here a form of the Godiva and Peeping Tom legend "where there is possibly a distant reflection of the punishment sometimes said to overtake those who gazed too curiously upon the swan maiden with her feathers."[2] The Godiva legend has been admirably illustrated by Mr. Hartland, who comes to the conclusion that it is the survival of an annual rite in honour of a heathen goddess and closely connected with these nudity observances which we are now discussing.[3] The difficulty however is to account for the nudity part of the ceremony. It may possibly be based on the theory that spirits dread indecency or rather the male and female principles.[4] This may be the origin of the indecencies of word and act practised at the Holí and Kajarí festivals in Upper India, which are both closely connected with the control of the weather. Among the Ramoshis of the Dakkhin the bridegroom is stripped naked before the anointing ceremony commences. The Mhárs of Sholapur are buried naked, even the loincloth being taken off. Barren women worship a naked female figure at Bijapur. At Dayamavá's festival in the Karnátak, women walk naked to the temple where they make their vows: and the Máng, who carries the scraps of holy meat which he scatters in the fields to promote fertility, is naked.[5] And in close connection with the question which we are considering, it may be noted that in Nepál temples are decorated with groups of obscene figures as a protection against lightning.[6]

---

[1] Conway, *Demonology*, I, 267.
[2] *Ibid*, I, 224.
[3] *Science of Fairy Tales*, 71, *sqq*.
[4] For some of these illustrations I am indebted to. Mr. Campbell, *Notes* 101, *sq*
[5] *Bombay Gazetteer*, XVIII--416: XX--180: XXIII--666. *Journal, Ethnological Society*, N. S. I., 98. In the *Katha Sarit Ságara* (*Tawney* I, 154) the Queen Kavalayávalí worships the gods stark naked.
[6] Wright, *History*, 10.

Nudity: rain-making in India.

The rain custom in India is precisely the same as those already described in Europe. During the Gorakhpur famine of 1873-74 there were many accounts received of women going about with a plough at night, stripping themselves naked and dragging it across the fields as an invocation to the rain god. The men kept carefully out of the way while this was being done. It was supposed that if the women were seen by men the spell would lose its effect. Mr. Frazer in this remarks that "it is not said that they plunge the plough into a stream or sprinkle it with water. But the charm would hardly be complete without it."[1] It was on my own authority that the custom which Messrs. Frazer and Hartland quote was originally recorded, and I do not remember at that time hearing of this part of the ritual. I am now able to supplement the existing evidence by other examples. In Sirsa, when a horse falls sick the cure is to kill a fowl or a goat and let its warm blood flow into the animal's mouth, but if this cannot be done quickly, it is sufficient for a man to take off all his clothes and strike the horse seven times on the forehead with his shoe.[2] Here the nudity is a charm to drive off the demon of disease. In Chhatarpur, when rain falls, a woman and her husband's sister take off all their clothes and drop seven cakes of cow dung into a mud reservoir for storing grain. If a man and his maternal uncle perform the same ceremony, it is equally effective: but, as a rule, women do it, and the special days for its performance are Sunday and Wednesday. Here we have the custom in process of modification, the substitution of males, one of whom is a relation in the female line, for the female officiants. Another account is given by Mrs. Fanny Parkes in her curious book entitled "Wanderings of a Pilgrim in search of the Picturesque."[3] "The Hindu women in the most curious way propitiate the goddess who brings the cholera into the bazár. They

---

[1] *Golden Bough*, I 17. Hartland, *Science of Fairy Tales*, 84, quoting *Panjáb Notes and Queries*, III, 41,115.

[2] *Settlement Report*, 207.

[3] I cannot lay my hands on a copy of the book: the quotation is given in *Calcutta Review*, XV, 486.

go out in the evening, about 7 P. M., sometimes two or three hundred at a time, each carrying a *lota* or brass vessel filled with sugar, water, cloves, etc. In the first place they make *púja;* then stripping off their sheets (*chádar*) and binding their sole petticoat round their waists, as high above the knee as it can be pulled up, they perform a most frantic sort of dance, forming themselves into a circle, while in the centre of the circle about five or six women dance entirely naked, beating their hands together over their heads, and then applying them behind with a great smack that keeps time with the music, and with the song they scream out all the time accompanied by native instruments played by men who stand at a distance, to the sound of which these women dance and sing, looking like frantic creatures. The men avoid the spot where the ceremony takes place, but here and there one or two men may be seen looking on, whose presence does not appear to molest the nut-brown dancers in the least; they shriek and sing and smack and scream most marvellously." Here we have the rule of privacy at these nudity ceremonies slightly relaxed. Of the nudity charm in cattle disease we have an instance from Jalandhar. In cattle disease "the remedy is for some one to strip himself and to walk round the patient with some burning straw or cane fibre in his hands."[1] Nudity also appears to be a condition of the erection of the pinnacle, the final act which completes a Hindu temple. "The temple at Arang in Ráepur district and that at Ḍeobálṇda, were built at the same time. When they were finished and the pinnacles (*kalas*) had to be put on, the mason and his sister agreed to put them on simultaneously at an auspicious moment. The day and hour being fixed by Bráhmans, the two, stripping themselves naked, according to the custom on such occasions, climbed up to the top: as they got up to the top each could see the other, and each through shame jumped down into the tank close to the respective temples, where they still stand turned into stone, and are visible when the tank water falls low in seasons of drought."[2] Of the regular nudity

[1] *Settlement Report*, 135.
[2] Cunningham, *Archæological Reports*, VII, 162.

spell in case of failure of rain, we have a good instance from Chunar in the Mirzapur district. "The rains this year held off for a long time and last night (24th July 1892) the following ceremony was performed secretly. Between the hours of 9 and 10 P.M., a barber's wife went from door to door and invited the women to join in ploughing. They all collected in a field from which all males were excluded. Three women from a cultivator's family stripped off all their clothes: two were yoked to a plough like oxen, and a third held the handle. They then began to imitate the operation of ploughing. The woman who had the plough in her hand shouted "O Mother Earth! bring parched grain, water and chaff. Our stomachs are breaking to pieces from hunger and thirst." Then the landlord and village accountant approached them and laid down some grain, water and chaff in the field. The women then dressed and returned home. By the grace of God the weather changed almost immediately, and we had a good shower."[1] Here we see that the ceremony is elaborately organized; that the privacy taboo is observed, and that the ritual is in the nature of sympathetic magic intended to propitiate Mother Earth. There can be no doubt that the ceremony prevails widely in Northern India, but, as might naturally be expected, it is very difficult to obtain exact information of what really goes on.

Other rain spells.

Besides these nudity spells there are numerous other spells for rain. Among the Bhíls in time of drought women and girls go out dancing and singing with bows and arrows, and, seizing a buffalo belonging to another village, sacrifice it to the goddess Kálí. The headman of the village to which the buffalo belongs seldom interferes. If he does, the women by abusing and threatening to shoot him almost always have their own way.[1] Analogous to this regular rain sacrifice is the custom at Ahmadnagar, where on the bright third of Baisákh (April-May), the boys of two neighbouring villages fight with slings

---

[1] *North Indian Notes and Queries,* I, 210.
[1] *Bombay Gazetteer,* III, 221.

and stones. The local belief is that if the fight is discontinued, rain fails, or if rain falls, that it produces a plague of rats. A good fight is supposed to cause abundant rain.[1] At Ahmadábád, again, there is a city headman known as the Nagar Seth or "chief man of the town." When rain holds off he has to perambulate the city walls pouring out milk to appease Rája Indra.[2] Here we reach the "sympathetic magic" type of observance under which most of the other practices may be classed, though here and there we seem to find the germ of the principle of vicarious sacrifice. Thus in the Panjáb the village girls pour down on an old woman as she passes some cow dung dissolved in water; or an old woman is made to sit down under the roof spout of a house and get a wetting when it rains. In the Muzaffarnagar district if rain fails they worship Rája Indra and read the story of the Megha Rája, or the lord of the rain. In his name they give alms to the poor and release a young bull or buffalo. Crushed grain is cooked on the edge of a tank in his honour and in the name of the rain god Khwája Khizr, and some offering is made to Bhúmiya, the lord of the soil. In Chhatarpur, on a wall facing the east, they paint two figures with cow dung, one representing Indra and the other Megha with their legs up and their heads hanging down. It is supposed that the discomfort thus caused to them will compel them to grant the boon of rain. The Mirzapur Korwas when rain fails get the Baiga to make a sacrifice and prayer to the sun godling (*Súraj deota*). Another common plan in Upper India is for a gang of women to come out to where a man is ploughing and drive him and his oxen by force back to the village where he and his cattle are well fed. Another device is to seize the blacksmith's anvil and pitch it into a well or the village tank. Here may be noticed, in the first place, the connection between wells and the rain god of which instances have been given by Mr. Gomme:[3] and in this connection we may note the case of the well in Farghana which caused rain if defiled;[4] secondly, the custom

---

[1] *Indian Antiquary*, V, 5.
[2] *Bombay Gazetteer*, IV, 114.
[3] *Ethnology in Folklore*, 94.
[4] Jarrett, *Aín-i-Akbari*, II, 408, quoting Alberuni, chapter VIII.

may have some connection with the use of iron as a fetish which scares evil spirits and to the widespread idea of the supernatural power of the blacksmith.[1] In the Panjáb an earthen pot of filth is carried to the door of some old woman cursed with a bad temper and thrown down so as to soil her threshold: if she then falls into a rage and gives vent to her feelings in abusive language, the rain will come down. Here, as in a case already given, the old woman is probably regarded as a sort of witch, who, if punished, will release the rain.[2] In Kangra there are some local gods whose temples are endowed with rent-free lands. When rain is wanted these deities are ordered to procure it, and if they fail they have to pay a fine into the Rája's treasury. This is the way the Chinese treat their gods who refuse to perform their duty.[3] The song of Alha and Udal, which describes the struggle between the Hindus and the early Muhammadan invaders, is sung in Oudh to procure rain. In the hills smart showers are attributed to the number of marriages going on in the plains. The bride and bridegroom, as we shall see in the legend of Dulha Deo, are particularly exposed to demoniacal influence of weather. In the eastern districts of the North-Western Provinces the people will not kill wolves, as they say that wherever a drop of wolf's blood falls there will be a scarcity of rain. To close this catalogue of rain spells, it is a common belief that sacred stones are connected with rainfall. The relics of Gautama Buddha were believed to have the same influence.[4] So the *linga* of Mahádeva, a thirsty deity, who needs continual cooling to relieve his distress, must be kept continually moist to avoid drought. Last year when rain failed at Mirzapur the people contributed to pay a gang of labourers who brought water to pour on a famous *linga*. Curiously enough the same custom prevails in Samoa. There, when there was excessive rain the stone representing the rain-making god was laid by the fire and kept warm till fine weather set in: but in

---

[1] *Folklore*, I, 273: Schrader, *Prehistoric Antiquities of the Aryan people*, 163, *sqq*.
[2] *Panjáb Notes and Queries*, I, 102.
[3] *Ibid*, II-41. Lyall, *Asiatic Studies*, 136.
[4] Beal *Fah Hian*, 78.

time of drought the priest and his followers dressed up in fine mats and went in procession to the stream, dipped the stone and prayed for a shower.[1]

Spells to cause rain to cease.

As in England, where "little children have a custom when it raines to sing or charm away the raine, joining in the chorus

"Raine! Raine! go away!
Come again a Saturday,"

so there are in India various spells intended to prevent the rain from falling. One is the reverse of the nudity charm which we have already discussed. In Madras a woman, generally an ugly widow, is made to dance, sometimes naked, with a burning stick in her hand and facing towards the sky. This is supposed to disgust Varuna, the sky god, who shrinks away at such a sight.[2] Another Madras method is to throw the two parts of a broken cocoanut over a shed as a propitiation to Varuna. In Muzaffarnagar the Muni or Rishi Agastya, who is a great personage in early folklore, is supposed to have power to stop the rain. When rain is in excess they draw a figure of him on a loin cloth and put it out in the rain. Some paint his figure on the outside of the house and let the rain wash it off. Others put some oil and water in a pot and shake them together till they are well mixed. Here we have possibly the idea that oil stills the raging waves. Another approved method is to put some water in a pot and bury it. This is believed to be a common practice with corn chandlers who love a drought, and when rain falls it is a common village phrase—"some rascal has been burying the water" (*páni gárná*). Another practice of evil-minded people is to fill lamp saucers with melted butter, and to light the wicks when clouds gather overhead. After a time they blow out the light and this causes the rain clouds to disperse. The theory is that the rain is ashamed at being liable to the suspicion

---

[1] Turner's *Samoa*, 45.

[2] *North Indian Notes and Queries*, I, 101: Aubrey, *Remaines*, 180: Henderson, *Folklore of the Northern Counties*, 24.

of putting out the sacred light. Another method is to take a piece of unleavened bread, to go into the fields and place it on the ground; or taking some sugar, rice, &c., to a place where four roads meet to defile it in a particularly disgusting way. On such substances it is believed that the rain is ashamed to fall. In Bombay a leaf plate filled with cooked rice and curds is placed in some open spot where the rain can see it and be off. If the rain should persist in coming, a live coal is placed on a tile and laid in an open space, where it is implored to swallow the hateful rain. All these practices are magic of the ordinary sympathetic kind.[1] Rain clouds are supposed also to be under the influence of the evil eye, and will blow over without giving rain if the malicious glance falls upon them. Hence, when rain is needed, if any one runs out of a house bareheaded while a shower is going on, he is ordered in at once, or he is made to put on his cap or turban, for a bareheaded man is apt to wish involuntarily that the rain may cease and thus injure his neighbours.

Hail and whirlwind.

The hail and the whirlwind are, like most of the natural phenomena which we have been discussing, attributed to demoniacal agency. Demons can, as we shall see later on, be dispersed by noise.[2] Hence one plan of driving off the hail demon is to take out an iron griddle plate and beat it with a bamboo. Here the use of the iron increases the efficiency of the spell. In a simpler form of the spell an unmarried girl is sent out of the house with an iron plate in her hand. In Muzaffarnagar when hail begins they pray at once to two noted demons, Ismáil Jogí and Noná Chamárin, and ring a bell in the nearest Saiva temple to scare the demon. In Mirzapur the Kharwárs throw the wooden peg on which the house flour mill works into the courtyard. In Multán it is believed that if you can catch a hail stone in the air before it reaches the ground and cut it in two with a pair of scissors, the hail will abate.[3] Not long ago a lady at Naini Tal, when a hailstorm came

[1] Aubrey, *Remaines*, 180; Henderson, *Folklore*, 24; *Panjáb Notes and Queries*, I, 65, 75, 109, 126.
[2] Henderson, *Folklore*, 4, 63; Farrer, *Primitive Manners*, 2, *sq.*
[3] Cunningham, *Archæological Reports*, V, 136.

on, saw her gardener rush into the kitchen and bring out the cook's chopper, with which he began to make strokes on the ground where the hail was falling. It appeared that he believed that the hail would dread being cut and cease to fall.[1] Whirlwinds also are the work of a demon. In Ireland it is believed that a whirlwind denotes that a devil is dancing with a witch: or that the fairies are rushing by, intent on carrying off some victim to the fairy mansions. The only help is to fling clay at the passing wind, and the fairies will be compelled to drop the mortal child or the beautiful young girl they have abducted[2]. In the Panjáb, Pheru, a saint well known in folklore,[3] is the deity of the petty whirlwinds which blow when the little dust clouds rise in the hot weather. Another whirlwind demon, the Saint Ráhma, was once neglected at the wheat harvest, and he raised a whirlwind which blew for nine days in succession. Since then his shrine receives the appropriate offerings.[4] On the same principle in Bombay whirlwinds are called Bagalya or devils.[5] Among the Mirzapur Korwas when a duststorm comes, the women thrust the house broom (*jhárú*) into the thatch so that it may not be blown away. The Ghasiyas make the women hold the thatch and stick an iron or wooden spoon into it to abate the wind. If a man were to touch it, the wind would rise and sweep the whole roof away. The Pankas in the same way make their women hold the thatch and throw a rice mortar and the flour mill pivot into the courtyard. The wind is ashamed of being defeated by the power of women, and ceases to blow. The residence of a soul in heaven is proportionate to his charities on earth, and when his allotted period is over, he falls as an aërolite. Many of these are worshipped as Linga, in Saiva shrines. An aërolite which fell at Sátímarhi in Bengal, in 1880, has now been deified and is worshipped as Adbhút Nátha or "the miraculous god[6]."

---

1 *North Indian Notes and Queries*, I, 13.
2 Lady Wilde, *Legends*, 128 : also see *Folklore*, I, 149, 153.
3 His legend is given by Temple, *Legends of the Panjáb*, II, 104, *sqq*; III, 301.
4 *North Indian Notes and Queries*, I, 39.
5 Forbes, *Oriental Memoirs*, I, 205.
6 Cunningham, *Archæological Reports*, XVI, 32.

CHAPTER II.

THE HEROIC AND VILLAGE GODLINGS.

Arma procul currusque virum miratur inanes :
Stant terrâ defixæ hastæ, passimque soluti
Per campum pascuntur equi.

ÆNEID, vi, 652—654.

The heroic godlings.

NEXT to those deities which have been classed as the godlings of nature come those which have a special local worship of their own. The number of these godlings is immense, and their functions and attributes so varied that it is extremely difficult to classify them on any intelligible principle. Some of them are pure village godlings of whom the last census has unearthed an enormous number all through the province. Some of them, like Hanumán or Bhímsen, are survivals in a somewhat debased form of some of the second-rate deities or heroes of the older mythology. Some have risen to the rank or are being gradully elevated to the status of tribal deities. Some are in all probability the local gods of the degraded races whom we may tentatively assume to be autochthynous. Many of these have almost certainly been absorbed into Bráhmanism at a comparatively recent period. Some are even now on their promotion for elevation into the orthodox pantheon. But it will require a much more deliberate analysis of the popular faith before it will be possible to classify this mob of divinities on any definite principle. The deities of the heroic class are as a rule benignant, and are generally worshipped by most Hindus. Those that have been definitely promoted into the respectable divine cabinet, like Hanumán, have Bráhmans or members of the ascetic orders as their priests, and their images, if not exactly admitted into the holy of holies of the greater shrines, are still allotted a respectable position in the neighbourhood, and receive a share in the offerings of the faithful. The local position of the shrine very often defines the status of the deity. To many godlings of this class is allotted the duty of acting as warders (*dwárapála*) to the temples of the great gods. Thus, at the Asthbhuja hill in Mirzapur the pilgrim to the shrine of the eight-armed Deví meets first on the road an image of the monkey god Hanumán before he comes into the immediate presence of the goddess. So at Benares Bhaironnáth is chief police officer (*kotwál*) or guardian of all the Saiva temples. Similarly at Jageswar beyond Almora we have Kshetrpál, at Bhadrináth Ghantakaran, at Kedárnáth Bhairava, and at Tungnáth Kál Bhairon[1]. In many places as the pilgrim ascends to the greater temples, he comes to a place whence the first view of the shrine is obtained. This is known as the *devadekhní* or spot from which the deity is viewed. This is generally occupied by some lower class deity who is just beginning to be considered respectable. Then comes the temple dedicated to the warden, and lastly the real shrine itself. There can be little doubt that this represents the process by which gods which are now admittedly within the circle of the deities of the first class, such as the beast incarnations of Vishnu, the elephant-headed Ganesa and the Saktis or impersonations of the female energies of nature, underwent a gradual elevation. This process is still going on before our eyes. Thus the familiar Gor Bába, a deified ghost of the aboriginal races, has in many places become a new manifestation of Siva as Goreswara. Similarly the powerful and malignant goddesses, who were by ruder people propitiated by the sacrifice of a buffalo or a goat, have been annexed to Bráhmanism as two of the numerous forms of Deví by the transparent fiction of a Bhainsásurí and Kálí Deví. In the case of the former her origin is clearly proved by the fact that she is regarded as a sort of tribal deity of the mixed class of Kánhpuriya Rájputs in Oudh.[2] Similarly Mahámáí or the "Great Mother," a distinctively aboriginal goddess, whose shrine consists of a low, flat mound of earth, with seven knobs of coloured clay in a single row at the head or west side, has been promoted into the higher pantheon as Jagadambá Deví, or "Mother of the World." Her shrine is still a simple, flat mound of earth with seven knobs

---

[1] Atkinson, *Himalayan Gazetteer*, II, 762.
[2] *Gazetteer*, I, 79.

at the top, and a flag in front to the east.[1] More extended analysis will probably show that the obligations of Bráhmanism to the local cultus are much greater than is commonly believed.

Hanumán.

First among the heroic godlings is Hanumán, "he of the large jaws," or as he is generally called Mahábír, "the great hero," the celebrated monkey chief of the Rámáyana, who assisted Ráma in his campaign against the giant Rávana to recover Sítá. Hardly any event in his mythology is more familiar to the Hindu peasant than this, because it forms the favourite subject of dramatic representation at the annual festival of the Dasahra. There Hanumán in fitting attire marches along the stage at the head of his army of bears and monkeys, and the play ends with the destruction of Rávana, whose great body formed of wicker work and paper is blown up with fireworks amidst the delighted enthusiasm of the excited audience. It is almost certain that the worship of Hanumán does not come down from the earliest ages of the Hindu faith, though it has been suggested that he is the legitimate descendant of Vrisha Kapi, the great monkey of the Veda.[2] One legend represents him as bringing during the great war from the Himalaya a mountain on which grew a tree which would relieve the wound of the hero Lakhshmana: but Bharata shot at him as he passed through the air, and wounding him, compelled him to drop a piece which formed the sacred hill at Govardhan. This is very like the story of the creation of the Vindhyan range to which reference has been already made. The more extreme school of modern mythologists would make out that Hanumán is only the impersonation of the great cloud monkey which fights the sun.[3] But the fact of monkey worship is susceptible of a much simpler explanation. The ape, from his appearance and human ways, is closely associated with man. It is a belief common to all folklore that monkeys were once human beings who have suffered degradation,[4] and according to one tradition stealers

---

[1] Cunningham, *Archæological Reports*, XVII, 141.
[2] Barth, *Religions of India*, 265.
[3] Gubernatis, *Zoological Mythology*, II, 99 *sq.*
[4] See the instances collected by Tylor, *Primitive Culture* I, 376 *sqq.*

of fruit become monkeys in their next incarnation: but the common theory that the monkey is venerated in memory of the demigod Hanumán is, as Sir A. Lyall[1] remarks, "plainly putting the cart before the horse, for the monkey is evidently at the bottom of the whole story. Hanumán is now generally supposed to have been adopted into the Hindu heaven from the non-Aryan or aboriginal idolators: though, to my mind, any uncivilized Indian would surely fall down and worship at first sight of an ape. Then there is the modern idea that the god was really a great chief of some such aboriginal tribe as those which to this day dwell almost like wild creatures in the remote forests of India: and this may be the nucleus of fact at the bottom of the legend regarding him. It seems as if hero worship and animal worship had got mixed up in the legend of Hanumán." At the same time it must be remembered that the so-called Aryans enjoy no monopoly of his worship. He is something like a tribal god of the Drávidian Suirís, and the wild Bhuiyas of Keonjhar identify him with Borám, the Sun god,[2] and it is at least a possible supposition that his worship was imported into Bráhmanism from some such source as these.

Hanumán as a village god.

Whatever may be the origin of the cult the fact remains that he is a great village god with potent influence to scare evil spirits from his subjects. His rude image smeared with oil and red ochre, meets one somewhere or other in almost every respectable Hindu village. In Bombay he is a giver of offspring, and barren women sometimes go to his temple in the early morning, strip themselves naked and embrace the god.[3] He is, as has been remarked, very popular among the Hinduised Drávidian races of the Vindhyan plateau. "The most awe-inspiring of their tremendous rocks are his fanes; the most lovely of their pools are sacred in virtue of the tradition of his having bathed in them." He was known as *Pawan ká pút* or "Son of the wind"; and the Bhuiyas of Singhbum, who are, Col.

[1] *Asiatic Studies*, 13*sq*.
[2] Buchanan, *Eastern India*, I, 467: Dalton, *Descriptive Ethnology*, 147.
[3] Campbell, *Notes*, 260.

Dalton gravely remarks, "without doubt the apes of the Rámáyana," call themselves Pawan bans or "sons of the wind" to this day.[1] But his chief function is as a warden or guardian against demoniacal influence, and at the Hanumángarhi shrine at Ajudhya, he is provided with a regular priesthood consisting of Kháki ascetics. The respect paid to the monkey does not need illustration. Everywhere in orthodox villages his life is protected by a most effective sanction. General Sleeman[2] tells the story of a Muhammadan Nawáb of Oudh who was believed to have died of fever, the result of killing a monkey. "Mumtaz-ud-daula" said his informant "might have been King of Oudh had his father not shot that monkey." In the Panjáb an appeal to a monkey overcomes the demon of the whirlwind. Where a monkey has been killed, it is believed, no one can live. His bones are also exceedingly unluckly, and a special class of exorcisors in Behár make it their business to ascertain that his bones do not pollute the ground on which a house is about to be erected.[3]

Bhímsen.

Another of these beneficent guardians or wardens is Bhímsen, "he who has a terrible army." He has now in popular belief very little in common with the burly hero of the Mahábhárata, who was notorious for his gigantic strength, great animal courage, prodigious appetite and irascible temper: jovial and jocular when in good humour, but abusive, truculent and brutal when his passions were roused.[4] He is now little more than one of the wardens of the household or village. In parts of the Central Provinces he has become degraded into a mere fetish, and is represented by a piece of iron fixed in a stone or in a tree.[5] Under the name of Bhímpen or Bhímsen his worship extends from Berár to the extreme east of Bastar, and not merely among the Hinduised aborigines, who have begun to honour Khandoba, Hanumán, Ganpati and their brethren, but among the rudest and most

---

1 *Descriptive Ethnology*, 140.
2 *Journey through Oudh*, II, 133.
3 Buchanan, *Eastern India*, II, 141*sq*. *Panjáb Notes and Queries*, IV, 9.
4 Dowson, *Classical Dictionary*, *sv*.
5 *Gazetteer*, 323.

savage tribes. He is generally adored under the form of an unshapely stone covered with vermilion, or of two pieces of wood standing from three to four feet out of the ground, which are possibly connected with the phallic idea towards which deities of this class so often diverge. Bhiwásu, the regular Gond deity, is identical with him. Mr. Hislop mentions a large idol of him eight feet high, with a dagger in one hand and a javelin in the other. He has an aboriginal priest known as Bhúmak or "he of the soil," and the people repair to worship on Tuesdays and Saturdays, offering he-goats, hogs, hens, cocks and cocoanuts. The headman of the village and the cultivators subscribe for an annual feast which takes place at the commencement of the rains, when the priest takes a cow from the headman by force and offers it to the godling in the presence of his congregation.[1] The Máriya Gonds worship him in the form of two pieces of wood previous to the sowing of the crops. The Naikude Gonds worship him in the form of a huge stone covered with vermilion. Before it a little rice cooked with sugar is placed. They then besmear the stone with vermilion and burn resin as incense in its honour, after which the victims—sheep, hogs and fowls, with the usual oblation of spirits—are offered. The god is now supposed to inspire the priest, who rolls his head, leaps frantically round and round, and finally falls down in a trance; when he announces whether Bhímsen has accepted the service or not. At night all join in drinking, dancing and beating drums. Next morning the congregation disperses. Those who are unable to attend this tribal gathering perform similar rites at home under the shade of a *mahua* tree *(bassia latifolia)*[2].

Pillar worship of Bhímsen.

The local worship of Bhímsen is specially in the form of pillars, which are known as Bhímláth or "Bhím's clubs." Many of these are really the memorial pillars erected by the great Buddhist King Asoka, but they have been appropriated by Bhímsen. Such are the pillars in the

---

[1] Hislop, *Papers*, 16.
[2] *Ibid* 23 *sqq*.

Bálaghát district of the Central Provinces, and at Kaháon in Gorakhpur. At Devadhura, in the lower Himalayas, are two boulders, the uppermost of which is called Ransila or the "Stone of War." On this rests a smaller boulder said to be the same as that used by Bhímsen to produce the fissures in the rocks: in proof of which the print of his five fingers is still pointed out.[1] Bhímsen is one of the special gods of the Bhuiyas of Keonjhur, and they consider themselves to be descended from him as he is the brother of Hanumán, the founder of their race.[2] According to the Hindu ritual he has his special feast on the *Bhaimy ekádashí* or eleventh of the bright fortnight in the month of Mágh. The Bengal legend tells that Bhímsen, the brother of Yudishthira, when he was sent to the snowy mountains and lay benumbed with cold, was restored by the saint Gorakhnáth, and made king of one hundred and ten thousand hills, stretching from the source of the Ganges to Bhután. Among other miracles Bhímsen and Gorakhnáth introduced the sacrifice of buffaloes in place of human beings, and in order to effect this Bhímsen thrust some of the flesh down the throat of the holy man. So, though they have both lost caste in consequence they are both deified. The saint is still the tutelary deity of the reigning family of Nepál, and all over that kingdom and Mithila Bhímsen is a very common object of worship. That mysterious personage Gorakhnáth flits through religious legend and folklore from postvedic to mediæval times, and little has yet been done to discover the element of historical truth which underlies an immense mass of the wildest fiction.[3]

Worship of Bhíshma.

In about the same rank as Bhímsen is Bhíshma, "the terrible one," another hero of the Mahábhárata. As having died childless, with no descendant to perform his funeral sacrifices, he is worshipped with libations of water on the *Bhíshma ashtamí*, or 23rd of the month of *Mágh*, but this

[1] Madden, *Journal, Asiatic Society, Bengal*, 1848, page 600.
[2] Dalton, *Descriptive Ethnology*, 147.
[3] Buchanan, *Eastern India*, III, 38: *Panjáb Notes and Queries*, I, 1, 25; II, 10, 45, 56, 83, 182; IV, 2, 24, 12, 63.

ceremony hardly extends beyond Bengal.[1] In Upper India five days in the month of *Kártik* (November-December), are sacred to him. This is a woman's festival. They send lamps to a Bráhman's house, whose wife during these five days must sleep on the ground on a spot covered with cowdung, close to the lamps which it is her duty to keep alight. The lamps are filled with sesamum oil and red wicks wound round sticks of the sesamum plant rest in the lamp saucers. A walnut, an *aonla* (the fruit of the *emblic myrobolon*), a lotus seed and two copper coins are placed in each lamp. Each evening the women come and prostrate themselves before the lamps or walk round them. They bathe each day of the feast before sunrise and are allowed only one meal in the day, consisting of sugarcane, sweet potatoes and other roots, with meal made of amaranth seed, millet and buckwheat cakes, to which the rich add sugar, dry ginger and butter. They drink only milk. Of course the Bráhman gets a share of these good things, to which the rich contribute in addition a lamp saucer made of silver, with a golden wick, clothes and money. At the early morning bath of the last day five lighted lamps made of dough are placed, one at the entrance of the town or village, others at the four cross roads, under the *pípal* or sacred fig tree, at a temple of Siva and at a pond. This last is put on a small raft made of the leaves of the sugarcane and floated on the water. A little grain is placed beside each lamp. After the lamps handed over to the Bráhman have burnt away or gone out, the black from the wicks is rubbed on the eyes and fingers of the worshippers, and their toe nails are anointed with the remainder of the oil. There is a legend connected with this feast. A childless Rája once threatened to kill all his queens unless one of them gave birth to a child. One of the Ránís, who had a cat, announced that she had been brought to bed of a girl, who was to be shut up for twelve years.[2] This was all very well, but the supposed girl had to be married, and here lay the difficulty.

---

[1] Wilson, *Essays*, II, 201; Growse, *Mathura*, 277*sq*.
[2] This is a common folklore incident: for the custom see Frazer, *Golden Bough*, II, 225 *sqq*.

Now this cat had been very attentive during this ceremony to Bhíshma, keeping the wicks alight by raising them from time to time with her paws and cleaning them on her body. So the grateful godling turned her into a beautiful girl, but her tail remained as before. However, the bridegroom's friends admired her so much that they kept her secret at the wedding and so saved the Rání from destruction, and when the time came for the bride to go to her husband, her tail dropped off too. So Hindu ladies use the oil and lamp black of Bhíshma's feast day as valuable aids to beauty.[1]

Worship of local gods.

We now come to the local or village gods. There is good reason to believe that most, if not all, of these deities, belong to the races whom it is convenient to call non-Aryan or aboriginal, or at least outside Bráhmanism, though some of them may have been from time to time promoted into the orthodox pantheon. This non-Bráhmanic character of the worship is implied by the character of their priesthood. In the neighbourhood of Delhi where the worship of Bhúmiya as a local god widely prevails, the so-called priest of his shrine, whose functions are limited to beating a drum during the service and receiving the offerings, is usually of the sweeper caste. Sir John Malcolm notes that the Bhopa of Central India, a functionary of the same class, is usually drawn from some menial tribe.[2] In the hill country of South Mirzapur the priest of the shrine of Gansám or Rája Lákhan, the tribal gods of the Drávidian races, is invariably selected from one of the most degraded of these races. Even the shrine erected in honour of Náhar Ráo, the famous king of Mandor, who met in equal combat the chivalrous Chauhán in the pass of the Aravalli range, is tended by a barber officiant.[3] Often in the same village one may see the shrine of the local god tended by his menial priest and the image of

---

[1] *Panjáb Notes and Queries*, III, 181, *sq*, Animals assisting the heroine and various forms of metamorphosis are common folklore incidents: Temple, *Wide-awake Stories*, 402, 420.

[2] *Central India*, II, 206.

[3] Tod, *Annals*, 1767: and for other examples, *Central Provinces Gazetteer*, 110: Buchanan, *Eastern India*, II, 131, 352, 478.

Mahádeva, Hanumán or Bhímsen, with a Bráhman attendant, and though the congregation of the meaner gods are looked on with some contempt or pity by their more respectable neighbours, little active hostility or intolerance is exhibited, and even in the eyes of the higher classes the miantenance of the village shrine for purely local purposes is generally supported and encouraged.

Village shrines.

The shrine of the regular village god (*gánw devata*) or rather godling in the Western Distircts of the North-Western Provinces, is generally a small square building of brick masonry, with a bulbous head and perhaps an iron spike as a finial. A red flag hung on an adjoining tree marks the shrine. In the interior lamps are occasionally lighted, fire sacrifices (*homa*) performed, and petty offerings made. The outside is often covered with rude representations of the mystical Swástika which has been already noticed in connection with sun worship. These shrines never contain idols which are placed only in the temples of the greater gods: but many of them have an inside platform on which the deity rests when he occupies the place. Speaking of this class of shrine Mr. Ibbetson remarks—"The Hindu shrine must always face east, while the Musalmán shrine is in the form of a tomb and faces the south. This sometimes gives rise to delicate questions. In one village a section of the commnuity had become Muhammadan. The shrine of the common ancestor needed rebuilding, and there was much dispute as to its shape and aspect. They solved the difficulty by building a Musalmán grave facing south, and over it a Hindu shrine facing east. In another village an Imperial trooper was once burnt alive by the shed in which he was sleeping catching fire, and it was thought best to propitiate him by a shrine, or his ghost might become troublesome. He was by religion a Musalmán, but he had been burnt, not buried, which seemed to make him a Hindu. After much discussion the latter opinion prevailed, and a Hindu shrine with an eastern aspect now stands to his memory.[1]" To the east of the North-Western

[1] *Panjáb Ethnography*, 114.

Provinces the village shrines are much less substantial erections. In the Gangetic valley where the population has been completely Hinduised, the shrine of the collective village deities known as the *deohár*, consists of a pile of stones collected under some ancient, sacred tree. Pieces of carved stone, the relics of some ruined temple, are constantly utilised for this purpose. Some of these stones, particularly those which retain some semblance to a figure or are decorated with ornamental carving, are occasionally smeared with oil and vermilion. Little clay images of horses and elephants and curious bowls with short legs known as *kalsa* are sometimes offered. These beehive shaped vessels appear to be used for the same purpose all along the Central Indian hills.[1] The little animal images are by some supposed to represent the equipage (*sawári*) of the deity. Others explain them by the fact that a person in distress vows a horse or elephant to the god, and when his wishes are realised, offers as a substitute this trumpery donation. On the neighbouring trees are often suspended miniature cots which commemorate the recovery of a patient from small-pox or other infectious disease. Among the semi-Hinduised Drávidian races of the Vindhyan range who worship Gansám Deva and Rája Lákhan, the shrine usually consists of a rude mud building, roofed with a rude thatch, which is often allowed to fall into disrepair, until the god reminds his votaries of his displeasure by an outbreak of epidemic disease or some other misfortune which attacks the village. This shrine is in charge of the village Baiga, who is invariably selected from among some of the ruder jungle tribes such as the Bhuiyá or Bhuiyár. Inside is a small mud platform which is known as "the seat of the godling" (*devata ká baithak*), on which are usually placed some of the curiously shaped earthen bowls already described, which are made specially for this worship and not used for ordinary domestic purposes. In these water is placed for the refreshment of the godling and they thus resemble the funeral vases of the Greeks. In ordinary cases the offering deposited on the altar platform consists of a thick griddle cake and a little milk: but in more serious cases where the deity

[1] *Bombay Gazetteer*, III, 220: *Rájputána Gazetteer*, III, 65.

makes his presence disagreeably felt, he is propitiated with a goat, pig or fowl, which is decapitated outside the shrine with the national and sacrificial axe. The head is brought inside dripping with blood, and a few drops of blood are allowed to fall on the platform. The head then becomes the perquisite of the Baiga and the rest of the meat is cooked and eaten near the shrine by the male worshippers, married women being carefully excluded from any share in the offering. The special regard paid to the head of the victim is quite in consonance with traditions of European paganism and folklore in several places.[1] Lower south beyond the river Son the shrine is of even a simpler type, and is there often represented by a few boulders near a stream where the worshippers assemble and make their offerings.

Localisation of the village god.

The non-Bráhmanic character of the worship is still further marked by the fact that no special direction from the homestead is prescribed in selecting the site for the shrine. No orthodox Hindu temple can be built south of the village site, as this quarter is regarded as the realm of Yama, the lord of the dead. In the more Hinduised village some attempt is occasionally made to conform to this rule, and occasionally as in the case of the more respectable Hindu shrines, the door faces the east. But this rule is not universal, and the site of the shrine is often selected under some suitable tree, whatever may be its position as regards the homestead, and it very often commemorates some half-forgotten tragedy, where a man was slain or murdered, where he fell from a tree or was drowned in a watercourse. Here some sort of a shrine is usually made with the object of appeasing the angry spirit of the dead man. These shrines have no idol, no bell to scare vagrant ghosts, and allow the godling to partake of the offerings or listen to the prayers of his votaries. If he is believed to be absent or sleeping, a drum is beaten to awake or recall him, and this answers the purpose of scaring off intruding spirits, who are always hungry and on the watch to appropriate the offerings of the faithful. There are also none of the sacrificial vessels which are

[1] Instances are given by Gomme, *Ethnology in Folklore*, 34, *sq.*

largely used in respectable fanes for cooling the idol with libations of water, and the instrument used for sacrificing the victim is only the ordinary axe which the dweller in the jungles always carries. There is one special implement which is very commonly found in the village shrines of the hill country south of the Ganges. This is an iron chain with a heavy knot at the end to which a strap like a Scotch tawse is often attached. The chain is ordinarily three and a-half feet long, the tawse two feet, and the total weight is about 7 lb. This is known as the *gurda*: it hangs from the roof of the shrine and is believed to be directly under the influence of the deity, so that it is very difficult to procure a specimen. The Baiga priest, when his services are required for the exorcism of a disease ghost, thrashes himself on the back and loins with his chain until he works himself up to the proper degree of religious ecstacy. Among the more primitive Gonds the chain has become a godling, and is regularly worshipped. In serious cases of epilepsy, hysteria and the like, which do not readily yield to ordinary exorcisms, the patient is taken to the shrine and severely beaten with the holy chain until the demon is expelled. This treatment is, I understand, considered particularly effective in the case of hysteria and kindred ailments under which young women are wont to suffer, and like the thong at the Lupercalia at Rome, a few blows of the chain are considered advisable as a remedy for barrenness.

Identification of the local godling.

The speciality of this class of godlings is that they frequent only particular places. Each has his separate jurisdiction, which includes generally one or sometimes a group of villages: and people to whom the local god is obnoxious and who fail to propitiate him by appropriate offerings can usually escape from his malignity by leaving his district This habit of emigration to escape the malignity of the offended godling no doubt accounts for many of the sites of deserted villages which are scattered all over the country. Hence it is absolutely essential that the local godling or group of godlings should be brought under proper control and carefully identified so as to ensure the safety and prosperity of the settlement. There are, as might be expected, various methods of securing this result. Thus in Northern Oudh, when a village is founded, the site is marked off by cross stakes of wood driven into the ground, which are solemnly worshipped on the day of the completion of the settlement, and then lapse into neglect unless some indication of the displeasure of the deity again direct attention to them. These crosses which are called *daharchandi*, are particularly frequent and well-marked in the villages occupied by the aboriginal Thárus in the sub-Himalayan Tarái, where they may be found in groups of ten or more on the edge of the cultivated lands. So among the Santáls, a piece of split bamboo about three feet high is placed in the ground in an inclined position and is called the *sipáhi* or sentinel of the hamlet,[1] and among the Gonds two curved posts, one of which is much smaller than the other, represent the male and female tutelary gods.

In the Eastern Districts of the North-Western Provinces a more elaborate process is carried out, which admirably illustrates the special form of local worship now under consideration. When the site of a new settlement is selected, an Ojha or sorcerer is called in to identify and mark down the deities of the place. He begins by beating a drum round the place for some days, which is understood to scare vagrant, outsider ghosts and to assemble the local deities. All the people assemble, and two men known as the *Mattíwáh* and *Pattíwáh* the "earthman" and the "leafman," who represent the gods of the soil and of the trees, soon become filled with the spirit and are found to be possessed by the local deities. They dance and shout for some time in a state of religious frenzy, and their disconnected ejaculations are interpreted by the Ojha, who suddenly rushes between them, grasps with his hands at the spirits which are supposed to be circling round them, and finally pours through their hands some grains of sesamum which is received in a perforated piece of the wood of the *gúlar* or sacred fig tree. The hole is immediately plastered up with a mixture of clay and cowdung, and the wood is carefully buried on the site selected

[1] Dalton, *Descriptive Ethnology*, 220, 281.

for the *deohár* or local shrine. By this process the deities are supposed to be fastened up in the sacred wood and to be unable to do any mischief, provided that the usual periodical offerings are made in their honour. This system does not appear to prevail among the Drávidian race of the Vindhyan plateau. Some time ago I discussed the matter with Hannu Baiga, the chief priest of the Bhuiyas beyond the Son, and he was pleased to express his unqualified approval of the arrangement. Indeed, he promised to adopt it himself, but unfortunately Hannu, who was a mine of information on the religion and demonology of his people, died before he could apply this test to the local deities of his parish. His wife has died also, and I understand that he is known to be the head of all the Bhúts or ghosts of the neighbourhood, while his wife rules all the Churels who infest that part of the country. At the same time to an ordinary Baiga the plan would be hardly as comfortable as the present arrangement. It would not suit him to have the local ghosts brought under any control, because he makes his living by doing the periodical services to propitiate them. Now-a-days he believes thoroughly in the influence of the magic circle and of spirits as ghost scarers.[1] So he is supposed once a year at least, or oftener in cases of pestilence or other trouble, to perambulate all round the village boundary, sprinkling a line of spirits on the ground as he walks. The idea is to form a magic circle impervious to strange and, in the nature of the case, necessarily malignant ghosts, who might wish to intrude from outside, and to control the resident ghosts and prevent them from contracting evil habits of mischief by wandering beyond their prescribed domains. The worst about this ritual is that the Baiga is apt to be very deliberate in his movements, to drink the liquor himself on the road, and to spoil the symmetry of the circle during his fits of intoxication. I know of one disreputable shepherd who was upwards of a fortnight getting round an ordinary sized village, and the levy on his parishioners to pay the wine bill was, as may easily be imagined, a very serious matter,

[1] For a number of instances of the use of spirits in this way, see Campbell, *Notes*, 128, *sqq*.

to say nothing of several calamities which occurred to the inhabitants in their unprotected state owing to his negligence. At present the feeling in his parish is very strong against him, and his constituents are seriously thinking of removing him, particularly as he has only one eye. This is a very serious deformity in ordinary people, but in a Baiga who is invested with religious functions, it is most objectionable and even dangerous.

In Hoshangábád a different system prevails. When a new village is founded by the aboriginal Kurkus, there is no difficulty in finding the abode of the godlings Dungar devata and Mátá, because you have only to look for and discover them upon their hill and under their tree. But Mutua devata has generally to be created by taking a heap of stones from the nearest stream and sacrificing a pig and seven chickens to him. "There is one ceremony, however, which is worth notice, not so much as being distinctively Kurku, but as illustrating the sense of mystery and chance which in the native mind seem to be connected with the idea of measurement, and which arises probably from the fact that with superficial measures, by heaping lightly or pressing down tight, very different results can be obtained. A measure is filled with grain to the level of the brim, but no head is poured on, and it is put before Mutua devata. They watch it all night, and in the morning pour it out and measure it again. If the grain now fills up the measure and leaves enough for a head to it, and still more if it brims and runs over, this is a sign that the village will be very prosperous, and that every cultivator's granaries will run over in the same way. But it is an evil omen if the grain does not fill up to the level of the rims of the vessel. A similar practice obtains in the Narbada valley when they begin winnowing, and some repeat it every night while the winnowing goes on."[1] The same custom prevails among the Kols in Mirzapur, who make the bride and bridegroom carry it out as an omen of their success or failure in life. By carefully packing and pressing down the grain, any chance of

[1] *Settlement Report*, 257.

an evil augury is easily avoided. We shall see later on that measuring the grain is a favourite device intended to save it from the depredations of evil-minded ghosts.

Dwára Gusáin.

A typical case of the worship of a local god is found among the Malers of Chutia Nágpur. His name is Dwára Gusáin or "lord of the house door." "Whenever from some calamity falling on the household, it is considered necessary to propitiate him, the head of the family cleans a place in front of his door, and sets up a branch of the tree called *mukmum*, which is held very sacred: an egg is placed near the branch, then a hog is killed and friends feasted: and when the ceremony is over the egg is broken and the branch placed on the suppliant's house."[1] Dwára Gusáin is now called Bárahduári, because he is supposed to live in a temple with twelve doors, and is worshipped by the whole village in the month of Mágh.[2] The egg is apparently supposed to hold the deity and this is, it may be remarked, not an uncommon folklore incident.[3]

Bhúmiya.

One of the most characteristic of the benevolent village godlings is Bhúmiyá—the godling of the land or soil (*bhumi*). He is very commonly known as Khetpál or Kshetrpál "the protector of the fields," Khera or "the homestead mound," Zamindár or the "landowner," and in the hills Saim or Sayam (Sanskrit *Syáma* black). In the neighbourhood of Delhi he is a male godling: in Oudh Bhumiya is a goddess, and is called Bhúmiyá Rání or "Soil Queen." She is worshipped by spreading flat cakes and sweetmeats on the ground, which having been exposed for some time to the sun, are eventually consumed by the worshipper and his family. To the west of the province the erection of Bhúmiyá's shrine is "the first formal act by which the proposed site of a new village is consecrated, and when two villages have combined their homesteads for greater security against the marauders of former days, the people of the one which moved still

---

[1] Shaw in *Asiatic Researches*, Vol. IV, quoted by Dalton.
[2] Risley, *Tribes and Castes of Bengal*, II, 58.
[3] Temple, *Wide-awake Stories*, 399.

worship at the Bhúmiyá of the deserted site. Bhúmiyá is worshipped after the harvests, at marriages, and on the birth of a male child: and Bráhmans are commonly fed in his name. Women often take their children to the shrine on Sundays, and the first milk of a cow or buffalo is always offered there." Young bulls are sometimes released in his honour, and the term *Bhúmiyá sánd* has come to be equivalent to our "parish bull."[1]

But this simple village godling is well on his way to promotion into the higher heaven. In Patna some have already begun to identify him with Vishnu.[2] In the hills also he is in a transitional stage: by some he is regarded as a beneficent deity who does not, as a rule, force his worship on any one by possessing them or injuring their crops. When a crop is sown a handful of grain is sprinkled over a stone in the field nearest to his shrine, in order to protect the crop from hail, blight, and the ravages of wild animals, and at harvest time he receives the first fruits to protect the garnered crop from rats and insects. He punishes the wicked and rewards the virtuous, and is lord of the village, always interested in its prosperity and a partaker of the good things provided on all occasions of rejoicing such as marriage, the birth of a child, or any great good fortune. Unlike the other rural deities he seldom receives animal sacrifices, but is satisfied with the humblest offering of the fruits of the earth. But he is on his promotion, and is beginning to be known as Saim, a corruption of Svayambhuva, the Bauddha form now worshipped in Nepál, and as such he gets offerings of kids. He sometimes possesses people, and his sign is that the hair of the scalplock becomes hopelessly entangled.[3] This reminds us of the English idea that those who have communication with fairies find their hair all tied in double knots, well known by the title of "elflocks."[4] It must also be noted that all over the world the hair is considered an inlet for spirits, possibly,

---

[1] *Oudh Gazetteer*, I, 518: Ibbetson, *Panjáb Ethnography*, 114.
[2] Buchanan, *Eastern India*, I, 190.
[3] Atkinson, *Himalayan Gazetter*, II, 825.
[4] Sir W. Scott, *Letters on Demonology*, 143.

as Mr. Campbell suggests, because it leads to the opening in the skull through which the dying spirit makes its exit. This may account for various customs of letting the hair loose, cutting it off or shaving.[1]

Bhairon.

Bhúmiyá, again, is often confounded with Bhairon, another warden godling of the land: while to illustrate the extraordinary jumble of these mythologies, Bhairon, who is almost certainly the "Karo Byro" (Kál Bhairon) of the Bhuiyas of Keonjhar, is identified by them with Bhímsen[2]. One of his most famous shrines is at Kalinjar, of which Abul Fazl says "marvellous tales are related."[3] Bhairon has a curious history. There is little doubt that he was originally a simple village deity: but with a slight change of name he has been adopted into Bráhmanism as Bhairava, "the terrible one," one of the most awful forms of Siva, while the female form Bhairaví is an equivalent for Deví, a worship specially prevalent among Jogis and Sáktas. On the other hand, the Jains worship Bhairava as the protector or agent of the Jain church and community, and do not offer him flesh or blood sacrifices, but fruit and sweetmeats.[4] In his Saiva form he is often called Svásva, "or he who rides a dog instead of a horse," and this vehicle of his marks him down as an offshoot from the rural Bhairon, because all through Upper India the favourite method of conciliating Bhairon is to feed a black dog until he is surfeited. One of his distinctive forms is Kál Bhairon, who is said in the Panjáb to frighten away death, but whom Colonel Tod, writing of Rájputána, calls "the bloodstained divinity of war."[5] The same godling is known as Bhairoba in Bombay, of whom Mr. Campbell[6] writes "He is represented as a standing male figure with a trident in the left hand and a drum (*damaru*) in the right, and encircled by a serpent. When thus represented, he is called Kála Bhairava.

---

[1] See the instances collected by Campbell, *Notes*, 173 *sqq.*
[2] Dalton, *Descriptive Ethnology*, 147.
[3] Jarrett, *Ain-i-Akbari*, II, 159: *Gazetteer, N.-W. P.*, I, 461.
[4] Wilson, *Essays*, I, 21: *Bombay Gazetteer*, XVI, 568.
[5] *Annals*, II, 515.
[6] *Notes*, 147.

But generally he is represented by a rough stone covered over with oil and red lead. He is said to be very terrible, and, when offended, difficult to be pleased. By some he is believed to be an incarnation of Siva himself, and by others as a spirit much in favour with the god Siva. He is also consulted as an oracle. When any one is desirous of knowing whether anything he is about to undertake will turn out according to his wishes, he sticks two unbroken betel nuts one on each breast of the stone image of Bhairava, and tells it, if his wish is to be accomplished, that the right or left nut is to fall first. It is said that, like other spirits, Bhairava is not a subordinate of Vetála; and that when he sets out on his circuit at night, he rides a black horse and is accompanied by a black dog." The same godling is in other forms known as Láth Bhairon, or "Bhairon of the club," which approximates him to Bhimsen, and as Battuk Bhairon or "the child Bhairon," and Nand Bhairon, in which we may possibly trace a connection with the legend of the divine child Krishna and his foster-father Nanda. In Benares, again, he is known as Bhaironnáth or "Lord Bhairon," or Bhút Bhairon, "Ghost Bhairon," and is regarded as the deified Magistrate of the city, who guards all the temples of Siva and saves his votaries from demons.[1]

Village worship of Bhairon.

But in his original character as a simple village godling, Bhairon is worshipped with milk and sweetmeats as the protector of the fields, cattle and homestead. Some worship him by pouring spirits at his shrine and drinking there: and on a new house being built he is propitiated to expel the local ghosts. He is respected even by Muhammadans as the Minister of the great Saint Sakhi Sarwar, and is usually called Bhairon Jati or "Bhairon the chaste."[2] But he is rapidly becoming promoted into the more respectable pantheon, and this will possibly finally take place at the great Saiva shrine of Mandháta on the Narbada with which a local legend closely

[1] Sherring, *Sacred City*, 119.
[2] *Panjáb Notes and Queries*, *I*, 35.

connects him.[1] All over Northern India his stone fetish is found in close connection with the images of the greater gods, to whom he acts the part of guardian, and this, as we have already seen, probably marks a stage in the process of his elevation.

Worship of the great mothers.

From these benevolent village godlings we pass on to a very obscure form of local worship, that of the great mothers. There can be very little doubt that this worship is founded on some of the very earliest beliefs of the race. No great religion is without its deified woman, the Virgin, Máya, Fátimah, and it may perhaps be suggested that it has come down from a time before the present organization of the family came into existence, and when descent through the mother was the only recognised form.[2] We have already met instances of this mother worship in the case of Gangá máí, "Mother Ganges," and Dhartí mátá "the Earth mother." We shall meet it again in Sítalá mátá, "the small-pox mother." In the older mythology Aditi or infinite space was regarded as Eternal Mother, and Prákrití was the Eternal Mother capable of evolving all created things out of herself, but never so creating unless united with the eternal spiritual principle embodied in the Eternal Male Parusha. Hence the dualistic idea in Bráhmanism of the androgynous Siva (*Ardhanari*). We shall meet later on with the ghost of the unpurified mother, the Churel, which is based on a different but cognate association of ideas. Akin to this again is the worship of the Satí, which will be discussed later on, and that of the Cháran women of Gujarát, who were obliged to immolate themselves to prevent outrage from the Kolis and other freebooters. This worship, probably originally derived from one of the so-called non-Aryan races, was subsequently developed into that of the female energies of the greater gods, as Bráhmání of Bráhma, Indrání of Indra, and so on : and thus the simple primitive worship of the mother has developed and degenerated into the abominations of the Tantras. These mothers are

---

1 *Central Provinces Gazetteer*, 259.

2 Lubbock, *Origin of Civilisation*, 146 : Starke, *Primitive Family*, 17 *sqq* : Letourneau *Sociology*, 384.

usually regarded as eight in number (*ashta mátri*), but the enumeration of them varies. Sometimes there are only seven—Bráhmí or Bráhmání, Máhesvarí, Kaumárí, Vaishnaví, Váráhí, Indrání or Aíndrí, or Máhendrí and Chámundá. Sometimes the number is eight—Bráhmání, Vaishnaví, Raudrí, Váráhí, Nárasinhiká, Kaumárí, Máhendrí, Chámundá, Chandiká. Sometimes sixteen—Gaurí, Padmá, Sachí, Medhá, Sávitrí, Vijayá, Jayá, Devasená, Svadhá, Sváhá, Sántí, Pushtí, Dhrití, Tushtí, Atmádevatá, Kuladevatá. They are closely connected with the worship of Siva and are attendants to his son Skanda or Kárttikeya, and rise in the later mythology to a much greater number.[1].

Mother worship in Gujarát.

But it is in Gujarát that this form of worship most widely prevails at the present day. Sir Monier Williams enumerates about one hundred and forty distinct mothers, besides numerous varieties of the more popular forms. They are all probably local dieties of the Churel type, who have been adopted into Bráhmanism. Some are represented by rudely-carved images, others by simple shrines, and others are remarkable for preferring empty shrines, and the absence of all visible representation. Each has special functions. Thus one called Khodiar or "mischief," is said to cause mischief unless propitiated : another called Antai causes and prevents whooping cough : another named Berai prevents cholera : another called Maraki causes cholera : Hadakái controls mad dogs and prevents hydrophobia : Asápura, represented by two idols, satisfies the hopes of wives by giving children. Not a few are worshipped either as causing or preventing demoniacal possession as a form of bodily disease. The offering of goat's blood to some of these mothers is regarded as very effectual. A story is told of a Hindu doctor who cured a whole village of an outbreak of violent influenza, attributed to the malignant influence of an angry

---

[1] Moiner Williams, *Sanskrit Dictionary*, s. v. *Matri* and for the Nepál enumeration Oldfield, *Sketches*, I, 151 ; for Bombay *Gazetteer*, XVII, 715. In the *Katha Sarit Ságara* (I, 552,) Náráyaní ; is their leader. There is a very remarkable story of the gambler who swindled the Divine Mother (*Ibid*, II, 574, *sqq*).

goddess, by simply assembling the inhabitants, muttering some cabalistic texts, and solemnly letting loose a pair of scapegoats in a neighbouring wood as an offering to the offended deity. One of these mothers is connected with the curious custom of the Couvade, which will be discussed later on.[1] Another famous Gujarát mother is Ambá Bhaváni. On the eighth night of the Naurátra the Rána of Dánta attends the worship, fans the goddess with a horse-hair fly flapper, celebrates the fire sacrifice, and fills with sweetmeats a huge cauldron which, on the fall of the garland from the neck of the goddess, the Bhíls empty. Among the offerings to her are animal sacrifices and spirituous liquor. The image is a block of stone roughly hewn into the semblance of a human figure.[2]

Mother worship in Upper India.

In the Hills what is known as the Mátri Púja is very popular. The celebrant takes a plank and cleans it with rice flour. On it he draws sixteen figures representing the Mátris, and to the right of them a representation of Ganesa. Figures of the sun and moon are also delineated, and a brush made of sacred grass is dipped in cow-dung, and the figures touched with it. After the recital of verses a mixture of sugar and butter is let drop on the plank three, five, or seven times. The celebrant then marks the forehead and throat of the person for whose benefit the service is performed with a coin soaked in butter, and keeps the money as his fee. The service concludes with a waving of lamps to scare vicious ghosts, singing of hymns and offering of gifts to Bráhmans.[3] In many parts of the plains Máyá, the mother of Buddha, has been introduced into the local woship as the *Gánwdeví* or village goddess. Her statues, which are very numerous in some places, are freely used for this purpose.[4]

---

[1] *Religious Thought in India*, 225, *sqq*. quoted by Campbell, *Notes*, 311: *Athenæum*, 6th *December* 1879. *Folklore Record*, III, Part I, 117, *sqq*.
[2] *Bombay Gazetteer*, V, 432, *sq*.
[3] Atkinson, *Himalayan Gazetteer*, II, 884.
[4] For instances, see Growse, *Mathura*, 116,125.

The jungle mothers.

As an instance of another type of this mother worship, we may take Porámái of Nadiya. She is represented by "a little piece of rough black stone painted with red ochre, and placed beneath the boughs of an ancient banyan tree. She is said to have been in the heart of the jungles with which Nadiya was originally covered, and to have suffered from the fire which Rája Kási Náth's men lighted to burn down the jungle."[1] She is, in fact, a mother goddess of the jungle of whom there are numerous instances. In the North-Western Provinces she is usually known as Banspatí or Bansaptí Má, "mistress of the jungle." Her shrine is generally a rude mass of stones and branches to which every passer-by contributes. When she is displeased she allows a tiger or leopard to kill her negligent votary. Sometimes she is identified with the Churel, more often with a mere ghost (*bhút*, *havva*) of some one who met untimely death in the forest. Akin to her is the Ghataut of Mirzapur, who is the deity of dangerous hill passes (*ghát*), and is worshipped in the same way, and Baghaut, the ghost of a man killed by a tiger. These all merge in character and function with the collective divine council (*deohár*) of villages on the borders of the jungle.

Other mothers.

Another of these mother goddesses, Mátá Januví or Janamí, the mother of births, is a sort of Juno Lucina among the Rájputs.[2] Her power rests in a bead, and all over Northern India midwives carry as a charm to ensure easy delivery a particular sort of bead known as *Kailás maurá* or "the crown of the sacred mountain Kailása." Another plan is to give the patient to drink out of a brass vessel engraved with spells and verses from the Qurán. In the Panjáb the washings of a brick from the fort of Chákabu of Amín near Pehoa are potent for the same purpose: or if any one knows how to draw a ground plan of the fort, the water in which the picture is washed off will be equally effective as a potion.[3] Dread famine has even become a mother

---

[1] Bholanáth Chandra, *Travels of a Hindu*, I, 38.
[2] Tod, *Annals*, I, 378.
[3] *Karnál Settlement Report*, 154.

goddess in the form of Bhúkhí Mátá, the mother of hunger, who like all the deities of dearth, is of a lean and starved appearance.[1] An interesting ceremony for the exorcism of famine is recorded from Bombay. The people subscribed to purchase ten sheep, fifty fowls, one hundred cocoanuts, betel nuts, sugar, clarified butter, frankincense, red powder, turmeric and flowers. A day previous to the commencement of the ceremony all the inhabitants of the village, taking with them their clothes, vessels, cattle and other moveable things, left their houses and encamped at the gate or boundary of the village. At the village gate a triumphal arch was erected, and it was adorned with garlands of flowers and mango leaves. Cocoanuts were hung from the arch, and the mango leaves were covered with red powder and turmeric. The villagers bathed, put on new clothes, and then a procession was formed. The village watchman walked in front, and next to him came the village headman, the crier and then the principal men of the village. On coming to the triumphal arch the whole procession stopped. A hole was dug in the ground and the village watchman put in it the head of a sheep, a cocoanut, betel nuts, and leaves and flowers. The arch was then worshipped by each of the villagers. The village watchman first entered the arch, and he was followed by the villagers with music, loud cheering and clapping of hands. The whole party then went to the village temple, bowed to the village god, and went to their respective houses. The blood of the ten sheep and fifty fowls was offered to the village gods, and the flesh was distributed among the villagers. A dinner was given to Bráhmans, and the ceremony came to an end.[2] Greatest of all the mother goddesses of the Rájputs is Mámá Deví, the mother of the gods. In one of her temples the goddess is represented in the midst of her numerous family, including the greater and minor divinities. Their statues are all of the purest marble, each about three feet high and tolerably executed, though evidently since the decline of the art.[3]

---

[1] Tod, *Annals*, II, 363*sq*; 763: Conway, *Demonology*, I, 54.
[2] Campbell, *Notes*, 145.
[3] Tod, *Annals*, I, 708; II, 670.

We now come to consider two divinities special to the Drávidian races who touch on the North-Western Provinces to the south across the Vindhyan and Kaimúr ranges, the physical as well as the ethnical frontier between the valleys of the Ganges and the Jumna and the mountain country of Central India. The chief Gond deity is Gansám Deo. Some vague attempt has been made to elevate him into the pantheon of Bráhmanism, and his name has been corrupted into Ghanasyáma, which means in Sanskrit "black like the thick heavy clouds of the rainy season," and is an epithet of Ráma and Krishna. One legend derives him from an actual Gond chieftain, just as many of the local gods whom we shall consider afterwards have sprung from real living personages of eminence or those who have lost their lives in some exceptional way. It is said that this chieftain was devoured by a tiger soon after his marriage. As might have been expected, his spirit was restless, and one year after his death he visited his wife and she conceived by him. "The descendants of this ghostly embrace are, it is said, living to this day at Amoda in the Central Provinces. He, about the same time, appeared to many of his old friends, and persuaded them that he could save them from the maws of tigers and other calamities, if his worship were duly inaugurated and regularly performed: and in consequence of this two festivals in the year were established in his honour: but he may be worshipped at any time, and in all sicknesses and misfortunes his votaries confidently appeal to him."[1] In the hill country of Mirzapur the shrine of Gansám is about one hundred yards from the village site and without any ornamentation; both inside and outside is a platform of mud on which the deity can rest when so disposed. The only special offerings to him are the curious water pot (*kalsá*) already described and some rude figures of horses and elephants which are regarded as the equipage (*sawári*) of the deity. In the Central Provinces, "a bamboo with a red or yellow flag tied to the end is planted in one corner, an old withered garland or two is hung up, a few blocks of rough stone, some smeared with

Gansam Deo.

---

[1] Dalton, *Descriptive Ethnology*, 232.

vermilion, are strewn about the place which is specially dedicated to Gansám Deo." [1]

Dulha Deo, the bridegroom god.

Another great god of the Drávidian races is Dulha Deo, "the bridegroom god." In his worship we have an echo of some great tragedy which still exercises a profound influence on the mind of the people. The bridegroom on his way to fetch his bride is, by established Hindu custom, treated with special reverence: and this unfortunate bridegroom, whose name is forgotten, is said to have been killed by lightning in the midst of his marriage rejoicings, and he and the horse he rode were turned into stone. In fact, like Ganymede or Hylas, he was carried off by the envy or cruel love of the merciless divine powers. He is now one of the chief household godlings of the Drávidian peoples. Flowers are offered to him on the last day of Phálgun (February), and at marriages a goat. Among some of the Gond tribes he has the first place, and is identified with Pharsipen, the god of war. In the native states of Ríwa and Sarguja, even Bráhmans worship him, and his symbol or fetish is the battle axe, the national weapon of the Drávidians, fastened to a tree [2] In Mirzapur he is pre-eminently the marriage god. In the marriage season he is worshipped in the family cook-room, and at weddings oil and turmeric are offered to him. When two or three children in the same hamlet are being married at the same time, there is a great offering made consisting of a red goat and cakes: and to mark the benevolent character of the deity as a household godling, the women, contrary to the usual rule, are allowed a share of the meat. This purely domestic worship is not done by the Baiga or devil priest, but by the eldest son (*tikait*) of the family. He is specially the tribal god of the Ghasiyas, who pour a little spirits in the cook-room in honour of him and of deceased relations. The songs in his honour lay special stress on the delicacies which the house matron prepares in his honour. Among the Kharwárs when the newly-married pair come home, he is worshipped near the family hearth. A goat is fed

[1] *Gazetteer*, 276.

[2] Dalton, *Descriptive Ethnology*, 134, 280 *sq*.

on rice and pulse, and its head is cut off with an axe with the invocation "take it, Dulha Deo!" On the day when this worship is performed the ashes of the fire-place are carefully removed with the hands, a broom is not used, and special precautions are taken that none of the ashes fall on the ground.

General Sleeman gives the legend of Dulha Deo in another form.

The Bhopal legend of Dulha Deo.

"In descending into the valley of the Narbada over the Vindhyan range from Bhopál, one may see on the side of the road upon a spur of the hill a singular pillar of sandstone rising in two spires, one turning and rising above the other to the height of some twenty to thirty feet. On the spur of a hill, half a mile distant, is another sandstone pillar not quite so high. The tradition is that the smaller pillar was the affianced bride of the larger one, who was a youth of a family of great eminence in those parts. Coming with his uncle to pay his first visit to his bride in the marriage procession, he grew more and more impatient as he approached nearer and nearer, and she shared the feeling. At last unable to restrain himself, he jumped from his uncle's shoulders, and looked with all his might towards the place above where his bride was said to be seated. Unhappily she felt no less impatient than he did, and they saw each other in the same moment. In that moment the bride, bridegroom, and uncle were, all three, converted into pillars, and there they stand to this day, a monument to warn mankind against an inclination to indulge in curiosity. It is a singular fact that in one of the most extensive tribes of the Gond population, to which this couple is said to have belonged, the bride always, contrary to the usual Hindu custom, goes to the bridegroom in procession to prevent a recurrence of this calamity."[1] This legend is interesting from various points of view. In the first place, it is an example of a process of thought which we shall find instances of when dealing with fetishism, whereby a legend is localised in connection with some curious phenomenon in the scenery which attracts general attention. Secondly, we have an instance of a

[1] *Rambles and Recollections*, I, 131.

primitive taboo which appears constantly in folklore, where, as in the case of Lot's wife, the person who shows indiscreet curiosity by a look, is turned into a stone or ashes.[1] Thirdly, it may represent a survival of a custom, to explain which a legend was invented, not uncommon among some primitive races where the marriage capturing is done, not by the bridegroom but by the bride. Thus among the Garos, all proposals of marriage must come from the lady's side, and any infringement of the custom can only be atoned for by liberal presents of beer given to her relations by the friends of the bridegroom, "who pretends to be unwilling and runs away, but is caught and subjected to ablution, and then taken in spite of the resistance and counterfeited grief and lamentations of his parents to the bride's house."[2] It may then reasonably be suspected that this custom of marriage prevailed among some branches of the Gond tribe, and that as they came more and more under Hindu influence, an unorthodox ritual prevailing in certain clans was explained by annexing the familiar marriage legend of Dulha Deo.

---

[1] Stokes, *Indian Fairy Tales*, 140*sqq*: Temple, *Widewake Stories*, 109, 302: *Indian Antiquary*, IV, 57.

[2] Dalton, *Descriptive Ethnology*, 64: and other instances in Westermarck, *History of human marriage*, 158*sq*.

CHAPTER III.

THE GODLINGS OF DISEASE.

Καὶ γὰρ τοῖσι κάκον χρυσόθρονος "Αρτεμις ὥρσεν
Χωσαμένη ὅ οἱ όυτι θαλύσια γουνῷ αλωῆς
'Οινεὺς ρέξ

ILIAD, ix, 533—35.

Sítalá, the small-pox goddess.

We now come to a special class of rural godlings, those that control disease. Of these the most familiar is Sítalá, "she that loves the cool," so called euphemistically in consequence of the fever which accompanies small-pox, the chief infant plague of India, which is under her control. She is thus the analogue of the Australian small-pox deity Budyah.[1] Sítalá has other euphemistic names. She is called Mátá, "the mother" *par excellence*, Jag Rání "the queen of the world," Máhá Máí, "great mother," Jagadambá, "mother of the earth," Phapholewálí "she of the vesicle," Kalejewálí "she of the liver." These euphemistic titles for the deities of terror are common to all the mythologies. The Greeks of old called the awful Erinyes the Eumenides. So the modern Greeks picture the small-pox as a woman, the enemy of children, and call her Sunchoremené, "indulgent or exorable" and Eulogia, "one to be praised or blessed," and the Celts address the fairies as "the men of peace" and "good neighbours."[2] In her original form as a village goddess she has seldom a special priest or a regular temple. A few fetish stones tended by some low caste menial constitute her shrine. As she comes to be promoted into some form of Kálí or Deví, she is provided with a regular fane. She receives little or no respect from men, but women and children attend her services in large numbers on "Sítalá's seventh" (*Sítalá-ki-saptamí*) which is her feast day. In Bengal she is worshipped on a piece of ground marked off and

---

[1] Tylor, *Primitive Culture*, I, 418.

[2] Grimm, *Teutonic Mythology*, II, 1161 : Tylor, *Early History*, 143 : Spencer, *Principles of Sociology*, I, 229 : Sir W. Scott, *Letters on Demonology*, 105.

smeared with cowdung. A fire being lighted and butter and spirits thrown upon it, the worshipper makes obeisance, bowing his forehead to the ground and muttering incantations. A swine is then sacrificed, and the bones and offal being buried, the flesh is roasted and eaten, but no one must take home with him any scrap of the victim.[1] There is a noted shrine dedicated to her in the Muzaffarnagar district under the name of Ujalí Mátá, or "the white mother," where she receives offerings of cakes, sweetmeats, and lumps of coarse sugar. When children get small-pox or scrofulous neck swellings, their parents pour water on the shrine and offer flowers, milk and Ganges water. Another favourite shrine is at Ráewála in Dehra Dún. There vast crowds assemble and make vows to procure children: and when a child is born they take it there and perform their vows. All the offerings are in fives, which is a lucky (*sawáyá*) number. In Chhatísgarh she is in process of elevation and is identified with Kálíká Bhavání. She is represented by a pebble with a trident, an earthen lamp, and a pot for milk and water as its adjuncts.[2] In the Panjáb, when a child falls ill of small-pox, no one is allowed to enter the house, particularly if he have bathed, washed or combed his hair: and if any one does come in he is made to burn incense at the door. Should a thunderstorm come on before the eruptions have fully come out, the sound is not allowed to enter the child's ear. Copper plates and utensils are violently beaten to drown the roar of the thunder. For six or seven days while the disease is at its height, the child is fed with raisins covered with silver leaf: when the eruption comes out clearly it is believed that Deví Mátá has arrived. When the disease has abated a little and the vesicles have become dry, some water is thrown over the body of the child. The parents then send for drummers and musicians and march in procession to the temple of Deví to which the child is carried dressed in saffron coloured clothes. A man goes in advance with a bunch of green grass in his hands from which he sprinkles a mixture of milk and water. In this way they visit

---

[1] Risley, *Tribes and Castes of Bengal*, I, 179.
[2] *Journal, Asiatic Society of Bengal*, 1890 p. 275.

some fig tree or other shrine of Deví, to which they tie red ribbons, besmear it with red lead, and paint and sprinkle it with curds.[1] The Khándhs, when the disease breaks out, desert the village leaving only a few persons to offer the blood of buffaloes, hogs and sheep, to the destroying power: and their neighbours bar out the spirit of the disease by laying thorns on the pathway which lead to the infected place. In Hoshangábád the goddess is supposed to live in the village and receives offerings of cocoanuts and sweetmeats, but no blood is shed at her shrine.[2] In the Hills she is represented as a woman dressed in yellow, with an infant in her arms, and is identified with the Háriti of the Nepál Buddhists. Her officiating priests are curriers and go through a rude form of the Sákti ceremonial.[3]

According to one story Sítalá is only the eldest of a band of seven sisters, by whom the pustular group of diseases is supposed to be caused. One list gives their names as Sítalá, Masání, Basantí, Mahá Máí, Polamde, Lamkariyá and Agwání.[4] We shall meet Masání or Masán, the deity of the cremation ground, in another connection. Basanti, is "the yellow goddess" so called probably on account of the colour of the skin in these diseases. Mahá Máí is merely "the great mother." Polamde is possibly "she that makes the patient soft or flabby," and Lamkariyá "she that hasteneth." Agwání is the fire goddess who heats the body with fever. Each of these is supposed to have special functions in connection with this group of diseases, but their authority is not very clearly defined. Their shrines cluster round the special shrine of Sítalá, and the villagers to the west of the North-Western Provinces call them her attendants (*khidmatgár*). In the Gurgaon district, accompanying images of Sítalá, is one of the Sedhu Lála, who is inferior to her and yet often worshipped before her, because he is regarded as her servant and intercessor. Copper coins are thrown behind her shrine

[1] Nur Ahmad Chishti; *Yádgár-i-Chishti.*
[2] *Settlement Report*, 255.
[3] Atkinson, *Himalayan Gazetteer*, II, 800.
[4] Ibbetson, *Panjáb Ethnography*, 114.

into a saucer which is known as her treasury (*málkhána*). Rice and other articles of food are placed in front of the shrine, and afterwards distributed to low-caste curriers (*Chamár*) and dogs.[1] Another list of the disease sisters which is plainly affected by Bráhmanical influence gives their names as Sítalá, Phúlmatí, Chamariyá, Durgá Kálí, Máhá Kálí, and Bhadrá Kálí. Chamariyá, who is apparently in some way connected with the Chamár or currier caste, is the elder, and Phúlmatí the younger sister of Sítalá. Phúlmatí brings the disease in its milder form, and the worst variety is the work of Sítalá in person. The special abode of Sítalá is the ním tree, and hence the patient is fanned with its leaves. A very bad form of confluent small-pox is the work of Chamariyá, who must be propitiated by the offering of a pig through a Chamár or other low-caste priest. The influence of Káli in her three-fold form is chiefly felt in diseases other than small-pox. Earthenware representations of elephants are placed at her shrine, and her offerings consist of cakes, sweetmeats, pigs, goats, sheep, and black fowls. Bhadrá Kálí is the least formidable of the three. The only person who has influence over Kálí as a disease goddess is the Ojha or exorcisor, who, when cholera and similar epidemics prevail, collects a subscription and performs a regular expiatory service.

Her connection with human sacrifice.

In her form as a household goddess Sítalá is often popularly known as Thandí or "the cool one," and her habitation in the house is behind the water pots in the cold damp place where the water drips. Here she is worshipped by the house mother, but only cold food or cold water is offered to her. There is, however, a darker side to the worship of Sítalá and the other disease godlings than this mild household service. In 1817 a terrible epidemic of cholera broke out at Jessore. "The disease commenced its ravages in August, and it was at once discovered that the August of this year had five Saturdays (a day under the influence of the ill-omened Sani). The number five being the express property of the destructive Siva, a mystical

[1] *Indian Antiquary*, VIII, 211.

connection was at once detected, the infallibly baneful influence of which it would have been sacrilege to question. On the night of the 27th a strange commotion spread through the villages adjacent to the station. A number of magicians were reported to have quitted Morelli with a human head in their possession, which they were to be directed by the presence of supernatural signs to leave in a certain, and to them unknown, village. The people on all sides were ready by force to arrest the progress of these nocturnal visitors, for the prophecy foretold that wherever the head fell, the destroying angel terminating her sanguinary course would rest, and the demon of death, thus satisfied, would refrain from further devastation in that part of the country. Dr. Tytler says that on that night, while walking along the road endeavouring to allay the agitation, the Judge and he perceived a faint light arising from a thick clump of bamboos. Attracted to the spot, they found a hut which was illuminated and contained images of five Hindu gods, one of which was Sítalá, the celebrated and formidable Aulá Bíbí, 'our lady of the flux'—an incarnation of Kálí, who, it is believed, is one day to appear riding on a horse for the purpose of slaughtering mankind and of setting the world on fire. In front of the idols a female child about nine years of age lay on the ground. She was evidently stupified with intoxicating drugs, and in this manner prepared to return responses to such questions as those initiated into the mysteries should think proper to propose." Dr. Chevers believes that the girl was intended to be a victim at the shrine, but this is far from certain.[1]

Small-pox worship in Bengal.

In Bengal the divine force antagonistic to Sítalá is Shasthí, who is regarded as the special guardian of children. In this exact form her worship does not appear to extend to Upper India, but this is probably the origin of what is known as the *Chhathi,* or ceremony on the sixth day after delivery, which is merely another form of the Bengáli word.[2] "In Bengal when small-pox rages the gardeners are

[1] *Medical Jurisprudence for India,* 415, *sq.*
[2] For Shashthí worship see Lál Behári De, *Govinda Samánta,* I, 62, *sqq.*

busiest. As soon as the nature of the disease is determined, the physician retires and a gardener is summoned. His first act is to forbid the introduction of meat, fish, and all food requiring oil or spices for its preparation. He then ties a lock of hair, a cowry shell, a piece of turmeric, and an articie of gold on the right wrist of the patient. • (The use of these articles as scarers of evil spirits will be considered later on.) The sick persons is then laid on the *májhpatta,* the young and unexpanded leaf of the plantain tree, and milk is prescribed as the sole article of food. He is fanned with a branch of the sacred *ním* (*azidirachta Indica*), and any one entering the chamber is sprinkled with water. Should the fever become aggravated and delirium ensue, or if the child cries much and sleeps little, the gardener performs the *Mátá Pújá.* This consists in bathing the image of the goddess causing the disease and giving a draught of the water to drink. To relieve the irritation of the skin, pease meal, turmeric, flour, or shell saw dustis sprinkled over the body. If the eruption be copious, a piece of new cloth in the figure of eight is wrapped round the chest and shoulders. On the night between the seventh and eighth days of the eruption the gardener has much to do. He places a waterpot in the sick room, and puts on it rice, a cocoanut, sugar, plantains, a yellow rag, flowers, and a few *ním* leaves. Having mumbled several spells (*mantra*) he recites the tale (*qissa*) of the particular goddess, which often occupies six hours. When the pustules are mature, the gardener dips a thorn of the *karaunda* (*Carissa*) in sesamum oil and punctures each one. The body is then anointed with oil and cooling fruits are given. When the scabs have peeled off, another ceremony called *godám* is gone through. All the offerings on the waterpot are rolled in a cloth and fastened round the waist of the patient. These offerings are the perquisite of the gardener who also receives a fee. Government vaccinators earn a considerable sum yearly by executing the Sítalá worship, and when a child is vaccinated a portion of the service is performed."[1] In Tirhut Sítalá has a special feast called *Júr Sital*, or "small-pox fever." The people bathe in water drawn the previous night, and

[1] Risley, *Bengal Tribes and Castes*, II, 62.

eat food cooked at that time after worshipping the goddess. Then, from morning till noon, all classes, rich and poor, cover themselves with mud and shower it on all whom they meet. No one is free from this mud bath, which is perhaps intended as a sort of personal penance, and partly an illustration of the protective powers of earth, of which some examples have already been given. In the afternoon they go out with clubs and hunt jackals, hares, and any animal they meet in the village: on their return they boast of their valour in having killed this or that jackal. This curious practice may possibly be analogous to the Irish and Manx custom of "hunting the wren."[1]

Mátangí Saktí, Masán.

We have already seen that Sítalá has been partly promoted to the Bráhmanical heaven. Here her special name is Mátangí Saktí, a word which has been connected with Masán, but is really derived from Mátá, the mother form of the goddess. Masán or Masání is quite a different godling. She resides at the cremation ground (*masán*), and is greatly dreaded. The same name is in the eastern districts of the North-Western Provinces applied to the shrine of the ghost of some low-caste man. Envious women will take the ashes from a burning place and throw them over an enemy's child. This is said "to cause them to be under the influence of the shadow" (*sáyá*), and to waste away by slow decline. This is a familiar idea in folklore. It rests, as Mr. Spencer says, on the theory that "primitive man, left to himself, necessarily concludes a shadow to be an actual existence which belongs to the person casting it."[2] Mátangí Saktí, again, appears in eight forms. Rauká Deví, Ghrauká Deví, Melá Deví, Mandlá Deví, Sítalá Deví, Sídalá Deví, Durgá Deví, and Sankará Deví, a collection of names which indiates the extraordinary mixture of beliefs, most of them obscure, and local manifestations of the deity, out of which this worship has been developed. She is described as having ears as large as a winnowing fan, projecting teeth, a hideous face with a

[1] Grierson, *Behár Peasant Life*, 401: Lady Wilde, *Legends*, 177.
[2] *Principles of Sociology*, I, 115.

wide open mouth. She rides on an ass, carries a broom in one hand, a pitcher and ewer in the other, and carries a winnowing fan with which she sifts mankind. This fan is, as we see later on, a most powerful fetish. All this is sheer mythology at its lowest stage, and represents the grouping of various local fetish beliefs on the original household worship.

Journey forbidden during an epidemic of small-pox.

During a small-pox epidemic no journey, not even a pilgrimage to a holy shrine, should be undertaken. General Sleeman[1] gives a curious case in illustration of this. "At this time the only son of Rámkrishna's brother, Khushhál Chand, an interesting boy of about four years of age, was extremely ill of small-pox. His father was told that he had better defer his journey to Benares till the child should recover, but he could neither sleep nor eat, so great was his terror lest some dreadful calamity should befall the whole family before he could expiate an unwilling sacrilege which he had committed, or take the advice of his high priest as to the best manner of doing it, and he resolved to leave the decision of the question to God himself. He took two pieces of paper, and having caused *Benares* to be written on one and *Jabalpur* on the other, he put them both in a brass vessel. After shaking the vessel well he drew forth that on which *Benares* had been written. 'It is the will of God,' said Rámkrishna. All the family, who were interested in the preservation of the poor boy, implored him not to set out lest the Deví who presides over small-pox should be angry. It was all in vain. He would set out with his household god, and, unable to carry it himself, he put it in a small litter upon a pole, and hired a bearer to carry it at one end while he supported it at the other. His brother Khushhál Chand sent his second wife at the same time with offerings to the Deví, to ward off the effects of his brother's rashness from the child. By the time his brother had got with his god to Adhartál, three miles from Jabalpur, he heard of the death of his nephew. But he seemed not to feel this slight blow in the

[1] *Rambles and Recollections*, I, 219.

terror of the dreadful but undefined calamity which he felt to be impending over him and the whole family, and he went on his road. Soon after, an infant son of his uncle died of the same disease, and the whole town at once became divided into two parties—those who held that the children had been killed by the Deví as a punishment for Rámkrishna's presuming to leave Jabalpur before they recovered, and those who held that they were killed by the god Vishnu himself for having been deprived of one of his arms. Khushhál Chand's wife sickened on the road and died on reaching Mirzapur; and as the Devi was supposed to have nothing to do with fevers, this event greatly augmented the advocates of Vishnu."

Preventatives of small-pox.

One method of protecting children from the disease is to give them opprobrious names and dress them in rags. This, with other devices for disease transference, will be discussed later on. We have seen that the *ním* tree is believed to influence the disease. The tender leaves are said to drop when an epidemic is about to occur, and some become spotted and eaten away as the body is marked by the disease. Hence, branches of the *ním* are hung over the door as a charm. Thunder disturbs the goddess who is in occupation of the patient; to remedy this the family stone flour mills are rattled near the ears of the child. Another device is to feed a donkey which is the animal on which Sítalá rides. This is specially known in the Panjáb as the *jandi pújá.*[1] In the same belief that the patient is under the direct influence of the goddess, if death ensues, the purification of the corpse by cremation is considered both unnecessary and improper. Like Gusáins, Jogis, and similar persons who are likewise regarded as inspired, those who die of this disease are buried, not cremated. As Sir A. C. Lyall observes: "The rule is ordinarily expounded by the priests to be imperative because the outward signs and symptoms mark the actual presence of divinity: the small-pox is not the god's work, but the god itself manifest: but there is also some ground for concluding that the process of

[1] *Panjáb Notes and Queries*, III, 42, 167.

burying has been found more wholesome than the hurried and ill-managed cremation which prevails during a fatal epidemic."[1] General Sleeman gives an instance of an outbreak of the disease which was attributed to a violation of this traditional rule.[2]

Minor godlings of disease.

There are a number of minor disease godlings, some of whom may be mentioned here. The Benares godling of Malaria is Jvaraharesvara "the lord who repels the fever." The special offering to him is what is known as *dúdhbhanga*, a confection made of milk, the leaves of the hemp plant and sweetmeats. Among the Kols of Chaibasa, Bangara is the god of fever, and is associated with Gohem, Chondu, Negra, and Dichali, who are considered respectively the gods of cholera, the itch, indigestion, and death. The Bengalis have a special ritual for the worship of Ghentu, the itch godling. The scene of the service is a dunghill. A broken earthenware pot, its bottom blackened by constant use for cooking, daubed white with lime, interspersed with a few streaks of turmeric, together with a branch or two of the *ghentu* plant, and last not least, a broomstick of the genuine palmyra or cocoanut stock, serve as the representation of the presiding deity of itch. The mistress of the family, for whose benefit the worship is done, acts as priestess. After a few doggrel lines are recited, the pot is broken and the pieces collected by the children, who sing songs about the itch godling.[3] Some of these godlings are like Shashtí, protectors of children from infantile disorders. Such are in Hoshangábád Bijaisen, in whose name a string, which, as we shall see, exercises a powerful influence over demons, is hung round the necks of children from birth till marriage,[4] and Kurdeo among the Kurkus who presides over the growth and health of the children in three or four villages together.[5] Acheri, a disease sprite in the hills, particularly favours those who wear red garments, and in his name a scarlet thread is tied round the throat as an

---

[1] *Asiatic Studies*, 57, *sq.*
[2] *Rambles and Recollections*, I, 221.
[3] *Calcutta Review*, XVIII, 68.
[4] *Hoshangabad Settlement Report*, 119.
[5] *Ibid.* 255.

amulet against colds and goitre. Ghanta Karana, "he who has ears as broad as a bell," or "who has bells in his ears," is another disease godling of the hills. He is supposed to be of great personal attraction, and is worshipped under the form of a water jar as the healer of cutaneous diseases. He is a gatekeeper, or, in other words, a godling on his promotion, in many of the Garhwál temples.[1] Among the Kurkus of Hoshangábád Mutua Deo is represented by a heap of stones inside the village. His special sacrifice is a pig, and his peculiar mission is to send epidemics, and particularly fevers, in which case he must be propitiated by extraordinary sacrifices.[2] In the same way Marí Mátá, the cholera mother of Berár, regulates the spread of the disease according to the attention she receives.[3]

Hardaur the cholera god.

But the great god of the cholera in Northern India is Harda or Hardaur Lála. It is only north of the Jumna that he is supposed to control this plague, and in his original home, Bundelkhand, he seems to have little or no connection with it. With him we reach a class of godlings quite distinct from nearly all those whom we have been considering. He is one of that numerous class who were in their lifetime actual historical personages, and who for some special cause, in his case from the tragic circumstances of his death, have been elevated to a seat among the hosts of heaven. Hardaur Lála or Díwán Hardaur was the second son of Bír Sinha Deva, the miscreant Rája of Orchha in Bundelkhand, who, at the instigation of Prince Jahángír, assassinated the accomplished Abul Fazl, the litterateur of the Court of Akbar.[4] His brother Jhajhár Sinh succeeded to the throne on the death of his father: and after some time, suspecting Hardaur of undue intimacy with his wife, he compelled her to poison her lover with all his companions at a feast in 1627 A.D. After this tragedy it happened that the daughter of the Princess Kanjávatí, sister of Jhajhár and Hardaur, was about to be married. Her

1 Atkinson, *Himalayan Gazetteer*, II, 833, 816, *sq.*
2 *Settlement Report*, 254, *sq.*
3 *Gazetteer*, 191.
4 Blockman, *Ain-i-Akbári, Introduction*, XXIV.

mother, accordingly, sent an invitation to Jhajhár Sinh to attend the wedding. He refused with the mocking retort that she would be wise to invite her favourite brother Hardaur. Thereupon, she in despair went to his cenotaph and lamented his tragical end. Hardaur from below answered her cries, promised to attend the wedding, and to make all the necessary arrangements. The ghost kept his promise and arranged the marriage ceremony as befitted the honour of his house. Subsequently he visited at midnight the bedside of the emperor Akbar,[1] and besought him to issue an order that platforms should be erected in his name, and honour be paid to him in every village of the empire, promising that if he were duly propitiated, a wedding should never be marred by storm or rain, and that no one who before eating presented a share of his meal to him should ever want for bread. Akbar, it is said, complied with these requests, and since then Hardaul's ghost has been worshipped in nearly every village in Upper India. He is chiefly honoured at weddings and in the month of May (*Baisákh*) when the women, particularly those of the lower classes, visit his shrine and eat there. His shrine is always erected outside the hamlet and is decorated with flags. On the day but one before the arrival of a wedding procession, the women of the family worship Hardaul, and invite him to the ceremony. If any signs of a storm appear he is propitiated with songs, one of the best known of which runs thus—

> Lála! Thy shrine is in every hamlet!
> Thy name throughout the land!
> Lord of the Bundelá land!
> May God increase thy fame![2]

Many of these shrines have a stone figure of the hero represented on horseback, set up at the head or west end of the platform. From his birthplace Hardaul is also known as Bundela, and one of the

---

[1] The chronology is hopeless. Akbar reigned from 1556 to 1605, and the death of Hardaur is fixed in 1627.

[2] Or in the local patois—
Gánwán chauntra, Lála desan nám!
Bundele des ke Raiya Ráu ke!
Tumhárí jay rakhe Bhagwán!

quarters in Mirzapur and in the town of Brindaban in the Mathura district, is named after him.[1]

But while in his native land of Bundelkhand Hardaul is a wedding godling, in the countries to the north of the Jumna it is on his power of influencing epidemics of cholera that his reputation mainly rests. The terrible outbreak of this pestilence which occurred in the camp of the Governor-General, the Marquess Hastings, during the Pindhári war, was generally attributed by the people to the killing of beef for the use of the British troops in the grove where Hardaul's ashes repose. Sir C. A. Elliott remarks that he has seen statements in the old official correspondence of 1828 A.D., when we first took possession of Hoshangábád, that the District Officers were directed to force the village headmen to set up altars to Hardaul Lála in every village. This was part of the system of "preserving" the cultivators, since it was found that they ran away if their fears of epidemics were not calmed by the respect paid to their local gods. But in Hoshangábád the worship of Hardaur Lála has fallen into great neglect of late, the repeated recurrence of cholera having shaken the belief in the potency of his influence over the disease.[2]

Exorcism of the cholera demon.

A disease so sudden and mysterious as cholera is naturally capable of superstitious explanation. Everywhere it is believed to be due to the agency of a demon which can be expelled by noise and special incantations, or removed by means of a scapegoat. This idea prevailed even among the Muhammadans at Herat.[3] All over Upper India when cholera prevails you may see fires lighted on the boundaries of villages to bar the approach of the cholera demon, and the people shouting and beating drums to hasten his departure. On one occasion I was present at such a ceremonial while out for an evening drive, and the grooms advised us to stop the horses to allow the demon to cross the road ahead of us without interruption.

---

[1] The chief authorities for Hardaul are Cunningham, *Archæological Reports*, XVII, 162, *sqq.* Mr. V. A. Smith, *Journal, Asiatic Society of Bengal*, 1875.

[2] *Settlement Report*, 119.

[3] Ferrier, *Caravan Journeys*, 451, *sq.*

This expulsion (*chalauwa*) of the disease spirit is often a cause of quarrels and riots, as villagers who are still safe from the epidemic strongly resent the introduction of the demon within their boundaries. In a recent case at Allahabad a man stated that the cholera monster used to attempt to enter his house nightly; that his head resembled a large earthen pot; and that he and his brother were obliged to bar his entrance with their clubs. Another attributed the immunity of his family to the fact that he possessed a gun, which he regularly fired at night to scare the demon. Not long ago some wise men in the same district enticed the cholera demon into an earthen pot by magic rites and clapping on the lid, formed a procession in the dead of night for the purpose of carrying the pot to a neighbouring village, with which their relations were the reverse of cordial, and burying it there secretly. But the enemy were on the watch and turned out in force to frustrate this fell intent. A serious riot occurred in which the receptacle containing the evil spirit was unfortunately broken, and he escaped to continue his ravages.[1] In Muzaffarnagar during an epidemic Kálí Devi is worshipped and a magic circle of milk and spirits is drawn round the village, over which the cholera demon does not care to step. They also have a reading of the scriptures in honour of Durgá, and worship the Satí shrine, if there be one in the village. Or a buffalo bull is marked with a red pigment and driven to the next village where he carries the plague with him. Last year at Meerut the inhabitants purchased a buffalo, painted it red and led the animal through the city in procession. Colonel Tod describes how Zálim Sinh, the celebrated regent of Kotah, drove cholera out of the place. "Having assembled the Bráhmans, astrologers, and those versed in incantations, a grand rite was got up, sacrifices made, and a solemn decree of banishment pronounced against Marí, the cholera goddess. Accordingly an equipage was prepared for her, decorated with funeral emblems, painted black and drawn by a double team of black oxen: bags of grain, also black, were put into the vehicle,

---

[1] *Allahabad Pioneer*, 10th March, 1891.

that the lady might not go out without food, and driven by a man in sable vestments, followed by the yells of the populace, Marí was deported across the Chambal river, with the commands of the priests that she should never again set foot in Kotah. No sooner did my deceased friend hear of her expulsion from that capital, and being placed on the road for Bundi, than the wise men ot this city were called on to provide means to keep her from entering therein. Accordingly all the water of the Ganges at hand was in requisition, an earthen vessel was placed over the southern portal from which the sacred water was continually dropping, and against which no evil could prevail. Whether my friend's supply of the holy water failed, or Marí disregarded such opposition, she reached the palace." [1]

Cholera caused by witchcraft.

In Gujarát, among the wilder tribes, the belief prevails that cholera is caused by old women who feed on the corpses of the victims. Formerly, when a case occurred, their practice was to go to the Soothsayer (*Bhagat*), find out from him who was the guilty witch, and kill her with much torture. Of late years this practice has to a great extent ceased. The people now attribute an outbreak to the wrath of the goddess Kálí, and, to please her, draw her cart through the streets, and lifting it over the village boundaries, offer up goats and buffaloes. Sometimes to keep off the disease they make a magic circle with milk or coloured threads round the village. [2] A visitation of the plague in Nepál was attributed to the Rája insisting on celebrating the Dasahra during an intercalary month. On another occasion the arrival of the disease was believed to have been caused by the evil eye of Saturn and other planets which secretly came together in one sign of the zodiac. A third attack was attributed to the king being in his eighteenth year and the year of the cycle being eighty-eight—eight being a very unlucky number. [3] So the Gonds try to ward off the anger of the evil spirits of cholera and

[1] *Annals*, II, 744.
[2] *Bombay Gazetteer*, VI, sq.
[3] Wright, *History*, 221, 267, 268.

small-pox by sacrifices and by thoroughly cleaning their villages and transferring the sweepings into some road or travelled track. Their idea is that unless the disease is communicated to some person who will take it on to the next village the plague will not leave them. For this reason they do not throw the sweepings into the jungle, as no one passes that way, and consequently the benefit of sweeping is lost.[1] An extraordinary case was recently reported from the Dehra Ismaíl Khán district. There had been a good deal of sickness in the village and the people spread a report that this was due to the fact that a woman, who had died some seven months previously, had been chewing her funeral sheet. The relatives were asked to allow the body to be examined, which was done, and it was found that owing to the subsidence of the ground through rain some earth had fallen into the open mouth of the corpse. A copper coin was placed in the mouth as a viaticum, and a fowl killed and laid on the body, which was again interred. The same result very often is believed to follow from burying persons of the sweeper caste in the usual extended position instead of a sitting posture or with the head downwards. Recently in Muzaffarnagar a corpse buried in the unorthodox way was disinterred by force and the matter came before the courts.

Demon of cattle disease.

In the same way cattle disease is caused by the plague demon. It is expelled in the same way as the cholera demon and removed by the agency of the scapegoat. In the western parts of these provinces you will often notice wisps of straw tied round the trunks of acacia trees as a spell to bar the murrain. Kásí Bába is the tribal deity of the Binds of Bengal. Of him it is said—a "mysterious epidemic was carrying off the herus on the banks of the Ganges and the ordinary expiatory sacrifices were ineffectual. One evening a clownish Ahír on going to the river saw a figure rinsing its mouth from time to time and making an unearthly sound with a conch shell. The lout, concluding that this must be the demon that caused the epidemic, crept up

[1] *Central Provinces Gazetteer*, 276.

and clubbed the unsuspecting bather. Kásí Náth was the name of the murdered Bráhman, and as the cessation of the murrain coincided with his death, the low Hindustáni castes have ever since regarded Kásí Bába as the maleficent spirit that sends disease among the cattle. Nowadays he is propitiated by the following curious ceremony. As soon as an infectious disease breaks out, the village cattle are massed together and cotton seed sprinkled over them. The fattest and sleekest animal being singled out is severely beaten with rods. The herd, scared by the noise, scamper off to the nearest shelter, followed by the scapebull: and by this means it is thought the murrain is stayed."[1]

Other cholera godlings.

Besides Hardaul Lála, the great cholera godling, Hulká Deví, the impersonation of vomiting, is worshipped in Bengal with the same object. Another cholera goddess is known as Marí or Marí Mái "mother death," or when promoted to Bráhmanism, Marí Bhavání. Among the jungle tribes of Mirzapur she is known as Obá, an Arabic name corrupted from the Arabic *wabá*, pestilence. Marí has a special shrine in the Sultánpur district in Oudh, erected to commemorate a fatal outbreak of cholera in Safdar Jang's army. There is no temple, but a *ním* tree is worshipped in which the deity is supposed to dwell.[2] In the Panjáb Marí is honoured with an offering of a pumpkin, a male buffalo, a cock, a ram, and a he goat. These animals must each be decapitated with a single blow before her altar. If more than one blow is required, the ceremony is a failure. Formerly in addition to these five kinds of offering, a man and a woman were sacrificed to make up the mystic number seven.[3]

Demoniacal theory of disease.

It is a commonplace of folklore and the beliefs of all savage races that disease and death are not the result of natural causes, but are the work of devils and demons, witchcraft, the Evil Eye, and so forth.[4] It is needless

---

[1] Risley, *Tribes and Castes of Bengal*, I, 132.

[2] *Oudh Gazetteer*, I, 355, 517; and Tod, *Annals*, II, 75.

[3] *Panjáb Notes and Queries*, I, 1: IV, 51.

[4] Grimm, *Teutonic Mythology*, II, 1153, *sqq.*: Black, *Folk Medicine*, 4: Tylor, *Primitive Culture*, I, 138: Conway, *Demonology*, I, 269: Lubboch, *Origin of Civilisation*, 25, 217: Spencer, *Principles of Sociology*, I, 230.

to say that the same idea extensively prevails in India. Thus in Rájputána sickness is popularly attributed to *Khor* or agency of the souls of deceased relations, and for treatment they call in a cunning man who propitiates the *Khor* by offering sweetmeats, milk, &c., and gives burnt ash and black pepper sanctified by charms to the patient.[1] Of similar beliefs in Western India a large collection has been made by Mr. Campbell.[2] So among the jungle tribes of Mirzapur the Korwas believe that all disease is caused by the displeasure of the collective village gods (*deohár*). These gods sometimes become displeased for no apparent reason, sometimes because their accustomed worship is neglected, and sometimes through the malignity of some witch. The special diseases which are due to the displeasure of these godlings are fever, diarrhœa, and cough. If small-pox comes of its own accord, it is harmless, but a more dangerous variety is attributed to the anger of these godlings. Cholera and fever are considered to be due to some malignant ghost (*bhút*). The Kharwárs believe that all disease is due to the Baiga not having paid proper attention to the village gods, Rája Chandol or some other godling. The Pankas think that disease comes in various ways—sometimes through ghosts or witches, sometimes because the godlings and deceased ancestors were not duly propitiated. Instances of similar beliefs might be almost indefinitely extended. Leprosy is a disease which is specially regarded as a punishment for sin, and a Hindu affected by this disease remains an outcaste until he can afford to undertake a purificatory ceremony. Even lesser ailments are often attributed to the wrath of some offended god or saint. Thus in Sátára the king Satesvar asked the saint Sumitra for water. But the sage was wrapped in contemplation and did not answer him. So the angry monarch took some lice from the ground and threw them at the saint, who cursed the king with vermin all over his body. He endured the affliction for twelve years, until he was cured by ablution at the sacred fountain of Devráshta.[3]

[1] *Gazetteer*, I, 175.
[2] *Notes*, 12, *sqq*.
[3] *Bombay Gazetteer*, XIX, 465.

Exorcism of disease.

The practice of exorcising these demons of disease has been elaborated into something like a science. Disease, according to the general belief of the rural population, can be removed by a species of magic usually of the variety known as sympathetic, or it may be transferred from the sufferer to some one else. The special incantations for disease are in the hands of low caste sorcerers, or magicians. Among the more primitive races, such as those of Drávidian origin in Central India, this is the business of the Baiga or aboriginal priest: but even here there is a differentiation of function, and though the Baiga is usually considered competent to deal with persons possessed by evil spirits, it is only special persons who can undertake the regular exorcism. This, among the lower tribes of Hindus, is the duty of the Syána or "cunning man" and the Oiha or "teacher."[1]

Powers, how acquired.

Exorcisors are both professional and non-professional. "Non-professional exorcisors are generally persons who get naturally improved by a guardian spirit (*deva*), and a few of them learn the art of exorcism from a teacher (*guru*). Most of the professional exorcists learn the art from a *guru* or teacher. The first study is begun on a lunar or on a solar eclipse day. On such a day the teacher, after bathing and without wiping his body or his head hair, puts on dry clothes and goes to the village godling's temple. The candidate, having done likewise, also goes to the temple. The candidate then spreads a white cloth before the god, and on one side of the cloth makes a heap of rice and on another a heap of *urad* (*phaseolus radiatus*), sprinkles red lead on the heaps, and breaks a cocoanut in front of the idol. The teacher then teaches him the incantation (*mantra*), which he commits to memory. An ochre-coloured flag is then tied to a staff in front of the temple, and the teacher and candidate come home. After this, on the first new moon which falls on a Saturday, the

---

[1] Some have attempted to derive *Ojha* from *ojh*, meaning entrails, because, as the Roman sorcerers did, he is supposed to inspect the entrails of the victim. This the Hindu *Ojha* never does. The name is really a corruption of the Sanskrit *upadhyáya* or teacher.

teacher and the candidate go together out of the village to a place previously marked out by them on the boundary. A servant accompanies them who takes a bag of *urad*, oil, seven earthen lamps, lemons, cocoanuts, and red powder. After coming to the spot the teacher and the candidate bathe, and then the teacher goes to the village temple and sits praying for the safety of the candidate. The candidate, who has been already instructed as to what should be done, then starts for the boundary of the next village accompanied by the servant. On his reaching the village boundary he picks up seven pebbles, sets them in a line on the road, and after lighting a lamp near them he worships them with flowers, red powder, and *urad*. Insense is then burnt and a cocoanut is broken near the pebbles which represent Vetála and his lieutenants, and a second cocoanut is broken for the village godling. When this is over he goes to a river, well, or other watering place, bathes, and without wiping his body or putting on dry clothes, proceeds to the boundary of the next village There he repeats the same process as he did before, and then goes to the boundary of a third village. In this manner he goes to seven villages and repeats the same process. All this while he keeps on repeating incantations. After finishing his worship at the seventh village, the candidate returns to his village, and going to the temple, sees his teacher and tells him what he has done. In this manner, having worshipped and propitiated the Vetála of seven villages, he becomes an exorcist. After having become able to exercise these powers he must observe certain rules. Thus, on every eclipse day he must go to a sea shore or a river bank, bathe in cold water, and while standing in the water repeat incantations a number of times. After bathing daily he must neither wring his head hair, nor wipe his body dry. While he is taking his meals he should leave off if he hears a woman in her monthly sickness speak, or if a lamp is extinguished. The Muhammadan methods of studying exorcism are different from those of the Hindus. One of them is as follows :—The candidate begins his study under the guidance of his teacher on the last day of the lunar month, provided it falls on a Tuesday or Sunday. The initiation takes place in a room, the walls and floors of which have been plastered with mud and here and there daubed with sandal paste. On the floor a white sheet is spread, and the candidate after washing his hands and feet and wearing a new waist-cloth or trousers, sits on the sheet. He lights one or two incense sticks and makes offerings of a white cloth and meat to one of the principal Musalmán saints. This process is repeated for from fourteen to forty days."[1] Few rural exorcisors perform these elaborate ceremonies, and most of them derive their reputation from a knowledge of a few charms of the *hocus pocus* variety, or from a cure in some particularly difficult case.

Methods of exorcism.

The methods of rural exorcism are various. Thus in Mirzapur when a person is known to be under the influence of a witch, the Ojha recites a spell which runs—"Bind the evil eye; bind the fist; bind the spell; bind the curse; bind the ghost and *churel;* bind the witch's hands and feet. Who can bind her? The teacher can bind her. I, the disciple of the teacher, can bind her. Go, witch, to wherever thy shrine may be, sit there, and leave the afflicted person." Then he sprinkles some grain on the ground and the charm is complete. So in cases of snake or scorpion bite the charm runs—"Black scorpion of the limestone! green thy tail and black thy mouth. God orders thee to go home. Come out scorpion at the spell. Come out, come out. If you fail to come out, Mahádeva and Párvatí will drive thee out." The number of such charms is legion. When the Ojha is called in to identify the demon which has beset the patient, he declares whether it is a local ghost or some outsider who has attacked him on a journey. Then he calls for some cloves and muttering a charm over them, ties them to the bedstead on which the sick man lies. Then the patient is told to name the ghost which has possessed him, and he generally names one of his dead relations, or the ghost of a hill, a tree, or a burial ground. Then the Ojha suggests an appropriate offering,

[1] Campbell, *Notes*, 192, *sqq*.

which, when bestowed, and food given to Bráhmans, the patient ought in all decency to recover. If he does not, the *Ojha* asserts that the right ghost has not been named, and the whole process is gone through again, if the necessary funds are forthcoming. The Baiga of Mirzapur, who very often combines the function of an Ojha with his own legitimate business of managing the local ghosts, works in very much the same way. He takes some barley in a sieve, which, as we shall see, is a very powerful fetish, and shakes it until only a few grains are left in the interstices. Then he marks down the intruding ghost by counting the grains and recommends the sacrifice of a fowl or a goat, or the offering of some liquor, most of which he usually consumes himself. If his patient die, he gets out of the difficulty by saying "such and such a powerful ghost (*bhút*) carried him off. What can a poor man, such as I am, do?" If a tiger or a bear kills a man, the Baiga tells his friends that such and such a malignant ghost was offended at no attention being paid to him, and in revenge entered into the animal who killed the deceased—the obvious moral being that in future more regular offerings should be made through the Baiga. In Hoshangábád the Bhomka sorcerer has a handful of grain waved over the head of the sick man. This is then carried to the Bhomka, who makes a heap of it on the floor, and sitting over it swings a lighted lamp suspended by four strings from his fingers. He then repeats slowly the names of the patient's ancestors and of the village and local godling, pausing between each, and when the lamp stops spinning, the name at which it halts is the name to be propitiated. Then in the same way he asks "what is the propitiation offering to be? A pig? A chicken? A goat? A cocoanut?" And the same mystic sign indicates the satisfaction of the god.[1] The Kol diviner drops oil into a vessel of water: the name of the deity is pronounced as the oil is dropped. If it forms one globule in the water, it is considered that the particular god to be appeased has been correctly named: if it splutters and forms several globules, another name is

[1] *Settlement Report*, 256.

tried. The Oraon Ojha puts the fowls intended as victims before a small mud image, on which he sprinkles a few grains of rice : if they pick at the rice it indicates that the particular devil represented by the image is satisfied with the intentions of his votaries, and the sacrifice proceeds.[1] The Panjáb sorcerer adopts a stock method common to such practitioners all over the world. He writes some spells on a piece of paper and pours on it a large drop of ink. Flowers are then placed in the hands of a young child, who is told to look into the ink and say "summon the four guardians!" He is asked if he sees anything in the ink, and according to his answers a result is arrived at.[2] The *modus operandi* of these exorcisors is in fact very much the same in India as in other parts of the world.[3]

Exorcism by dancing and flagellation.

Two special methods of expelling these diseases may be briefly discussed. An important part of the ritual is the dance of ecstasy in which the person supposed to be under the direct influence of the deity moves according to some rude rhythmic measure and announces the pleasure of the deity. This religious dance is common all the world over.[4] Iron is a well known scarer of evil spirits, and this accounts for the efficacy of the *Gurda* or sacred chain of the Mirzapur Baiga already referred to, with which he soundly thrashes patients attacked with epilepsy, hysteria, and similar ailments which from their nature are obviously due to demoniacal agency. There are numerous instances of the use of flagellation for the exorcism of evil spirits. In Jaunpur the Ojhas use this method at the shrine of Ghauspur.[5] The records of Roman Catholic hagiology, and of the special sect of the flagellants will furnish numerous parallel instances.[6]

---

[1] Dalton, *Descriptive Ethnology*, 188, 257.

[2] *North Indian Notes and Queries*, I, 85.

[3] See Yule *Marco Polo*, II, 71 *sq.*, with note : Tylor, *Primitive Culture*, I, 127 : Lubbock, *Origin of Civilisation*, 237 : Farrer, *Primitive Manners*, 159, *sq.*

[4] See copious instances collected by Campbell, *Notes*, 72, *sqq.*

[5] See Knighton's account in *Nineteenth Century*, 1880.

[6] See Cooper, *Flagellation and the Flagellants* : Dalton, *Descriptive Ethnology*, 256 : Campbell, *Notes*, 44 *sq.*, and for restoration to life by beating see Tawney, *Katha Sarit Ságara*, II. 245.

Treatment of exorcisors.

While the sorcerer by virtue of his profession is generally respected and feared, in some places they have been dealt with rather summarily. Sudarsan Sáh rid Garhwál of them by summoning all the professors of the black art with their books. When they were collected he had them bound hand and foot and thrown with their books and implements into the river.[1] This same monarch also disposed very effectually of a case of possession in his own family. One day he heard a sound of drumming and dancing in one of his courtyards, and learnt that a ghost named Goril had taken possession of one of his female slaves. The Rája was wroth, and taking a thick bamboo he proceeded to the spot and laid about him so vigorously that the votaries of Goril soon declared that the deity had taken his departure. The Rája then ordered Goril to cease from possessing people; and nowadays if any Garhwálí thinks himself possessed, he has only to call on the name of Sudarsan Sáh and the demon departs.[2]

Appointment of Ojhas.

The mode of succession to the dignity of an Ojha varies in different places. In Mirzapur the son is usually educated by his father and taught the various spells and modes of incantation. But this is not always the case; and there at the present time the institution is in a transitory stage. South of the Son we have the Baiga who usually acts as an Ojha also; and he is invariably drawn from the aboriginal races. Further north he is known as Náya (Sanskrit *nayaka*) or "leader." Further north again, as we leave the hilly country and enter the completely Bráhmanised Gangetic valley, he changes into the regular Ojha, who is always a low-class Bráhman. In one instance which came under my own notice the Náya of the village had been an aboriginal Kol, and he before his death announced that "the god had sat on the head" of a Bráhman candidate for the office, who was duly initiated and is now the recognised village

[1] Atkinson, *Himalayan Gazetteer*, II, 833.
[2] *Ibid.* II, 823.

Ojha. This is a good example of the methods by which Bráhmanism annexes and absorbs the demonolatry of the lower races. Similarly in Hoshangábád the son usually succeeds the father, but a Bhomka does not necessarily marry into a Bhomka family, nor does it follow that "once a Bhomka, always a Bhomka." On the contrary, the position seems to be the result of the special favour of the god of the particular village in which he lives; and if the whole of the residents emigrate in a body, then the gods of the new village site have to be consulted afresh as to the servant whom they choose to attend upon them. "If a Bhomka dies, or goes away, or a new village is established, his successor is appointed in the following way. All the villagers assemble at the shrine of Mutua Deo, and offer a black and white chicken to him. A Parihár or priest should be enticed to grace the solemnity and make the sacrifice, but if that cannot be done, the oldest man in the assembly performs it. Then he sets a wooden grain measure rolling along the line of seated people, and the man before whom it stops is marked out by the intervention of the deity as the new Bhomka."[1] It marks perhaps some approximation to Hinduism that this priest when inspired by the god wears a string made of the hair of a bullock's tail, unless this is based on the common use of thread as a scarer of demons, or is some token or fetish peculiar to the race. At the same time the non-Bráhmanic character of the worship is proved by the fact that the priest when in a state of ecstasy cannot endure the presence of a cow or a Bráhman. "The god," they say "would leave their heads if either of these came near." On one occasion when Sir C. A. Elliott saw the process of exorcism, the man did not actually revolve when "the god came on his head." He covered his head up well in a cloth, leaving space at the top for the god to approach, and in this state he twisted and turned himself about rapidly, and soon sat down exhausted. Then from the pit of his stomach he uttered words which the bystanders interpreted to direct a certain line of conduct for the sick man to pursue. "But perhaps the

---

[1] *Settlement Report*, 256, *sq.*

occasion was not a fair test, as the Parihár strongly objected to the presence of an unbeliever, on the pretence that the god would be afraid to come before so great an official." This has always been the standing difficulty in Europeans obtaining a practical knowledge of the details of rural sorcery, and when a performance of the kind is specially organized it will usually be found that the officiant performs the preliminary ceremonies with comparative success, but breaks down when the ecstatic crisis should have commenced. This is always attributed to the presence of an unbeliever, however interested and sympathetic. The same result usually happens at spiritualistic *séances*, when any one with even an elementary knowledge of physics or mechanics happens to be one of the audience.

Fraud in exorcism.

The question naturally arises—are all these Ojhas and Baigas conscious hypocrites and swindlers? Dr. Tylor shrewdly remarks that "the sorcerer generally lessens his time-honoured profession in good faith, and retains the belief in it more or less from first to last. At once dupe and cheat, he combines the energy of a believer with the cunning of a hypocrite.[1]" This coincides with the experience of most competent Indian observers. Captain Samuells who repeatedly witnessed these performances distinctly asserts that it is a mistake to suppose that there is always intentional deception.[2]

Disease charms.

Next to the services of the professional exorcisor for the purpose of preventing or curing disease, comes the use of special charms for this purpose. There is a large native literature dealing with this branch of science. As a rule most native patients undergo a course of this treatment before they visit our hospitals; and the result of a recourse to European medical science is hence occasionally disappointing. One favourite talisman of this kind is the magic square which consists

[1] *Primitive Culture*, I, 134, and compare Lubbock, *Origin of Civilisation*, 251.
[2] Quoted by Dalton, *Descriptive Ethnology*, 232.

of an arrangement of certain numbers in a special way.[1] In the case of cattle disease some numbers are written on a piece of tile and beneath them are inscribed some gibberish which pretends to be Arabic or Sanskrit and appeals to Ismáil Jogí or Noná Chamárin, two noted disease demons. This is hung on a rope over the village cattle-path and a ploughshare is buried at the entrance to make the spell more powerful. When cattle are attacked with worms the owner fills a clean earthen pot with water from the well with one hand; he then mutters a blessing and with some sacred *dábh* grass sprinkles a little water seven times along the back of the animal. The number of these charms is legion. Many of them merge into the special preservatives against demoniacal influence or the evil-eye, which will be discussed later on. Thus the bázár merchant writes the words *Rám! Rám!* several times near his door, or he makes a representation of the sun and moon or a rude image of Ganesa, the God of luck, or draws the mystical Swástika.

Rag offerings

Next come the arrangements by which disease may be expelled or transferred to some one else. This appears to be at least one explanation of the custom of hanging rags on trees which prevails nearly all over the world.[2] Thus in Persia, they fix rags on bushes in the name of the Imám Raza. They explain the custom by saying that the eye of the Imám being always on the top of the mountain, the shreds which are left there by those who hold him in reverence, remind him of what he ought to do in their behalf with Muhammad, Ali, and the other holy personages who are able to propitiate the Almighty in their favour.[3] Moorcroft in his journey to Ladákh describes how he propitiated the evil spirit of a dangerous pass with the leg of a pair of worn out nankin trousers.[4] Among the Mirzapur Korwas

---

[1] For examples see Herklot's *Qánún-i-Islám*, Chap. XXXII.

[2] Black, *Folk Medicine*, 40: Tylor, *Primitive Culture*, II, 150: Henderson, *Folklore of the Northern Counties*, 230: Gregor, *Folklore of N.-E. Scotland*, 40: Lubbock, *Origin of Civilisation*, 287: Lady Wilde, *Legends of Ireland*, 237.

[3] Ferrier, *Caravan Journeys*, 113.

[4] *Travels in the Himálayas*, I, 428.

the Baiga hangs rags on the trees which shade the village shrine as a spell to bring health and good luck. These rag shrines are to be found all over the province and are generally known as Chithariyá or Chithraiyá Bhawání—"our Lady of Tatters." Some of these *deæ loci* have been annexed to Bráhmanism as a manifestation of Kálí. Many of them are situated on jungle pathways and are doubtless intended as a means of transferring disease to some passer-by, who in order to avoid the spells adds a rag on his own account. Others are probably connected with tree worship. Thus Colonel Tod describes the trees in a sacred grove in Rajputána as decorated with shreds of various coloured cloth, "offerings of the traveller to the forest divinity for protection against evil spirits."[1] In the Panjáb the trees on which rags are hung are known as Lingrí Pír or the Rag Saint.[2] The same custom prevails at various Himálayan shrines, and at the Vastra harana or sacred tree at Brindaban near Mathura, which is now invested with a special legend as commemorating the place where Krishna carried off the clothes of the milkmaids when they were bathing.[3] In Berár a heap of stones daubed with red and placed under a tree fluttering with rags represents Chindiya Deo or "the Lord of Tatters" where, if you present a rag in due season you may chance to get good clothes.[4] This usage often merges into actual tree worship, as among the Mirzapur Patáris, who, when fever prevails, tie a cotton string which has never touched water round the trunk of a *pípal* tree and hang rags from the branches; the Kharwárs have a particular sacred *mahua* tree known as the *Byáhi mahua* or *mahua* of marriage on which threads are tied at marriages. At almost any holy bathing place women may be seen winding a cotton thread round the trunk of a *pípal* tree. From these rags, supposed to be occupied by the spirits of disease, the transition to the ordinary relic fetish, many of which if touched cure sickness, is capable of easy explanation.

---

[1] *Annals*, II, 717.
[2] O'Brien, *Multán Glossary*, 218.
[3] Madden, *Journal Asiatic Society, Bengal*, 1848. p. 415; Bholanáth Chandra, *Travels*, II, 62.
[4] *Gazetteer*, 191.

Disease transference.

Disease is also transferred in an actual, physical way. Thus, in Ireland, a charm or curse is left on a gate or stile, and the first healthy person who passes through will, it is believed, have the disease transferred to him. So in Scotland, if a child is affected with the whooping cough, it is taken into the land of another laird, and there the sickness is left.[1] Similarly in Mirzapur, one method of transferring disease is to fill a pot with flowers and rice and bury it in a pathway with a flat stone to cover it. Whoever touches this is supposed to contract the disease. This is known as *chalauwa,* which means "passing on" the disease. This goes on daily in Upper India. Often when walking in a bázár in the early morning, you will see a little pile of earth decorated with flowers in the middle of the road. This usually contains some of the scabs or scales from the body of a small-pox patient, which are placed there in the hope that some one may touch them, contract the malady, and thus relieve the sufferer. In 1883 it was officially reported that at Cawnpore small-pox had greatly increased from the practice of placing these scabs on the roads. At the instance of Government the matter was investigated, and it was found that in the early stages of the disease the Diuli ceremony is performed at cross-roads; and that at a later period the crusts from small-pox patients mixed with curdled milk and cocoanut juice are carried to the temple or platform of the small-pox goddess and are dedicated to her.[2] One morning in a village near Agra, I came across two old women fiercely quarrelling. On making enquiries I found that one of them had placed some small-pox crusts off her child on her neighbour's threshold. The people agreed that this was a wicked act, as it displayed special animus against a particular person. If they had been placed on the cross-road, and any one had been unlucky enough to touch them and contract the disease, it would not have mattered so much—that was the will of God. Connected with this are other practices such as the following. In the hills in case of illness a stake is driven down into the earth where four

---

[1] Gregor, *Folklore of N.-E. Scotland,* 46, 157.
[2] *Panjáb Notes and Queries,* II, 42.

roads meet, and certain drugs and grains are buried close by which are speedily disinterred and eaten by crows. This gives immediate relief to the sufferer.[1] The idea apparently is, that the disease is thus transferred to the crow, a sacred bird, and in close communion with the spirits of the sainted dead. So in cases of cattle disease, a buffalo's skull, a small lamb, vessels of butter and milk, fire in a pan, wisps of grass, and sticks of the *siras* tree (*acacia speciosa*) are thrown over the boundary of a neighbouring village. This often causes a riot.[2] In the same way killing buffaloes and putting their heads in the next village removes cholera, and by pouring oil on grain and burning it, the disease flies elsewhere in the smoke.

Scapegoats.

This brings us to the regular scapegoat. At shrines of Sítalá, the small-pox goddess, sweepers bring round a small pig. Contributions are called for from the worshippers, and when the value of the animal is made up, he is driven by the people into the jungle, pursued by an excited crowd who believe that the creature has taken the disease with it. General Sleeman gives an excellent example of this :—" More than four-fifths of the city and cantonments of Ságar had been affected by a violent influenza, which, commencing with a distressing cough, was followed by fever and in some cases terminated in death. I had an application from the old Queen Dowager of Ságar to allow of a noisy religious procession for the purpose of imploring deliverance from this great calamity. The women and children in this procession were to do their utmost to add to the noise by raising their voices in psalmody, beating upon their brass pans and pots with all their might, and discharging firearms where they could get them. Before the noisy crowd was to be driven a buffalo which had been purchased by general subscription, in order that every family might participate in the merit. They were to follow it out eight miles, where it was to be turned out for any one who would take it. If

[1] Madden, *Journal Asiatic Society, Bengal,* 1848, p. 583.
[2] *Panjáb Notes and Queries,* I, 64.

the animal returned, the disease must return with it, and the ceremony be performed over again. I was requested to intimate the circumstance to the officer commanding the troops in cantonments, in order that the noise they intended to make might not excite any alarm and bring down upon them the visit of the soldiery. It was, however, subsequently determined that the animal should be a goat, and he was driven before the crowd. Accordingly I have on several occasions been requested to allow of such noisy ceremonies in cases of epidemics, and the confidence the people feel in their efficacy has no doubt a good effect."[1]

Demons scared by noise.

This leads incidentally to the discussion of another question—that evil spirits are scared by noise. In the first place this appears largely to account for the use of bells in religious worship. There is, besides, the additional fact that they are composed of metal, which, as we shall see elsewhere, is a well known scarer of demons. The use of the bell or resounding shell trumpet is common everywhere. The intention is to call the divinity to the feast which has been prepared by his votaries, and to scare vagrant ghosts who would otherwise partake of the meal. The Gonds have elevated the bell into a Deity in the form of Ghagarapen, and one special class of their devil priests, the Ojhyáls, always wear bells.[2] So the Patári priest of Mirzapur and many classes of ascetics throughout the country carry bells or rattles made of iron—a powerful demon fetish—to scare demons. The ringing of bells is everywhere common for the same purpose. Milton speaks of—

> "The bellman's drowsy charm;
> To bless the doors from nightly harm."[3]

The passing bell protects the departing soul as it flies through the air from demoniacal influence, and the keening at an Irish wake is probably a survival of the same custom. But Panjábi Musalmáns

---

[1] *Rambles and Recollections*, I, 214.
[2] Hislop, *Papers*, 6, 47.
[3] *Penseroso*, 83-84.

have a prejudice against beating a brass tray as it is believed to disturb the dead, who wake, supposing the day of judgment has arrived.[1] We have already seen that noise scares the demon of the hail Demons are always particularly dangerous during the more serious crises of life. Thus drums are beaten and songs are sung at marriages to protect the youthful pair from evil. When a child is born, guns are fired to scare demons from the mother and child, and it is a very common idea that disease is removed by volley firing. This principle accounts for a number of other curious and obscure practices which need not be discussed in detail.[2]

Disease scapegoats.

To return to the scapegoats. In Berár, if cholera is very severe, the people get a scapegoat or young buffalo, but in either case it must be a female and as black as possible. They then tie some grain, cloves, and red lead in a yellow cloth on its back and turn it out of the village. A man of the gardener class takes the goat outside the boundary and it is not allowed to return.[3] So among the Korwas of Mirzapur when cholera begins, a black cock, and when it is severe, a black goat is offered by the Baiga at the shrine of the local Deity, and he then drives them off in the direction of some other village. After it has gone a little distance, the Baiga, who is protected from evil by virtue of his holy office, follows it, kills and eats it. Among the Patárís, in a cholera epidemic, the elders of the village and the Ojha wizard feed a black fowl with grain and drive it beyond the boundary, ordering it to take the plague with it. If a resident of another village finds such a fowl and eats it, cholera comes into his village. Hence when disease prevails people are very cautious in meddling with stray fowls. When these animals are sent off, a little oil, red lead, and a woman's forehead spangle are put upon it. When such an animal comes into a village the Baiga takes it to the local shrine, worships it, and

---

[1] *North Indian Notes and Queries*, I, 16.
[2] Numerous examples are given in *Calcutta Review*, April 1884 : *Panjáb Notes and Queries*, II, 21, *sq.* : Campbell's *Notes*, 45, 108, 407.
[3] *Panjáb Notes and Queries*, III, 81.

then passes it on quietly outside the boundary. Among the Kharwárs, when disease attacks the cattle, they take a black cock, put some red lead on its head, some antimony on its eyes, a spangle on its forehead, and fixing a pewter bangle to its leg, let it loose calling to the disease—"Mount on the fowl and go elsewhere into the ravines and thickets; destroy the sin." This dressing up of the scape animal in women's ornaments and trinkets is possibly a relic of some grosser form of expiation in which a human being was sacrificed. So, in the Panjáb when cholera prevails, a man of the Chamár or currier class is branded on the buttocks and turned out of the village.[1]

Modified forms of the scapegoat.

A curious modification of the ordinary scapegoat, of which it is unnecessary to give further instances, comes from Kulu. "The people occasionally perform an expiatory ceremony with the object of removing ill-luck or evil influence which is supposed to be brooding over the hamlet. The godling (*deota*) of the place is, as usual, first consulted through the disciple (*chela*) and declares himself also under the influence of a spell and advises a feast which is given in the evening at the temple. Next morning a man goes round from house to house, a creel on his back, into which each family throws all sorts of odds and ends, parings of nails, pinches of salt, bits of old iron, handfuls of grain, &c. The whole community then turn out and perambulate the village, at the same time stretching an unbroken thread round it fastened to pegs at the four corners. This done, the man with the creel carries it down to the river bank and empties the contents therein, and a sheep, fowl, and some small animals are sacrificed on the spot. Half the sheep is the property of the man who dares to carry the creel, and he is also entertained from house to house on the following night."[2] He is, in fact, as is shown by the mystic articles which he carries with him, the bearer of the guilt of the village, like the Sineaters of English rural life who took upon their own shoulders the guilt of the dead man.

---

1 *Panjáb Notes and Queries*, I. 27.
2 *Settlement Report*, 155.

The scapegoat merging into a sacrifice.

In the final stage we find the scapegoat merging into a regular expiatory sacrifice. Thus at one of their festivals, the Bhúmij used to drive two male buffaloes into a small enclosure, while the Rája and his suite witnessed the proceedings. They first discharged arrows at the animals, and the tormented and enraged beasts fell to and gored each other while arrow after arrow was discharged. When the animals were past doing very much mischief, the people rushed in and hacked them to pieces with axes. This custom is now discontinued.[1] Similarly, in the hills at the Nand Ashtami, or feast in honour of Nanda, the foster father of Krishna, a buffalo is specially fed with sweetmeats, and after being decked with a garland round the neck is worshipped. The headman of the village then lays a sword across its neck and the beast is let loose, when all proceed to chase it, pelt it with stones, and hack it with knives until it dies. In other villages when a man dies, his relations assemble at the end of the year in which the death occurred, and the nearest male relative dances naked (a custom of which other instances have been already quoted) with a drawn sword in his hand, to the music of a drum, in which he is assisted by others for a whole day and night. The following day a buffalo is brought and made intoxicated with Indian hemp (*bhang*) and spirits, and beaten to death with sticks, stones, and weapons.[2] Similarly the Hill Bhotiyas have a feast in honour of the village god, and towards evening they take a dog, make him drunk with spirits and hemp, and kill him with sticks and stones, in the belief that no disease or misfortune will visit the village during the year.[3] At the periodical feast to the mountain goddess of the Himalaya, Nandá Devi, it is said that a four-horned goat is invariably born and accompanies the pilgrims. When unloosed on the mountain the sacred goat suddenly disappears and as suddenly reappears without its head, and then furnishes food to the party.

---

1 Dalton, *Descriptive Ethnology*, 176.
2 Atkinson, *Himalayan Gazetteer*, II, 851, *sq.*
3 *Ibid.* II, 871.

CHAPTER IV.

THE WORSHIP OF THE SAINTED DEAD.

Αἶψα δ' ἵκοντο κατ' ἀσφοδελὸν λειμῶνα,
Ἔνθα τε ναίουσι ψυχαί, εἴδωλα καμόντων.

ODYSSEY, xxiv, 12—14.

Ancestor worship: its origin.

The worship of ancestors is one of the main branches of the religion of the Indian races. "Its principles are not difficult to understand, for they plainly keep up the arrangements of the living world. The dead ancestor, now passed into a deity, simply goes on protecting his own family, and receiving suit and service from them as of old; the dead chief still watches over his own tribe, still holds his authority by helping friends and harming enemies; still rewards the right and sharply punishes the wrong."[1] It is, in fact, the earliest attempt of the savage to realise the problems of human existence, as the theology of the Vedas or Olympos is the explanation which the youth of the world offers of physical phenomena. The latter is primitive physics, the former primitive biology, and it marks a stage in the growth of anthropomorphism when the worship of unseen spirits in general passes to that of unseen spirits in particular.

Ancestor worship among Aryans.

It is admitted that this form of worship was general among the Aryan nations,[2] but it is a mistake to suppose, as is too often done, that the worship was peculiar to them. That such is not the case can be proved by numerous examples drawn from the practices of aboriginal tribes in India, who have lived in such complete isolation that the custom can hardly have been due to modern imitation of the

---

[1] *Primitive Culture*, II, 113.

[2] Hearn, *Aryan Households*, 18: Spencer, *Principles of Sociology*, I, 270, *sq.*: Whitney, *Oriental and Linguistic Studies*, 1st *ser.*, 59: Mommsen, *History of Rome*, I, 73.

ritual of their Hindu neighbours. Thus, the Korwas of Mirzapur worship their dead relations in February with an offering of goats. This is done by the eldest son of the dead man in the family cook-house. Their ancestors do not appear in the flesh after death, but show themselves in dreams. On the day on which they are expected to appear, the householder makes an offering of cakes to them in the family kitchen. The Pataris and Majhwárs believe that the dead do not visit their family homes, but come into the neighbourhood on certain days when worship is being done. At other times they remain in the sky or wander about on the mountains. Sometimes they appear to some of their descendants and say "Worship us, give us food and drink." If they are not propitiated they give trouble and cause sickness. The Bhuiyárs sacrifice a fowl and make a burnt offering. As they pray they say "You are our father and mother. Watch us and save us from evil." The Kharwárs, who are more completely Hinduised, worship the Pitri at weddings in the courtyard. The worship is done by the head of the family. Balls of rice are boiled in milk by the house-master, and then a Bráhman repeats some texts. They have the usual ceremony in honour of the dead at the Pitra paksha or fortnight of the dead in Kuár (August). The Kisáns and Bhuiyárs of Chutia Nágpur adore their ancestors, "but they have no notion that the latter are now spirits, or that there are spirits or ghosts, or a future state, or anything." The Bhuiyas revere their ancestors under the name of *vira* or "hero," a term which is elsewhere applied to ghosts of a distinctly malignant character. The Kharrias put the ashes of their dead into an earthen vessel and throw it into the river. They afterwards set up in the vicinity slabs of stone, and to these they make daily oblations. The only worship performed by the Korwas of Chutia Nágpur is that of their deceased relations. The same is the case with other allied races such as the Bhíls and Santáls.[1] The Gonds propitiate for at least one year the spirits of their departed friends, even though they have been men of no note; but when a person has been in any way distinguished, if,

[1] Dalton, *Descriptive Ethnology*, 132, 133, 139, 160, 229: Campbell, *Notes* 2, *sqq.*: Tylor, *Primitive Culture*, II, 117.

for example, he has founded a village or been its headman or priest, then he is treated as a god for years, and a small shrine of earth is erected to his memory at which sacrifices are annually offered.[1] It is said that the Juángs, who, until quite recently used to dress in garments of leaves, are the only one of these tribes who do not practise this form of worship[2]: but these races are particularly reticent about their beliefs and usages, and it is more than probable that further enquiry will show that they are not peculiar in this respect.

Worship of ancestors among Bráhmanised Hindus.

The ordinary worship of ancestors among the Bráhmanised Hindu races has been so often described in well known books as to need little further illustration. The spirits of departed ancestors attend on the Bráhmans invited to the ceremony of the *sráddha* "hovering round them like pure spirits, and sitting by them when they are seated." "An offering to the gods is to be made at the beginning and end of the *sráddha;* it must not begin and end with an offering to ancestors, for he who begins and ends it with an offering to the Pitri quickly perishes with his progeny." The place where the oblation is to be made is to be sequestered, facing the south and smeared with cowdung. The use of this substance is easily accounted for, without following the remarkable explanation of a modern writer, who connects it with the dropping of the Aurora.[3] "The divine manes are always pleased with an oblation in empty glades, naturally clean, on the banks of rivers and in solitary spots." The ceremony is to be performed by the eldest son, which furnishes the Hindu with the well known argument for the necessity of marriage and the procreation of male issue.[4] The orthodox Hindu besides the annual *sráddha,* in connection with his daily worship, offers an oblation of water (*tarpana*), to the sainted dead. The object of the annual *sráddha* is to accelerate the progress (*gati*) of the soul through the various stages of bliss known as *salokya, samípya* and *sarúpya,* and by its performance at Gaya

[1] Hislop, *Papers*, 16, *sq.*
[2] Dalton, *op cit.*, 158.
[3] Gubernatis, *Zoological Mythology*, I, 276.
[4] Manu, *Institutes*, III, 189, 205.

the wearied soul passes into Vaikuntha or the paradise of Vishnu. It may also be noted that the sacred grains used in the performance of the *sráddha* are barley and sesamum. We have seen that the annual ceremony is performed by orthodox Hindus until the spirit attains beatification. This usually takes place after three generations, and the soul then passes into felicity and ceases to influence its descendants for good or evil. The more primitive races believe that the spirit like themselves is mortal. The Kunbis of Bombay believe that a ghost cannot trouble a man for more than twelve years; in the Dakkhin their life is limited to three or four generations. The Kurkus of Central India worship the dead for only one year.[1] Hindus do not allow their sons during the fortnight sacred to the manes to wash their bodies or clothes, shave or bathe, as they believe that the dirt thus removed will reach and annoy the sainted dead. The story goes that Rája Karan made a vow that he would not touch food until he had given a maund and a quarter (about one hundred pounds) of gold daily to Bráhmans. When he died he went to heaven and was there given a palace of gold to live in, and gold for his food and drink as this was all he had given away in charity in his mortal life. So in his distress he asked to be allowed to return to earth for fifteen days. His prayer was granted, and he occupied himself during his time of grace in giving nothing but food in charity, being so busy that he neglected to bathe, shave, or wash his clothes.[2]

Special forms of ancestor worship.

The worship which has been thus described readily passes into other and grosser forms. Thus, in the family of the Gáikwárs of Baroda when they worship Mahádeva they think of the greatest of this line of princes. The temple contains a rudely executed portrait of Khanderáo, that to the left the bed, garments and phial of Ganges water which commemorate his mother Chimnábái. Govindráo has an image dressed

[1] See the instances collected by Campbell, *Notes*, 12: Tylor, *Primitive Culture*, II, 116.
[2] *North Indian Notes and Queries*, I, 95.

up and Fateh Sinh a stone face.[1] In Central India, Rájputs wear the figure of a distinguished ancestor or relation engraved in gold or silver. This image, usually that of a warrior on horseback, is sometimes worshipped, but its chief utility is as a charm to keep off ghosts and evil spirits.[2] The aboriginal Bhuiyás of Chutiá Nágpur "after disposing of their dead, perform a ceremony which is supposed to bring back into the house the spirit of the deceased, henceforward an object of household worship. A vessel filled with rice and flour is placed for the time on the tomb, and when brought back a mark of a fowl's foot is found at the bottom of the vessel, and this indicates that the spirit of the deceased has returned."[3] We shall meet other instances of similar practices when we consider the malignant variety of ghosts. A curious illustration of the popular form of ancestor worship is given by General Sleeman. "Rám Chandra the Pandit said that villages which had been held by old Gond proprietors were more liable than any others to visitation from local ghosts: that it was easy to say what village was, or was not, haunted; but often exceedingly difficult to say to whom the ghost belonged. This once discovered, the nearest surviving relation was, of course, expected to take steps to put him to rest. 'But,' said he, 'it is wrong to suppose that the ghost of an old proprietor must be always doing mischief. He is often the best friend of the cultivators, and of the present proprietor too, if he treats him with proper respect; for he will not allow the people of any other village to encroach upon the boundaries with impunity, and they will be saved all expense and annoyance of a reference to the judicial tribunals for the settlement of boundary disputes. It will not cost much to conciliate these spirits, and the money is generally well laid out.'" He instances a case of a family of village proprietors "who had for several generations at every new settlement insisted upon having the name of the spirit of the old proprietor inserted in the lease instead of their own, and thereby secured his good graces on all occasions." A cultivator who

[1] *Bombay Gazetteer*, VII, 16, *sq*.
[2] Malcolm, *Central India*, I, 144.
[3] Dalton, *Descriptive Ethnology*, 148.

trespassed on land believed to be in charge of such a spirit had his son bitten by a snake, and his two oxen were seized with the murrain. "In terror he went off to the village temple, confessed his sin, and vowed to restore not only the half acre of land, but to build a very handsome temple on the spot as a perpetual sign of his repentance. The boy and the bullocks all then recovered, the shrine was built, and is, I believe, still to be seen as a boundary mark."[1]

Worship of special ancestral ghosts.

From this family worship of deceased relations, the transition to the worship of special persons of high local reputation in life, or who have died in some remarkable way, is easy. The intermediate links are the Sádhu and the Satí, and the cultus finally culminates in a creed like that of the Jainas, who worship a pantheon of deified saints, that of the Lingayat worship of Siva incarnated in Chambasápa, or the godlike weaver Kabír of the Kabírpanthis.

The Sádhu.

The Sádhu is a saint who is regarded as "the great power of God." He is a visible manifestation of the divine energy acquired by his virtue and self-devotion. We shall meet later on instances of deified holy men of this class. Meanwhile, it may be noted, we see around us the constant developement of the cultus in all its successive stages. Thus in Berár at Askot the saint is still alive; at Wadnera he died nearly a century ago, and his descendants live on the offerings made by the pious. At Jalgánw a crazy vagabond was canonised on grounds which strict people consider quite insufficient. There is, of course, among the disciples and descendants of these local saints a constant competition going on for the honour of canonisation, which, once secured, the shrine may become a very valuable source of income and reputation. But the indiscriminate and ill-regulated deification of mortals is one of the main causes of the weakness of modern Hinduism, because by a process of abscission, the formation of multitudinous sects which take their titles

---

[1] *Rambles and Recollections*, I, 287, 289, 291.

and special forms of belief from the saint whose disciples they profess to be, is promoted and encouraged. Thus, as has been well remarked, Hinduism lies in urgent need of a Pope or acknowledged orthodox head "to control its wonderful elasticity and receptivity, to keep up the standard of deities and saints, and generally to prevent superstitions running wild into a tangled jungle of polytheism."[1]

These saints have wrested from the reluctant gods, by sheer piety and relentless austerity, a portion of the divine thaumaturgic power which exhales after their death from the places where their bodies are laid. This is the case with Muhammadans as well as Hindus. Thus at Chunár there is a famous shrine in honour of Sháh Qásim Sulaimáni, a local saint whose religious opinions were displeasing to Akbar, who imprisoned him there until his death in 1614 A.D.[2] His cap and turban are still shown at his tomb, and when these are gently rubbed by one of his disciples, the divine influence exudes through the assembled multitude of votaries, many of whom are Hindus. Hindu saints of the same class are so directly imbued with the divine afflatus that they need not the purifying influence of fire, and are buried, not cremated. Their last resting place (*samádh*) is usually represented by a pile of earth or a tomb or tumulus of a conical or circular form. Others again, like some of the Gusáins, are after death enclosed in a box of stone and consigned to the waters of the Ganges. These shrines are generally occupied by a disciple of the saint and there vows and prayers are made and offerings presented.

The Sati.

The second link between ancestor worship and that of special deceased worthies is seen in the Satí or "faithful wife," who, before the practice was prohibited by our Government, was bound to bear her deceased lord company

---

[1] *Berár Gazetteer*, 191.

[2] For a complete account of this saint see *North Indian Notes and Queries*, vol. I.

to the world of spirits for his consolation and service.[1] The small shrines in honour of the Satí are found often in considerable numbers on the banks of tanks. They are visited by women at marriages and other festivals, and are periodically repaired and kept in order. According to Mr. Ibbetson, in the Delhi territory, these shrines take the place of those dedicated to the sainted dead or Pitri.[2] They often contain a representation in stone of the lord and his faithful spouse, and one of his arms rests affectionately on her neck. Sometimes, if he died in battle, he is mounted on his war steed and she walks beside him, but her worshippers are not always careful in identifying her shrine, and I have seen at least one undoubted revenue survey pillar doing duty as a monument of some unnamed local divinity of this class. Among the warlike tribes of Rajputána the Satí shrine usually takes the form of a monument on which is carved the warrior on his charger, with his wife standing beside him, and the images of the Sun and Moon on either side, emblematical of never-dying fame. Such places are the haunted ground of many a ghostly legend. "Among the altars on which have burnt the beautiful and the brave, the harpy (*Dákini*) takes up her abode, and stalks forth to devour the heart of her victims." The Rájput never enters these places of silence, but to perform stated rites or anniversary offerings of flowers and water to the manes of his ancestors.[3] There is a peculiarly beautiful Satí necropolis at Udaypur,[4] and the Satí Burj or tower at Mathura, erected in honour of the Queen of Rája Bihár Mall of Jaypur in 1570 A.D., is one of the chief ornaments of the city.[5]

The Satí is regarded as having secured the honour of deification by her sacrifice, and is able to protect her worshippers and gratify their desires. Some are even the subject of special honour,

---

1 For illustrations of this idea see Spencer, *Principles of Sociology*, I, 187, *sq.*: Lubbock, *Origin of Civilisation*, 284: Tylor, *Primitive Culture*, I, 458, *sqq*.

2 *Panjáb Ethnography*, 115.

3 Tod, *Annals*, I, 79.

4 Ferguson, *History of Indian Architecture*, 470: *Rájputána Gazetteer*, III, 46.

5 Growse, *Mathura*, 138.

such as Sakhu Bái, who is worshipped at Akola.[1] Even the aboriginal Kaurs of Sirguja worship a deified Satí. She has a sacred grove, and every year a fowl is sacrificed to her, and every third year a goat. Colonel Dalton observes that the Hindus who accompanied him were intensely amused at the idea of offering fowls to a Satí who is accustomed to the simpler bloodless tribute of milk, cakes, fruit, and flowers. This is the rule at Jilmili, the Satí shrines belonging to the family of the local Rája.[2] The curses of a dying Satí were greatly feared, and in popular belief usually brought ruin on those who were responsible for her death. Colonel Tod gives many instances of this.[3] In Jesalmer, a curious variation of the Satí ceremony seems to have prevailed: mothers used to sacrifice themselves with their dead children.[4]

Modern saints, Gauhar Sháh; Shekh Burhan.

We have already noticed some instances of the modern canonisation of saints and holy men. Of worthies of this kind who have received semi-divine honours, the name is legion. A few examples may be given to illustrate this phase of the popular faith. Thus, one Gauhar Sháh was canonised quite recently at Meerut because he made a prophecy that a windmill belonging to a certain Mr. Smith would soon cease to work. The fulfilment of his prediction was ample evidence of his sanctity. Just before his death this holy man directed that he should be removed from an inn which immediately fell down. Another saint of the same place is said to have been generous enough to give five years of his life to the notorious Begam Samru who died in 1836, in all the odour of sanctity. Shekh Búrhan, a saint of Amber, was offered a drink of milk by Mokul, one of the Shekháwat chiefs, and immediately performed the miracle of drawing a copious stream of milk from the udder of an exhausted female buffalo. "This was sufficient to convince the old chief that he could work other miracles,

---

1 *Berár Gazetteer*, 191.
2 *Descriptive Ethnology*, 138.
3 *Annals*, II, 544, 546, 676; for similar cases in Nepál, see Wright, *History*, 159, 212.
4 *Panjáb Notes and Queries*, IV, 44, *sq.* In the *Katha Sarit Ságara* (Tawney, II, 254), a mother proposes to go into the fire with her dead children.

and he prayed that through his means he might no longer be childless. In due time he had an heir, who, according to the injunction of Búrhan, was styled after his own tribe Shekh, whence the title of the clan. He directed that the child should wear the crosstrings (*baddiya*) worn by Muhammadan children, which, when laid aside, were to be deposited in the saint's shrine, and further, that he should assume the blue tunic and cap, abstain from hog's flesh, and eat no meat in which the blood remained. He also ordained that at the birth of every Shekháwat a goat should be sacrificed, the Islamite creed (*kalima*) recited, and the child sprinkled with the blood." These customs are still observed and the Shekh's shrine is a sanctuary while his descendants enjoy lands specially assigned to them.[1] This power of conferring male offspring has made the reputation of many saints of this class, like the famous Salím Chishti of Fatehpur-Sikri, whose prayers were efficacious in procuring an heir for the Emperor Akbar. Up to the present day childless women visit his shrine and hang rags on the delicate marble traceries of his tomb to mark their vows.

Harshu Pánre.

Besides this sainthood which is based on sanctity of life and approved thaumaturgic powers, the right of deification is conferred on persons who have been eminent or notorious in their lives, or who have died in some extraordinary or tragical way. All or nearly all the deified saints of Northern India may be grouped under one or other of these categories. We have already given one instance of the second class in Hardaul Lála, the cholera godling. Another example is that of Harshu Pánré or Harshu Bába, the local god of Chayanpur near Sahsarám in Bengal, whose worship is now rapidly spreading over Northern India, and promises to become as widely diffused as that of Hardaul himself. He was a Kanaujiya Bráhman, the family priest of Raja Sáliváhana of Chayanpur. The Rája had two queens one of whom was jealous of the priest's influence. About this time the priest built a fine house close to the palace and one night the

[1] Tod, *Annals*, II, 430, *sq.*

Rája and Rání saw a light from its upper storey gleaming aloft in the sky. The Rání hinted to the Rája that the priest had designs of ousting the monarch from his kingdom, so the Rája had his house demolished and resumed the lands which had been conferred on him. The enraged Bráhman did *dharna*, in other words, fasted till he died at the palace gate. This tragical event occurred in 1427 A.D., and when they took his body for cremation to Benares, they found Harshu standing in his wooden sandals on the steps of the burning *ghát*. He informed them that he had become a Brahm or Bráhman ghost. The Rája's family was destroyed except one daughter who had been kind to the Bráhman in his misfortunes, and through her the family continues to this day. Harshu is now worshipped with the fire sacrifice and offerings of Bráhmanical cords and sweetmeats. If any one obtains his desire through his intercession, he offers a golden Bráhmanical cord and a silken waist-string and feeds Bráhmans in his name.[1] Another saint whose legend much resembles that of Harshu is Ratan Pánré, who revenged the seduction of his daughter on the Kalhans Rája of Gonda by the destruction of his palace.[2]

Maheni.

There is a similar case among the Hayobans Rájputs of Gházipur. In 1528 A.D. their Rája, Bhopat Deva, or perhaps one of his sons, seduced Mahení, a Bráhman girl, a relation of their family priest. She burned herself to death, and in dying imprecated the most fearful curses on the Hayobans clan. In consequence of a succession of disasters which followed, the tribe completely abandoned their family settlement at Ballia, where the woman's tomb is worshipped to this day: and even now none of the clan dares to enter the precincts of their former home.[3]

Nahar Khán.

Of the same type is the case of the celebrated Jaswant Sinh of Márwár, who had an intrigue with the daughter of one of his chief officers. "But

[1] Cunningham, *Archæological Reports*, XVII, 160 *sqq.*: Buchanan, *Eastern India*, I, 488: *North Indian Notes and Queries*, II, 38.

[2] *Oudh Gazetteer*, I, 540, *sq.*

[3] Oldham, *Memoir of Gházipur*, I, 55, *sq.*

the avenging ghost of the Bráhman interposed between him and his wishes : a dreadful struggle ensued, in which Jaswant lost his senses, and no effort could banish the impression from his mind. The ghost persecuted his fancy, and he was generally believed to be possessed of a wicked spirit, which, when exorcised, was made to say he would depart only on the sacrifice of a chief equal in dignity to Jaswant. Nahar Khán, 'the tiger lord,' chief of the Kumpáwat clan, who led the van in all his battles, immediately offered his head in expiation for his prince : and he had no sooner expressed this loyal determination than the holy man who exorcised the spirit caused it to descend into a vessel of water, and having waved it thrice round his head they presented it to Nahar Khán, who drank it off, and Jaswant's senses were instantly restored. This miraculous transfer of the ghost is implicitly believed by every chief of Rájasthán, by whom Nahar Khán is called " the faithful of the faithful, and worshipped as a local god.[1]

Vyása Válmíki and Dattátreya.

Next come those mortals who have been deified on account of the glory of their lives. Vyása, the compiler of the Vedas, has been canonised, and there is a temple in his honour both at Benares and Rámnagar. In the latter place he has been promoted to the dignity of an incarnation of Siva, whereas in Benares he has a temple of his own. His worship extends as far as Kulu, where he has an image near a stream. Pilgrims offer flowers in his name and set up a stone on end in commemoration of their visit.[2] So with Valmíki, the author of the Rámáyana, who has a shrine at Bálu in the Karnál district and has now, by an extraordinary freak in hagiolatry, become identified with Lál Beg, the low caste god of the sweepers.[3] In the same way from the Himalaya to Bombay Dattátreya, a deified mortal, is reverenced by the Vaishnavas as a partial manifestation of Vishnu, and by the Saivas as a distinguished authority on the Yoga philosophy. He has temples both in Garhwál and in the

---

[1] Tod, *Annals*, II, 40.
[2] Sherring, *Sacred City*, 118, 174 : Moorcroft, *Journey to Ladakh*, I, 190.
[3] *Panjáb Notes and Queries*, I, 1 : *Indian Antiquary*, XI, 290 : *Gazetteer, North-Western Provinces*, VI, 634 : *Dabistán*, II, 24, *sq*.

Konkan, like Parásara Rishi, the reputed author of the Vishnu Purána, who wished to make a sacrifice to destroy the Rákshasas, but was dissuaded by the saints, and then scattered the fire over the slope of the Himalaya, where it still blazes forth at the phases of the moon.[1]

Ganga Náth, Bhola Náth, Bhairwanand, the Mughal of Ganor.

Two other hill godlings owe their promotion to the tragic circumstances of their death. Ganga Náth was a Rája's son who quarrelled with his father and became a religious mendicant. He subsequently fell into an intrigue with the wife of an astrologer who murdered him and his paramour. They both became malignant ghosts, to whom numerous temples were erected. When any one is injured by the wicked or powerful, he has recourse to Ganga Náth, who punishes the evil-doer. Of the same type is Bhola Náth, whose brother, Gyán Chand, one of the Almora princes, had him assassinated with his pregnant mistress, both of whom became malignant ghosts, and are particularly obnoxious to gardeners, one of whom murdered them. This caste now specially worships them, and a small iron trident is sometimes placed in the corner of a cottage, and resorted to in their names when any sudden or unexpected calamity attacks the occupants.[2] Similar is the case of Bhairwanand, the tribal deity of the Raikwár Rájputs of Oudh. He was pushed into a well by his brother in order to fulfil a prophecy, and has since been deified.[3] So with the Queen of Ganor who was obliged to surrender herself to her Mughal conqueror. She killed him by means of a poisoned robe. He died in extreme torture and was buried on the road to Bhopál. A visit to his grave is believed to cure tertian ague.[4]

Bandit godlings.

Even the thieving tribes have, as their godlings, deified bandits. Such is Salhes, the godling of the criminal Doms and Dusádhs of Behár. He was a

---

[1] Atkinson, *Himalayan Gazetteer*, II, 805: *Bombay Gazetteer*, XI, 300, 302.
[2] Atkinson, *loc. cit.*, II, 817, *sqq.*
[3] *Oudh Gazetteer*, I, 284.
[4] Tod, *Annals*, I, 659, *sq.*

great hero and the first watchman. He fought a famous battle with Chuhar Mal of Mohâma and is the subject of a popular epic in Tirhút. With his worship is associated that of his brother, Motirám, another worthy of the same kind.[1] At Sherpur near Patna is the shrine of Gauraiya or Goraiya, a Dusádh bandit chief to which members of all castes resort, the clean making offerings of meal, the unclean sacrificing a swine or several young pigs and pouring out libations of spirits on the ground. Even a godling like Salhes is in process of promotion, because, according to some, he was the porter of Bhím Sen.[2] Another bandit godling is Mitthu Bhúkhiya, a freebooter, worshipped by the Banjáras or wandering carriers. He has a special hut in which no one may drink or sleep, and which is marked with a white flag. The clan always worship here before committing a crime. They assemble together and an image of a famous tribal Satí is produced. Butter is put into a saucer and in this a light is placed, very broad at the bottom and tapering upwards. The wick standing erect is lit, an appeal is made to the Satí for an omen, and those worshipping mention in a low tone to the godling where they are going, and what they propose to do. The wick is then carefully watched, and should it droop at all, the omen is propitious. All then salute the flag and start on their marauding expedition.[3] So the Dhánuks of Patna have a shrine to one of their chiefs who was killed in a skirmish with the Muhammadans six hundred years ago, and whose ghost has since then been troublesome. He is worshipped in a shrine of brick and a member of the tribe acts as his priest.[4]

Rája Lákhan.

The tribal god of the Mirzapur Kols is Rája Lákhan. The tribe nowadays can give no satisfactory account of him. One story is that he came from Lucknow, a legend based of course on the similarity of the name. But there can be no reasonable doubt that he was really Lakhana

---

[1] Cunningham, *Archæological Reports*, XVI, 28: Grierson, *Behár Peasant Life*, 407: *Maithili Chrestomathy*, 3, *sqq*.
[2] Risley, *Bengal Tribes and Castes*, I, 256.
[3] *Berar Gazetteer*, 199, sq.
[4] Buchanan, *Eastern India*, I, 83.

Deva, the son of the famous Rája Jaychand of Kanauj, who is known in song as the Kanaujiya Ráe. He was perhaps taken to Dehli and converted to Islám, but the popularity of his name in local legends points to the possibility that he was a leader of the Hindus against the Muhammadan invaders. At any rate it is curious that he, a Rájput, as much a stranger to the Drávidian Kols as his Muhammadan rival, should have been deified by these primitive dwellers in the jungle.[1]

Nathu Kahár.

We shall come elsewhere on instances of the belief that human beings were sacrificed under the foundations of important buildings. Nathu Kahár is the deity of the Oudh boatmen, and is said to have been buried alive under the foundation of the fort of Akbarpur, in the Fyzábád District, where a fair is held in his honour.[2]

Rámása Pír.

The godling or saint invoked by Pindhári women when their husbands went on marauding expeditions, was Ramása Pír. He was a well known warrior killed in battle at Ranuja near Pushkar. Saturday is his day for prayer, on which occasions small images of horses in clay or stone are offered at his shrine. The figure of a man on horseback stamped in gold or silver representing the godling was found on the necks of many of the Pindháris killed in the great campaign of 1817-18. He is now known as Deva Dharma Rája, which is one of the titles of Yama, the god of death, and Yudisthira, his putative son.[3]

Ráe Sinh.

Another local godling of the same class is Ráe Sinh, whose legend is told by General Sleeman. "At Sanoda there is a very beautiful little fortress or castle, now unoccupied, but still entire. It was built by an officer of Rája Chhattar Sál of Bundelkhand about 1725 A.D. His son,

---

[1] For his history in connection with the inscribed pillar ta Bhuili in the Mirzapur district, see *Archæological Reports*, XI, 129, *sq*.

[2] *Oudh Gazetteer*, I, 517.

[3] Malcolm, *Central India*, II, 177, *sq*.

by name Ráe Sinh, was, soon after the castle had been completed, killed in an attack upon a town near Chhattarkot, and having in the estimation of the people become a god, he had a temple and a tomb raised to him. I asked the people how he became a god, and was told that some one who had been long suffering from a quartan ague went to the tomb one night and promised Ráe Sinh, whose ashes lay under it, that if he could contrive to cure his ague for him, he would during the rest of his life make offerings at his shrine. After this he never had an attack and was very punctual in his offerings. Others followed his example and with like success, till Ráe Sinh was recognised universally among them as a god, and had a temple raised to his name." "This is the way," remarks General Sleeman, "gods were made all over the world and are now made in India."[1]

Miscellaneous godlings.

It would be easy to add largely to the catalogue of local godlings who have been deified in this way: to consider, for instance, Náth Bába, the tribal god of the Sengar Rájputs of Gházipur: Lot, the deity of the Chauháns of Ajmere: the Katyúri Rájas of Kumaun: Hindupat of Oudh, and so on. But the instances already given will probably be sufficient to illustrate this form of the local worship of deified worthies.[2]

The Pirs and Sayyads.

We now come to a more miscellaneous class—the Pírs and Sayyads. Some of these we have encountered already. These saints are usually of Muhammadan origin, but most of them are worshipped indiscriminately both by Musalmáns and low class Hindus. The word Pír properly means "an elder," but, according to the Súfi belief, is the equivalent of *Murshid* or "religious leader." Sayyad, an Arabic word, meaning "Lord" or "Prince," is probably in many cases a corruption of *Shahíd*, "a martyr of the faith," because many of these worthies owe their reputation to the fact of their having lost their lives in the early struggles between Islám and idolatry. This worship illustrates in

[1] *Rambles and Recollections*, I, 123.

[2] Oldham, *Gházipur Memoir*, I, 57, *sq.*: Tod, *Annals*, II, 489: Atkinson, *Himalayan Gazetteer*, II, 831: *Oudh Gazetteer*, I, 563.

an admirable way the extreme receptivity of the popular belief. We have here a body of saints many of whom were deadly enemies of the Hindu faith who are now worshipped by Hindus. The peculiarity of the cultus is its extreme catholicity. "The *'Urs* or annual ceremony of one of these saints, like the Martyr's day of St. Edmund or St. Thomas of Canterbury, has degenerated into much that is mere carnal traffic and pagan idolatry, a scandal to the rigid Islámite. Yet, if he uplifts his voice against such soul-destroying abuses he may be hooted by loose living Musalmáns as a Wahhábi who denies the power of intercession, while the shopkeepers are no worse than Ephesian silversmiths at crying down an inconvenient religious reformer"[1] and the writer illustrates the fusion of the two creeds in their lower forms by the fact that the holy Hindu now in the flesh at Askot has only recently taken over the business, as it were, from a Muhammadan Faqír whose disciple he was during life, and now that the Faqír is dead, Narsinh Báwa presides over the annual veneration of his slippers. Similarly at the Muharram celebrations and at the pilgimages to tombs like those of Gházi Miyán, a large number of the votaries are of Hindus. In many towns the maintenance of these Muhammadan festivals mainly depends on the assistance of the Hindus, and it is only recently that the unfortunate concurrence of these exhibitions with special Hindu holidays has, it may be hoped only temporarily, interrupted the tolerant and kindly intercourse between the followers of the rival creeds. In many of these shrines the actual or pretended relics of the deceased worthy are exhibited. Under the shadow of the famous fortress of Chunár, in the Mirzapur district, is the shrine of Sháh Qásim Sulaimáni, of whom mention has been already made. The guardian of the shrine shows to pilgrims the turban of the saint who was deified about three hundred years ago, and the conical cap of his supposed preceptor the eminent Pír Jaháníya Jahángasht, but as in many such cases the chronology is hopeless.

[1] *Berár Gazetteer*, 195.

The most noted of the Pírs are, of course, the Panj Pír, or five original great saints of Islám. They were—the Prophet Muhammad, 'Ali his cousin-german and adopted son, Fátima daughter of the Prophet and wife of 'Ali, and their sons Hasan and Husen whose tragical fate is commemorated with such ardent sympathy at the Muharram.[1] But by modern Indian Musalmáns the name is usually applied to five leading saints—Bahá-ul-haqq of Multán, Sháh Ruqa-i-Álam Hazrat of Lucknow, Sháh Shams Tabríz of Multán, Makhdúm Jahániya Jahán Gasht of Multán, and Bába Shekh Faríd-ud-dín Shakkarganj of Pák Patan. Another enumeration makes the Chár Pír or four great saints to be—'Ali and his successors in saintship—Khwája Hasan Basri, Khwája Habíb Ázami, and Abdul Wáhid Kúfi. Another list of the Pírs of Upper India gives—Ghàzi Miyán, Pír Hathíli, sister's son of Ghàzi Miyán, Pír Jalíl of Lucknow, and Pír Muhammad of Jaunpur. Islám is, in fact, no less subject to periodical change than other religions organized on a less rigid system.[2]

The Panj Pír.

The worship of the Pírs has however undergone a grievous degradation. Thus, in the Panjáb, nearly every caste has its own Pír. The Dyers venerate Pír Ali Rangrez, the Lohárs Hazrat Dáúd or the Lord David, the Mehtars or sweepers, Lál Pír and Bába Faqír. In almost every Muhammadan house is a dreaded spot called the Pír's corner, where the owner erects a little shelf, lights a lamp every Thursday night, and hangs up garlands of flowers. Shekh Saddu is a favourite Pír with the women, especially those who wish to obtain an undue ascendancy over their husbands. When a woman wishes to have a private entertainment of her own she pretends to be shadow-smitten, that is, that the shadow of some Pír, usually Shekh Saddu, has fallen upon her, and her husband is bound to give an entertainment, known as "a session" (*baithak*), for the purpose of exorcising

Modern Pír worship.

[1] For a concise account see the Persian *Miracle play* translated by Sir Lewis Pelly; Intro. XI, *sqq*, quoted by Hughes, *Dictionary of Islám*, 185, *sq*.

[2] The five Pírs give their name to the Pír Panjal pass in Kashmir (Jarrett, *Ain-i Akbari*, II, 348). For another list of the Panj Pír see Temple, *Legends of the Panjáb*, II, 372, note.

him, to which no male is allowed admittance. At these rites of the Bona dea, it is believed that the Pír enters the woman's head and that she becomes possessed, and in that state of frenzy can answer any question put to her. All her female neighbours accordingly assemble to have their fortunes told by the Pír, and when they are satisfied they exorcise him with music and singing.

The Pachpiriyas.

But it is in the eastern part of the North-Western Provinces that the worship has reached its most degraded form. The worship of the so-called five saints prevails largely among the lower Hindu castes. But it is almost impossible to get any consistent account of these worthies, and the whole cultus has become imbedded in a mass of the wildest legend and mythology. Thus, in Benares, there are no less than five enumerations of the Pánch Pír :—

(1) Ghási Miyán, Aminá Satí, Suthán, Ajab Sálár, and Palihár.

(2) Ghazi Miyán, Aminá Satí, Suthán, Ajab Sálár, and Buahna.

(3) Ghází Miyán, Aminá Satí, Buahna, Bhairon, and Bande.

(4) Ghází Miyán, Aminá Satí, Palihár, Kálika, and Shahza.

(5) Ghází Miyán, Suthán, Ajab Sálár, Buahna, and Bahláno.

Here we have much that is distinctively Hindu and little derived from the real Islámitic saints.[1] In Behár again the five saints are Ghází Miyán, Hathíla, Parihár, Sahjá Máí, and Ajab Sálár, and with them are associated Aminá Satí, Langra Tár, who is represented by a piece of crooked wire, and Sobarna Tír, the bank of the Sobarna river.[2] Here we reach an atmosphere of the crudest fetishism. To go further still the title of the Pánch Pír or five saints has been applied to five Rájput heroes—Rámdeo, Pábu, Harbu, Mallináth, and Guga.[3] In Eastern India the priests of the faith are drawn from the Dafáli or drummer caste, who go about singing

---

[1] The whole cultus has been admirably described by Mr. R. Greeven in *North Indian Notes and Queries*, Vol. II, separately republished as "Heroes Five."

[2] Grierson, *Behar Peasant Life*, 405.

[3] *Panjáb Notes and Queries*, IV, 64.

and reciting the tale of Ghávi Miyán and his martyrdom. An iron bar wrapped in red cloth and adorned with flowers represents Ghází Miyán, which is taken round from house to house, drums are beaten, and petty offerings of grain levied from the villagers. Low caste Hindus, like Pásis and Chamárs, worship them in the form of five wooden pegs fixed in the courtyard of the house: and the Barwárs, a low criminal tribe in Oudh, build in their houses an altar in the shape of a tomb, at which yearly in August the head of the family sacrifices in the name of the Pírs a fowl and offers some thin cakes which he makes over to a Muhammadan beggar who goes about from house to house beating a drum.

Gházi Miyán.

The whole worship centres round Ghází Miyán. His real name was Sayyad Sálár Masaud, and he was nephew of Sultán Mahmúd of Ghazni. He was born in 1015 A.D., was leader of one of the early invasions of Oudh, and is claimed as one of the first martyrs of Islám in India. He was killed in a battle with the Hindus of Bahraich in 1034 A.D. Close to the battlefield was a tank with an image of the sun on its banks, a shrine sacred in the eyes of all Hindus, and Masaud whenever he passed it, was wont to say that he wished to have this spot for a dwelling place, and would, if it so pleased God, through the power of the spiritual sun, destroy the worship of the material. He was buried by some of his followers in the place which he had chosen for his resting-place, and tradition avers that his head rests on the image of the sun, the worship of which he had given his life to destroy. In fact there seems some reason to connect his worship nowadays with that of the sun. He is the type of youth and valour in militant Islám, and in Hinduism assumes the form of one of those godlike youths like Krishna or Dulhadeo, snatched away by an untimely and tragical fate in the prime of boyish beauty. So, though he was a fanatical devotee of Islám, his tomb is visited as much by Hindus as by Muhammadans. Besides his regular shrine at Bahraich, he has cenotaphs in various places, as at Gorakhpur and Bhadohi, in the Mirzapur district, where annual fairs are held in his honour. The worship of Masaud, which is now discouraged by Muhammadan puritans, embodied even in early times so much idolatry and fetishism as to be obnoxious to purists: it fell under the censure of the authorities, and Sikandar Lodi interdicted the possession of his spear.[1] Nowadays at his festivals a long spear or pole is paraded about, crowned at the top with bushy hair representing the head of the martyr, which, it is said, kept rolling on the ground long after it was severed from the trunk.[2]

Sakhi Sarwar.

Sakhi Sarwar or "generous leader," the title of a saint whose real name was Sayyad Ahmad, is held in great reverence in the Panjáb. His father is said to have been a native of Bághdád, and he flourished about the middle of the twelfth century. Another legend represents him as a disciple of the celebrated Pír Dastagír of Bághdád. The hill that overlooks his tomb is said to have been infested by a fearful giant. This monster used at night to stand on the hill-top and with a torch lure unwary travellers to their destruction. Against him Sakhi Sarwar and his four companions waged war, but all except the saint were killed: and such was the fall of the monster that the hill trembled to its base. Within an enclosure are seen the tombs of the saint, his lady Bíbí Ráé, and a Jinn who fell before the onset of the hero. The walls are hung with offerings of small pillars of various degrees of ornamentation. Persons who suffer from ophthalmia vow gold or silver eyes for their recovery. The hair of an expected child is vowed to be shaved at a certain time at the temple, and its weight in gold or silver is given to the saint. Some childless parents vow to him their first child, and on its birth take it to the temple with a cord round its neck. There are numbers of sacred pigeons attached to the shrine which are supported by an allowance realised from certain dedicated villages. The mark of Ali's fingers and the print of his foot are still shown to the devout in consideration of a fee to the guardians of the shrine, a visit to which is considered peculiarly efficacious for the

---

[1] Brigg's *Farishta*, I, 587.

[2] For the history of Masaud see *Oudh Gazetteer*, I, 111, *sqq.*: Sleeman, *Journey through Oudh*, I, 48: Elliot, *Supplemental Glossary*, *sv.*

cure of demoniacal possession, exhibiting itself in the form of epilepsy or hysteria. As a curious illustration of the catholicity of the worship of these saints, we find a shrine of Bába Nának, the founder of Sikhism, and a temple to Vishnu close to the tomb of Sakhi Sarwar. In the neighbourhood of Delhi he is not held in so much respect, but shrines in his honour are common, vows and pilgrimages to him are frequent, and Bráhmans tie threads on the wrists of their clients on a fixed day in his name. He is also known as Lakhdáta or "the giver of lakhs," and in this form has become the patron deity of athletes and especially of wrestling.[1]

Guga Pír.

Another noted local saint is Gúga Pír, also known at Záhir Pír, "the Saint apparent," or in the Panjáb as Bágarwála, as his grave is near Dadrewa in Bikáner, and he is said to have reigned over the Bágar or great prairies of Northern Rájputána. He flourished about the middle of the twelfth century when Indian hagiolatry was at its zenith. He is said to have been really a Hindu with the title of Gúga Bír or "Gúga the hero," but he is worshipped by Muhammadans as well as Hindus, and according to one local story he was converted to Islám. "He is said to have killed his two nephews and to have been condemned by their mother to follow them below. He attempted to do so, but the earth objected that he being a Hindu, she was quite unable to receive him till he should be properly burnt. As he was anxious to re-visit his wife nightly, this did not suit him, and so he became a Musalmán, and her scruples being thus removed, the earth opened and swallowed him and his horse alive. He is to the Hindus of the Eastern Panjáb the greatest of the snake Kings."[2] His shrine is often found in association with that of Nara Sinha, the man lion incarnation of Vishnu, and of Gorakhnáth, the famous ascetic whose disciple he is said to have been—another instance of the curious mixture of Hindu and Musalmán hagiology. He is represented on horseback with his

---

[1] *Calcutta Review*, LX, 78, *sqq.*: Ibbetson, *Panjáb Ethnography*, 115: Oldham, *Contemporary Review*, XLVII, 412: *Panjáb Notes and Queries*, II, 181, *sq.*: Temple, *Legends of the Panjáb*, I, 66, *sqq.*

[2] Ibbetson, *Panjáb Ethnography*, 115, *sq.*

mother trying to detain him as he descends to the infernal regions. He holds as a mark of dignity a long staff in his hands, and over him two snakes meet, one being coiled round his staff. Both Hindu and Muhammadan faqírs take the offerings devoted to him, and carry his standard (*chhari*), covered with peacocks' feathers, from house to house in the month of August. It is significant of the association of his worship with some early non-Aryan beliefs that the village scavenger is considered to be entitled to a share in the offerings.[1]

Another legend represents Gúga to be the son of a certain Rání Báchhal and fixes his birthplace at Sirsawa in the Sahāranpur district. About the time of the invasion of Mahmúd of Ghazni, she married Vatsa, the Rája of Bagardes, or the Rájputána desert. By the influence of the ubiquitous Saint, Gorakhnáth, she conceived in spite of the intrigues of her sister, and her child was called Gúga, because the saint gave his mother as a preservative a piece of gum resin (*Gúgal*). His cousins attacked him and tried to rob him of his kingdom, but Gúga defeated them and cut off their heads which he presented to his mother. She, in her anger, ordered him to go to the place where he had sent her nephews: so he requested the earth to receive him into her bosom, which she refused to do until he became a convert to Islám. He then went to Mecca and became a disciple of one Ratan Haji, and on his return the earth opened and received him with his famous black mare Javádiyá. The mare has, of course, a story of her own. Gúga had no children, and lamenting this to his guardian deity he received from him two barley-corns, one of which he gave to his wife and the other to his famous mare who gave birth to his charger, hence known as Javádiyá or "barley-born."

---

[1] *Indian Antiquary*, XI, 33, *sq.*: Cunningham, *Archæological Reports*, XVII, 159: *Panjáb Notes and Queries*, II, 1. The story of Guga engulphed is of the Curtius type: Temple, *Legends of the Panjáb*, I, 121, *sqq.*; III, 261 *sqq.* Tod, *Annals*, II, 492. The lowest form of the legend is in Muzaffarnagar, where he is said to have jumped into a heap of cowdung (*mánd*), where he disappeared. *North Indian Notes and Queries*, I, 39.

The snake godlings.

The connection of Gúga with snake worship will have been noticed. Another godling of the same kind is Tejají, the Ját snake godling of Márwár. He lived about nine hundred years ago. One day he noticed that a Bráhman's cow was in the habit of going to a certain place in the jungle where milk fell from her udder into the hole of a snake. Teja agreed to supply the snake daily with milk and thus save the Bráhman from loss. Once when he was preparing to visit his father-in-law, he forgot the compact, and the snake appearing declared that it was necessary he should bite Teja. He stipulated for permission first to visit his father-in-law, to which the snake agreed. Teja proceeded on his journey and on the way rescued the village cattle from a gang of robbers, but was desperately wounded in the encounter. Mindful of his promise, he, with difficulty, presented himself to the snake, who, however, could find no spot to bite, as Teja had been so grievously wounded by the robbers. Teja, therefore, put out his tongue which the snake bit, and so he died. He is now a protector against snake bite, and is represented as a man on horseback with a drawn sword, while a snake is biting his tongue.[1] Tejají, as a snake godling, thus ranks with Bhajang, the snake god of Kathiáwár, who is the brother of Seshanága, and with Manasá, the snake goddess of Bengal.[2]

Bába Faríd Shakkarganj.

Bábá Faríd, known as Shakkarganj or "fountain of sweets," the saint of Pákpatan in the Montgomery district of the Panjáb, is another worthy who enjoys a high reputation throughout Northern India. He was the disciple of the famous Qutub-ud-dín, who again sat at the feet of Muín-ud-dín of Ajmere, also a great name to swear by. Faríd's disciple was Nizám-ud-din Auliya, who has a lovely tomb near Delhi. Faríd is said to have had the "the hidden hand" (*dast-i-ghaib*), a sort of magic bag which gave him anything he wished which is like the inexhaustible pot, a stock element in

---

[1] *Rájputána Gazetteer*, II, 37.

[2] *Bombay Gazetteer*, V, 218: Risley, *Tribes and Castes of Bengal*, I, 41.

Indian folk-lore.[1] The Emperor determined to humble him when he came to Delhi, but he answered in the famous proverb *Delhi dúr ast*—"Delhi is far away," the oriental equivalent to Rob Roy's "It is a far cry to Lochow." The Muhammadan Thags looked on him as the founder of their system, and used to make pilgrimages to his tomb. He is believed to have been connected with the Assassins or disciples of the "Old man of the mountain."[2] "Every devotee who contrives to get through the door of his mausoleum at the prescribed time of his feast, is assured of a free entrance into Paradise hereafter. The crowd is, therefore, immense, and the pressure so great that two or three layers of men, pushed closely over each other, generally attempt the passage at the same time, and serious accidents notwithstanding every precaution taken by the police are not uncommon."[3] He has another famous Dargáh at Shekhsir in Bikáner, which is called after him, and the Játs used to esteem him highly until "the Bona dea assumed the shape of a Játni, to whom in the name of Kiraní Mátá," our mother of the ray, "all bend the head."[4] Another legend fixes his tomb at Girar in the Wardha district of the Central Provinces. The zeolitic concretions of the Girar hill are accounted for as the petrified cocoanuts and other articles of merchandise belonging to two travelling dealers who mocked the saint, on which he turned their whole stock of trade into stones as a punishment. They implored his pardon and he created a fresh stock for them from dry leaves, on which they were so struck by his power that they attached themselves to his service till they died.[5] In the western part of the North-Western Provinces the first fruits of the sugarcane crop are dedicated to him. He was a thrifty saint, and for the last thirty years of his life he supported himself by holding to his stomach

---

[1] Temple, *Wideawake Stories*, 423, with references: and for the wishing hat and inexhaustible purse, Tawney, *Katha Sarit Ságara*, I, 14, note, 571.

[2] For whom see Yule, *Marco Polo*, I, 132, *sq*.

[3] Ibbetson, *Panjáb Ethnography*, 115.

[4] Tod, *Annals*, II, 199, note.

[5] *Central Provinces Gazetteer*, 197, *sq*., 515.

wooden cakes and fruits whenever he felt hungry.[1] In this he resembled Khwája Qutub-ud-dín Ushi, who was able by a miracle to produce cakes for the support of his family and himself.[2]

Minor Saints.

Of the minor saints the number is legion. Only a few instances can be given. In the North-Western Provinces the tomb of Zindah Sháh Madár at Makkhanpur in the Cawnpore district is held in great honour. He gives his name to the Madári Muhammadan faqírs.[3] Mírán Sáhib is also a great name to swear by. He was a magician and subdued to his service a Jinn named Zain Khan whom he treated with great cruelty. One day the Jinn surprised his master in a state of uncleanness and slew him, but even then he was unable to escape from the influence of this arch-magician who rules him in the world of spirits. Mírán Sáhib is buried at Ajmere and has Dargáhs at Amroha near Morádábád, and at Búndi. In Karnál he is said to have been a saint of Bághdád. He is often identified with Hazrat Píran Pír of the Panjáb, but this is doubtful. He led the Sayyad army against the Rája of Tharwa and had his head carried off by a cannon ball during the battle. He did not mind this and went on fighting. Then a woman in one of the Rája's villages said, "Who is this fighting without his head?" Upon which the body said *Haqq! Haqq!* "The Lord! the Lord!" and fell down dead calling out "What! are not these villages upside down yet?" Upon which every village in the Rája's territory was turned upside down and every one killed except a Bráhman girl, the paramour of the Rája. Their ruins remain to authenticate the story. Now the saint and his sister's son Sayyad Kabír are jointly worshipped. We shall meet this headless hero again in the case of the Dúnd. Many ancient ruins, like those at Bakhira Tál in the Basti district, are said to represent cities

---

[1] For the history of Faríd see *Indian Antiquary*, XI, 33, *sq.* Thomas, *Chronicles of the Pathán Kings*, 205: Ibbetson, *Panjáb Ethnography*, 115: Sleeman, *Rambles and Recollections*, II, 249: Crooke, *Rural Glossary*, sv. *Farídí*.

[2] Jarrett, *Ain-i-Akbari*, II, 303.

[3] Crooke, *Handbook of Ethnography*, sv, *Madári*: Tod, *Annals*, I, 395.

overturned, generally because the Rája seduced a Bráhman girl.[1] Bo 'Ali Qalandar is hardly known beyond the Panjáb. He used to ride about on a wall, but finally settled at Pánipat. He prayed so constantly that it became laborious to get water for his ablutions each time, so he stood in the Jumna which then flowed past the town. After standing there seven years the fishes had gnawed his legs and he was so stiff that he could hardly move: so he asked the Jumna to step back seven paces. She in her hurry to oblige the saint went back seven *kos* or ten miles and there she is now. He gave the Pánipat people a charm which dispelled all the flies from the city, but they grumbled and said they rather liked flies. So he brought them back a thousandfold. He was buried first at Karnál, but the Pánipat people claimed his body and opened his grave, whereupon he sat up and looked at them till they felt ashamed. They then took away some bricks for the foundation of a shrine: but when they got to Pánipat and opened the box they found his body in it, so that he now is buried in both places. There is also a shrine created over the wall on which he used to ride.[2] Malámat Sháh is treated with much respect in the Bára Banki district of Oudh. The disciple in charge of his tomb calls the jackals with a peculiar cry at dusk. They devour what is left of the offerings, but will touch only such things as are given with a sincere mind and not to be seen of men. A religious tiger is also said to come over from Bahraich and pay an annual visit to the shrine.[3] At Qasúr is the tomb of the saint Miyán Ahmad Khán Darvesh, on which the attendants place a number of white pebbles. These are called "Ahmad Khán's lions" and are sold to people who tie them round the necks of children troubled in their sleep.[4] Shekh Saddu has been already mentioned in another connection. His visitations cause melancholy and hypochondria. He is exorcised by the distribution of sweets to the poor and the sacrifice of a black goat. He

---

[1] Cunningham, *Archæological Reports*, XXII, 71, and for Mírán Sáhib, *Rájputána Gazetteer*, I, 237: *Karnál Settlement Report*, 152.

[2] Karnál *Settlement Report*, 153.

[3] *Oudh Gazetteer*, I, 92.

[4] *Panjáb Notes and Queries*, III, 81.

once found a magic lamp, like that of Aladdin, the powers of which he abused and was torn to pieces by the Jinn.[1] In the Etáh district is the tomb of Kalyán Bhárthi, a Hindu ascetic. He was buried alive at his own request about four hundred years ago. Before his interment he announced that exactly six months after he was actually dead the arch of his tomb would crack, and so it happened. Now a mound of earth in the centre is supposed to mark the head of the saint. The virtue of his shrine is such that if any one take a false oath within its precincts he will die at once. The tomb is hence largely used for settlement of disputes and many a wearied District Officer longs that there were more such places throughout the land.

Shrines which cure disease.

Many of these local shrines owe their reputation to notorious cures which have been performed by the intervention of the resident saint. Thus, a shrine in Berár is noted for its power in cases of snakebite and scrofula. A large two-storeyed gate of its enclosure owes its erection to the gratitude of a wealthy tailor who was here cured of sore disease of the loins.[2] At the tomb of Pír Jahániya in the Muzaffargarh district people suffering from leprosy and boils get the incumbent to prepare baths of heated sand in which the diseased part or the whole body is placed. The efficacy of the remedy is ascribed to the thaumaturgic power of the saint.[3] The tomb of Makhdúm Sáhib in the Fyzábád district is famous for the exorcism of evil spirits, a reputation which it shares with the shrine of Bairám at Bidauli in Muzaffarnagar, and that of Bíbí Kamál at Káko, halfway between Gaya and Patna.[4] So in Bengal the chief disease shrines are those of Tárakesvara in Hughli sacred to Mahádeva, of Vaidyanátha in the Santál parganas, and Gondalpára in Hughli, famous in cases of hydrophobia. "The device followed at the last place is for the bitten

---

[1] Mr. Mírs Hasan Ali, *Observations on the Muhammadans of India*, II, 324, *sqq.* gives the full account of him.

[2] *Berár Gazetteer*, 192.

[3] O'Brien, *Multáni Glossary*, 146.

[4] *Oudh Gazetteer*, I, 334: Cunningham, *Archæological Reports*, XVI. 5, and for the Chánod shrine, *Bombay Gazetteer*, VI. 160.

person, after fasting, to defray the expense of a special service, and to receive a piece of red broadcloth impregnated with the snuff of a lampwick and secreted in the heart of a plantain. As long as this charm is preserved and the patient abstains from the eating of this variety of plantain, the effects of the bite are warded off. Another plan is for the patient to take a secret medicine, probably cantharides pounded, with twenty-one pepper-corns before the twenty-first day. This causes the patient to throw off some mucus, known as "the dog's whelp" and this leads to cure."[1] The tomb at Fyzábád known as Fazl-ul-haqq or "Grace of God," brings good luck if sweetmeats are offered every Thursday, and another called 'Ilm Bakhsh or "wisdom giver" causes boys who are taken there to learn their lessons quickly.[2] Dr. Buchanan gives a case at Patna of a certain Sayyad Yúsuf who manifested himself to a poor blind weaver and told him that he would recover his sight next day. At the same time the saint ordered his patient to search for the tomb and proclaim its virtues. The weaver, on recovering his sight, did not fail to obey the orders of his benefactor, and he and his descendants have since then lived at ease on the contributions of the faithful, though his tomb is a mere heap of clay and has no endowment.[3]

The nine yard tombs.

There is a special class of tombs notorious for their physical peculiarity. These are known as "the nine yard long" tombs (*naugaza, naugaja*) where the giants of olden time rest. There is one of these at Nágaur in Rájputána, and many others have been met with in the course of the Archæological Survey.[4] Five of them at Vijhi measure respectively 29, 31, 30, 30, and 38 feet. Mr. W. Simpson calls these tombs Buddhistic, but this is very doubtful.[5] Curiously enough, some of these tombs have grown considerably in quite modern times. Thus, the tombs said to be those of Seth and Job at Ajudhya, which

[1] Risley, *Tribes and Castes of Bengal*, I, 367.
[2] *Panjáb Notes and Queries*, III, 143.
[3] *Eastern India*, I, 82, *sq*.
[4] *Report*, I, 98, *sq.*: 130, *sq.*: XIV, 41: XXIII, 63.
[5] *Journal, Asiatic Society of Bengal*, XIII, 205: *Panjáb Notes and Queries*, I, 109.

are now 17 and 12 feet long respectively, were in the time of Abul Fazl only 10½ and 9 feet in length.[1] Of another class is that of Sayyad Mahmúd at Jhanjhána in the Muzaffarnagar district. He was buried next to one of his disciples, but the latter is too modest to place himself on an equality with his master; so his tomb, however much it is repaired, always sinks to a lower level than that of his preceptor.

Shrines with images or relics.

The reputation again of many shrines rests on the assumed discovery, generally by means of a dream, that an ancient image or the bones of a martyr are buried on the site, and in their honour a shrine is established. Thus, the great temple at Bandakpur in the Damoh district owes its origin to the fact that a Pandit in 1781 A.D. dreamed a dream, that in a certain spot lay buried in the earth an image of Jageswar Mahádeva, and that if he built a suitable temple over the place indicated, the image would make its appearance. On the strength of this dream the Pandit built a temple, and it is asserted that in due course of time the image developed itself without the aid of man.[2] So the Bhairava temple on the Langúr peak owes its establishment to a cowherd having found on the spot a yellow coloured stick, which, on his attempting to cut it with an axe, poured out drops of blood. Frightened at the sight, the cowherd fled, only to be visited at night by the god in his terrible form, who commanded him to set up his shrine here. A similar legend is attached to the Náráyana image in Nepál.[3] The celebrated shrine of Hanumán at Beguthua was miraculously discovered in the last century by a wandering ascetic.[4] Another tomb at Fyzábád is now honoured, because some time ago the metal top of one of the pinnacles took to shaking, which had such an effect on the superstition of the weaver population that they have since levied a tax on every piece of cloth they make for its repair.[5] The Mahárája of Balrámpur some time ago

---

[1] Oudh Gazetteer, I, 11, *sq.*
[2] *Central Provinces Gazetteer*, 175.
[3] Atkinson, *Himalayan Gazetteer*, II, 777: Wright, *History*, 114, 124.
[4] *Oudh Gazetteer*, I, 38.
[5] *Settlement Report*, 18?

noticed a rude shrine of Bijlesvari Devi, the goddess of lightning, and remarked that he would build a handsome temple in her honor, were it not for the sacred banyan tree which shaded it and prevented the erection of the spire to the proper height. That very night the tree was uprooted by a hurricane, and a handsome temple was erected, this manifestation of her power having made the goddess more popular than ever. Lightning is very generally considered the infant sister of Krishna, and in Bombay the leaves of the *Bauhinia tomentosa* and the *Mimosa Suma* are regarded as amulets against it.[1] Mistakes are, however, sometimes made. This was the case some time ago at Ajudhya, where certain images were discovered and worshipped until a learned Pandit ascertained that they were actually the deities of the aboriginal Bhars, who used to sacrifice Bráhmans to them. They were really Jaina images, but it is needless to say that their worship was immediately abandoned.[2]

Shrines on probation.

As is only natural, shrines which have been discovered in this way rest at the outset under a certain degree of suspicion, and have to make their reputation by works of healing and similar miracles. If they fail to do so they sink into disrepute. Such was the case with a very promising shrine supposed to be that of the saint Ashraf Ali, whose bones were found accidentally not long ago at Ahraura in the Mirzapur district. It enjoyed considerable reputation for a time, but failing to keep up its character, was discredited and abandoned. The competition is in fact so keen, and the pecuniary value of a successful institution of the kind so considerable, that the saint has to give unequivocal proofs of his presence and influence in order to secure that continuous respect which is readily accorded to respectable ancient saints and local godlings who have in an extended course of usefulness long since established their claims to recognition by a series of exhibitions of their thaumaturgic virtues.

[1] *Oudh Gazetteer* I, 210, *sq.*: Campbell, *Notes*, 142.
[2] *Oudh Gazetteer*, I, 8, *sq.*

Shrines which cure barrenness.

Barrenness in popular belief is a disease mainly due to the agency of evil spirits, and the desire for male offspring is so intense among Hindus that the keepers of these shrines deal in multitudinous nostrums to secure this object. One extraordinary method of procuring children which long troubled our Magistrates in Upper India was for the would-be mother to burn down the hut of some neighbour. This practice under the reign of English law has almost entirely ceased. The Khándh priest takes a woman to the confluence of two streams, sprinkles water over her, and makes an offering to the god of births. The Panjábi woman, who is prevented from burning her neighbour's roof, now takes a little grass from seven thatches and burns it.[1] Another plan is to bathe underneath a person who has been hanged, and women of the middle classes try to obtain a piece of the wood of the gallows. In Gujarát, when an ascetic of the Dúndiya sect dies, women who seek the blessing of a son strive to secure it by creeping under his litter.[2] Along the roads may be seen trees almost destroyed by a noxious creeper known as the *Ákás bel*. Women in hope of offspring often transplant this from one tree to another and are thus a decided nuisance to a District Magistrate with a taste for arboriculture. But the best plan is to visit a shrine with a reputation for healing this class of malady, and there the patient is given a cocoanut from the holy of holies, a flower, a *lichi* fruit, or even a barley-corn.[3] The same idea recurs constantly in folklore. The barren queen is given the juice of a pomegranate by a faqír, or the king plucks one of the seven mangoes which grow on a special tree, or a beggar gives the princess the drug which causes her to give birth to twins.[4] Some holy men do not, it must be admitted, escape the tongue of slander for their doings in this department of their business.

---

1 *North Indian Notes and Queries*, I, 50.
2 Forbes, *Rás Málá*, II, 332, quoted by Campbell, *Notes*, 15.
3 See Temple, *Legends of the Panjáb*, I, Intro., XXIII.
4 Lál Bihári De, *Folk Tales of Bengal*, I, 117, 187 : Tawney, *Katha Sarit Ságara*, I, 52, 172, 355, 382 ; II, 216.

Harmless saints and godlings.

Most of these saints and godlings whom we have been considering are comparatively harmless, and even benevolent. Such is nearly always the case with the ghosts of the European dead who are constantly deified. Perhaps because the Sáhib is such a curiously incomprehensible personage to the rustic he is believed to retain his powers in the after world. But it is a remarkable and unconscious tribute to the foreign ruler that his ghost should be beneficent. The gardener in charge of the station cemetery in Mirzapur recently informed me that he constantly sees the ghosts of the ladies and gentlemen buried there coming out for a walk in the hot summer nights and that they never harm him. But with ordinary graves it is necessary to be cautious. If you visit an old tomb it is well to clap your hands as the ghost sometimes re-visits its resting place, and if discovered in *déshabille*, is likely to resent the intrusion in a very disagreeable manner. In fact for this reason tombs are to be visited with caution, and instances have occurred of cases of epilepsy and hysteria which are due to some petty insult to the dead.

Variations in local worship.

This branch of the cultus of the local deities is thus in a constant state of flux and flow. Discredited saints and shrines are always passing into contempt and oblivion: new worthies are being constantly canonized. The worst part of the matter is that there is no official controller of the right to deification, no *advocatus diaboli* to dispute the claims of the candidate to celestial honors: At the same time the system, though often discredited by fraud, admirably illustrates the elastic character of the popular creed. Hinduism would hardly be so congenial to the minds of the masses if some rigid supervising agency disputed the right of any tribe to worship its hero, of any village to canonize its local worthy. The steady popularity of the system, for the present at least, shows that it satisfactorily provides for the religious wants of the people.

CHAPTER V

THE WORSHIP OF THE MALEVOLENT DEAD.

Πρωτη δὲ ψυχὴ Ἐλπήνορος ἦλθεν ἑταίρου,
Οὐ γὰρ πω ἐτέθαπτο ὑπὸ χθονὸς εὐρυοδείης.

ODYSSEY, xi, 51—52.

The malevolent dead.

THESE deified ghosts and saints whom we have been discussing, though occasionally touchy and sensitive to insult or disrespect, are as a rule benevolent. But there is another class of beings at whose feet the rustic lies in grievous and perpetual bondage. These are the malevolent dead. It is not difficult to understand why the spirits of the dead should be regarded as hostile. A stranger is, in the belief of all primitive people, synonomous with an enemy : and the spirit of the departed having abandoned his own and joined some other and invisible tribe whose domains lie outside the world of sense is sure to be considered inimical to the survivors left on earth. As we have already seen, even the usually kindly spirit of the departed household dead requires propitiation and resents neglect ; much more those of a different tribe or family. Again, those disembodied souls in particular whose departure from earth occurred under unexpected or specially tragical circumstances are naturally considered to have been ejected against their will from their tenement of clay, and as for many of them the proper funeral rites have not been performed, they carry with them into the next world an angry longing for revenge.[1] The possibility of the permanent separation of the spirit from the flesh and its independent existence rests on the familiar conception of the relations between soul and body. This may be illustrated by the savage theory of dreams.

[1] See Lubbock, *Origin of Civilisation*, 220 : Tylor, *Primitive Culture*, II. 27 : Spencer, *Principles of Sociology*, I. 215, *sq.* : Sir W. Scott, *Letters on Demonology*, 90.

The theory of dreaming.

Many savages believe that the evidence of dreams is sufficient to prove that the soul wanders about during sleep, and that the dream is the record of its actual experiences in hunting, dancing, visiting friends, and so on.[1] The rustic Hindu pushes the principle a step farther and believes that in the absence of a man's proper soul his body may be occupied by a strange and consequently malignant ghost. Hence come the nightmare and evil dreams. Thus the Korwas of Mirzapur believe that a *bhútin* or dangerous female ghost named Reiyá besets them at night at the orders of some witch, and attacks people's joints with the rheumatism. The Majhwárs believe that the Rákshasa attacks them in dreams. He comes in the shape of an old man with enormous teeth, brown colour, black, entangled hair, and sometimes swallows his victims. It is fear of him that brings the fever, and he can be exorcised only by the Baiga with an offering of rice and pulse. The Dáno also comes in dreams, squeezes a man's throat, and stops his breath. The Bhuiyárs have adopted from the Hindu mythology Jam or Yama, the God of Death as one of their dream ghosts. He sits on his victim's breast in sleep, and it is impossible to shake him off or make an alarm. Sometimes these night ghosts come as tigers, wolves, or bears, and hunt a man down in his sleep. Many of these people again believe that a man's separable spirit is represented by his shadow or reflection. Hence they are cautious not to tread on the shadow of another in the sunshine, dislike looking into other people's mirrors, and think that if their picture is taken some of the spirit goes away with it and the result is weakness or perhaps death.

The Bhút.

The general term for these spirits is *Bhút* (in Sanskrit *bhúta*), which means "formed or created." In the earlier Hindu writings the word is applied to the powers of Nature and even to deities. Siva himself is called

[1] In the Panchatantra there is a tale of a king who lost his soul, but afterwards recovered it. According to Appollonius, the soul of Hermotimos of Klazomenæ left his body frequently, resided in different places, uttered all kinds of predictions, returning to his body which remained in his house. At last some spiteful persons burnt his body in the absence of his soul.—Tawney, *Katha Sarit Ságara*, I, 22, note.

Bhútesvara or "Lord of Spirits": but as the Greek Dæmon acquired a less respectable meaning in the later ages of the nation's history, so Bhút has now come to mean a malignant evil spirit. But Bhút is a general term which includes many grades of malignant spirits which it is necessary to distinguish. We shall first, however, consider certain characters common to Bhúts in general. The proper Bhút is the spirit emanating from a man who has died a violent death, either by accident, suicide, or capital punishment. Such a soul reaches an additional grade of malignancy if he has been denied proper funeral ceremonies after death. This is one of his special wants which deprive the spirit of its longed for rest.[1] Thus we read in Childe Harold: "Unsepulchred they roamed and shrieked each wandering ghost." This idea is at the basis of the Hindu funeral ceremonies and of the periodical *sráddha*. Hence arose the conception of the Gayál or "sonless ghost." He is the spirit of a man who has died without any issue competent to perform the customary rites: hence he is spiteful and is especially obnoxious to the lives of the young sons of other people. Accordingly in almost every Panjáb village may be seen small platforms with rows of little hemispherical depressions into which milk and Ganges water are poured, and by which lamps are lit and Bráhmans fed to conciliate the Gayál: "while the careful mother will always dedicate a rupee to him and hang it round her child's neck till he grows up." Mr. Ibbetson suggests that this may have been the origin of the mysterious so-called "cup-marks" described by Mr. Rivett-Carnac. But this is far from certain: they may equally well have been used for sacrifices to Mother Earth, or in any other primeval form of worship.[2]

General characters of Bhúts.

Bhúts are most to be feared by women and children, and especially immediately after eating sweets, "so that if you treat a school to sweetmeats the sweetmeat seller will also bring salt, of which he will give a pinch

---

[1] See Tylor, *Primitive Culture*, II, 27.
[2] *Panjáb Ethnography*, 116.

to each boy to take the sweet taste out of his mouth."[1] Salt is, as we shall see later on, particularly inimical to evil spirits.[2] Women who have married a second time are specially liable to the envious attacks of the first husband. If in Bombay "a Mahadeo Koli widow bride or her husband sicken it is considered the work of the former husband." Among the Somavansi Kshatriyas there is a strong belief that when a woman marries another husband, her first husband becomes a ghost and troubles her. This fear is so thoroughly rooted in their minds that whenever a woman of this caste sickens she attributes her sickness to the ghost of her former husband and consults an exorcist as to how she can get rid of him. The exorcist gives her some charmed rice, flowers, and basil leaves and tells her to enclose them in a small copper box and wear it round her neck. Sometimes the exorcist gives her a charmed cocoanut which he tells her to worship daily, and in some cases he tells the woman to make a copper or silver image of the dead and worship it every day."[3] So in Northern India people who marry again after the death of their first wife wear what is known as the *saukan maura* or second wife's crown. This is a little silver amulet generally with an image of Deví engraved upon it. This is hung round the husband's neck; all presents made to the second wife are first solemnly dedicated to this, and the illness or death of the second wife or her husband soon after marriage is attributed to the jealousy of the ghost of the first wife which has not been suitably propitiated. In the Panjáb, on the same principle, if a man has lost two or three wives in succession he gets a woman to catch a bird and adopt it as her daughter. He then pays the dower, marries his bird bride, and immediately divorces her. By this means the malignant influence of the ghost is checked.[4] In short, as we shall notice more than once, it is at the main crises of life—marriage, birth, and the hour of death—that demoniacal influence is most powerful.

---

1 *Panjáb Ethnography*, 117.
2 Aubrey, *Remaines*, 121: Lady Wilde, *Legends*, 44, 233.
3 Campbell, *Notes*, 171.
4 *Panjáb Notes and Queries*, I, 13: *North Indian Notes and Queries*, I, 15.

Food of Bhúts.

Like evil spirits all the world over, Bhúts will eat filthy food, but they are very fond of fresh milk, and so no Panjábi woman likes her child to leave the house soon after drinking milk. If she cannot prevent it from going she puts some salt or ashes into its mouth to scare the Bhút.[1]

Posture of Bhúts.

Bhúts can never sit on the ground apparently because, as has been shown already, the earth personified as a goddess scares away evil influence. Hence near the low caste shrines a couple of pegs or bricks are set up for the Bhút to rest on, or a bamboo is hung over it on which the Bhút perches when he visits the place.[2] On the same principle the Oráons hang up the cinerary urn containing the bones of the dead man on a post in front of the house,[3] and the person who is going on a pilgrimage or conveying the bones of a relative to the Ganges, sleeps on the ground, but the bones must not rest on the ground; they are hung on a branch of a tree, so that their late owner may re-visit them if so disposed. Near shrines where Bhúts are always about on the chance of appropriating some of the offerings, it is expedient to sleep on the ground. So the bride and bridegroom rest and the dying man is laid at the moment of dissolution.

Tests for Bhúts.

There are three infallible tests by which you may recognise a a Bhút. In the first place, he casts no shadow as he walks; secondly, he can stand almost anything in his neighbourhood, but the scent of burning turmeric, which is a demon scarer apparently by virtue of its yellow colour; thirdly, a genuine Bhút always speaks with a nasal twang. It is possibly for this last reason that the term for the gibberish in the mediæval Hindu plays and for modern English is *Pisácha bhásha* or the language of goblins.[4] Some, like the Churel whom we shall meet later on, have their feet turned backwards. Some, like Bráhman

---

[1] *Panjáb Notes and Queries*, IV, 51.
[2] See Cunningham, *Archæological Reports*, XVII, 147.
[3] Dalton, *Descriptive Ethnology*, 261.
[4] *Panjáb Notes and Queries*, IV, 51: Lál Bihári De, *Folk Tales*, 199: *Govinda Samanta*, I, 109: 152, *sq.*: 157: *Northern Indian Notes and Queries*, I, 83.

ghosts, are wheat coloured or white; others like the Káfari or ghost of a murdered negro are black and particularly dreaded. A famous ghost of this class haunts a lane in Calcutta which takes its name from him. Vetála, the, king of the Bhúts, is green and rides a green horse.[1]

Spirit entries—the head.

Spirits enter a person in various ways. They enter by the head, and this is the reason why the skull has sutures which are broken during cremation to allow the spirit to escape. When the chief teacher of the Bráhmans in Bombay dies the successor breaks a cocoanut on his skull and makes an opening in which the sacred *Sálagrama* stone is laid.[2] At a Gond wedding the old man who officiates knocks the heads of the bride and bridegroom together.[3] At a Hindu marriage in Upper India the mother of the bridegroom as he leaves the house and when he returns with his bride waves lamps, a brass tray, grain, and a rice pounder, round his head to drive off Bhúts. He wears a marriage crown on the same principle, which also accounts for much of the customs of blessing and anointing which are common all over the world. The hair too is an entry for Bhúts. Hence ascetics and exorcisors wear it loose and Hindus allow one lock to remain uncut.[4] The same idea is the basis of the custom of shaving at puberty and during mourning.

Spirit entries—the mouth.

As might have been expected, Bhúts are fond of entering a man through the mouth. Hence arises much of the mouth washing which is part of the daily ritual of the Hindu and many of the precautions taken at meals. We shall discuss this in connection with the Evil eye. Hence too it is very dangerous to yawn lest a Bhút may go down your throat: so you should put your hand to your mouth and say *Náráyan!* "Great God!" afterwards, or crack your fingers

[1] For other instances see Campbell, *Notes*, 156, *sq*.
[2] *Bombay Gazetteer*, XV, 150: Campbell, *Notes*, 172.
[3] Hislop, *Notes*, I, 3.
[4] In the *Katha Sarit Ságara* (Tawney, I, 30) Chánakya, when he makes a solemn vow, unlooses his scalp lock.

which scares the evil spirit. This idea is the common property of folklore.[1] So sneezing is due to demoniacal influence, but opinions differ as to whether it is caused by a Bhút entering or coming out of the nose. In Bombay it is considered very ominous to sneeze on the threshold, which is a sacred place.[2] Many omens are taken from sneezing. One sneeze is ominous, but if in starting on a journey he sneezes twice, he may go in peace. When you sneeze your friends should congratulate you, and say "May you live a thousand years!" The sneezing superstition is in India at least as old as the Buddhist Jattakas, and like many ideas of the same kind perhaps about the earliest property of the race.[3] On the whole, sneezing is auspicious, because it is probable that it means the expulsion of a Bhút. So it was in the days of Homer—"Even so she spoke and Telemachus sneezed loudly and around the roof rang wondrously, and Penelope laughed and straightway spoke to Enmœus winged words—'Go call me the stranger, even so into my presence! Dost thou not mark how my son has sneezed a blessing on all my words?'"[4]

Spirit entries—the hands, feet, and ears.

The hands and feet are also means by which Bhúts enter. Hence much of the ablution at prayers and meals: the passing of the hand over the head, the cracking of the fingers to scare evil spirits, the hand pledging at marriages, the ceremonial washing of the bridegroom's feet by his father-in-law at a wedding, the lifting of the bride over the threshold, and perhaps the marking of the wall with hand prints to avoid demoniacal influence, with numerous allied customs in the ordinary ritual.[5] And so with the ears, which are believed to communicate direct with the brain and are kept carefully covered with cloth on chilly mornings. Hence the custom of ear piercing (*kanchhedan*), which is in Upper India about the only survival of

---

[1] *Panjáb Notes and Queries*, II, 114, 167: Tylor, *Primitive Culture*, I, 102: Aubrey, *Remaines*, 177, 194: Campbell, *Notes*, 177.
[2] Campbell, *Notes*, 176.
[3] Fansboll, *Jattaka*, II, 15, *sq.*: Ibbetson, *Panjáb Ethnography*, 118.
[4] *Odyssey*, XVII, 541, *sq.*: *Marco Polo*, II, 351: Aubrey, *Remaines*, 177.
[5] For numerous other examples see Campbell, *Notes*, 177, *sqq.*

the common procedure when males attain puberty, and of wearing earrings and similar ornaments which is habitual with all classes of Hindus and specialized among the Kanphata Jogís who take their name from this practice.

The Bengali variety of Bhút.

In Bengal the ordinary Bhút is a member of the Kshatriya, Súdra, or Vaisya class. The Brahman Bhút, or Brahmadaitya, is quite another variety. The ordinary Bhúts are as tall as palmyra trees, generally thin and very black. They usually live on trees, except those which the Brahmadaitya frequents. At night, and especially at the hour of midnight, they wander about the fields, frightening travellers. They prefer dirty places to those which are clean, and have never been seen in the temples of the gods, though, as we have seen, they often sneak about in the neighbourhood in quest of offerings. They are always stark naked, and are fond of women, whom they possess and abduct. They eat rice and all sorts of human food, but their favourite dish is fish. Hence no Bengali, except for a considerable bribe, will take about fish at night. If two Bhúts attack a person they quarrel among themselves and allow him to escape. The best protection is to invoke the gods and goddesses, especially Kálí, Durgá, and Siva, the last of whom, as already noted, is the Lord of Bhúts.[1]

Varieties of Bhúts: Vetála.

Bhúts are of many varieties. Vetála or Baitál, their leader, is familiar to every one in the Baitál Pachísí. He is not regarded as particularly offensive, but usually he is a vagrant Bhút which enters the body of some one when the real owner is absent. More frequently he is the spirit of some living person dissatisfied with his lodgings on earth, who leaves his own body and occupies a corpse. He, in company with the Vasus, Yakshas, Bhútas, and Gandharvas, has passed into the degraded Tantrika worship.[2]

---

1 *Govinda Savanta*, I, 115, *sqq*.

2 Wilson, *Essays*, 1, 26. The spirit entering the body of a dead man forms the leading incident in the tale of Fadlallah in the Arabian Nights, and for Indian examples see Tawney, *Katha Sarit Ságara*, I, 21, 74, 132. He remarks (*ibid*., II, 208) that these stories disprove the assertion that among races which burn their dead little is known of regular corpse spectres or that they are special to lands tenanted or influenced by Slavonians.

The Pret.

The term Pret or Preta, which simply means "deceased" or "departed," properly represents the state of the soul between the moment of death and the completion of its obsequies. During this period it wanders in the air round its original home and is popularly believed to be no larger than a man's thumb. The term, however, is sometimes extended to the spirit of a deformed or crippled person, or one defective in some limb or organ, or of a child that dies prematurely owing to the omission of the prescribed ceremonies during the formation of the embryo. Among some of the jungle tribes it is even believed that there is no need to protect a child from evil spirits until it begins to eat grain, because up to that time it is nothing more than a Bhút itself. The Pret is occasionally under provocation malignant, but as it partakes to some degree of the functions of the ancestral household spirit, it is not necessarily malicious or evil disposed towards living persons. The Pret is specially worshipped at Gaya at the hill known as Pretsila or "the rock of the Pret," and a special class of Bráhmans at Patna call themselves Pretiya, because they worship the ghost of some hero or saint.[1]

Pisácha.

Next comes the Pisácha, which is more of the ogre type. Properly speaking it is an evil spirit produced by man's vices, the ghost of a liar, adulterer, or criminal of any kind, or of one who has died insane. But his functions do not appear to be very accurately defined, and he merges into the general crowd of Bhúts.[2]

The Rákshasa.

The Rákshasa, again, a word that means, "the harmer" or "the destroyer," is of the ogre-vampire type. He goes about at night, haunts cemeteries, disturbs sacrifices and devout men, animates dead bodies, ensnares

[1] Buchanan, *Eastern India*, I, 65, 166.

[2] In Folklore Pisáchas cure disease. "Rise up in the last watch of the night, and with dishevelled hair and naked, and without rinsing your mouth, take two handfuls of rice as large as you can grasp with the two hands, and muttering a form of words, go to a place where four roads meet and there place the two handfuls of rice and return, in silence without looking behind you. Do so always until that Pisácha appears and says 'I will put an end to your ailment.' Then receive his aid gladly, and he will remove your complaint."—Tawney, *Katha Sarit Ságara*, I, 255, *sq.*

and even devours human beings, and is generally hostile to the human race. He is emphatically a devourer of raw flesh, and eats carrion. Some have long arms; some are fat; some thin; some dwarfish; others enormously tall or hump backed. Some have only one eye, others only one ear; some have enormous paunches, projecting teeth, and crooked thighs; others can on occasion assume noble forms and are beautiful to look at.[1] He is the great *Deus ex machiná* of folklore. He can change into almost any form as he pleases, his breath is a roaring wind, he can lengthen his arms to eighty miles, and he can smell out human beings like Giant Blunderbore. The female, the Rákshasí, sometimes marries the hero, has mortal children, which she devours, but sometimes befriends human creatures, and even acts as a maid. But as a rule she is malignant and often besets some city where she demands the daily tribute of a human being.[2] The idea of the Rákshasa comes from the earliest times. Some have thought them to be types of the early Dravidian opponents of the Hindus. Nirriti is a Rákshasa deity in the Veda, and Dr. Muir has traced the various stages by which the Rákshasa was developed into a godling. Thus, in the Mahábhárata Jará is called a household goddess, and is represented as seeking to requite by benefits the worship which was paid to her.[3] Manu prescribes a special oblation for "the spirits which walk in darkness." The blood in the sacrifices is, according to the old ritual, presented to each evil spirit, though even here we notice the transition from animal to corn offerings.[4] Like all other demons Rákshasas are scared by light, and hence the lamp is known as *rákshogna* or destroyer of demons.

The modern Rákshasa.

Nowadays Rákshasas live in trees and cause vomiting and indigestion to those who trespass on their domains at night. They mislead night

---

1 Monier Williams' *Sanskrit Dictionary*, sv.

2 Temple, *Wideawake Stories*, 395, *sqq.* And for other examples—Tawney, *Katha Sarit Ságara*, I, 25. A boy becomes a Rákshasa by tasting the brains of a corpse, *ibid.* *I*, 210: II, 318.

3 *Journal, Royal Asiatic Society*, N. S. II, 300: *Ancient Sanskrit Texts*, IV 247: Wilson, *Rig Veda*, I, 107.

4 Manu, *Institutes*, III, 90: Haug, *Aitareya Bráhmanam*, II, 87, 90, *sq.*

travellers like Will o' the wisp, and they are always greedy and in quest of food. So, if a man is eating by lamplight, and the light goes out, he will cover the dish with his hands, which are, as we have already seen, scarers of demons, to preserve the food from the Rákshasas.[1] And Bengali women go at night with a lamp into every room to expel the evil spirits.[2] The Rákshasas are always fighting with the gods, and their blood still remains on many of these ghostly battlefields. In the hills this is believed to be the cause of the red ferruginous clay which is occasionally observed, and the Lohu or "blood red" river has a similar origin.[3] In folklore the Rákshasas have kingdoms and possess enormous riches, which they bestow on those whom they favour like Tára Bai in the story of Seventee Bai. In this they resemble the Irish fairies, who hide away much treasure in their palaces underneath the hills and in the lakes and sea. "All the treasure of wrecked ships is their's: and all the gold that men have hidden or buried in the earth when danger was on them, and then died and left no sign to their descendants. And all the gold of the mine and the jewels of the rocks belong to them, and in the Sifra or fairy house the walls are silver and the pavement is gold, and the banquet hall is lit by the diamonds that stud the rocks."[4] Their finger nails, as those of Europeans in popular belief, are a deadly poison, and the touch of them produces insensibility or even death.[5] They often take the disguise of old women and have very long hair, which is a potent charm. These old Rákshasas, however, in spite of their malignity and power of working harm, are, like evil spirits all over the world, usually fools, and readily disclose the secrets of their enchantments to the distressed hero or heroine who is unlucky enough to fall into their power.[6] They are, as has been said already, usually cannibals. In the

---

[1] *Pánjáb Notes and Queries*, II, 132.
[2] Lál Bihári De, *Govinda Samanta*, I, 117. Numerous other instances are given by Campbell, *Notes*, 24, *sqq*.
[3] *Journal, Asiatic Society, Bengal*, 1847, p. 582.
[4] Miss Frere, *Old Deccan Days*, 41, 195: Wright, *History of Nepal*, 175: Lady Wilde, *Legends*, 257.
[5] Miss Frere, *loc. cit.*, 82.
[6] Miss Frere, *loc. cit.*, 58, 62, 208, 268, *sqq*.

great Panjáb legend of Rasálu he conquers the seven Rákshasas who used to eat a human being every day, and there is a Nepál story of the Rákshasa Gurung Mápa who used to eat corpses. He was propitiated by a grant of land to live on and an annual offering of a buffalo and some rice.[1] All ghosts, as we shall see later on, have the power of lengthening themselves like the Naugaza, whom we have already mentioned. For this reason demons are, as a rule, of gigantic form, and many of the enormous fossil bones found in the Siwálik hills were confidently attributed to the Rákshasas, which reminds us of the story of the smith in Herodotus, who found the gigantic coffin seven cubits long containing the bones of Orestes.[2] Like the ghost in Hamlet, the angel that visited Jacob, and the destroying night spirits of Sodom, the Rákshasas always depart at dawn. They invariably travel through the air and are supposed to keep their souls in birds and trees—a fertile element in folk tales which is called by Major Temple "The Life Index."[3]

Rákshasas as architects.

Rákshasas again are often represented as the architects of ancient buildings. Thus, at Ramtek in the Central Provinces, there is a curious old temple built of hewn stones, well fitted together without mortar. From its shape and structure it is probably of Jaina origin, though local tradition connects it with the name of Hemádpant the Rákshasa. He is an example of Rákshasas developed in comparatively recent times from a historical personage. He was probably the Minister of Mahádeva (1260—1271 A.D.), the fourth of the Yádava Kings of Deogiri. According to the common story, he was a giant or a physician who brought the current Maráthi character from Ceylon. The Dakkhin swarms with ancient buildings attributed to him.[4] Such is also the case with another class of demons,

[1] Atkinson, *Himalayan Gazetteer*, II, 352, Note: Cunningham, *Archæological Reports*, II, 21.

[2] Tylor, *Early History*, 316: Herodotus, I, 68.

[3] *Wideawake Stories*, 404, *sqq.*: Miss Stokes, *Fairy Tales*, 261: Tylor, *Primitive Culture*, I, 161: Wright, *History of Nepal*, 175: Lady Wilde, *Legends* 253: Tawney, *Katha Sarit Ságara*, I, 42-47.

[4] *Central Provinces Gazetteer*. 428: Cunningham, *Archæological Survey*, IX, 142, XVII, 5: *Indian Antiquary*, VI, 366: *Bombay Gazetteer*, XII, 449: and compare Tylor, *Primitive Culture*, I, 394, *sq.*: Wright, *History of Nepal*, 175.

the Asuras or rivals of the gods. In Mirzapur the ancient embankment at the Karsota lake is their work. Once upon a time two of these demons vowed that whoever first succeeded in building a fort should be the conqueror, and that his defeated rival should lose his life. So they set to work in the evening, one on the Bijaigarh hill, and the other on the opposite peak of Kunda Kot about twelve miles distant. The demon of Bijaigarh, having lost his tools in the dark, struck a light to search for them. His adversary, seeing the light and imagining that the sun was rising and his rival's work completed, fled precipitately. The Bijaigarh fort was finished during the night and stands to the present day, while on Kunda Kot you see only a few enormous blocks of stone which was all the vanquished Asura had time to collect. Many buildings again are attributed to personages who succeeded in getting an Asura under his influence, and being obliged to find work for him, compelled him to occupy his time in architecture. In "The Lay of the Last Minstrel" Michael Scott got out of the dilemma by making the demons twist ropes of sand. So in Patna the Asura Jarasandha is the reputed builder of an enormous embankment which is called Asuren after him, and another demon of the same class is said to be the architect of an ancient fortification in Puraniya.[1]

Development of Rákshasas.

Rákshasas are developed even in this prosaic age of ours. The ghost of some Musalmáns is believed by Hindus to become a most malignant Rákshasa. Such a ghost is conciliated by being addressed by the euphemistic title of Mamdúh, "the praised one." Bisaldeva, the famous king of Ajmer, was turned into a Rákshasa on account of his oppression of his subjects, in which condition he resumed the evil work of his earthly existence, "devouring his subjects" until one of his grandchildren offered himself as a victim to appease his insatiable appetite. "The language of innocent affection," says Colonel Tod, "made its way to the heart of the Rákshasa, who recognised his offspring and winged his flight to

[1] Buchanan, *Eastern India*, I, 88 : III, 56.

the Jumna."[1] Young men who are obliged to travel at night have reason to be cautious of the Rákshasí as well as of the Churel with whom she is occasionally identified. She takes the form of a lovely woman and lures away her victims to destruction. At the mound of Bilsar in the Etah district lived a Rája whose house overlooked that of a Brahman named Púran Mall. The Bráhman asked the Rája to change the position of his sitting room, and when his request was refused, poisoned himself with opium. His body turned blue like indigo and he became a most malignant demon or Bír known as the Brahm Rákshasa or Bráhman Ogre which caused the death of the Rája and his family, and forced his successors to remove to a distance from their original family residence.

The Deo, Bír, Dáno.

Closely connected with the Rákshasas are various classes of demons known as Deo, Dáno, or Bír. The Deo is a survival of the Deva or "shining ones" of the old world mythology. It is another of the terms which have suffered grievous degradation. It originally was applied to the thirty-three great divinities, eleven of which inhabited each of the three worlds. Now the term represents a vague class of the demon Ogre family. The Deo is a cannibál, and were he not exceedingly stupid, could do much harm, but in the folk tales he is always being deceived in the most silly way. He has long lips, one of which sticks up in the air while the other hangs down pendent. Like many of his kinsfolk all over the world, he is a potent cause of tempests.[2] The Bír who takes his name from the Sanskrit *víra*, "hero," is a very malignant village demon. In one of the Mirzapur villages is the shrine of Kharbar Bír or "the noisy hero." No one can give any satisfactory account of him, but it is quite certain that if he is not propitiated by the Baiga, he brings disease on men and cattle. Genda Bír, a woman who was tired of life, and instead of burning herself threw herself down from a tree, is

---

[1] *Annals*, II, 382, note: for a similar story see Wright, *History of Nepal*, 86.
[2] Lál Bihári De, *Folk Tales*, 257: Miss Stokes, *Fairy Tales*, 273, 291: Tylor, *Primitive Culture*, II, 98, *sq.*, 378.

worshipped near Nágpur.[1] Kera Bir, a demon of the same sort, is worshipped at Jaunpur, and it is said that the English Engineers tried in vain to blow up his shrine when the Fort was taken. In Bombay there are seven Bírs who go about together and scour the fields and gardens by night.[2] The Dáno represents the Danava of the old mythology. They are the foes of the gods and often confounded with the Daityas and Asuras. He is worshipped at Hazáribágh in the form of a stone daubed with five streaks of red lead and set up outside the house.[3] The Daitya is in much the same class. In Mirzapur he lives in a tree : in front he looks like a man, but seen from behind he is quite hollow, only a mere husk without a backbone. At midnight he shows himself in his tree in a flash of fire and smoke and sometimes flies to another tree, a short distance off. He is worshipped with holy water pots (*kalsa*), and some greens. In one village he is called Beohár Bába or "Lord of Merchandise." Colonel Tod describes a place in the table land of Central India known as Daitya-ká-hár or "the demon's bone," on which those who are in search of ease jump from above. Although most of the leapers perish, some instances of escape are recorded. The hope of obtaining offspring is said to be the most usual motive for the act.[4]

The Headless Horseman or Dúnd.

Nowadays the most dreaded of these creatures is perhaps the Headless Horseman, who is popularly known as Dúnd or truncated. By one account he took his origin from the wars of the Mahábhárata. However this may be, he appears periodically in the form of a headless trunk seated on horseback, with the head tied before it on the pommel of the saddle. He makes his rounds at night and calls to the householder from outside: but woe to any one who answers him, for this means death. The belief in these visionary death summonses is very common.[5] The Irish Banshee howls at night and announces

---

[1] Cunningham, *Archæological Reports*, XVII, 1.
[2] *Gazetteer*, XI, 308.
[3] Risley, *Tribes and Castes of Bengal*, I, 303.
[4] *Annals*, II, 631.
[5] Sir W. Scott, *Letters on Demonology*, 40, *sq.*: Tylor, *Primitive Culture*, I, 145.

death. In Mirzapur, Baghesar, or the tiger demon, lives on the Churni hill. He sometimes comes down at night in human form and calls people by name at their doors. If any one answers him he becomes sick. The Bengali believes that Nisi or Night personified stands at the doors of simple folk, calls them from their beds, and decoys them to pools and tanks where they are drowned.[1] In 1882 quite a panic was caused in the neighbourhood of Agra by a visit from the Dúnd. Every one shut up their houses at sunset and no one on any consideration would answer a call from outside after nightfall. It was shrewdly suspected at the time that this rumour was spread by some professional burglar who made a harvest while the scare lasted.[2]

There are numerous other versions of the Headless Horseman story in Northern India. In a fight in Khandesh the Gávli prince engaged in personal conflict with the Saint Sayyad Saadat Pír and struck off his head. The headless body continued to fight and the Hindu army fled in panic. The trunk then snatched up the head and led his victorious troops to a neighbouring hill where the earth opened and swallowed it.[3] So in Oudh Malik Ambar, the companion of Salar Masaud. was, it is said, killed with his master at Bahraich, but wandering back to Bijnor a headless trunk on horse back, he at length reached the place where his tomb now stands, when the earth opened and received him and his horse.[4]

The Ghostly Army.

Closely connected with this are the numerous legends of the Ghostly Army. Thus, at Fyzabad, the country people point out a portion of the Queen's highway along which they will not pass at night. They say that after dark the road is thronged with troops of headless horsemen, the dead of the army of Prince Sayyad Sálár. The

---

[1] Lal Bihári De, *Govinda Samanta*, I, 9.
[2] The Legends of the Headless Horseman have been discussed at length by Major Temple in *Calcutta Review*, CLIII, 158, *sqq.*: also see *Panjáb Notes and Queries*, III, 78, and for the English version Henderson, *Folklore of the Northern Countries*, 270, 326, *sq.*
[3] *Bombay Gazetteer*, XII, 457.
[4] *Oudh Gazetteer*, I, 308, 311.

great host moves on with a noiseless tread: the ghostly horses make no sound, and no words of command are shouted to the headless squadrons. Another version comes from Ajmer. There for some time past a troop of four or five hundred horsemen armed and dressed in green issue from a valley in the neighbourhood of the city, and after riding about for some time mysteriously disappear. They are believed to be the escort of the Imám Husen whose tragical death is commemorated at the Muharram. The same legend prevails all through Upper India, and, indeed, all the world over. If you walk nine times round Neville's Cross, you will hear the noise of the battle and the clash of armour, and the same tale is told of the ghostly combatants who fight the battle of Marathon over again, which a recent prosaic authority attributes to the beating of the waves on the shore, while others say that these spectral armies of the sky are nothing more than wild geese or other migratory birds calling in the darkness.[1]

The Skandhaháta.

The Dúnd is apparently a close relation to the Skandhaháta of Bengal who goes about with his head cut off from the shoulders. They dwell in low moist lands outside a village, in bogs and fens, and go about in the dark rolling on the ground with their huge arms stretched out. Woe betide the belated peasant who falls within their grasp![2]

Masán.

Masán, a word which properly means "a place for cremation," is usually regarded as the malignant ghost of a child. As we have already noticed, the jungle tribes of Mirzapur consider a child to be a Bhút until it begins to eat grain. The accounts of Masán differ in various places. He is occasionally the ghost of a low caste man, very often for some unexplained reason that of an oilman, who, from the dirt accompanying his trade, is generally held unlucky. By another account such ghosts prowl about in villages in the hills in the form of bears and

[1] For England, see Henderson, *Folklore,* 308: for Marathon, Grote, *History of Greece,* IV, 285, *Folklore* I, 167: and for Páuipat and Chillianwála, Cunningham, *Archæological Reports,* XX, 96.

[2] Lal Bihari De, *Govinda Savanta,* I, 159.

other wild animals.[1] Others say that he is of black and hideous appearance, comes from the ashes of a funeral pyre, and chases people as they pass by. Some die of fright from his attacks, others linger for a few days, and some even go mad. "When a person becomes possessed of Masán, the people invoke the beneficent spirit of the house to come and take possession of some member of the family and all begin to dance. At length some one works himself into a state of frenzy, and commences to torture and belabour the body of the person possessed by Masán, until at length a cure is effected or the patient perishes under this drastic treatment. Khabísh resembles Masán in his malignant nature and fondness for burial grounds. He is also met with in dark glens and forests in various shapes. Sometimes he imitates the bellow of a buffalo or the cry of a goatherd or neatherd, and sometimes he grunts like a pig. At other times he assumes the disguise of a religious mendicant and joins travellers on their way: but his conversation is, like that of ordinary Bhúts, always unintelligible. Like Masán he often frightens people and makes them ill, and sometimes possesses unfortunate travellers who get benighted."[2]

Influence of Masán.

Children afflicted by Masán are said "to be under his shadow" (*chháya*), and waste away by a sort of consumption. Here we have an instance of the idea common to many primitive races, that the shadow represents the actual soul.[3] This malady is believed to be caused by some enemy flinging the ashes from a cremation place over a child, and the cure is to weigh the child in salt, a well known scarer of demons, and give it away in charity. It is believed when thieves enter a house that they throw over the inmates some Masán or ashes from a burning ground which makes them unconscious while the robbery goes on. This resembles the English "Hand of Glory" of which other instances will be given in another connection. As a good instance of this theory of the shadow a Nepál legend describes

---

[1] Traill, *Asiatic Researches*, XVI, 137, *sq.*
[2] Atkinson, *Himalayan Gazetteer*, II, 820.
[3] Tylor, *Primitive Culture*, I, 428, *sq.*

how a Láma arrested the flight of a Bráhman by piercing his shadow with a spear.[1]

Tola.

Tola is a sort of "Will o' the wisp" in the hills. According to one account, he is, like the Gayál, of whom we have spoken already, the ghost of a bachelor, and other ghosts refuse to associate with him: so he is seen only in wild and solitary places. Others say that he belongs to the class of children ghosts who have died too young to undergo the rites of tonsure or cremation. They are harmless and not dreaded. After a child undergoes the specified religious ceremonies its soul is matured and fitted either to remain with the spirits of the sainted dead or to assume a new existence by transmigration. The estate of the Tola is only temporary, and after a time it, too, enters another form of existence.[2]

Airi.

Another famous hill Bhút is Airi. He is the ghost of some one who was killed in hunting. Like the European legend of the Wild Huntsman, he haunts the forest in which the accident occurred, and is sometimes heard hallooing to his dogs.[3] His companions are fairies, who, like the Churel, have their feet turned backwards. He is accompanied by two litter bearers and a pack of hounds with bells round their necks. Whoever hears their bark is certain to meet with calamity. Airi is much given to expectoration, and his saliva is so venomous that it wounds those on whom it falls. Incantations must be used, and the affected part swept or rubbed with the branch of a tree. If this be not done at once, the injured man dies, and in any case he must abstain from rich food for several days. "Those who see Airi face to face are burnt up by the flash of his eye, or are torn to pieces by his dogs, or have their livers extracted and eaten by the fairies who accompany him. But should any one be fortunate

---

[1] Wright, *History*, 153.

[2] Traill, *Asiatic Researches*, XVI, 137, *sq.*: *North Indian Notes and Queries*, II, 27.

[3] Sir W. Scott, *Letters on Demonology*, 41, *sq.*: Henderson, *Folklore*, 129, *sq.*, who, quoting Yarrell, asserts that this legend is based on the weird noise caused at night by flocks of bean geese.

enough to survive, the Bhút discloses hidden treasures to him. The treasure-trove thus disclosed varies in value from gold coins to old bones. His temples are always in deserted places. A trident represents the god, and a number of surrounding stones his followers. He is worshipped once a year by lighting a bonfire round which all the people sit. A kettle drum is played, and one after another they become possessed, and leap and shout round the fire. Some brand themselves with heated iron spoons and sit in the flames. Those who escape burning are believed to be truly possessed, while those who are burned are considered mere pretenders to divine frenzy." This closely resembles the worship of Ráhu already described. "The revels usually last for about ten nights, and until they are ended, a lamp is kept burning at the shrine of the god. Those possessed dye a yard of cloth in red ochre and bind it round their heads, and carry a wallet in which they place the alms they receive. While in this state they bathe twice and eat but once in the twenty-four hours. They allow no one to touch them, as they consider other men unclean, and no one but themselves is permitted to touch the trident and stones in Airi's temple, at least as long as the festival lasts. The offerings, goats, milk, &c., are consumed by the worshippers. The kid is marked on the forehead with red, and rice and water are thrown over him. If he shakes himself to get rid of it, the god has accepted the offering, whereupon his head is severed with a knife. If he does not shake himself or bleats, it is a sign that the offering is not accepted, and the victim escapes."[1]

Acheri, Deo, Rúniya.

Other Bhúts in the hills are Acheri—the ghosts of little girls who live on the tops of mountains, but descend at night to hold their revels in more convenient places. To fall in with their train is fatal, and they have a particular antipathy to red colour. When little girls fall suddenly ill the Acheri is supposed to have thrown its shadow over them. The Deo are the regular demons already described: some are obnoxious to men, some to cattle. The Rúniya moves about at

[1] Atkinson, *Himalayan Gazetteer*, II, 825, *sqq.*: Madden, *Journal, Asiatic Society, Bengal*, 1847, p. 599, *sq.*

night and uses a huge rock as his steed, the clattering of which announces his approach. He is the demon of the avalanche and landslip. Should he take fancy to a woman she is haunted by his spirit in his dreams and, gradually wasting away, finally falls a victim to her passion.[1]

Birth fiends—the Jilaiya, Chordevan.

Another of these night fiends is the Jilaiya of Bihár, which takes the shape of a night bird and is able to suck the blood of any person whose name it hears. Hence women are very careful not to call their children by name at night. It is believed that if this bird fly over the head of a pregnant woman her child will be born a weakling.[2] Hence it closely approximates to the birth fiends who beset the mother and child during the period of parturition impurity. Thus the Oraons of Chutia Nágpur believe that the fiend Chordevan comes in the form of a cat and tears the mother's womb.[3] The Bráhman, Prabhu, and other high caste women of Bombay believe that on the fifth and sixth day after birth the mother and child are liable to be attacked by the birth spirit Satvái, who comes in the shape of a cat or a hen. Consequently they keep a watch in the lying-in room during the whole night, passing the time in playing, singing, and talking. The Maráthas of Násik believe that on the fifth night, at about twelve o'clock, the spirit Sathi accompanied by a male fiend called Burmiya, comes in the lying-in room, makes the mother insensible, and either kills or disfigures the child. The Vádvals of Thána think that on the fifth night the birth spirit Sathi comes in the form of a cat, hen, or dog, and devours the heart and skull of the child. They therefore surround the bed with strands of a creeper, place an iron knife or scythe on the mother's cot, an iron bickern at the entrance of the lying in room, and keep a watch for the whole night. All this is akin to the belief in fairy changelings, and the malignant influences which surround the European mother and child.[4]

---

[1] Traill, *Asiatic Researches*, XVI, 137, *sq.*: Atkinson, *loc. cit.*, II, 831.
[2] Grierson, *Bihár Peasant Life*, 408.
[3] Dalton, *Descriptive Ethnology*, 251.
[4] For numerous instances see Campbell, Notes, 387, and Hartland, *Science of Fairy Tales*, 93, *sqq.*

The Pari and the Jinn.

Little reference has yet been made to the Pari or fairies and the Jinn or genii, because they are in their present shape at least of exotic origin, though their original basis probably lies in the various Bhúts and spirits who are common in Indian folklore. Fairies are of many varieties. One is Sháhpasand, "the beloved of the king," who takes the air in the shape of a pigeon and kisses the beautiful hero: others are the attendants of the Court of Indra, who occasionally bestows one on the hero who wins his favour or influences him by spells or by the agency of some noted faqír. They are of surpassing loveliness, with white skins and always dressed in red.[1] With the Jinn we reach a chapter of folklore of great extent and complexity. They are usually divided into the Jánn, who are the least powerful of all, the Jinn, the Shaitán or devils, the 'Ifrít and the Maríd, the last of whom rule the rest. The Jánns, according to the prophet, were created out of a smokeless fire. Jánn is sometimes identified with the serpent and sometimes with Iblís, who has been imported direct from the Greek *diabolos*. The Jinns were the pre-adamite rulers of the world and for their sins were overcome by the angels and taken prisoners and driven to distant islands. They appear as serpents, scorpions, lions, wolves, or jackals. One kind rules the land, another the air, a third the sea. There are forty troops of them, each consisting of six hundred thousand. Some have wings and fly, others move like snakes and dogs, others again like men. They are of gigantic stature, sometimes resplendently handsome, sometimes horribly hideous. They can become invisible and move on earth where they please. They ride the whirlwind like Indian demons, and direct the storm. Their chief home is the mountains of Qáf, which encompass the earth. Besides these there is a troop of minor demons such as the Ghúl, the English Ghoul, who is a kind of Shaitán, eats men, and is variously described as a Jinn or an enchanter. The Ghúl is properly a female and the male is the Qutrub. They are the offspring of Iblís and his wife. The Silát or Silá lives in forests, and when it captures a man makes him dance and plays with him as the cat

[1] Temple, *Wideawake Stories*, *passim*. They are the equivalent of the Apsarases who dance at Indra's Court: Tawney, *Katha Sarit Ságara*, I, 238.

plays with the mouse. Similar to this creature is the Ghaddár, who tortures and terrifies men, the Dalhám who is in the form of a man and rides on an ostrich, and the Shiqq and Nasnás who are ogres or vampires. But these are little known in Indian folklore except that directly imported from Arabic sources.[1]

The Baghaut.

As an instance of the respect paid to the ghosts of those who have died an untimely death, we may instance the Baghaut. This is usually erected on the place where a man has been killed by a tiger, but it sometimes merges into the common form, as in a case given by Dr. Buchanan,[2] where a person received the same honour because he had been killed by the aboriginal Kols. Every passer by throws a stone upon the pile, and the shrine is in charge of the Baiga or aboriginal priest, who offers upon it a cock, or a pig, or some spirits, and lights a little lamp there occasionally. Many such shrines are to be found in the Mirzapur jungles. In the Central Provinces they are known as Pát, a term applied in Chutia Nagpur to holy heights dedicated to various divinities.[3] They are erected in a place where a man has been killed by a tiger or snake : sometimes no reason whatever is given for the selection. "In connection with these shrines they have a special ceremony for laying the ghost of a tiger. Until it is gone through neither Gond nor Baiga will go into the jungles if he can help it, as they say not only does the spirit of the dead man walk, but the tiger is also possessed, for the nonce, with an additional spirit of evil [by the soul of the dead man entering into him], which increases his power of intelligence and ferocity, rendering him more formidable than usual, and more eager to pursue his natural enemy, man. Some of the Baigas are supposed to be gifted with great powers of witchcraft, and it is common for a Baiga medicine man to be called in to bewitch the tigers and prevent them carrying off the village cattle. The Gonds thoroughly believe in the powers of these men."[4] I myself

---

[1] Hughes, *Dictionary of Islám* sv. Genii quoting Lane, *Arabian Nights* and *Modern Egyptians*.
[2] *Eastern India*, I, 106.
[3] Dalton, *Descriptive Ethnology*, 132.
[4] *Central Provinces Gazetteer*, 280.

came across a singular instance of this lately. I was asking a Baiga of the Chero tribe in South Mirzapur what he could do in this way, but I found him singularly reticent on the subject. I asked the Superintendent of the Dudhi Estate, who was with me, to explain the reason. "Well," he answered, "when I came here first many years ago a noted Baiga came to me and proposed to do some witchcraft to protect me from tigers, which were very numerous in the neighbourhood at the time. I told him I could look after myself and advised him to do the same. That night a tiger seized the wretched Baiga while he was on his way home, and all that was found of him were some scraps of cloth and pieces of bone. Since then I notice that the Baigas of these parts do not talk so loudly of their power of managing tigers when I am present."

The Churel.

More dreaded even than the ghost of a man who has been devoured by a tiger is the Churel, a name which has been connected with that of the Chúhra or sweeper caste. The ghosts of all low caste people are notoriously malignant, and for this reason they are always buried face downwards, or their corpses are cremated in order to prevent the evil spirit from escaping. Riots have taken place in the Panjáb and the authority of Magistrates has been invoked to prevent a Chúhra being buried face upwards.[1] The Churel, who corresponds to the Jakhái, Jokhái, Mukái and Navlái of Bombay,[2] is the ghost of a woman dying while pregnant, or on the day of her child's birth, or within the prescribed period of impurity. The superstition is based on the horror felt by all savages at the blood or even touch of a woman while ceremonially impure.[3] The idea is common in India. The woman in her menses is carefully secluded and not allowed to do cooking or any other domestic work. The birth impurity usually lasts for twelve days after parturition. The Churel is particularly malignant to her own family. She appears in various forms. Sometimes she is fair in front and black behind, but she invariably has her

[1] Ibbetson, *Panjáb Ethnography*, 117.
[2] Campbell, *Notes*, 149.
[3] For instances see Fraser, *Golden Bough*, I, 185, 187 : II, 238.

feet turned round, heels in front and toes behind. This idea prevails in other places. The Gira, a water spirit of the Konkan, has his feet turned backward.[1] In the Teignmouth story of the devil, he leaves his backward footsteps in the snow. Pliny so describes the anthropophagi of Mount Imœus, and Megasthenes speaks of a similar race on Mount Nilo.[2] She generally, however, assumes the form of a beautiful young woman and seduces youths at night, particularly those who are good looking. She carries them off to some kingdom of her own, keeps them there till they lose their manly beauty, and then sends them back to the world grey haired old men who, like Rip Van Winkle, find all their friends dead long ago. I had a smart young butler at Etah who once described to me vividly the narrow escape he had from the fascinations of a Churel who lived in a pípal tree near the cemetery. He saw her sitting on a wall in the dusk and entored into conversation with her : but he fortunately observed her tell-tale feet and escaped. He would never again go by that road at night without an escort. So the fairies of England and Ireland look with envy on the beautiful boys and girls and carry them off to fairy land, where they keep them till youth and beauty have departed.[3] The Korwas of Mirzapur say that if a woman dies in the lying-in room (*saurhi*), she becomes a Churel, but they know no more about her. The Patáris and Majhwárs think that if a woman dies within the period of pregnancy or uncleanness she becomes a Churel. She comes in the form of a pretty little girl in white clothes and seduces them away to the mountains until the Baiga is called in to sacrifice a goat and releases her victim. The Bhuiyárs go further still and say that little baby girls who die before they are twenty days old become Churels. They live in stones in the mountains and cause pain to men. The remedy is for the afflicted one to put some rice and barley on his head, turn round two or three times. and shake off the grain in the direction of the jungle, when she releases her victim. But she continues to visit him in dreams and

---

[1] Campbell, *Notes*, 156.
[2] Tylor, *Primitive Culture*, I, 307 : Pliny, *Natural History*, VII, 2.
[3] *Folklore*, II, 288 : Lady Wilde, *Legends*, 7, 39.

requires propitiation. Churel has been very generally enrolled among the regular village gods and resides with them in the common shrine. Any one who sees a Churel is liable to be attacked by a wasting disease, and, as in the case of the Dúnd, to answer her night summons brings death.

Means of baffling the Churel.

There are fortunately various remedies which are effective in preventing a woman who dies under these special conditions from becoming a Churel. One way is that practised by the Majhwárs of Mirzapur, which resembles that for laying the evil spirit of a sweeper, to which reference has been made already. They do not cremate the body, but bury it, fill the grave with thorns, and pile heavy stones above to keep down the ghost. Among the Bhandáris of Bengal, when a pregnant woman dies before delivery, her body is cut open and the child taken out, both corpses being buried in the same grave.[1] In the hills if a woman dies during the menstrual period or in childbirth the corpse is anointed with the five products of the cow and special texts are recited.. A small quantity of fire is then placed on the chest of the corpse, which is either buried or thrown into flowing water.[2] Here we have the three great demon scarers—fire, earth, and water—combined. In another device iron, which has similar virtue, is used. Small round headed iron spikes, specially made for the purpose, are driven into the nails of the four fingers of the corpse, while the thumbs and great toes are securely fastened together with iron rings. The ground in which the woman died is carefully scraped and the earth removed. The spot is then sown with mustard (*sarson*), which is also sprinkled along the road traversed by the corpse on its way to the burial ground. The reason given for this is twofold. Firstly, the mustard blossoms in the world of the dead, and its sweet smell pleases the spirit and keeps her content: secondly, the Churel rises from her grave at nightfall and seeks her former home; she sees the minute grains of the mustard scattered abroad and stoops to pick it up, and while

[1] Risley, *Tribes and Castes*, I, 94.
[2] Atkinson, *Himalayan Gazetteer*, II, 932.

so engaged cock-crow comes, she is unable to visit her home, and must return to her grave. This is another instance of the rule that evil spirits move about only at night.[1] Though the Churel is regarded with disgust and terror, curiously enough a family of Chauhán Rájputs in Oudh claim one as their ancestor.[2] We have here another example of the use of *sarson* or mustard as a scarer of demons. In all principal Hindu ceremonies in Western India grains of *Sarshapa* or *sarson* (*sinapis dichotoma*) and parched rice are scattered about to scare fiends. Akbar used to have *sipand* or *sarson* burnt on a hot plate to keep off the evil eye (*nazar-i-bad, chashm rasídan*) from his valuable horses.[3]

The couvade.

In connection with this subject of parturition impurity, the very remarkable custom of the couvade may be referred to here. This is the rule by which at the birth of a child the father is treated as an invalid instead of or in addition to the mother :—[4]

"When Chineses go to bed,
"And lie in in their ladies' stead."

Marco Polo writing of Zardandan gives a good example. "When one of their wives has been delivered of a child, the infant is washed and swathed, and then the woman gets up and goes about her household affairs, whilst the husband takes to bed with the child by his side, and so keeps his bed for forty days: and all the kith and kin come to visit her and keep up a great festivity. They do this because, they say, the woman has had a hard time of it, and it is but fair that the man should have his share of suffering."[5] Professor Max Müller thinks that it is clear that the poor husband was at

---

[1] *Panjáb Notes and Queries*, II, 168, *sq.* Tylor, *Primitive Culture*, II, 67.
[2] *Oudh Gazetteer*, II, 418 : and for more information about the Churel see Calcutta Review, LXVIII, 180, *sq.*: Dalton, *Descriptive Ethnology*, 258.
[3] Blockmann *Ain-i-Akbari*, I, 139 : Campbell, *Notes*, 24 : Tawney, *Katha Sarit Ságara*, I, 133, 287, 290, II, 136.
[4] For the couvade in general see Lang : *Custom and Myth*, II, 223, *sqq.*: Conway, *Demonology*, II, 99 : Tylor, *Early History*, 288 : Max Müller, *Chips*, II, 287 Starke, *Primitive Family*, 51, *sqq.*: Westermarck, *History of Human Marriage*, 106, *sqq.*, and for a recent English case *Academy*, 23rd February 1884.
[5] Colonel Yule's *Edition*, II, 70, with *Note*.

first tyrannized over by his female relations, and afterwards frightened into superstition. He then began to make a martyr of himself, till he made himself really ill or took to his bed in self-defence. The custom appears, however, to rest on a much more primitive set of ideas. It partly implies, perhaps, the transition from that social state in which, owing to the laxity of the connection between the sexes, the only recognised form of descent was through the mother, and partly the kindred conception that the father has more to do with the production of the child than the mother, and that the father must at the critical period of the baby's existence exercise particular caution that through his negligence no demoniacal influence may assail the infant.

It is curious that in India itself so few actual instances of the couvade have been discovered. But that the custom generally prevailed is quite certain, and in Upper India, at least, it seems to have been masked by special birth ceremonies of great stringency and elaborate detail, but of distinctly later date than the very primitive usage with which we are now concerned. One instance of the actual couvade is given by Professor Sir Monier Williams. Among a very low caste of basket makers in Gujarat it is the usual practice for a wife to go about her work immediately after delivery, as if nothing had occurred. "The presiding mother (*máta*) of the tribe is supposed to transfer the weakness to her husband, who takes to his bed and has to be supported for several days with good nourishing food."[1] Again, among the Kols of Chutia Nagpur *father* and mother are considered impure for eight days, during which period the members of the family are sent out of the house and the husband has to cook for his wife. If it be a difficult case of parturition the malignancy of some spirit of evil is supposed to be at work, and after divination to ascertain his name, a sacrifice is made to appease him.[2] Among many of the Dravidian races of Mirzapur when the posset or spiced drink is prepared for the mother after

---

[1] *Athenæum*, 6th December 1879: *Folklore Record*, III, Part I, 117, *sqq.*: *Religious Life*, 229.

[2] Dalton, *Descriptive Ethnology*, 191: Risley, *Tribes and Castes*, I, 323.

delivery, the *father* is obliged to drink the first sup of it.[1] Among all these people the father does not work or leave the house during the period of parturition impurity and cooks for his wife. When asked why he refrains from work, they simply say that he is so pleased with the safety of his wife and the birth of his child that he takes a holiday: but some survival of the couvade is probably at the root of the custom. The same idea prevails in a modified form in Bombay. "The Pomaliyas, gold washers of South Gujarat, after a birth take great care of the husband, give him food, and do not allow him to go out."[2] The same idea that the infant is likely to receive demoniacal influences from his father appears to be the origin of another class of birth ceremonies. In Upper India, in respectable families, the father does not look on the child until the astrologer selects a favourable moment. If the birth occur in the unlucky lunar asterism of Múl, the father is not allowed to see his child often for years. So in Bombay, "the Belgaum Chitpávans do not allow the father to look on the new born child, but at its reflection in butter. The Dharwár Radders do not allow the father to see the lamp being waved round the image of Satvái. If the father sees it, it is believed that the mother and child will sicken. The Karnátak Jainas allow any one to feed the new born babes with honey and castor oil, except its father. Among the Beni Israels when the boy is being circumcised the father sits apart covered with a veil. Among the Púna Musalmáns friends are called to eat the goat offered as a sacrifice on the birth of a child. All join the feast except the parents, who may not eat the sacrifice."[3] Probably on the same principle among most of the lower castes the father and mother do not eat on the wedding day of their children, until the ceremony is over.

Places infested by Bhúts: burial grounds, deserts.

There are, of course, certain places which are particularly infested by Bhúts. To begin with, they naturally abound in the neighbourhood of burial

[1] A similar custom prevails among the Korvi basket makers of Madras. Tylor, *Primitive Culture*, I, 84.

[2] Campbell, *Notes*, 410.

[3] *Ibid.*

places, cremation grounds, and in all deserts as the great desert of Lop where Marco Polo assures us they are constantly seen at night. In the Western Panjáb deserts during the prairie fires and in the dead of night, the lonely herdsmen used to hear cries arising from the ground and shouts of *Már! Már!*—"Strike! Strike!" which were ascribed to the spirits of men who had fought and been killed in former frontier raids. Such supernatural sounds were heard by the early settlers within the last fifty years, and until quite recently the people were afraid to travel without forming large parties for fear of encountering the supernatural enemies who frequented these uninhabited tracts.[1] So among the Mirzapur jungle tribes, the wild forests of Sarguja are supposed to be infested with Bhúts, and if any one goes there rashly, he is attacked through them with diarrhœa and vomiting. The site of the present British Residency at Kathmandu, in Nepal, was specially selected by the Nepalese as it was a barren patch supposed to be the abode of demons. So in Scotland, the local spirit lives in a patch of untilled ground known as the Gudeman's field or Cloutie's Croft.[2] The goblins of the churchyard type very often take the form of owls and bats who haunt the abodes of the dead. "Screechowls are held unlucky in our days," says Aubrey.

Sedit in adverso nocturnus culmine bubo.
Funcreosque graves edidit ore sonos.[3]

The *strix* or screechowl in Roman folklore was supposed to suck the blood of young children. Another form of the word in Latin is *striga*, meaning a hag or witch. The Lilith of the Jews, the "night monster" of our latest version of the Old Testament, becomes in the Rabbinical stories Adam's first wife, "the Queen of demons and murderess of young children." She is the "night hag" of Milton.[4] The Kumaun owl legend is that they originally had no plumes of their own, and were forced to borrow those of their

---

[1] *Sirsa Settlement Report*, 32.

[2] Wright, *History*, 15: Yule's *Marco Polo*, I, 203: Spencer, *Principles of Sociology*, I, 249, *sq.*: Henderson, *Folklore*, 278.

[3] *Remaines*, 109, *sq.*: Spencer, *loc. cit.*, I, 329: Farrer, *Primitive Manners*, 24: *ibid.*, 225, *sq.*

[4] *Isaiah*, XXXIV, 14: Mayhew, *Academy*, 14th June 1884: Conway, *Demonology*, II, 91, *sqq.*: Gubernatis, *Zoölogical Mythology*, II, 202.

neighbours, who pursue them if they find them abroad at daylight. Owl's flesh is a powerful love phyltre, and the eating of it makes a man a fool and causes loss of memory: hence women give it to their husbands, that by the mental weakness it produces they may be able to carry on their flirtations with impunity. On the other hand, the owl is the type of wisdom, and eating the eyeballs of an owl gives the power of seeing in the dark, an excellent instance of sympathetic magic. If you put an owl in a room, go in naked, shut the door, and feed the bird with meat all night you acquire magical powers. I once had a native clerk who was supposed to have gone through this ordeal, and was much feared in consequence[1] —another instance of the nudity charm.

To return to the connection of ghosts with burial grounds. At Bisheshar in the hills the Hindu dead from Almora are burnt. The spirits of the departed are supposed to lurk there, and are occasionally seen. Sometimes under the guidance of their leader Bholanáth, whom we have mentioned already, they come some in palanquins and some on foot, at night to the Almora bazár and visit the merchants' shops. Death is supposed to follow soon on a meeting with their processions. These ghosts are supposed to be deficient in some of their members. One has no head, another has no feet, and so on: but they can all talk and dance. This illustrates another principle about ghosts—that mutilation during life is avoided as being likely to turn the spirit into a malignant ghost after death. This explains the strong feeling among Hindus against execution by decapitation and the dread which Muhammadans exhibit regarding the cremation of the dead,[2] and accounts, in all probability, for the lame demons which abound all the world over, like Hephaistos, Wayland Smith, the Persian Aeshma, the Asmodeus of the book of Tobit, and the club footed devil of Christianity.[3] The prejudice against amputation

[1] Madden, *Journal, Asiatic Society, Bengal*, 1848, p. 626: *Panjáb Notes and Queries*, I, 89, IV, 67: Chevers, *Indian Medical Jurisprudence*, 105: Miss Frere, *Old Deccan Days*, 76: Gubernatis, *Zoölogical Mythology*, II, 248, *sq.*

[2] *Journal, Asiatic Society, Bengal*, 1848, p. 609: Benjamin, *Persia*, 192: Tylor, *Primitive Culture*, I, 451.

[3] Tylor, *loc. cit.*, II, 230: *Early History*, 358: Cox, *Mythology of the Aryan Nations*, II, 327: Conway, *Demonology*, I, 18.

based on this idea is one of the many difficulties which meet our surgeons in India.

The ghosts of old ruins.

Another place where ghosts, as might have been expected, resort is old ruins. Many ancient buildings are, as we have seen, attributed to the agency of demons, and in any case interference with them is resented by the Deus loci who occupies them. Dr. Buchanan describes how on one occasion no one would assist him in digging out an ancient stone image. The people told him that a man who had made an attempt to do so some time before had met with sudden death. The landlord of the village stated that he would use bricks from their ruins to build his house were he not afraid of the consequences. So in Bombay, interference with the bricks of an ancient dam brought Guinea worm and dysentery into a village, and some labourers were cut off who meddled with some ancient tombs at Ahmadnagar.[1] General Cunningham in one of his reports describes how on one occasion when carrying on some excavations, his elephant escaped, and was recovered with difficulty: the people unanimously attributed the disaster to the vengeance of the local ghosts who resented his proceedings. The people who live in the neighbourhood of the old city of Sahet Mahet are, for the same reason, very unwilling to meddle with its ruins, or even to enter it at night. When Mr. Benett was there a storm which occurred, was generally believed to be a token of the displeasure of the spirits at intrusion.[2] In the Konkan it is believed that all treasures buried under ground, all the mines of gold, silver, and precious stones, all old caves, and all ruined fortresses are guarded by underground spirits in the shape of a hairy serpent or frog. These spirits never leave their places, and they attack or injure only those persons who come to remove the things they are guarding.[3] In short, these places are like the Sith Bhruaith mounds in Scotland, which were respected, and it was deemed unlawful and dangerous to cut wood, dig earth there,

---

[1] *Eastern India*, I, 414: *Bombay Gazetteer*, XII, 13, XVII, 703.
[2] *Oudh Gazetteer*, III, 286.
[3] Campbell, *Notes*, 150, *sq.*

or otherwise disturb them. In the same way the sites of ancient villages which abound in Upper India are more or less respected. They were abandoned on account of the ravages of war, famine, or pestilence and are guarded by their spirits, these calamities being self-evident proofs of their malignity and displeasure.[1]

Mine spirits; cave spirits.

We have already noticed incidentally the mine spirits. They are usually malignant and resent trespass on their domains. Of a mine at Patna Dr. Buchanan writes: "A stone cutter who was in my service was going into one of the shafts in order to break off a specimen, when the guide, a Muhammadan trader, acquainted with the fears of the workmen, pulled him back in alarm and said, 'Pull off your shoes! Will you profane the abode of the gods?'" The idea may have its origin, as Mr. Spencer suggests, in the practice of cave burial.[2] The belief is very general that spirits and deities live in caves. There is a whole cycle of fairy legend centering round the belief that some of the heroes of old live still in caves surrounded by their faithful followers, and will arise one day to win back their kingdom. Thus, Bruce and his enchanted warriors lie in a cave in Rathlin island, and one day they will arise and win back the island for Scotland.[3] The same tale is told of Arthur, Karl the Great, Barbarossa, and many other heroes.[4] So in India many deities live in caves. Among the Korwas of Chutia Nágpur their bloodthirsty divinity has a cave as her residence. Talao Daitya, a noted demon in Káthiawár, lives in a cave where a lamp is lit which never goes out however violently the wind may blow or the rain may fall. Saptasrí Deví, a much dreaded spirit in the Konkan, lives in a cave[5]: such is also the case with the eight armed Deví at Ashtbhuja in the Mirzapur district. Her devotees have to creep through a narrow passage into what is now the shrine of the goddess, but is said to have been originally a cave.

---

[1] On this see Sir W. Scott, *Letters on Demonology*, 79: Tylor, *Primitive Culture*, II, 25.
[2] *Principles of Sociology*, I, 201.
[3] Lady Wilde, *Legends*, 86.
[4] See Hartland, *Science of Fairy Tales*, 207, *sqq*.
[5] Atkinson, *Himalayan Gazetteer*, II, 321, *sq.*: Dalton, *Descriptive Ethnology*, 229: *Bombay Gazetteer*, VIII, 660: XI, 383.

When the Mirzapur Korwas have to enter a cave they first arm themselves with an axe and rude spear as a protection against Bhúts. There are two haunted caves in the Mircha and Banka hills in Sarguja. The Mircha cave is inhabited by a demon called Mahádáni Deo, who is much feared. Not even a Baiga can enter this cave, but many of them have seen his white horse tied up near the entrance and green grass and horse dung lying there. In the cave on the Banka hill lives a Dano whose name no one knows or dares to tell. No one ventures to enter his cave, and he worries people in dreams and brings sickness unless a Baiga periodically offers a cock with black and white feathers below the cave, makes a fire sacrifice, and throws some grains of rice in the direction of the mountain. When this Dáno is enraged a noise like *Gudgud! Gudgud!* comes from the cave. He is also heard shouting at night, and when cholera is coming he calls out *Khabardár! Khabardár!* "Be cautious! Be cautious!" Any one who goes near this cave gets diarrhœa. Captain Younghusband has recently solved the mystery of the famous Lamp Rock of Central Asia, which is simply the light coming through a concealed aperture at the rear of the entrance.[1] Many caves again have acquired their sanctity by being occupied by Jogis and Saints. Such are many of the Buddhist caves found in many places. Such is a cave at Bhuili in the Mirzapur district, which has a very narrow entrance, but miraculously expands to accommodate any possible number of pilgrims. These cave spirits are common to European folklore.[2] Such are the Kobolds of Germany. Burton[3] sums up the matter. "Subterranean devils are as common as the rest, and do as much harm. Olaus Magnus makes six kinds of them—some bigger, some less. These (Saith Munster) are commonly seen among mines of metals, and are some of them noxious; some again do no harm. The metal men in many places account it good luck, a sign of treasure and rich ore, when they see them. Georgius Agricola reckons two

[1] *North Indian Notes and Queries*, I, 103, *sq.*
[2] Henderson, *Folklore*, 322: Conway, *Demonology*, I, 233, *sq.*: Sir W. Scott. *Letters on Demonology*, 103.
[3] *Anatomy of Melancholy*, 126.

more notable kinds of them—Getuli and Cobali: both are clothed after the manner of metal men, and will many times imitate their works. Their office, as Pictorius and Paracelsus think, is to keep treasure in the earth, that it be not all at once revealed."

Bhúts guarding treasure.

This leads us to the common idea that Bhúts are the guardians of treasure. Ill-luck very often attaches to treasure trove. Some years ago a Chamár dug up some treasure in the ancient fort of Atranji Khera in the Etah district. He did his best to purge himself of the ill omen attaching to it by giving away a large portion in charity. But he died a beggar, and the whole country side attributes his ruin to the anger of the Bhúts who guarded the deposit. Not long ago an old man came into my court at Mirzapur and gave up two old brass pots, which he had found while ploughing about a year before. Since then he had suffered a succession of troubles, and his son who was with him when he found the property died. He then called a conference of sorcerers to consider the matter, and they advised him to appease the Bhút by giving up the treasure. He further remarkod that the Sarkár (Government) knew some spell (*mantra*), which prevented any harm to it from taking over such dangerous property. Treasure is often kept thus guarded in sacred caves. At Jaynagar is said to be the treasury of Indradyumna, sealed with a magic seal. The spot presents the appearance of a plain smooth rock, perhaps artificially smoothed. It is said that Indradyumna had a great warrior whom he trusted fully and raised to the highest honour. At last the man began to entertain the idea of asking his master's daughter in marriage. The king, hearing of this, was sore wroth, but his dependent was too powerful to be easily subdued. So he contrived that a cavern should be excavated, and here he removed all his treasure, and when all was secured, he invited the warrior to the place. The man unsuspectingly went in, when Indradyumna let fall the trap door and sealed it with a magic seal: but he was punished by defeat at the hands of the Muhammadans.[1] The Irish Leprehaun is

[1] *Archæological Reports*, X, 117.

also a treasure guardian, and he has his counterparts in Northern Britain.[1]

In connection with these treasure guardians, we reach another cycle of folklore legends—that of gifts or robberies from fairyland. In one version from Patna it is said that one day a corpse came floating down the river and a faqír announced that this was Chán Hájí. He was duly buried and honoured, and in many places he used to keep silver and gold vessels for the use of travellers. If any one wanted a vessel, he had only to say so, and one used to float out of the water, but a covetous man appropriated one, and since then the supply has ceased.[2] The same legend is told of the great Karsota lake in Mirzapur and of numbers of others all over the country. The culprit is generally a Banya or corn chandler, the type of sneaking greediness. The same story appears constantly in European folklore, as is shown by Mr. Hartland's admirable summary.[3] Another version current in India also corresponds with the western tradition. This is where a person receives a gift from the fairies which he does not appreciate and so loses. Thus in a tale from Raepur, in the Central Provinces, a goatherd used to watch a strange goat which joined his flock. One day it walked into the tank and disappeared. While the goatherd was looking on in wonder a stone was thrown to him from the water and a voice exclaimed "This is the reward of your labour." The disappointed goatherd knocked the stone back into the water with his axe. But he found that his axe had been changed by the touch into gold. He searched for the stone, but could never find it again. In another tale a cowherd tends the cow of the fairy and following the animal into a cave gives him some golden wheat as his reward, which he unthinkingly barters for tobacco. In a third version the fool throws away a handful of golden barley and only comes to know of his mistake when his wife finds that some fuel cakes

The fairy gift legend.

---

[1] Lady Wilde, *Legends*, 56 : Henderson, *Folklore*, 320, *sq*.
[2] *North Indian Notes and Queries*, II, 58.
[3] *Science of Fairy Tales*, Chapter VI.

on which he had laid his blanket had turned into gold.[1] We have this underground fairy kingdom in a legend preserved by the old Buddhist traveller, Hwen Thsang.[2] There was a herdsman who tended his cattle near Bhágalpur. One day a bull separated from the rest of the herd and roamed into the forest. The herdsman feared that the bull was lost, but in the evening he returned radiant with beauty. Even his lowing was remarkable, and the rest of the herd feared to approach him. At last the herdsman followed him into a cleft of the rock where he found a lovely garden filled with fruits exquisite of colour and unknown to man. The herdsman plucked one, but was afraid to taste it, and as he passed out a demon snatched it from his hand. He consulted a doctor who advised him next time to eat the fruit. When he again met the demon who tried to snatch it from his hand the herdsman ate the fruit. But no sooner had it reached his stomach than it began to swell inside him, and he grew so enormous that though his head was outside his body was jammed in the fissure of the rock. His friends in vain tried to release him, and he was gradually changed into stone. Ages after a king who believed that the stone must have medicinal virtues, tried to chisel away a small portion, but the workmen after ten days' labour were not able to get even a pinch of dust.

Bhúts of roads, cross-roads, and boundaries.

Bhuts are also found at roads, cross-roads, and boundaries. Thus in the hills an approved charm for getting rid of disease of diabolical origin is to plant a stake where four roads meet and to bury grains underneath which crows disinter and eat. The same custom prevails as far as Madras.[3] The custom of laying small-pox scabs on roads has been already noticed. The same idea is probably at the root of the old English plan of burying suicides at cross-roads with a stake driven through the chest of the corpse. So in the eastern parts of the North-Western Provinces we have Sewanriya, who, like Terminus, is a special god of the boundary (*Siwána*), whose function it is to keep foreign

---

[1] *Archæological Reports*, XXIII, 91 : XVII, 31 : X, 72.
[2] Julien's *translation*, I, 179.
[3] *North Indian Notes and Queries*, I, 100.

Bhúts from intruding into the village under his charge. For the same reason the Baiga pours a stream of liquor round the boundary. This is probably the origin of a whole series of special ceremonies performed when the bridegroom reaches the boundary of the bride's village. Of the Khándh god of boundaries we read, "He is adored by sacrifices, human and bestial. Particular points upon the boundaries of districts fixed by ancient usage, and generally upon the highways, are his altars, and these demand each an annual victim, who is either an unsuspecting traveller struck down by the priests or a sacrifice provided by purchase."[1]

Haunted houses.

Bhúts particularly infest old empty houses. If a house is unoccupied for any time a Bhút is sure to take up his quarters there. Such houses abound. The old fort at Agori on the Son is said to have been deserted because of the malignancy of its Bhúts. Not long ago a merchant built a splendid house in the Mirzapur Bázár and was obliged to abandon it for the same reason. Many European houses are haunted. There is one in Jhánsi Cantonment where a Bhút, in the form of a faqír, dressed in white clothes, appears at night. Fortunately he is of a kindly disposition.

Bhúts in flowers.

Bhúts occasionally take up their abode in sweet smelling flowers, and hence it is dangerous to allow children to smell them. But, on the other hand, as we shall see elsewhere, flowers and fruits are scarers of demons.

Bhúts, cooking.

Bhúts, it is believed, do their cooking at noon and evening; so women or children should be cautious about walking about at such times, lest they tread unwittingly on this ghostly food and incur the resentment of its owners.[2]

Haunts of Bhúts—hearth, unclean places, roof, &c.

There are numerous other places frequented by Bhúts. Among these is the house hearth. This probably in a large measure accounts for the precautions

[1] Macpherson, *Khonds*, 67, *sq*.
[2] *Panjáb Notes and Queries*, IV, 132.

taken by the Hindu in preparing and protecting the family cooking place and plastering it with fresh cowdung, which is a scarer of demons. The idea was common to all the Aryan races,[1] but it is found also among the aboriginal tribes, who perform much of the worship of Dulha Deo and similar family guardians at the family cooking place. In Upper India, when a bride first goes to the house of her husband she is not permitted to cook. On an auspicious day announced by the family priest she commences her duties and receives presents of money and jewelry from her relations. Among low castes at marriages a special ceremony—that of the *matmangara* or "lucky earth"—is performed, when the earth to prepare the fireplace on which the wedding feast is cooked is brought home. So in Behár, after bathing the bride or bridegroom the mother or female guardian brings home a clod of earth out of which a rude fireplace is prepared, on which butter is burnt and paddy parched on the threshold of the kitchen where the spirit is supposed to dwell. A goat is sacrificed at the same time, and some of this parched paddy is kept to be used at the ceremony on the following day.[2] For the same reason special care is taken of the ashes of the house hearth, which must be carefully removed and not spilt on the ground. When the ancestral ghosts are about these ashes are spread on the floor and the manes make a mark on them at night which shows they have visited their former home. Connected with the same train of ideas is the belief that dinner time is a period at which caution against demoniacal influence is requisite. Most Hindus particularly dislike being watched at their meals and make a pretence of eating in secret. If in a walk round your camp you come on one of your servants cooking, he pretends not to recognise his master and his hangdog look is the equivalent of the ordinary salaam. The Vaishnava sect of Ramánujas are very particular in this respect. They cook for themselves, and should the meal during its preparation, or while they are eating, attract even the looks of a stranger, the operation is instantly

[1] Hearn, *Aryan Household*, 55, *sq.*
[2] Risley, *Tribes and Castes*, I, 456.

stopped and the food buried in the ground.[1] Bhúts again frequent privies and dirty places of all kinds. Hence the caution with which a Hindu performs the offices of nature, his aversion to going into a privy at night, and the precaution he uses of taking a brass vessel with him as a scarer of demons. Mr. Campbell takes this to depend on the experience of the disease-bearing power of dirt. "This belief explains the puzzling inconsistency of Hindus of all classes that the house, house door, and a little in front is scrupulously clean, while the yard may be a dung heap or a privy. As long as the house is clean the Bhút cannot come in. Let him live in the privy: he cannot do much harm there."[2] So with the house roof. We have already seen that some of the Dravidian races will not let their women touch a roof during a whirlwind. So most people particularly object to strangers standing on their roofs. Truculent beggars sometimes do this in order to extort alms. If a buffalo calf gets on the thatch it is considered particularly unlucky.

[1] Wilson, *Essays*, I, 39.
[2] *Notes*, 169.

CHAPTER VI.

THE EVIL EYE AND THE SCARING OF GHOSTS.

Nescio quis teneros oculus mihi fascinat agnos.

ECLOGUES, iii, 103.

The evil eye.

The belief in the baneful influence of the Evil Eye prevails widely.[1] According to Pliny[2] it was one of the special superstitions of the people of India, and in the present day it forms an important chapter in the popular belief. But the investigation of its principles is far from easy. It is very closely connected with a number of kindred ideas connected with diabolical influence, and few natives care to speak about it except in a furtive way. In fact it is far too serious a matter to be discussed lightly. Walking about villages you will constantly observe special marks on houses and symbols of various kinds which are certainly intended to counteract diabolical influence: but hardly any one cares directly to explain the real motive, and if you ask the meaning of them you will almost invariably be told that they are purely decorative or made with some purpose other than that for which they are really intended.

Theories of the evil eye.

One and perhaps the most common theory of the Evil Eye is that "when a child is born an invisible spirit is born with it: and unless the mother keeps one breast tied up for forty days, while she feeds the child with the other (in which case the spirit dies of hunger), the child grows up with the endowment of the Evil Eye, and whenever any person so endowed looks at anything constantly, something will happen to it."[3] So in Ireland we are told "the gift comes by

---

[1] For some of the literature of the Evil Eye see Tylor, *Early History*, 134: Henderson, *Folklore of the Northern Countries*, 187, *sq.*: Westropp, *Primitive Symbolism*, 58, *sqq.*: Gregor, *Folklore of N.-E. Scotland*, 8: Tennent, *Ceylon*, II, 176: Virgil, *Eclogues*, III, 103: Persius, *Satires*, II, 34: Horace, I, *Epist.*, 141, 37: *Proverbs*, XXVII, 22; *St. Mark*, VII, 22.

[2] *Nat. Hist.*, VII, 2.

[3] Ibbetson, *Panjáb Ethnography*, 117.

nature and is born with one, though it may not be called into exercise unless circumstances arise to excite the power; then it comes to act like a spirit of bitter and malicious envy that radiates a poisonous atmosphere, which chills and blights everything within its reach."[1] In Bombay "the blast of the Evil Eye is supposed to be a form of spirit possession. In Western India all witches and wizards are said to be, as a rule, evil-eyed. Of the rest those persons only who are born under certain circumstances are believed to be evil-eyed. The circumstances are as follows. Among the Hindus it is believed that when a woman is pregnant she begins to conceive peculiar longings from the day of conception or from the fifth month. They consist in eating various fruits and sweetmeats, in walking under deep shades or in gardens where brooks gurgle, or in putting on rich clothes or ornaments, and in many other like things. If in the case of any woman these desires are not gratified, the child whom she gives birth to becomes weak and voracious and is said to have an evil eye. If such a person sees a man or woman eat anything which he feels a longing for, the eater either vomits what he or she has eaten, or falls sick. By some it is believed that if a person comes from without at the time of dinner, and enters the house without washing his feet, the man who is eating becomes sick or vomits the food he has eaten or does not feel longing for food for some time until the blast of the Evil Eye is warded off." Mr. Campbell explains this on the principle that "as he comes from places where three or four roads meet, and which are spirit haunts, an evil spirit accompanies him without entering his body, from the place of its residence by which he has passed. If he washes his feet the spirit goes back; but if he enters the house with spirit-laden feet, the spirit enters the house with him and affects any one of the persons eating."[2]

Evil eye resulting from covetousness.

The real fact seems to be that the evil eye is generally the result of the feeling of covetousness.[3] Thus a man blind of an eye, no matter how well

[1] Lady Wilde, *Legends*, 24.
[2] Campbell, *Notes*, 207.
[3] On this see valuable notes by W. Cockburn, in *Panjáb Notes and Queries*, I, 14.

disposed he may be, is almost certain to envy a person blessed with a peculiarly good pair of eyes. But if the blind man's attention had been distracted by something conspicuous in the appearance of the other, such as lampblack on his eyelids, a mole or a scar, the feeling of dissatisfaction which is fatal to the complete effect of the envious glance is certain to arise. This theory that the glance may be avoided or neutralised by some blot or imperfection is at the basis of many of the popular remedies or prophylactics invented with the object of averting its influence.

Blots or imperfections as a prophylactic.

Hence comes the device of making an intentional blot in anything a person values, so that the glance of the Evil eye may be deprived of its complete satisfaction. Thus most people put lampblack on the eyes of their children as a protection against fascination, because black is a colour hateful to evil spirits: it has the additional advantage of protecting the eye from the fierce heat of the Indian summer. It is also believed that a person whose eyelids are encircled with lampblack, is incapable of casting the evil eye himself: and it is considered nice in a woman to ornament herself in this way, since because she herself is not liable to fascination, except at some special crisis of her life, such as marriage or parturition, it shows her indisposition to covet the beauty of others with the inference that she has no need to do so.

Use of opprobrious names.

On the same principle, when a parent has lost a child by any disease which, as is usually the case, can be attributed to fascination or other demoniacal influence, it is a common practice to call the next baby by some opprobrious name with the intention of so depreciating it that it will be regarded as worthless and protected in future. Thus, a male child is called Kuriya or "Dunghill," Kadheran or Ghasíta—"He hat has been dragged along the ground," Dukhi or Dukhita—"The tafflicted one," Phatingua—"Grasshopper," Jhingura—"Cricket," Banka—"Dumb," Bhikhra or Bhikhu—"Beggar," and so on: while gilrs are called Andhrí—"Blind," Tínkauriyá or Chhahkauriyá—

"She that was sold for three or six cowry shells," Dhuriyá—"Dusty," Machhiyá,—"Fly" and so on.[1] All this is connected with what the Scotch call "forespeaking" when praise beyond measure, praise accompanied with a sort of amazement or envy is considered likely to be followed by disease or accident. So in Ireland, to avoid being suspected of having the evil eye, it is necessary when looking at a child to say, "God bless it!": and when passing a farmyard where the cows are collected for milking to say, "The blessing of God be on you and on all your labour!"[2] Thus, if a native gentleman brings his child to visit a European, he dislikes to hear it praised unless the praise is accompanied with some pious ejaculation, and it is safer to speak in a complimentary way of some conspicuous ornament or piece of dress which is always put on as a preservative. In connection with this question of names, it may also be noticed that it is a common habit to have two names for children—one for ordinary use and the other carefully concealed. Many contractions and perversions of ordinary names as well as nicknames or childish titles of endearment are also freely used. This is done on the principle that it is very dangerous for a wizard to obtain knowledge of a person's real name, as he is thus enabled to acquire control over the owner.[3] This accounts for the taboo by which a Hindu woman is prevented from using the name of her husband. To this, however, there is one notable exception—"At marriages, coming of age, first pregnancy, and festive days, as the Nágpanchmi and Mangala Gauri in August, it is usual for the woman to recite or sing a couplet or verse in which the husband's name occurs. At marriages this naming is in practice little more than a game. An old man or an old lady gets close to the door and refuses to allow the young women to go unless they have told their husbands' name. At the pregnancy ceremony the same custom is observed." Mr. Campbell takes this to be "part of a ceremony whose

[1] Numerous lists of such names have been collected, which may be consulted by the curious. Temple, *Proper Names of Panjábis*, 22, *sqq.*: *Indian Antiquary*, VIII, 321, *sq.*: X, 321, *sq.*: *Panjáb Notes and Queries*, I, 26, 51; III, 9.

[2] Gregor, *Folklore of N.-E. Scotland*, 35: Lady Wilde, *Legends*, 20.

[3] *Folklore*, I, 273: Spencer, *Principles of Sociology*, I, 242: Lubbock, *Origin of Civilisation*, 243: Farrer, *Primitive Manners*, 119, *sq.*

object is to drive to a distance any spirits whose influence might blight the tender life of the unborn child. This seems natural when it is remembered that the names of men are either the names of gods, of precious stones, or of spices, all of which have a power to scare spirits: and as repeating the thousand names of Mahádeva is a service in which he greatly delights, apparently because it keeps spirits at a distance, so this repeating of the husband's and wife's name seems to have the same object."[1] At the same time, it seems equally possible that we have here, as in the case of the couvade to which reference has been already made, a survival of the custom of distinctly admitting maternity and paternity, which is the first stage out of the state of what has been euphemistically called communal marriage.

Other imperfection blots.

Another plan of protection from demoniacal influence based on the same idea is to dress up a child in filthy clothes to disguise its appearance: or a boy is dressed as a girl during the period of infancy. This is done because little girls are supposed to be naturally protected from the evil eye or other malignant influences. This may possibly explain a series of obscure customs which prevail among the lower castes of Northern India. Thus, at marriages among Chamárs, boys dress as girls, and perform a rude and occasionally obscene dance. Among tho Modh Bráhmans of Gujarát, at marriages the bridegroom's maternal uncle, whose special position is almost certainly a survival from times when descent through the mother was the only recognised form, dresses as a Jhanda or Pathán Faqír, whose ghost is dangerous, in woman's clothes from head to waist, and in men's clothes below, rubs his face with oil, daubs it with red powder, and then, armed with a sword, goes with the bride and bridegroom to a place where two roads cross (which, as we have seen, is a haunt of spirits), and stays there till the pair offer the goddess food.[2] For the same purpose of disguise, it is in many places usual to bore the

[1] *Notes*, 400 *note*.
[2] *Bombay Gazetteer*, V, 45, *sq*.

nose of a long wished for son as soon as he is born, and thus to make him look like a girl: and some people, with the same idea, will not wash a little boy's face till he is six years old.[1] Similarly, young men, if vigorous and stout, consider themselves very liable to the fascination of lean people, and tie a rag round the left arm, or a blue thread round their necks, often twisting the blue feathers of the jay into the thread, as an additional precaution. Nor do they care to expose their bodies to the public gaze, but wear a light shawl of a gaudy colour, even in the warmest season of the year. Should such a youth, if sufficiently conceited about his personal appearance, detect a suspicious person looking at him, he will immediately pretend to limp, or contort his face and spasmodically grasp his ankle or his elbow as if he were in pain, to distract and divert the attention he fears.

So all natives dread being stared at, particularly by Europeans: and you will often see a witness cast his eyes on the ground when the magistrate looks at him full in the face, sometimes because he knows he is lying and dreads the consequences, but it is often done through fear of fascination. A European, in fact, to the rustic, is a strange, inscrutable personage, gifted with many occult powers for good or for evil, and there are numerous extraordinary legends current about him. We shall return to this in dealing with the wonderful *Momiái* legend. Here it may be noted that in popular belief his nails, like those of the Rákshasa, distil a deadly poison, and hence he is afraid to eat with his fingers, as all reasonable people do, and prefers to use a knife and fork.

A few other examples illustrating the same principle may be given. When a man is copying a manuscript he will sometimes make an intentional blot. A favourite trick is to fold the paper back before the ink of the last line is dry, so as to blot and at the same time make it appear the result of chance. Similarly an intentional irregularity is introduced in printing chintzes and like

[1] *Panjáb Notes and Queries,* II, 42.

handicrafts, and this goes a long way to explain the occasional and almost unaccountable defects to be found in some native work. The letter from a Rája is spotted with gold-leaf as a preservative, partly to divert the glance of fascination and partly because gold is a scarer of demons. The ugly figure of a *churel* or a caricature of a European is drawn on the walls of the house, which by the way is always on the same principle left unfinished. Confectioners, when one of their vessels of milk is exposed to the public view, put a little charcoal in it, as careful Scotch mothers do with the water in which they wash their babies.[1] If a cow gives a large quantity of milk the owner tries to hide it, and if it chances to get sour, he attributes the loss to the malignant influence of some enemy, witch, or demon. A mother while dressing her baby makes a black mark on its cheek, and before a man eats betel he pinches off a corner of the leaf as a safeguard. When food is taken to the labourer in the field, a piece of charcoal or a copper coin is placed in the basket, and when horses while feeding throw a little grain on the ground, it is not replaced because the horse is believed to do this in order to avoid fascination. Grooms with the same object throw a dirty duster over the withers of a horse while it is feeding, and when food is purchased in the open market a little is thrown into the fire. So, when a person is having a particular good dinner, he should select an auspicious moment and do the same. Orthodox Hindus pretend that this is intended as an offering to Annadeva, the god of food: but here many varied beliefs, such as fear of fascination, earth and fire worship appear to combine to establish these and kindred practices.[2]

Articles which scare spirits: iron.

We now come to consider the various articles which are believed to possess the power of scaring spirits, and counteracting demoniacal influence of different kinds. First among these is iron. Why iron has been regarded as a scarer of demons has been much debated. Natives of India will tell you that it is the material out of which

---

[1] Gregor, *Folklore of the North of Scotland*, 7.

[2] See *Panjáb Notes and Queries*, I, 75, 87, 89, 101, 103, 113; III, 16; Tod, *Annals*, I, 357, *Note*.

arms are made and that an armed man should fear nothing. Others say that its virtues depend on its black colour, which, as we shall see, is obnoxious to evil spirits. Mr. Campbell thinks the reason to be that in all cases of swooning and seizures iron is of great value either applied hot or as a lancet to let blood.[1] This perhaps accounts for the practice of branding followed by many Hindu ascetics. A sword or knife is always placed in the bed of the young mother and her baby. She, at this crisis of her life, is particularly exposed to the evil influence of spirits. In the same way the Scotch fairies are particularly fond of milk, and hence try to gratify their desires on "unsained" or unchurched women.[2] There is a case in the Indian Law Reports where the knife thus placed near the woman was used to murder her.[3] Pliny advises that a piece of iron should be put in the nest of a sitting hen to save her eggs from the influence of thunder. This is now done in Sicily, with the object of absorbing every noise that might be injurious to the chickens.[4] The knife and sword have particular potency in this way. We have seen that beating an iron tray scares the hail demon; so the Indians in Canada put out swords in a storm to frighten off the demon of thunder.[5] The common belief is that the evil spirit is such a fool that he runs against the sharp edge of the weapon and allows himself to be wounded. The magic sword is a stock element in Indian folklore.[6] In the Panjáb while a house is being built an iron pot, or a pot painted black which is good enough to scare the demon, is always kept on the works, and when it is finished the young daughter of the owner ties to the lintel a charm used on other occasions also, the principal virtue of which lies in a small iron ring. Here is combined the virtue of the iron and the ring which is a sacred circle. In India iron rings are constantly worn with this object. They scare evil and disease, as in Ireland an iron ring worn on the fourth finger cures rheumatism. The bridegroom in the marriage procession

[1] *Notes*, 34.
[2] Gregor, *Folklore of N.-E. Scotland*, 5, 60, 62.
[3] Reg. *v.* Lalla, *Nizámat Adálat Reports*, N.-W. P., 22nd September 1853.
[4] Gubernatis, *Zoological Mythology*, II, 281.
[5] *Folklore*, I, 154.
[6] Tawney, *Katha Sarit Ságara*, I, 386, 575; II, 64.

carries a sword as a preservative, and magistrates in India are constantly asked to grant licenses for this purpose. If the license is not granted the bridegroom carries a sword of lath, but the object is partially attained if it has a spike of iron attached to it.[1] It is probably on the same principle that the blacksmith's anvil is used as a rain spell, and that if any one insults it by sitting on it he is believed to suffer from boils. We have already noticed the value of iron nails for the purpose of laying the ghost of the *churel*, and such nails are very commonly driven into the doorpost, or into the legs of the bed, with the object of resisting evil spirits.

Iron horse shoes.

The uses of iron in this way are most numerous but need no further illustration. The horse shoe is one special form of the spell. Why this should be so has been much debated. Mr. Farrer thinks that it may be connected with the respect paid to the horse in folklôre.[2] The Irish say that the reason is that the horse and the ass were in the stall when Christ was born, and hence are blessed for evermore.[3] The idea that its shape connects it with the *yoni* and phallicism hardly deserves mention. One thing is clear, that the element of luck largely enters into the matter—the shoe must have been found by chance on the road,[4] and this combined with the general protective power of iron is possibly a sufficient explanation of the practice. The custom is common in India. The great gate of the mosque at Fatehpur-Sikri is covered with them, and the practice is general at many shrines.

Iron converted into gold.

There is also a cycle of legends which connect iron with the philosopher's stone and transformation into gold. Laliya, a blacksmith at Ahmadabád, made an axe for a Bhíl, who returned and complained that it would not cut. Laliya on looking at it found that the blade had been

[1] Lady Wilde, *Legends*, 202 : *Panjáb Notes and Queries*, I, 123 : Ibbetson, *Panjáb Ethnography*, 117 : O'Brien, *Multáni Glossary*, 15.
[2] *Primitive Manners*, 293.
[3] Lady Wilde, *Legends*, 181.
[4] Lady Wilde, *loc. cit.* Aubrey, *Remaines*, 27 : Gregor, *Folklore of N.E. Scotland*, 117.

turned into gold. On questioning the Bhíl he ascertained that he had tried to sharpen it on what turned out to be the philosopher's stone. Laliya by possession of the stone acquired great wealth and was at last attacked by the King's troops. At last he was obliged to throw the stone into the Bhadar river, where it still lies, but once some iron chains were let down and touching it the 'inks were turned into gold.'[1]

Gold and silver as protectives.

Gold, and in a less degree silver, have a similar protective influence. The idea is apparently based on their scarcity and value, and on their colour, yellow and white being obnoxious to evil spirits. Hence a little bit of gold is put into the mouth of the dying Hindu. These metals are particularly effective in the form of ornaments, many of which have some mystic significance or are formed in imitation of some sacred leaf, flower, or animal. This is one main cause of the recklessness with which rich natives load their children with masses of ornaments, though they are well aware that the practice often leads to robbery and murder.

Copper and brass as protectives.

Next come copper and brass. The use of copper in the form of rings or amulet cases is very common. Many of the vessels used in the daily service of the gods, such as the *argha*, with which the daily oblations are done, are formed of this metal. So with brass or various kinds of alloy used for drinking and cooking utensils. The common brass *lota* is always carried about by a man during the period of mourning as a preservative against the evil spirits, which surround him until the ghost is laid. Copper rings are specially worn as an antidote to pimples and boils, while those of iron are supposed to weaken the influence of the planet Sani or Saturn, which is proverbially unlucky and malignant. His evil eye in particular brings misfortune at intervals of twenty-four years: all offerings to him are black and consequently ill-omened, such as black cloth, sesamum

[1] *Bombay Gazetteer,* V, 123, and for another instance see Jarrett, *Ain-i-Akbari,* II, 197.

oil, iron, charcoal, buffaloes, and black salt: and only the Dakaut, the lowest class of Bráhman menial priest, will accept such offerings.[1]

Coral and other marine products.

Next in value to these metals come coral and other marine products, which probably derive their virtue from being strange to an inland dwelling people, and as connected with the great ocean, the final home of the sainted dead. Coral is particularly valued in the form of a necklace by those who cannot afford the costlier metals, and its ashes form a chief part of various rural remedies and stimulants. So with shells, particularly the *sankha* or conch shell, which is used for oblations and is regarded as sacred to Vishnu. It is blown at his temples when the deity receives his daily meal, in order to scare vagrant spirits, who would otherwise consume or defile the offering. So with the cowry shell which is worn round the neck by children as an antidote to the Evil eye or diabolical influence, and is hung with the same object round the neck or pasterns of a valued horse, or on a cow, or buffalo. The shell armlet worn by Bengali women has the same protective influence.[2]

Precious stones.

Precious stones possess similar value. In one special combination of nine varieties, known as the *nau ratana,* they are specially efficacious—the ruby sacred to the Sun, the pearl to the Moon, coral to Mars, emerald to Mercury, topaz to Jupiter. diamond to Venus, sapphire to Saturn, amethyst to Rahu, cat's eye to Ketu. The *naulakha* or nine lakh necklace constantly appears in Indian folklore. In the story of Princess Aubergine we read that "inside the fish there is a bumble bee, inside the bee a tiny box, and inside the box is the wonderful nine lakh necklace. Put it on and I shall die," and in one of Somadeva's stories, at the marriage Jaya gives the bride a necklace of such a kind that as long as it is upon a person's neck hunger, thirst, and death, cannot harm them.[3] The wearing of a

[1] Lál Bihári De, *Folk Tales*, 108, *sqq.*: Wilson, *Indian Caste*, II, 174.

[2] For further examples see Campbell, *Notes*, 126, *sqq.*

Temple, *Wideawake Stories*, 83: Tawney, *Katha Sarit Ságara*, I. 173.

ring of sapphire, sacred to Sani or Saturn, is supposed to turn out lucky or unlucky according to circumstances. For this reason the wearer tries it for three days, that is, he wears it on Saturday, which is sacred to Saturn, and keeps it on till Tuesday. During this time, if no mishap befalls him, he continues to wear it during the period when the planet's influence is unfavourable: but should any mishap befall him during the three days, he gives the ring to a Bráhman.[1] So the onyx, known as the Sulaimání or stone of Solomon, has mystic virtues, as according to Burton[2] carbuncles and coral, beryl, pearls, and rubies were believed to drive away devils, to overcome sorrow, and to stop dreams.

Beads.

With poorer people beads take the place of gems, and in particular the curious enamelled bead, which possibly came from China and is still found on old deserted sites mostly of Buddhistic origin, enjoys special repute. We have already met with the parturition bead. In Scotland the lambber bead cures inflamed eyes and sprains.[3] As an antidote to the Evil eye blue beads are particularly valued, and are hung round the necks and pasterns of horses and other valuable animals. This belief in the efficacy of beads is at the basis of the use of rosaries, which as used in Europe are almost certainly of eastern origin, imported in the middle ages in imitation of those worn by Buddhistic or Hindu ascetics who ascribe to them manifold virtues. Such are those of the *tulasi* used by Vaishnavas and those of the ***rudrák-sha*** berry worn by Saivas.

Blood.

A curious Evil eye spell is recorded from Allahabád. A woman of the Chamár or currier caste gave birth to a dead child. Thinking that this was due to fascination she put a piece of the cloth used at her confinement down a well, having previously enclosed in it two leaves of betel, some cloves, and a piece of castor oil plant.[4] Here we have in the first place a

---

[1] Campbell, *Notes*, 119.
[2] *Anatomy of Melancholy*, 434.
[3] Henderson, *Folklore of Northern Counties*, 146.
[4] *Panjáb Notes and Queries*, III, 67.

case of well worship: secondly, the use of betel, cloves, and the castor oil plant—all scarers of evil spirits: and thirdly, an instance of the use of blood for the same purpose. We have elsewhere noticed the special character attached to the menstrual or parturition blood. But blood itself is most effective against demoniacal influence. There are cases in which blood is drunk or rubbed on the body as an antidote to disease. In Bombay some Maráthas give warmed goat's blood in cases of piles, and in typhus or red discoloration of the skin with blotches the patient is cured by killing a cock and rubbing the patient with blood. Others use the blood of the great lizard in cases of snake bite.[1] Similarly among the Dravidian races the Kos drink the blood of the sacrificial bull: the Malers cure demoniacs by giving the blood of a sacrificed buffalo: the Paháriyas in times of epidemics set up a pair of posts and a cross beam and hang on it a vessel of blood.[2] We shall meet with other instances of this when dealing with the blood covenant, as, for instance, when some of lower castes in Upper India mark the forehead of the bride with blood or vermilion, and when red paint is smeared on the village god in lieu of a blood sacrifice. This idea of the efficacy of blood to scare evil spirits is possibly the basis of much of the animal sacrifice performed at the numerous shrines. Numerous similar instances might be collected from the ritual of the Jews and other ancient races, and until quite recently among ourselves bleeding was regarded as a means of letting out the devil.

Incence.

Similarly with the use of incense, which is intended partly to please the divinity who is being worshipped and partly to scare demons who steal or defile the offerings. So bad smells repel demons. Thus in Ireland if a child is sick they take a piece of the cloth worn by the person supposed to have overlooked the infant and burn it near him. If he sneezes he expels the spirit and the spell is broken, or the cloth is burned to ashes and given to the patient, while his forehead is rubbed with

[1] Campbell, *Notes*, 49, *sq.*
[2] Dalton, *Descriptive Ethnology*, 115, 270, 272.

spittle. In Northern India, if a child is sick, a little bran, pounded chillies, mustard, and sometimes the eyelashes of the child are passed round its head and burned. If the burning mixture does not smell very badly, which it is needless to say is hardly ever the case, it is a sign that the child is still under the evil influence : if the odour is abominable, that the attack has been obviated.[1] Similarly in Bengal red mustard seed and salt are mixed together, waved round the head of the patient, and then thrown into the fire.[2] We have noticed the use of spittle for this purpose in Ireland. The same idea prevails in India. Spittle is regarded as impure : hence a native cleans his mouth daily with a fresh twig of the *nim* tree and regards the European's constant use of the same toothbrush day after day as one of the numerous extraordinary impurities which we permit. Hence, too, the practice of spitting when any person who is feared or detested passes by. In Bombay spittle, especially fasting spittle, is used to rub on wounds and cure them : it cures inflammation of the eyes, which was an idea familiar to the Jews : it guards children against the Evil eye. In the Konkaṇ, when a person is affected by the Evil eye, salt and mustard seed are waved round his head, thrown into the fire, and he is told to spit. In Gujarát, when an orthodox Shiah Musalmán travels with a Sunni he spits, and among the Roman Catholics of Kánara at baptism the priest wets the thumb with spittle and with it touches the child's ears and nostrils.[3]

Salt.

We have already had an instance of the use of salt as a demon scarer in the case of children who have eaten sweets. Many classes of Hindu ascetics bury their dead in salt. It is waved round the head of the bride and bridegroom, and buried near the house door as a charm. In classical antiquity it was mixed with water and sprinkled on the worshippers. The idea is probably based on its power of preventing decay.[4]

---

[1] *Panjáb Notes and Queries*, I, 51.
[2] Risley, *Tribes and Castes*, II, 209.
[3] Campbell, *loc. cit.*, 131 : Tylor, *Primitive Culture*, II, 439.
[4] For a similar belief in Ireland, see Lady Wilde, *Legends*, 44, 233.

Another series of prophylactics depends on the idea that the spirits flutter in the air round a person exposed to their influences. Hence a long series of customs known as *parachhan* performed at Hindu marriages in Upper India, when lights, a brass tray, grain, and household implements, like the rice pounder, are waved round the head of the bride and bridegroom as a protective. This is perhaps one explanation of the use of flags at temples and village shrines, though in some cases they appear to be used as a perch on which the deity sits when he makes his periodical visits. Hence, too, feathers have a mystic significance, though in some cases, as in those of the peacock and jay, the colour is the important part. Hence the waving of the fan and *chauri* over the head of a great man. A woman carrying her child on her return from a strange village, lest she should bring the evil influence of any foreign evil spirit with her, will before entering her own homestead pass seven little stones seven times round the head of the baby, and throw them in different directions so as to pass away any evil that may have been contracted. When a sorcerer is called in to attend a case attributed to demoniacal possession he whisks the patient with a branch of the *ním*, *madár* or camel thorn, all of which are more or less sacred trees and have acquired a reputation as preservatives. With this is combined the aspersion of the afflicted one, be he man or beast, with some water from the blacksmith's shop, in which iron has been repeatedly plunged and has bestowed additional efficacy upon it. This respect for the forge of the backsmith is a curious survival from the time of the early handicrafts. In Scotland the same idea prevails about water from the forge, and in Ireland no one will take anything by stealth from such a place.[1] In all the mythologies the idea is widespread that the art of smithying was first discovered and practised by supernatural beings. We see this through the whole range of Folklore from the Cyclopes to Wayland Smith who finally came to be connected with the Devil of Christianity.[2]

Waving.

---

[1] Gregor, *Folklore of N.-E. Scotland*, 45 : Lady Wilde, *Legends*, 205.

[2] For a full discussion of the evidence in support of this see Schrader, *Prehistoric Antiquities of the Aryan Peoples*, 163, *sqq*.

Water.

We have already referred to water as a protective against the influence of evil spirits. Thus in Upper India on a lucky day fixed by the Pandit the ceremony of *Nahâwan* or bathing is performed for the protection of the young mother and her child two or three days after her confinement. Both of them are bathed in a decoction of the leaves of the *nîm* tree. Then a handful of the seeds of mustard and dill is waved round the mother's head, and then thrown into a vessel containing fire. When the seeds are consumed the cup is upset and the mother breaks it with her own foot. Next she sits with grain in her hand while the household brass tray is beaten and the midwife throws the child into the air. All this takes place in the open air in the courtyard of the house. Here we have a series of antidotes to demoniacal influence, the purport of which will be easily understood on principles which have been already explained.

Grain.

With the use of grain we meet another valuable antidote. When parched and purified by the influence of fire it acquires additional efficacy. At low caste marriages in Upper India rice is parched with special ceremonial precautions and scattered by the brothers of the bride on her and her bridegroom as they revolve in the marriage shed. The idea is familiar in folklore.[1] Another common plan is to make a pile of rice with a knot of turmeric, and a copper coin concealed in it. This the bride knocks down with her foot. The same custom prevails as far as Bombay.[2] All through Upper India the exorciser shakes grain in a fan, which as we shall see is a potent fetish, and by the number of grains which remain in the interstices calculates which particular ghost is worrying the patient. On the same principle the Orâons put rice in the mouth of the corpse, and the Koiris when they marry walk round a pile of water pots and scatter rice on the ground.[3] Barley, another sacred grain, is rubbed over the corpse of a Hindu and sprinkled on the head before the cremation rite is performed, and in

[1] For instances see Tawney, ***Katha Sarit Sâgara***, I, 478; II, 167.
[2] *Gazetteer*, XVIII, 399 *sq*.
[3] Dalton, *Descriptive Ethnology*, 261, 321.

Hoshangabád they tie a sheaf of corn on a pole and fasten it to the cattle shed.[1] The uses of various kinds of grain for this purpose are infinite, and the instances in support of it could be almost indefinitely extended.

Products of the cow.

So with the products of the sacred cow, which are, as might have been expected, most valuable for this purpose. Hence the use of ghi, or clarified butter, in the public or domestic ritual. Milk for the same reason is used in offerings, and sprinkled on the ground as an oblation. Cow dung, in particular, is regarded as efficacious. After the death or birth impurity the house is carefully plastered with a mixture of cow dung and clay. No cooking place is pure without it, and the corpse is cremated with cakes of cow dung fuel. Even the urine of the cow is valued as a medicine and a purificant: and every rich native keeps a cow, so that his glance may fall on her when he wakes from sleep, and regards her as the guardian of the household.

Colours.

Colours again are scarers of evil spirits. They particularly dread yellow, black, red, and white. The regard for yellow explains the common use of turmeric in the domestic ritual. Combined with oil, which is also efficacious, the bride and bridegroom are carefully rubbed before marriage with this condiment which is known as *abtan*. Five roots of turmeric are sent to complete the betrothal. This explains the use of yellow clothes by various classes of ascetics, and of *chandan* or sandalwood in making caste marks and for various ceremonial purposes. So the corpse is covered with turmeric before cremation,—a custom which is certainly not of Aryan origin, because it prevails among the Thárus, one of the most primitive tribes of the Sub-Himálayan forests. Yellow and red again are the usual colours of the marriage garments. The parting of the bride's hair is stained with vermilion, though here, perhaps, the practice is based on the symbolical belief in the blood covenant. And the same idea is probably at the basis of the flinging of red powder and water coloured

[1] *Settlement Report*, 274.

with turmeric at the Holi or spring festival. Black again is feared by evil spirits, and the husbandman hangs a black pot in his field as a spirit scarer, and young women and children have their eyelids marked with lampblack. So in the Mirzapur Baiga's sacrifice a black fowl or a black goat is the favourite victim. Charcoal is, on the same principle, valued and some is always put into milk as a preservative or buried under the threshold to guard the household from harm.

Grasses, sacred.

For the same reason various kinds of grass are considered sacred, such as the *kusa*, the *durva*, the *darbha*. Some of these form an important ingredient in the *sráddha* offerings to the sacred dead, some are used in the marriage and cremation ritual, on some the dying man is laid at the moment of dissolution.

Caste marks and tattooing.

Next come certain special marks made on the body. Such are the marks branded on their bodies by various classes of ascetics and the widespread custom of tattooing. It has been suggested that many of these marks are of totemistic origin. That this is so among races other than those of India is almost certainly the case.[1] But though tattooing very possibly originated in totemism, as far as has hitherto been ascertained, no trace remains of a tribal tattoo, and it is safer at present to class marks of this kind in the general category of devices to repel evil spirits. Among purely sectarial marks we have the forehead mark of the Saivas composed of three curved lines like a half moon, to which is added a round dot on the nose: it is made with the clay of the Ganges, or with sandalwood, or ashes of cow dung. The mark of the Vaishnavas is two lines rather oval drawn the whole length of the nose and carried forward into straight lines across the forehead. It is generally made with the clay of the Ganges, sometimes with the powder of sandalwood. The Sákta forehead mark is a small semicircular line between the eyebrows and a dot in the middle.

[1] Frazer, *Totemism*, 26, *sq.*

The practice of tattooing[1] is common both among the Aryan and Dravidian races, but is more general among the lower than the higher castes. Thus the Juáng women tattoo themselves with three strokes on the forehead just over the nose, and three on each of the temples. They attach no meaning to the marks, have no ceremony in adopting them, and are ignorant of the origin of the practice. The Kharria women make three parallel lines on the forehead, the outer lines terminating at the outer ends in a crook, and two on each temple. The Ho women tattoo themselves in the form of an arrow, which they regard as their national emblem. The Birhor women tattoo their chests, arms, and ankles, but not their faces. The Oráon women have three marks on the brow and two on each temple. The young men burn marks on their fore-arms as parts of the ordeal ceremony; girls when adult, or nearly so, have themselves tattooed on the arms and back. The Kisán women have no such mark: if a female of the tribe indulges in the vanity of having herself tattooed she is at once turned adrift as having degraded herself.[2]

Among the Dravidian tribes of the North-Western Provinces the Korwas get their women tattooed by a woman of the Bádi sub-division of Nats. They are tattooed only on the breast and arms, not on the thighs. There are no ceremonies connected with it, nor any special pattern. Any girl gets herself tattooed in any figure she approves for a small sum. Well-to-do women always get it done; but if a woman is not tattooed, it is not considered unlucky. Men are not tattooed. The Ghasiya women tattoo themselves on the breast, arms, thighs, and feet. They say that when a woman dies who is not tattooed, the Great Lord Paramesar is displeased and turns her out of heaven or has her branded with the thorns of the acacia. So with Chamárs. When a woman who has not been tattooed dies, Paramesar asks her where are the marks and signs which she ought to possess to show that she has lived in the world. If she cannot show them she will, in her

---

[1] On tattooing see Fraser, *loc. cit.*: Tylor, *Primitive Culture*, I, 393: Lubbock, *Origin of Civilisation*, 61, *sqq*.
[2] Dalton, *Descriptive Ethnology*, 157, 161, 191, 219, 251.

next birth, be reborn as a Bhútní, Pretní or Rákshasí. At present among low caste women the process of tattooing is regarded as a species of initiation and usually marks the attainment of puberty. It thus corresponds with the ceremony of ear piercing among males. To the east of the North-Western Provinces a girl is not allowed to cook until she is tattooed with a mark supposed to represent the cooking house of Sítá (*Sítá ki rasoí*), and in Bengal high caste people will not drink from the hands of a girl who does not wear the *ullikhi* or star-shaped tattoo mark between her eyebrows. A Chamár woman who is not tattooed at marriage will not, it is believed, see her father and mother in the next world. This reminds us of the idea prevalent in Fiji that women who are not tattooed are liable to special punishment in the next world.[1] In Bombay the custom has been provided with a Bráhmanical legend. One day Lakshmí, the wife of Vishnu, told her husband that whenever he went out on business or to visit his devotees she became frightened. Hearing this Vishnu took his weapons and stamped them on her body, saying that the marks of his weapons would save her from evil.

Forms of tatoo marks.

Hence women in Bombay tattoo themselves with the figures of the lotus, conch shell, and discus, and from this the present custom originated.[2] In Upper India the forms of the tattoo marks fall into various classes. Some are rude or conventialised representations of animals, plants, or flowers: The operators carry round with them sketches of the different kinds of ornament, and the girl selects these according to taste. The peacock, the horse, the serpent, the scorpion, tortoise, centipede, appear constantly in various forms.[3] Others again are representations of jewelry actually worn—necklaces, bracelets, armlets, or rings. Others again are purely religious, such as the trident or matted hair of Siva, the weapons of Vishnu, and the cooking house of Sítá, the stock type of wifely virtue. Some of these marks were originally, it is most probable, of totemistic association, but

[1] Bholanáth Chandar, *Travels of a Hindu*, I, 326 : *Panjáb Notes and Queries*, I, 27, 99 : Farrer, *Primitive Manners*. 125.

[2] Campbell. *Notes*, 134

they have now become merely ornamentative, as was the case in Central Asia in the time of Marco Polo, where they were regarded only as "a piece of elegance or a sign of gentility", and among the Thracians as described by Herodotus.[1] It may be noticed that in the time of Marco Polo people used to go from Upper India to Zayton in China to be tattooed.[2] These animal forms of tattooing are found also among the Dravidian races of the Central Provinces, where the forms used are a peacock, an antelope or a dagger, and the marks are made on the back of the thighs and legs. In Bengal tattooing is used as a cure for goitre.[3]

Miscellaneous spirit scarers.

We may close this long catalogue of devices intended to scare spirits with a number of miscellaneous examples. With this object the merchant pastes on the walls of his shop the gaudy labels off his cloth bales. Poor people in Upper India place on their houses an old shoe heel upwards. This is perhaps based on the principle that spirits fear leather. We have had an example of this already in the procedure of the Baiga, who flagellates people suffering from demoniacal possession with a tawse or leathern strap. In the Dakkhin a person troubled with nightmare sleeps with a shoe under his pillow, and an exorcist frightens evil spirits by threatening to make them drink water from a tanner's well. The Púna Kunbis believe that a drink of water from a tanner's hand destroys the power of a witch, and a man, if he feels he has been struck by an incantation, at once takes hold of an upturned shoe.[4] In the Panjáb if a man sits on a currier's stone he gets boils.[5] This idea also possibly accounts for much of the fear or contempt felt regarding shoe-beating, and for the flinging of the slipper or old shoe when the English bride and bridegroom leave for the honeymoon. Again, various skins, such as those of the tiger and antelope, are worn by, or used as a seat, by some classes of ascetics. Garlic, again, probably from its pungent nature,

---

[1] Yule, *Marco Polo*, II, 69, 99: Herodotus, V, 6: also for the Dacians, see Pliny *Nat. Hist*, VII, 10: XXII, 2.
[2] *Loc. cit.* II, 218.
[3] Hislop, *Papers*, 11, note: Risley, *Tribes and Castes*, I, 292.
[4] Campbell, *Notes*, 105.
[5] *North India Notes and Queries*, I, 86.

is a preservative. It is known in Sanskrit as *mlechcha kanda* "or the foreigner's root," and its virtues are generally recognised.[1] Possibly for the same reason onions are with many castes a forbidden article of food. Glass in the form of beads, mirrors, &c., has similar qualities : and pieces of horn, such as that of the jackal and deer, are widely used for the same purpose. Garlands of flowers possess the same property, and so do various fruits, such as dates, cocoanuts, betel nuts, and plantains which are put in the lap of the bride or pregnant woman to scare the evil spirits which cause barrenness, and sugar is distributed at marriages.

Persons naturally protected against spirits.

Some persons have a natural protection against the influence of fascination in the shape of some physical deformity which relieves them of the danger of being envied. Men with double thumbs are considered particularly lucky in this respect, and a bald man is similarly protected. On the other hand, a one-eyed man is dreaded because he is naturally envious of people who possess good sight, and he is proverbially a scoundrel. People who are born within the period of the Solono festival in August are not only protected from, but possess the power of casting, the evil eye : and the same is the case with those who have accidentally eaten ordure in childhood. We have already noticed the mystic power of cow dung. Dung generally is offensive to spirits, partly because it is dirty and partly because it is in some instances used as a medicine. Women who eat dung possess, as we shall see elsewhere, the power of witchcraft.

Fascination among the Gonds.

The Gonds have a special procedure in cases of deaths which they believe to have occurred through fascination. The burning of the body is postponed until it is made to point out the delinquent. The relations solemnly call upon the corpse to do this, and the theory is that if there has been foul play of any kind, the body, on being taken up, will force the bearers to convey it to the house of the person by whom the spell was cast. If this be three

[1] Gubernatis, *Zoological Mythology*, I, 281.

times repeated, the owner of the house is condemned, his property is destroyed, and he is expelled from the neighbourhood.[1]

Amulets.

In ordinary cases, however, most people find it advisable to carry an amulet of some kind as a preservative. An amulet is primarily a portion of a dead man or dead animal by which hostile spirits are coerced or their good offices secured.[2] Though Mr. Ferguson may be correct in his statement that prior to the distribution of the remains of the great Buddha at Kusinagara we have no historical record of the worship of relics, still the idea must have prevailed widely among the Hindu races, out of whom the votaries of the new faith were recruited. With some of these relics of the Buddha, such as his begging bowl which was long kept in a Dagoba or Vihára erected by King Kanishka, then removed for a time to Benares, and finally to Kandahár, where it is now held in the highest respect by Muhammadans, and has accumulated round it a cycle of legends like those connected with the Sangrail, we reach the zone of pure fetishism.[3] The amulet then, which is in its original conception a portion of a dead body, is supposed to concentrate within itself the virtues and powers of the man or animal of which it formed a part. Hence tiger's claws, which represent in themselves the innate strength and bravery of the animal, are greatly esteemed for this purpose, and the sportsman when he shoots a tiger has to count over the claws carefully to the coolies in charge of the animal or they will certainly misappropriate them. In the same way a portion of the umbilical cord is placed among the clothes of the infant and its mother to avert the Evil eye.

Religious amulets.

Another form of Evil eye amulet is a piece of metal, stone, bone, or similar substance worn on the person with an invocation inscribed on it to some special god. This is a very common form among Muhammadans.[4] On the same principle Hindus head their letters with the words

---

[1] Dalton, *Descriptive Ethnology*, 283.
[2] Spencer, *Principles of Sociology*, I, 254, note: 301.
[3] *History of Indian Architecture*, 57, *sqq.*: Cunningham, *Archælogical Reports*, II, 87: XVI, 8, *sqq.*
[4] For examples, see Herklot, *Qánún-i-Islám*, app. XXV: 239 *sqq.*

Srí Rámjí "the great god, Rama," or with the figures 74, of which one not very probable explanation is that they represent the weight in maunds of gold earrings taken from the Rájput dead at the famous seige of Chithor.

The equilateral triangle.

The equilateral triangle is another favourite mystic sign. According to Christian ideas the figure of three triangles intersected and containing five lines, is called the pentangle of Solomon, and when it is deliniated on the body of a man it marks the five places in which Our Saviour was wounded, and it was therefore regarded, as a *fuga demonum*, or a means of frightening demons.[1] Similarly in Northern India the equilateral triangle is considered to be a mystic sign, and the little broadcloth bags hung round the necks of children to avert the Evil eye are made in this shape. The diamond shape is also approved, because it contains two equilateral triangles base to base.

The spread hand.

Another form of amulet or mystic sign is the mark of the spread hand with the fingers extended. This is made by the women of the family on the outer wall of the house and round the doorpost, and is considered to be particularly efficacious. Mr. Campbell suggests that the custom is based on the belief in the hand being a spirit entry.[2] However this may be, the custom is very generally prevalent. The Bloody Hand of Ulster worn as a crest by the Baronets of one creation is well known.[3] The Uchlas of Púna strew sand on the spot where the dead breathed his last. They cover the spot with a basket which they raise next morning in the hope of finding the mark of a palm, which shows that the dead is pleased and brings vigour on the family: and the Thákurs on the fifth day after the birth of a child dip a hand in red powder and water and make a mark on the wall of the lying-in room which they worship.[4] At the rock-cut temple of Tilok Sendur in

[1] Aubrey, *Remaines*, 57.
[2] *Notes*, 177.
[3] Westropp, *Primitive Symbolism*, 58, *sqq.*: 61, *sqq.*: *Panjáb Notes and Queries*, I, 137.
[4] *Bombay Gazetteer*, XVIII, 473, 426.

Hoshangábád an annual festival is held, and those who come to demand any special benefit, such as health or children, mark their vow by stamping their hand dipped in red paint against the rock wall, fingers upward. If the prayer is heard they revisit the place and make the same mark, this time with the fingers downwards: but whether Mahadeva is not gracious to his votaries, or whether it is that the sense of favours to come is not keen enough after the prayer of the moment has been granted, the hand-stamps pointing downwards are not a tenth in number of those pointing upwards.[1] The stamping of the hand and five fingers immersed in a composition of sandal wood has always been regarded as a peculiarly solemn mode of attesting an important document, and it is said that Muhammad himself adopted this practice.[2]

Protective amulets.

There are numerous varieties of these protective amulets. Thus the Mirzapur Korwas tie on the necks of their children roots of various jungle plants such as the *siyár singhí*, which owes its name and repute to its resemblance to the horn of the jackal. In cases of disease the Kharwars wear leaves of the *bel* tree, cloves and flowers selected by a Bráhman. The Gújars of Hazâra hang the berries of the *batkar* tree (*celtis caucasia*) round the necks of men and animals to protect them from the Evil eye.[3] Among Muhammadans little stone or glass tablets are freely used for the same purpose. Some have a hocus-pocus inscription purporting to be a verse of the Qurán in Arabic: others have the name of Fátima coupled with those of the famous martyrs Hasan and Husen. Another amulet of a very elaborate kind is described as containing a piece of the umbilical cord encased in metal, a tiger's claw, two claws of the large horned owl turned in opposite directions and encased in metal, a stone known as the *athráhd ká manká*, because it has the property of turning eight colours according to the light in which it is placed (probably a tourmaline or quartzoze pebble),

[1] *Settlement Report*, 59 *sqq.*
[2] Tod, *Annals*, I, 383, note: 411, note.
[3] *Panjáb Notes and Queries*, II, 44.

and a special evil eye destroyer in the shape of a jasper or marble bead. These five articles are necessaries, but as an extra precaution the amulet contained some crude gold, a whorled shell, an ancient copper coin, a cowry, some ashes from the fire of a Jogi ascetic, and the five ingredients of the sacred incense. The owner admitted that it would have improved had it also contained a magic square.[1] This reminds us of the necklace of amber beads hung round the neck of Scotch children to keep off ill luck and the Irish scapular, a piece of cloth on which the name of Mary is written on one side and I. H. S. on the other, which are preservatives against evil spirits.[2]

Magic circle.

One of the most valuable of these protectives is the magic circle which appears in various forms throughout the whole range of folklore. We have seen how the Baiga perambulates his village and drops a line of spirits along the boundary to repel foreign ghosts. It is believed that evil spirits cannot pass a line thus made. This accounts for the numerous European and Indian stone circles which in Ireland are the resort of the fairies.[3] We have constant references in the folktales to the circle within which the ascetic or magician sits while he is performing his sorceries. Thus, in the story of Nischayadatta the ascetics "quickly made a great circle with ashes and entering into it they lighted a fire with fuel, and all remained there muttering a charm to protect themselves." In the tales of the Vetála we find the mendicant under a banyan tree engaged in making a circle, and Ksántisila makes a circle of the yellow powder of bones, the ground within which was smeared with blood and which had pitchers of blood placed in the direction of the cardinal points.[4] The same idea appears in the magic circle used as an ordeal or to compel payment of a debt. Thus we read in Marco Polo,[5] "If a debtor have been several times asked by his creditor for payment

---

[1] *Panjáb Notes and Queries*, III, 186.
[2] *Folklore*, II, 75: Lady Wilde, *Legends*, 110.
[3] Lady Wilde, *loc. cit.* 79.
[4] Tawney, *Katha Sarit Ságara*, I, 337; II, 233, 358.
[5] II, 279.

and shall have put him off day by day with promises, then if the creditor can once meet the debtor and succeed in drawing a circle round him, the latter must not pass out of this circle until he shall have satisfied the claim or given security for its discharge. If he in any other case presume to pass the circle he is punished with death as a transgressor against right and justice." In Northern India this circle is known as a *gururu* or *gaurua*, and a person who takes an oath stands within it or takes from inside an article which he claims. In one form of this ceremony the circle is made by an unmarried girl on the ground with calf's dung and in the centre is placed a vessel of water. If money is in dispute the amount claimed is placed in the water vessel by the defendant. The narrator tells a story to prove the efficacy of the rite. "My father owed a Kalwár one rupee and the Kalwár claimed five. The matter was brought before the tribal council, and the Kalwár swore to the five rupees upon the *gaurua*. Within an hour his boy, while playing behind the house, was carried off by a wolf He was rescued, but he was under the curse of the *gaurua*, and shortly after he put his finger into a rat-hole, was bitten by a snake, and died within the hour."[1]

Rings, bracelets, knotted strings.

From the same principle arises the belief in the magic virtue of the ring, the bracelet, and the knotted string. To begin with rings. A woman's nose ring has special respect paid to it, and for a stranger even to mention it is a breach of delicacy.[2] It is the symbol of married happiness, and is removed when the wearer becomes a widow. Among Muhammadans Shiah women remove their nose rings during the Muharram as a sign of mourning. A ring of *Kusa* grass is put on the finger during the most sacred ceremonies and at marriage. It represents an imperishable bond between the giver and the receiver, and is a symbol of the original blood covenant, which is an important element in the belief of all primitive people.[3] The idea of the magic power of the ring appears constantly in folklore. Thus,

[1] *North Indian Notes and Queries*, I, 61.
[2] Tod, *Annals*, I, 457.
[3] Trumbull, *Blood Covenant*, 65 : Lubbock, *Origin of Civilisation*, 25 : Tylor, *Early History*, 128 *sq.* : Jones, *Finger Ring Lore*, 91, *sqq.*

we have the ring placed in a sacred square and sprinkled with buttermilk, which gives immediately whatever the owner demands.[1] So in Somadeva Srídatta places a ring on the finger of the unconscious princess and she immediately revives: the disloyal wife here, as in the Arabian Nights, takes a ring from each of her lovers.[2] The same idea attaches to the bracelet, which is in close connection with the soul of the wearer. Such is the *chandanhár* or sandal-wood necklace of Chandan Rája, and Sodewá Bai is born with a golden necklace round her neck, concerning which her parents consulted the astrologers. They announced, " This is no common child : the necklace of gold about your daughter's neck contains your daughter's soul. Let it therefore be guarded with the utmost care : for if it were taken off and worn by another person she would die. "[3] The Máls of Birbhúm exchange necklaces at marriages,[4] and the princess Kalingasená wears a bracelet and necklace of lotus fibres to secure relief from the pains of love.[5] The same idea appears in the use of strings and knots. In Northern India a piece of bat's bone is tied by a string round the ankle as a remedy for rheumatism, and answers to the eelskin which is used for the same purpose in England.[6] In Ireland a strand of black wool is tied round the ankle, and a charm is recited to cure a sprain : a red string is tied round a child's neck in chincough and epilepsy.[7] In Hoshangábád a thread is tied round the ankle as an antidote to fever. If possible a bit of *ashtara* root should be fastened in the knot, and before tying it an oblation of butter is burnt before it. Similarly a peacock's feather tied on the ankle cures a wound.[8] In the Panjáb it is a charm against snakebite to smoke one of the tail feathers of a peacock in a tobacco pipe.[9] The Rájput father binds round the arm of his new born infant a root

---

[1] Temple, *Wideawake Stories*, 199.
[2] Tawney, *Katha Sarit Ságara*, I, 61 : II, 80 (Lane, *Arabian Nights*, I, 9).
[3] Miss Frere, *Old Deccan Days*, 230, 236.
[4] Risley, *Tribes and Castes*, II, 49.
[5] Tawney, *loc cit.*, I, 300.
[6] Crooke, *Rural Glossary* sv *Guriyá* : Henderson, *Folklore of Northern Counties*, 155 : Gregor, *Folklore of N.-E. Scotland*, 145.
[7] Lady Wilde, *Legends*, 195, 197, 199.
[8] *Settlement Report*, 278, 286.
[9] *North Indian Notes and Queries*, I, 15.

of that species of grass known as the *amardúb* or "imperishable" *dúb*, well known for its nutritive qualities and luxuriant vegetation, in the same way as Scotch women wear round their necks blue woollen threads or small cords until they wean their children.[1] We have already noticed the efficacy of various grasses as spirit scarers.

Further developements of the magic circle.

This belief in the efficacy of the magic circle accounts for a variety of other customs. Thus, in a family sacrifice among the Chakmas of Bengal round the whole sacrificial platform had been spun from the house mother's distaff a long white thread which encircled the altar, and then carried into the house, was held at its two ends by the good man's wife. Among the Haris at marriages, the right hand little finger of the bridegroom's sister's husband is pricked, and a few drops of blood allowed to fall on threads of jute which are rolled up in a tiny pellet. This the bridegroom holds in his hand while the bride attempts to snatch it from him. Her success in the attempt is deemed to be of good omen for the happiness of the marriage. Here we have a survival of descent in the female line, the blood covenant, and the magic influence of the cord all combined.[2] Connected with this is the belief in the forming a connection by knotting the magic string. Thus, among the Karans of Bengal the essential part of the marriage ceremony is believed to be the laying of the bride's right hand in that of the bridegroom and binding their two hands together with a piece of string spun in a special way.[3] This belief in knots is common to all folklore.[4] This accounts for the knotting together of the clothes of the bride and bridegroom in Northern India as they move round the sacred fire. A similar belief explains the wearing of the *janeú* or sacred thread by high caste Hindus. The knots on it, known as *Brahma granthi* or "the knots of the Creator," repel evil influences, and Muhammadans on their

[1] Tod, *Annals*, I, 415: Henderson, *Folklore of Northern Counties*, 20.
[2] Risley, *Tribes and Castes*, I, 173, 315.
[3] *Ibid.*, I, 425.
[4] Tawney, *Katha Sarit Ságara*, I, 576, quoting Lenormant *Chaldæan Magic and Sorcery*, 41: Ralston, *Songs of the Russian People*, 288.

birthdays tie knots in a cord which is known as the *sálgirah* or "year knot."

Face covering.

Another device is to cover the face which prevents the evil glance reaching its victim. Thus, at widow marriages in Northern India the bride and bridegroom are covered with a sheet during the ceremony, probably in order to avert the envious or malignant influence of the spirit of the woman's first husband: and the same belief is almost certainly at the root of much of the customs of *parda* or seclusion of women. It is as much through fear of fascination as modesty that women draw their sheet across the face when they meet a stranger in the streets.[1] We come across the same feeling in the rule by which all doors were closed when the princess in the Arabian Nights went to the bath, and when not long ago the Mikado of Japan and other eastern potentates took their walks abroad. We thus reach by another route the cycle of Godiva legends.

Omens.

Closely connected with the class of ideas which we have been discussing is the belief in omens. This constitutes a very important branch of Indian folklore. The success of a journey or enterprise is believed, in a great measure, to depend on the object which is seen first in the morning, or observed on the road at an early period of the march. Thus, the face of a Teli or oil maker, perhaps from the dirt which accompanies his business, is about the worst which can be seen in the early morning, but, with the curious inconsistency which crops up everywhere in phases of similar belief, that of a sweeper is lucky. His face should always be looked at first, but on meeting a Bráhman, the glance should start from his feet. The Thags, like all criminal tribes of the present day, were great believers in what Dr. Tylor calls *angang* or meeting omens.[2] With them if a wolf crossed the path from left to right, it was considered a bad omen: if from right to left the import was uncertain. The call of the wolf was considered ominous; if heard during the day, the gang had immediately to leave the neighbourhood. The same idea

[1] For numerous examples see Hartland, *Science of Fairy Tales*, 79, *sqq*.
[2] *Primitive Culture*, I, 120.

attached to a crow sitting silent on a tree, or a man having his turban knocked off by accidentally touching a branch. The jungle tribes have a strong belief in such omens. The Korwas of Mirzapur abandon a journey if a jackal cross the road from the right, or if a little bird known as the *suiya* or small parrot calls in the same direction. The Patáris and Majhwárs return if a *nílgái* cross the road from the right. All natives have more or less the same feeling, and scientific treatises have been compiled on the subject. Mentioning a monkey in the morning brings starvation for the rest of the day: though looking at its face only is deemed lucky. Hence monkeys are commonly tied in stables to protect horses, and an old adage says that "the evil of the stable is on the monkey's head." If a dog flaps its ears and shakes its head while any business is going on, disaster is sure to follow, and people careful in such matters will stop the work if they can. The baying of a dog at night indicates death and misfortune, an idea common to British folklore.[1] The Bengalis regard the twittering of the little house lizard as very unlucky and postpone a journey when it is heard.[2] The hare is always a bad omen. He is a god among the Kalmucs, who call him Sakya Muni or the Buddha, and say that on earth he allowed himself to be eaten by a starving man, for which gracious act he was raised to domineer over the moon, where they profess to see him. There are traces of the same idea in Upper India.[3] The sites of many cities are said to have been founded where a hare crossed the path of the first settler.[4] The hare is detested by the agricultural and fishing population of the Hebrides: and it is one of the usual disguises of the witch in European folklore.[5] Black is, of course, ill-omened, and if a man, when digging the foundations of a new house, turns up a piece of charcoal, it

---

[1] Henderson, *Folklore of the Northern Counties*, 48: Lady Wilde, *Legends*, 146, *sqq*.

[2] Lál Bihári De, *Govinda Samanta*, I, 12.

[3] Tawney, *Katha Sarit Ságara*, II, 66. It has been suggested the idea arose from the Sanskrit word *sasin*, meaning "hare marked" or "the moon," but this seems rather putting the cart before the horse: see Conway, *Demonology*, I, 125: Gubernatis, *Zoological Mythology*, II, 8: Aubrey, *Remaines*, 20, 109.

[4] For example, Lunáváda in Riwa Kantha. *Bombay Gazetteer*, VI, 126.

[5] Gregor, *Folklore of N.-E. Scotland*, 128: Lady Wilde, *Legends*, 179.

is advisable to change the site. Owls are also naturally of evil omen. Even the stout-hearted old Zálim Sinh, the famous regent of Kotah, abandoned his house because an owl hooted on the roof.[1] To see a Dhobi or washerman who is associated with foul raiment is exceedingly dangerous. I once had a bearer who was sadly afflicted because while on tour he had to sleep in the same tent with a Dhobi. The old man was constantly bruising his shins over the ropes and pegs because he was in the habit of stumbling out before dawn with his hands tightly pressed over his eyes to protect himself from the sight of his ill-omened companion. A one-eyed man is, as we have already said, very unlucky. When Jaswant Rao Holkar lost one eye he said, "I was before bad enough, but now I shall be the guru or preceptor of rogues."[2] I once had an office clerk afflicted in this way, and his colleagues refused to sit in the same room with him because their accounts always went wrong when he looked at them. When it was found impossible to provide any other accommodation for him, they insisted that he should cover the obnoxious organ with a handkerchief when he had to work in their neighbourhood. One of the last of the Anglo-Indians who had become thoroughly orientalized used to insist on his valet, when he came to wake him, holding in his hand a tray containing some milk and a gold coin, so that his first glance on waking might fall on these lucky articles.

Lucky and unlucky days and marks.

So there are days which are lucky and unlucky. A Persian couplet lays down that one should not go east on Saturday and Monday: west on Friday and Sunday: north on Tuesday and Wednesday: south on Thrsday. To avoid this some article is sent on in advance to a friend's house on the road and the journey is supposed to commence when it was sent. Even Akbar prescribed that the clothes which came on the first day of the month Farwardín were the most lucky.[3] So with moles and other marks on the body which have their significance. The idea widely prevails in Indian and

[1] Tod, *Annals*, II, 577, *sq*.
[2] Malcolm, *Central India*, I, 253, note.
[3] Blockmann, *Aín-i-Akbari*, I, 91

European folklore. The mark of the quoit or discus is emblematical of coming royalty.[1]

Effect of this belief.

The catalogue of these superstitions might be almost indefinitely extended. The principles on which most of them depend are clear enough. They rest on a sort of "sympathetic magic": things which are good looking, people who are healthy or prosperous, or who live by cleanly occupations give favourable omens: while those that are ugly, or of low caste, or associated with menial or unpleasant duties and so on, are ominous. Europeans in India usually quite fail to realize the influence which such ideas exercise over the people. Most of us have been struck by the almost unaccountable failure of natives to keep an appointment, to meet a European Officer for the inspection of a school or market, to attend a summons from the Courts. If enquiries are made it will often be found that some idea of the kind explains the matter. Thus Colonel Tod describes how he had a visit from Mánik Chand. "He looked very disconsolate and explained that he had seven times left his tent and as often turned back, the bird of omen having each time passed him on the adverse side: but that at length he had determined to disregard it, as having forfeited confidence he was indifferent to the future."[2]

Unlucky names and persons.

The same idea of good or evil omen attaches to many places and persons. "Nolai was built by Rája Nol. Its modern appellation of Barnagar has its origin in a strange, vulgar superstition of names of ill-omen, which must not be pronounced before the morning meal. The city is called either Nolai or Barnagar according to the hour at which the mention becomes necessary."[3] So with the town of Jammu in Kashmír, which is unlucky from its association with Yama, the god of death, with Talwára in the Hoshyárpur district, with Rohtak,

---

[1] Tawney, *Katha Sarit Ságara*, I, 469 (quoting Dyer, *English Folklore*, 280): 433: II, 376: I, 103, 105: II, 11.
[2] *Annals*, I, 694.
[3] Malcolm, *Central India*, I, 12, note.

which should be called Rustájgarh, and with numerous other places in Northern India.[1] So there is hardly a village in which it is not considered ominous to name before breakfast some one who from his misery, rascality, or some other reason is considered unlucky. In Mathura there is a tank built by Rája Patni Mall. "Should a stranger visit it in the morning and enquire of any Hindu by whom it was constructed, he will have considerable difficulty in eliciting a straightforward answer. The Rája, it is said, was of such a delicate constitution that he could never at any time take more than a few morsels even of the simplest food: hence arises the belief that any one who mentions him the first thing in the morning will, like him, have to pass the day fasting."[2] When we wonder at people suffering bondage of this kind we must not forget that similar beliefs prevail in our own country. "In Buckie there are certain family names which no fisherman will pronounce. The bann lies particularly heavy on Ross. Coull also bears it, but not to such a degree. The folks of that village talk of spitting out the bad name."[3]

Euphemism in regard to animals.

A similar euphemistic form of expression is often used in regard to animals. The Mirzapur Patáris, when they have to mention a monkey in the morning, call him *Hanumán* and the bear *jatari* or "he with the long hair," or *dím khaiya*, "the eater of white ants": the Pankas call the camel *lambghincha* or "long-necked." "I asked the Rája," says General Sleeman, "whether we were likely to fall in with any hares, making use of the term *khargosh* or 'ass-eared.'" "Certainly not," said the Rája, "if you begin by abusing them by such a name, call them *lambkanna* or 'long-eared' and you will get plenty."

Helps to the departing soul.

Leaving now the question of ghost scaring, we come to consider various means adopted to facilitate the journey of the departing soul, and to prevent it from returning as a malignant ghost to bring suffering,

[1] *Panjáb Notes and Queries*, I, 15, 87, 137; *North Indian Notes and Queries*, I, 137, 207: II, 28, 30, 66.
[2] Growse, *Mathura*, 128.
[3] Gregor, *Folklore of N.-E. Scotland*, 200 *sq.*

disease, or death on the survivors. First comes the placing of the dying man on the ground at the moment of dissolution. This is done, partly, as we have seen, through some feeling of the sanctity of Mother Earth, and, partly, that the spirit may meet with no obstruction in its passage through the air. Mr. Frazer has shown that customs based on this principle prevail widely.[1]

Lighting the spirit on its way.

Another device is to light the spirit on its way. Thus, when a Hindu dies, a lamp made of flour is placed in his hands to light his ghost to the realm of Yama. Devout people believe that the ghost takes three hundred and sixty days to make the journey, so an offering of that number of lamps is made. In order, also, to keep him on his way, in the case of a man, they feed a Bráhman, or if the deceased was a woman, a Bráhmani every day for a year. The lamps are lighted facing the south, and this is the only occasion on which this is done, because the south is the realm of death, and no one will sleep or have their house door opening toward that ill-omened quarter of the sky.

Keening.

Similarly the relations howl during the burial ceremonies, like keeners at an Irish wake, in order to scare evil spirits who would obstruct the progress of the ghost to his final home.[2]

Carrying corpse by special way.

Another plan is to carry out the corpse by a special way which is then barred up, so that it may not be able to find its way back. The same end is attained by carrying the corpse out feet foremost. Thus, Marco Polo writes, "Sometimes their sorcerers shall tell them that it is not good luck to carry the corpse out by the door; so they have to break a hole in the wall, and to draw it out that way when it is taken to the burning."[3] It is needless to say that the same custom prevails in

---

[1] *Contemporary Review*, XLVIII, 108: Gregor, *Folklore of N.-E. Scotland*, 206.
[2] See Spencer, *Principles of Sociology*, I, 153.
[3] *Marco Polo*, I, 208, with Yule's note.

Great Britain.[1] The Banjáras of Khándesh reverse the process. They move their huts after a death, and make a special entrance to be used instead of the ordinary door, which is supposed to be polluted by the passage of the spirit of the dead.[2] A somewhat similar custom prevails among the Maghs of Bengal. When the friends return from the cremation ground, if it is the master of the house who has died, the ladder leading up to the house is thrown down, and they must effect an entrance by cutting a hole in the back wall and so creeping up.[3]

Barring the return of the ghost.

The most careful precautions are, however, devoted to barring out the ghost and preventing its return to its original home. It is through fear of the spirit's return that Hindu mourners do not look back on their return from the cremation ground lest their souls should be detained among the spirits of the dead.[4] There are also physical obstructions placed in the way of the ghost. Thus in the Himálayas, when a man has attended the funeral ceremonies of a relative, he takes a piece of the shroud worn by the deceased, and hangs it on some tree near the cremation ground as an offering to the spirits which frequent such places. On his return, he places a thorny bush on the road wherever it is crossed by another path, and the nearest male relative of the deceased on seeing this, puts a stone on it, and pressing it down with his feet, prays the spirit of the dead man not to trouble them.[5] Among the Bengal Limbus the Phedangma attends the funeral, and delivers a brief address to the departed spirit on the general lot of mankind and the doom of birth and death, concluding with the command to go where his fathers have gone and not to come back to trouble the living with dreams.[6] Practically the same custom still prevails in Ireland. When a corpse

[1] Gregor, *loc. cit.* 206 : Frazer, *loc cit.* : Conway, *Demonology*, I, 53 : Farrer, *Primitive Manners*, 23.
[2] *Bombay Gazetteer*, XII, 107.
[3] Risley, *Tribes and Castes of Bengal*, II, 34.
[4] For examples, see Wilson, *Essays*, II, 292 : Spencer, *Principles of Sociology*, I, 147.
[5] Atkinson, *Himalayan Gazetteer*, II, 832 : for a similar practice among the Khonds, see Tylor, *Primitive Culture*, II, 126.
[6] Risley, *Tribes and Castes of Bengal*, II, 19.

is carried to the grave, it is the rule for the mourners to stop half-way while the nearest relatives build up a small monument of loose stones, and no hand would dare to touch or disturb this monument while the world lasts.[1]

Many other mourning customs appear to be based on analogous principles. In Upper India, among the lower Hindu castes, when the mourners return after the ceremony, they bathe, water being a scarer of ghosts, and at the house door they touch a stone, cow dung, iron, fire, and water, which have been placed outside the house in readiness when the corpse was removed. They then touch each their left ears with the little finger of the left hand, chew leaves of the bitter *ním* tree as a sign of mourning, and after sitting some time in silence disperse. This sitting in silence is commonly explained merely as a mark of sympathy for the bereaved relatives; but an analogous custom in Ireland leads to the inference that the real reason is to give the ghost time to depart, and not to interrupt its passage in any way. On the west coast of Ireland, after the death no wail is allowed to be raised until three hours have elapsed, because the sound of the crying would hinder the soul from speaking to God when it stands before him, and would waken up the great dogs that are watching for the souls of the dead to devour them.[1] The same idea of barring the return of the ghost by the agency of fire is found among the Nats of Káthiawár, who burn hay on the face of the corpse before burning it, and among the Thoris, who brand the great toe of the right foot of the deceased.[2]

We have in these ceremonies and in the ordinary ritual some further illustrations of the protective influences of various articles which scare evil spirits. Thus, after the cremation the officiating Bráhman touches fire and bathes in order to purify himself and bar the return of the ghost: and the relative who lights the funeral pyre, keeps a piece of iron with him, and goes about with a brass drinking vessel in his hand as a preservative against evil spirits

---

[1] Lady Wilde, *Legends*, 83.
[2] *Bombay Gazetteer*, VIII, 159.

while the period of mourning lasts. The system of protection is exactly the same as in the case of the young mother and her child during the period of impurity consequent on parturition. As the Hedley Kow, the North British goblin, is particularly obnoxious at childbirth, so the Rákshasí of Indian folklore carries off the baby if the suitable precautions to repell her are neglected.[1]

Other means of barring or keeping ghost.

Another method of barring the return of the ghost is to bury the dead face downwards. This is common among sweepers of Upper India, whose ghosts, as is seen in the probable connection between Chúhra and Churel, are always malignant. The same custom prevails among the Charan Banjárás of Khándesh.[2] With this may be contrasted the Irish custom of loosening the nails of the coffin before interment in order to facilitate the passage of the soul to heaven.[3] Similar to this is the plan pursued by the Mangars of Bengal: "One of the maternal relatives of the deceased, usually the maternal uncle, is chosen to act as priest for the occasion, and to conduct the ritual appointed for the propitiation of the dead. First of all he puts in the mouth of the corpse some silver coins and some coral, which is much prized by the Himalayan races. Then he lights a wick soaked in clarified butter, touches the lips with fire, scatters some parched rice about the mouth, and lastly, covers the face with a cloth. Two bits of wood, about three feet long, are set up on either side of the grave. In the one are cut nine steps or notches forming a ladder for the spirit of the dead to ascend to heaven; on the other every one present at the funeral cuts a notch to show that he has been there. As the maternal uncle steps out of the grave, he bids a solemn farewell to the dead, and calls upon him to ascend to heaven by the ladder that stands ready for him. When the earth has been filled in, the stick notched by the funeral party is

---

[1] Henderson, *Folklore of Northern Counties*, 14, 271: Tawney, *Katha Sarit Ságara*, I, 546, and generally for these protectives Tawney, *ibid.*, I, 305: Tylor, *Primitive Culture*, II, 194, *sq.*: 439 *sq.*: Frazer, *Contemporary Review*, XLVIII, 113: Grierson, *Behár Feasant Life*, 388: *Folklore*, II, 26: 294.

[2] *Bombay Gazetteer*, XII, 109. The Thags treated their victims in the same way. *Illustrations of the History and Practices of the Thags*, 9.

[3] *Folklore*, II, 26.

taken away to a distance and broken in two pieces, lest by its means the dead man should do the survivors a mischief. The pole used to carry the corpse is also broken up, and the spades and ropes are left in the grave."[1]

The tombstone and cairn.

The same idea of barring the return of the ghost accounts for the tombstone and cairn. British evil spirits have been secured in this way. Mr. Henderson tells of a vicious spirit which was entombed under a large stone for the space of ninety years and a day. Should any luckless person sit on that stone, he would be unable to quit it for ever.[2] When a Ho or Munda dies, a very substantial coffin is constructed and placed on faggots of brushwood. The body carefully washed and anointed with oil and turmeric is reverently laid in this coffin, and all the clothes, ornaments, and agricultural implements that the deceased was in the habit of using are placed with it, and also any money that he had about him when he died. Then the lid of the coffin is put on and the whole is burned. The bones are collected, taken in procession to the houses of friends, to his fields, and every place which the deceased was in the habit of visiting. They are finally buried under a large slab, and a megalithic monument is erected to the memory of the dead. A quantity of rice, cooked and uncooked, is thrown into the grave with other food.[3]

Laying of ghosts among Korkus.

The Korkus of Hoshangábád have a curious method of laying the ghost. "Each clan has a place in which the funeral rite of every member of that clan must be performed: and however far the Korku may have wandered from the original centre of his tribe, he must return there to set his father's spirit to rest, and enable it to join its own family and ancestral ghosts. In this spot a separate stake (*mundu*) is set up for every one whose rites are separately performed, and if a poor Korku performs them for several ancestors at once, he still puts up only one stake. It stands two or two and a half feet above the ground, planed

[1] Risley, *Tribes and Castes*, II, 75.
[2] *Loc. cit.*, 264.
[3] Dalton, *Descriptive Ethnology*, 202 *sq.*

smooth and squared at the top: on one side is carved at the top the likeness of the sun and moon, a spider, and a wheat ear, and below it a figure representing the principal person in whose honour it is put up, on horseback, with weapons in his hands. If more than one person's death is being celebrated, the rest are carved below as subordinate figures. I could not learn that the spirits are supposed to specially haunt this grove of stakes, or that Korkus have any dread of going near it at night; but they are far bolder than Hindus in this respect. When the funeral rite is to be performed, the first thing is to cut a bamboo and take out the pith which is to represent the bones of the deceased, unless he has been burnt, in which case the bones themselves will have been preserved. A chicken is then sacrificed on the grave, and all that night the mourners watch and dance, and sing and make merry. Next day they go out very early, and cut down some perfectly unblemished tree, either teak or *salui*, not hollow or decayed or marked with an axe, which they cut to make the *munda* stake. It is brought home at once and fashioned by a skilful man. In the afternoon it is taken to the place where cattle rest outside the village at noontide, and is washed and covered with turmeric like a bridegroom, and five chickens are sacrificed to it. It is then brought home again, and the pith representing the bones is taken outside the village and hung to some tree for safety during the night. [The idea, as we have elsewhere seen, is more probably to allow the ghost an opportunity of revisiting them.] All the friends and relations have by this time assembled, and this evening the chief funeral dinner is given. Next day the whole party set out for the place where the stakes of their clan are set up, and after digging a hole and putting two copper coins in it and the bones of the deceased or the pith which stands for them, they put the stake in and fix it upright. Then they offer a goat or chickens to it, which are presently eaten close by, and in the evening the whole party return home."[1] All these proceedings carried out by a most primitive tribe admirably illustrate the principles which have been already discussed.

[1] *Settlement Report*, 263, *sq.*

Similar customs prevail among other aboriginal races of the Central Provinces. In some places they burn their dead, and then erect platforms, at the corners of which they place tall, red stones. In other places a sort of low square mound is raised over the remains of the deceased, at the corners of which are erected wooden posts, round which thread is wound, and a stone is set up in the centre. Here offerings are presented as in the jungle worship of their deities, of rice and other grains, fowls, or sheep. On one occasion after the establishment of the Bhonsla or Mahratta Government in Gondwána, a cow was sacrificed to the manes of a Gond; but this having come to the notice of the authorities, the relations were publicly whipped, and all were interdicted from doing such an act again. To persons of more than usual reputation for sanctity offerings continue to be presented annually for many years after their decease. In the district of Bhandára rude collections of coarse earthenware in the shape of horses may be seen, which have accumulated from year to year on the tombs of such men.[1] The Pauariyas of Chota Nágpur bury their dead, except the bodies of their priests, which are carried on a cot into the forests, covered with leaves and branches, and kept there, the reason assigned being that if laid in the village cemetery, their ghosts are exceedingly troublesome. The bodies of people who die of contagious diseases are similarly disposed of.[2]

Customs among other aborigines.

In a country where immediate burial or cremation is necessary and habitual, we need not expect to meet with the customs, of which Mr. H. Spencer[3] gives examples, of placing the body on a platform or the like in order to secure its personal comfort and conciliate the spirit. But the Thárus of the sub-Himalayan Tárai have a custom of placing the corpse on the village fetish mound during the night after death, and then the mourning goes on. Among all Hindus, of course, as

Respect paid to corpse.

[1] Hislop, *Papers*, 19.
[2] Dalton, *Descriptive Ethnology*, 274.
[3] *Principles of Sociology*, I, 161.

far as the exigencies of rapid disposal of the remains permit, it is a general rule to treat the dead with respect: corpses are carefully covered with red cloth, and removed reverently for burial or cremation.

Fasting.

The custom of fasting as a sign of mourning has now disappeared, unless the final feast after the termination of the funeral ceremonies be regarded as a survival of the celebration of a close of a period of fasting. More probably, however, it is based on the principle that evil spirits are repelled by cooked food. Fasting is generally believed to bring on preternatural excitement, which is regarded as inspiration, and it is supposed to induce what is technically known as *laghima* or independence of the laws of gravitation.[1]

Mutilation.

Similarly the only distinct survival of the ceremonial mutilation, so common among savages as a sign of mourning, is the shaving which is compulsory on all the clansmen who have shared in the death pollution.[2] This ceremonial shaving is also perhaps the only survival in Northern India of the puberty initiation ceremonies. The hair cut appears to be regarded as a sacrifice. Between the ages of two and five the Bhíls shave the heads of their children. The child's aunt takes the hair in her lap, and wrapping it in her clothes, receives a cow, buffalo, or other present from the child's parent.[3] The hair is in fact, as in the Samson-Delilah story, regarded as embodying the strength of its owner. This is perhaps the idea at the basis of our custom of keeping hair as a relic of the dead in lockets and bracelets. In the folk tales an important form of the *deus ex machinâ* is hair, human for choice, but any kind will do.[4] One curious instance of mutilation regarded as a charm may be quoted from Bengál. Should a woman give birth to several still-born children

---

[1] Tylor, *Primitive Culture*, II, 410, *sqq.*: Spencer, *Principles of Sociology*, I, 261 *sq.*: Monier Williams, *Religious Life*, 428. A list of Hindu fasts is given in *Panjáb Notes and Queries*, III, 56.
[2] Spencer, *loc. cit.*, I, 163, *sq.*: 267.
[3] *Bombay Gazetteer*, III, 220.
[4] Temple, *Wideawake Tales*, 414: *Legends of the Panjáb*, I, Intro., XIX: *Folklore*, II, 236.

in succession, the popular belief is that the same child re-appears on each occasion, when, to frustrate the designs of the evil spirit that has taken possession of the child, the nose or a portion of an ear is cut off and the body is cast away on a dunghill.[1]

Food for the dead.

Another means for conciliating the spirit of the deceased is to lay up food for its use. This is a custom very common among primitive races.[2] The Hos told Colonel Dalton that the reason of this was that they were unwilling to derive any immediate benefit by the death of a member of the family. Hence they burn his wearing apparel and personal effects, but they do not destroy clothes and other things which have not been worn. For this reason old men of the tribe, in a spirit of careful economy, avoid wearing new clothes, so that they may not be wasted at the funeral.[3] The custom still survives in Ireland, where it is a very prevalent custom during some nights after a death to leave food outside the house—a griddle cake or a dish of potatoes. If it is gone in the morning, the spirits must have taken it, for no human being would touch the food left for the dead. On November Eve food is also laid out in the same way.[4] There are numerous instances of similar practices in India. The Khándesh Mhárs, when they remove a corpse, put in its mouth *pán* leaf with a gold bead from his wife's necklace. At the grave the brother or son of the dead man wets the end of his turban and drops a little water on the dead man's lips.[5] In the Panjáb it is a common practice to put into the mouth of a corpse the *pancharatna* or five jewels—gold, silver, coral, copper, and pewter. The leaves of the sweet basil (*tulasi*) and Ganges water are put into the mouth of a dying man, and the former into the ears and nostrils also. These are said to be offerings to Yama, god of death, who on receiving them, shows mercy to the soul of the deceased.[6] The same

[1] Risley, *Tribes and Castes*, I, 211.
[2] Spencer, *op. cit.* I, 157, 206: Tylor, *Primitive Culture*, I, 482: Lubbock. *Origin of Civilization*, 37: Farrer, *Primitive Manners*, 21, *sq.*
[3] *Descriptive Ethnology*, 205.
[4] Lady Wilde, *Legends*, 118, 140.
[5] *Bombay Gazetteer*, XII, 118.
[6] *North Indian Notes and Queries*, I, 16.

customs generally prevail among Hindus in Northern India. Among the Buddhists of the Himalaya Moorcroft was present at the consecration of the food for the dead. The Lama consecrated barley and water and poured them from a silver saucer into a brass basin, occasionally striking two brass cymbals together, reciting or chanting prayers, to which an inferior Lama from time to time uttered responses aloud, accompanied by the rest in an under tone. This was intended for the use of the souls in hell, who would starve were it not provided.[1] The Mirzapur Korwas, when burning a corpse, place with it the ornaments and clothes of the deceased, and an axe. This they do not break, as other savages often do. They say that the spirit of the dead man will want it to hack his way through the jungles of the other world. When the Bhuiyárs cremate a corpse they throw near the spot an axe if the deceased was a man, and a *khurpi* or weeding spud if a woman. No one would dare to appropriate such things. Where the corpse is burned they leave a platter made of leaves containing a little boiled rice, and they sprinkle on the ground all the ordinary kinds of grain and some turmeric and salt as food for the dead in the next world. All these tribes and many low caste Hindus in Upper India lay out platters of food under the eaves of the house during the period of mourning, and they ascertain by particular marks which they examine next day whether the spirit has partaken of the food or not. Among the jungle tribes there is a rule that the food for the dead is prepared not by the house mother, but by the senior daughter-in-law, and even if incapacitated by illness from performing this duty, she is bound at least to commence the work by cooking one or two cakes, and the rest are prepared by one of the junior women of the family. Among the more Hinduised Majhwárs and Patáris we reach the stage where the clothes, implements of the deceased, and some food are given to the Patári priest, who, by vicariously consuming them, lays up a store for the use of the dead man in the other world. This is the principle on which food and other things are given to the Mahábrahman or ordinary Hindu funeral

[1] Moorcroft and Trebeck, *Travels in the Himalaya*, I, 342.

priest at the close of the period of mourning. So among the Bhumij of Bengal, at the funeral ceremony, an outsider who is often a Láya or priest comes forward to personate the deceased, by whose name he is addressed, and asked what he wants to eat. Acting thus as the dead man's proxy, he mentions various articles of food which are placed before him. After making a regular meal he goes away, and the spirit of the deceased is believed to go with him. So among the Chakmas a bamboo post or some other portion of a dead man's house is burned with him, probably in order to provide him with shelter in the next world. Among the Kámis, before they can partake of the funeral feast, a small portion of every dish must be put on a leaf plate and taken out into the jungle for the spirit of the dead man, and carefully watched until a fly or other insect settles on it. The watcher then covers up the plate with a slab of stone, eats his own food, which he brings with him to the place, and returns to tell the relatives that the dead man's spirit has received the offering set for him. The fly here represents the spirit,—an idea very common in folklore, where an insect often represents the life index. An English lady has been known to stop playing lawn tennis because a butterfly settled on the court. The Mál Pahariyas pour the blood of goats and fowls of their ancestral monumental pillars that the souls may not hunger in the world of the dead.[1] In the same way the *ghant* or water vessel hung by Hindus on a *pipal* tree after a death is intended to refresh the soul on its journey to the other world.

Recalling the ghost.

But while it is expedient by some or other of these devices to bar or lay the ghost, or prevent its return by providing for its journey to, and accommodation in, the next world, some tribes have a custom of making arrangements to bring back the soul of the deceased to the family abode, where he is worshipped as a household spirit. Some of the Central Indian tribes catch the spirit re-embodied in a fowl or fish, some bring it home in a pot of water and flour.[2] Among the

[1] Risley, *Tribes and Castes*, I, 126: 174, 395: II, 71.
[2] Tylor, *Primitive Culture*, II, 152.

Tipperahs of Bengal, when a man dies in a strange village separated from his home by a river, they stretch a white string from bank to bank along which the spirit is believed to return.[1] This illustrates an idea common to all folklore that the ghost cannot cross running water without some material assistance. Among the Hos on the evening of the cremation day certain preparations are made in anticipation of a visit from the ghost. Some boiled rice is laid apart for it, and ashes are sprinkled on the floor, in order that should it come, its footsteps may be detected. On returning they carefully scrutinise the ashes and the rice, and if there is the faintest indication of these having been disturbed it is attributed to the action of the spirit, and they sit down shivering with horror and crying bitterly, as if they were by no means pleased with the visit though it be made at their earnest solicitation.[2]

Use of ashes in ghost finding.

This use of ashes, as a means of identifying the ghost, constitutes in itself quite an important chapter in folklore. It reminds us of the Apochryphal legend of Bel and the Dragon.[3] The idea probably arises from the respect paid to the ashes of the house fire by primitive races among whom the hearth and the kitchen are the home of the household godlings. So in Manxland the ashes are carefully swept to the open hearth and nicely flattened down by the women before going to bed. In the morning they look for foot marks on the hearth, and if they find such footmarks directed to the door, it means in the course of the year a death in the family, and if the reverse they expect an addition to it by marriage. In Ireland similar omens are taken on May Eve by sprinkling ashes on the threshold.[4] So at the annual feast of the dead, the jungle tribes of Mirzapur spread ashes on the floor, and a mark generally like that of a chicken's foot shows that the family ghosts have visited the house. "On New Year's Eve," says Aubrey, "sift or smoothe the ashes and leave it so when you go to bed : next morning look, and if you find there

---

[1] Risley, *Tribes and Castes*, II, 326.
[2] Dalton, *Descriptive Ethnology*, 204, *sq.*
[3] I, 14 : see Tylor, *loc. cit.*, II, 197.
[4] *Folklore*, II, 310 : Lady Wilde, *Legends*, 105.

the likeness of a coffin, one will die; if a ring, one will be married."[1] In North Scotland, on the night after the funeral bread and water were placed in the apartment where the body lay. The dead man was believed to return that night and partake of the food; unless this were done, the spirits could not rest in the unseen world. This probably accounts for the so-called "food vases" and "drinking cups" found in the long barrows.[2] All Hindus believe that the ghosts of the dead return on the night of the Diwálí or feast of lamps.

Replacing of household earthen vessels.

After a death all the household earthen pots are broken and replaced. It has been suggested that this is due either to the belief that the ghost of the dead man is in some of them: or the custom may have some connection with the idea of providing the ghost with utensils in the next world.[3] In popular belief, however, the custom is explained by the death pollution attaching to all the family cooking utensils, which, if of metal, are purified with fire. The same idea prevailed among the Hebrews, among whom an earthen vessel remaining in a tent in which a person died was considered to be unclean for seven days.[4]

Cremation in effigy.

When a person dies at a distance from home, and it is impossible to perform the funeral rites over the body, it is cremated in effigy. The special term for this is *Kusaputra* or son of the *Kusa* grass. Colonel Tod relates an instance of a similar ceremony when King Ummeda of Búndi abdicated. "An image of the prince was made, and a pyre was erected on which it was consumed The hair and whiskers of Ajít, his successor, were taken off and offered to the Manes: lamentations and wailing were heard in the Queen's apartments, and the twelve days of mourning were passed as if Ummeda had

---

[1] *Remaines*, 95: Henderson, *Folklore of the Northern Counties*, 57.
[2] Gregor, *Folklore of N.-E. Scotland*, 213.
[3] Frazer, *Contemporary Review*, XLVIII, 117: Spencer, *Principles of Sociology*, I, 195.
[4] *Numbers*, XIX, 15.

really deceased: on the expiration of which the installation of his successor took place."[1]

Measuring of corpses.

Ghosts, as we have already remarked in the case of the Naugaza, have the powers of lengthening themselves. Some can grow to the length of ten yojanas or eighty miles,—a faculty which reminds us of the Ifrít of the Arabian Nights. In one of the Bengal tales a ghost is identified because she was able to stretch out her hands several yards for a vessel.[2] Such ghosts possess the very dangerous power of entering human corpses, like the Vetála, and swelling to an enormous size. The Kharwárs of Mirzapur have a wild legend how long ago an unmarried girl of the tribe died and was being cremated. While the relations were collecting wood, a ghost entered the corpse, but the friends managed to expel him: since then great care is taken not to leave the bodies of women unwatched. So in the Panjáb, when a great person is cremated, the bones and ashes are carefully watched till the fourth day, to prevent a magician interfering with them. If he has a chance he can restore the deceased to life, and ever after retain him under his influence. But the best plan is, if the corpse cannot be immediately disposed of, to measure it carefully, and then no malignant Bhút can occupy it. We have already met with instances of mystic effect supposed to follow on measuring or weighing grain.

Friendly ghosts.

Most of the ghosts whom we have been already considering are malignant. There are, however, others, which, like our Robin Goodfellow, Puck or Brownie or the Phouka or Leprehaun of Ireland, are friendly. Such, in one of his many forms, is the Brahmadaitya or ghost of a Bráhman who has died unmarried. He appears to be about the only respectable bachelor ghost. In one of the folk tales a ghostly reaper of this class assists his human friend, and can cut as much of the crop in a minute as an ordinary person can in a day. This

---

[1] *Annals*, II, 542.
[2] Lál Bihári De, *Folk Tales of Bengal*, 198, 274: Lane, *Arabian Nights*, I, 71.

Brahmadaitya is the leader of the other ghosts; he lives in a tree, and, unlike other varieties of Bhúts, does not eat all kinds of food, but only such as are considered ceremonially pure. He never, like common Bhúts, frightens men, this being considered beneath his dignity, but is harmless and quiet, never injuring benighted travellers, nor entering into the bodies of living men or women: but if his dignity be insulted or any one trespass on his domains, he wrings their necks. Hence in regard to trees great caution is required. A Hindu will never climb one of the varieties of fig, the *ficus cordifolia,* except through dire necessity, and if a Bráhman is forced to ascend the *bel* tree or *ægle marmelos* for the purpose of obtaining the sacred trefoil so largely used in Siva worship, he only does so after offering prayers to the gods in particular and to the Brahmadaitya in particular who may have taken up his abode in that special tree.[1] These tree ghosts are, it is needless to say, very numerous. Hence most local shrines are constructed under trees; and in one particular tree, the *bíra,* the jungle tribes of Mirzapur localize Bágheswar, the tiger god, one of their most dreaded deities. These divinities who reside in trees are of various kinds and appear constantly in folklore. Thus, Devadatta worships a tree which one day suddenly clave open and a nymph appeared, who introduced him inside the tree, where was a heavenly palace of jewels, in which, reclining on a sofa, appeared Vidyatprabhá, the maiden daughter of the king of the Yakshas: and in another story the mendicant hears inside a tree a Yaksha joking with his wife.[2]

Malignant Bráhman ghosts.

But there is another variety of Bráhman ghost, who is much dreaded. Such is the Brahmaparusha or Brahma Rákshasa. In one of the folk tales he appears black as soot, with hair yellow as the lightning, looking like a thunder-cloud. He had made himself a wreath of entrails: he wore a sacrificial cord of hair: he was gnawing the flesh of a man's head and drinking blood out of a skull. In another story these

[1] Lál Bihári De, *Folk Tales of Bengal,* 198, 206: *Govinda Samanta,* I, 135.
[2] Tawney, *Katha Sarit Ságara,* I, 229: II, 116, who quotes other authorities: Tylor, *Primitive Culture,* I, 476: II, 148, 215.

Brahma Rákshasas have formidable tusks, flaming hair, and insatiable hunger. They wander about the forests catching animals and eating them.[1] Mr. Campbell tells a Marhatta legend of one of these who became a Brahma parusha in order to teach grammar to a pupil. He haunted a house at Benares, and a pupil went to take lessons from him. He promised to teach him the whole science in a year on condition that he never left the house. One day the boy went out and learned that the house was haunted, and that he was being taught by a ghost. The boy returned and was ordered by the preceptor to take his bones to Gaya, and perform the necessary ceremonies for the emancipation of his soul. This he did and the uneasy spirit of the learned man was laid.[2] We have already encountered similar angry Bráhman ghosts, such as Harsha Pánre and Mahení.

The Ják, Jákni, Chordeva, Chordeví.

The really friendly agricultural sprites are the pair known in some places as Ják and Jákní, and in others as Chordeva and Chordeví. Chordeva means "the thief godling." With the Ják we come on another of those curious survivals from the older mythology in a sadly degraded form. As Varuna, the god of the firmament, who has been reduced in these latter days to Barun, a petty weather godling, so the Ják is the modern representative of the Yaksha who in better times was the attendant on Kuvera, the god of wealth, in which duty they are assisted by the Guhyakas. In the folk tales the Yakshas, it must be admitted, have an equivocal reputation. In one story the female or Yakshiní bewilders travellers at night, makes horns grow on their foreheads, and finally devours them: in another the Yakshas have, like the Churel, feet turned the wrong way and squinting eyes: in a third they separate the hero from the heroine because he failed to make due offerings to them on his wedding day. On the other hand, in a fourth tale the Yakshiní is described as possessed of heavenly beauty; she appears again when a sacrifice is made in a cemetery to get her into the hero's power as a heavenly maiden beautifully adorned, seated in a chariot of gold,

[1] Tawney, *loc. cit.*, II, 338, 511.
[2] Campbell, *Notes*, 146, *sq.*

surrounded by lovely girls: and lastly, a Bráhman meets some Buddhist ascetics, performs the Uposhana vow, and would have been born a god had it not been that a wicked man compelled him by force to take food in the evening, and so he was re-born as a Guhyaka. The heroes rescue him, he becomes a god, and gives his preservers the boon of inexhaustible wealth.[1] In the modern folklore of Kashmír, the Yaksha has turned into the Yech or Yách, a humorous though powerful spirit in the shape of a civet cat of a dark colour with a white cap on its head. Its feet are so small as to be almost invisible, and it squeaks in a feline way. It can assume any shape, and if its white cap can be secured, it becomes the servant of the possessor, and the white cap makes him invisible. In the Vishnu Purána we read that Vishnu created the Yakshas as beings emaciate with hunger, of hideous aspect, and with long beards, and that from their habit of crying for food they were so named.[3] By the Buddhists they were sometimes regarded as benignant spirits. One of them acts as a sort of chorus in the Meghadúta or "Cloud Messenger" of Kalidása. Yet we read of the Yaka Alawaka, who, according to the Buddhist legend, used to live in a banyan tree, and slay any one who approached it: while in Ceylon they are represented as the demons whom Buddha destroyed.[4] In later Hinduism they are generally of fair repute, and one of them was appointed by Indra to be the invisible attendant of the Jaina Saint Mahávíra.[5]

Benevolent field sprites.

At any rate the modern Ják and Jákní, Chordeva and Chordevi are eminently respectable and kindly sprites. The Ják is condemned to live apart from the Jkní in adjoining villages, but he is an uxorious husband, and robs his own village to supply the wants of his consort. So if you see a comparatively barren village, which is next to one more productive, you may be sure that the Ják lives in the former and the Jákní

[1] Tawney, *Katha Sarit Ságara*, I, 337, 204: II, 427: I, 467: II, 83.
[2] Temple, *Wideawake Stories*, 317: *Indian Antiquary*, XI, 260, *sq.*
[3] As if from *jaksh* "to eat": a more probable derivation is *yaksh* "to move, to worship."
[4] Spence Hardy, *Manual of Buddhism*, 269: Conway, *Demonology*, I, 151, *sq.*
[5] Wilson, *Essays*, I, 293. It is curious that in Gujarát the term Yaksha is applied to Musalmans, and in Cutch to a much older race of northern invaders. *Bombay Gazetteer*, V, 133, 236.

in the latter. The same is the character of the Chor or Chordeva and the Chorní or Chordeví of the jungle tribes of Mirzapur.

Benevolent cattle godlings.

In the hills there are various benevolent ghosts or godlings who protect cattle. Such is Nagardeo in Garhwál, who is represented in nearly every village by a three-pronged pike (*trisúla*) on a platform. When cows and buffaloes are first milked, the milk is offered to him. So with Chaumú or Baudhán. He has a shrine in almost every village, and every one is supposed to see that these places are kept clean and holy. Lamps are lighted, sweetmeats and the first fruits of cattle offered. When a calf dies the milk of the mother is considered unholy till the twelfth day, when some is offered to the deity. He also recovers lost animals, if duly propitiated, but if neglected, he brings disease on the herd.[1] Another cattle god in the hills is Kalbisht or Kaluva, who lived on earth some two hundred years ago. His enemies persuaded his brother-in-law to kill him. After his death he became a benevolent spirit, and the only people he injured were the enemies who compassed his death. His name is now a charm against wild beasts, and people who are oppressed resort to his shrine for justice.[2]

Children's bugaboos.

We close this long catalogue of ghostly personages with those who are merely bugaboos to frighten children. Such are Hawwa, probably a corruption through the Prákrit of the Sanskrit *bhúta*, and Humma or Húmu, the ghost of the Emperor Humayun, who died an untimely death. They are to Bengáli matrons what Old Scratch and Red Nose and Bloody Bones are to English mothers.[3] Akin to these is Ghoghar, which represents *ghugghu* or the hooting of the owl:[4] Nekí Bíbí or "the good lady": Máno or the cat: Bhákur: Bhokaswa: and Dokarkaswa "the old man with the bag," who carries off naughty children, who is the Mr. Miacca of the English nursery.[5]

---

[1] *North Indian Notes and Queries*, I, 56: Atkinson, *Himalayan Gazetteer*, II, 833.

[2] Atkinson, *loc. cit.*, II, 828.

[3] Henderson, *Folklore*, 253: Aubrey, *Remaines*, 59.

[4] In Bombay Ghoghar takes the form of a native seaman or lascar. *Gazetteer*, IV, 343.

[5] Jacobs's *English Fairy Tales*.

CHAPTER VII.

TREE AND SERPENT WORSHIP.

Sylvarum numina, Fauni.

Et Satyri fratres.

OVID METAMORP., iii, 163.

Αυτὰϱ ἐπ' ἄυτοῦ
Κυάνεος ἐλέλικτο δράκων, κεφαλαὶ δέ οἵ ἦσαν
Τρεῖς ἀμφιστρεφέες, ἑνὸς αὐχένος ἐκπεφυυῖαι.

ILIAD, xi, 38—40.

The worship of trees and serpents may be conveniently considered together: not that there is much connection between these two classes of belief, but because this course has been followed in Mr. Ferguson's elaborate monograph on the subject.

Basis of tree worship, various theories.

The worship of trees appears to be based on many converging threads of thought, which it is not easy to disentangle. Mr. H. Spencer[1] classes it as an aberrant species of ancestor worship. "A species somewhat more disguised externally, but having the same internal nature: and though it develops in three different directions, still these have all one common origin. First, the toxic excitements produced by certain plants are attributed to the agency of spirits or demons: secondly, tribes that have come out of places characterised by particular trees or plants, unawares change the legend of emergence from them into the legend of descent from them: thirdly, the naming of individuals after plants becomes a source of confusion." According to Dr. Tylor,[2] again, the worship depends on man's animistic theory of nature. "Whether such a tree is looked on as inhabited like a man by its own proper life and soul, or as possessed

[1] *Principles of Sociology*, I, 359.
[2] *Primitive Culture*, II, 221, *sq.*

like a fetish by some other spirit which has entered it and used it for a body, is often hard to determine." "The tree may be the spirit's perch or shelter (as we have seen is the case with the Churel or Rákshasa), or the sacred grove is assumed to be the spirits' resort."

Summary.

The basis of the cultus of trees may then perhaps be stated as follows—There is, first, the respect paid to memorial trees, where the people assemble, as at the village pípal, which is valued for its shade and beauty and its long connection with the social life of the community. This would naturally be regarded as the abode of some god and forms the village shrine, a convenient centre for the religious worship of the local deities, where they reside and accept the offerings of their votaries. It may again be the last survival of the primeval forest where the dispossessed spirits of the jungle find their last and only resting place. Such secluded groves form the only and perhaps the earliest shrine of many primitive races.[1] Secondly, an allegorical meaning would naturally be attached to various trees. It is invested with a mystic power owing to the mysterious waving of its leaves and branches, the result of superhuman agency: and this would account for the weird sounds of the forest at night. It is an emblem of life, reproducing itself in some uncanny fashion with each recurring spring. It has some mystic connection with the three worlds—

Quantum vertice ad auras
Ætherias tantum radice in Tartara tendit.

Like Yggdrassil, it connects the world of man with the world of gods, and men may, like Jack of the Bean Stalk, climb by its aid to heaven. Thirdly, it embodies in itself many utilities necessary to human life and many qualities which menace his existence. Its wood is the source of fire, itself a fetish. Its fruit, flowers or bark are sources of food or possess intoxicating or poisonous attributes, which are naturally connected with demoniacal influences. Fourthly, trees often develop into curious or uncanny forms which compel fear or adoration. Thus, according to the old ritual, trees

[1] This is discussed at length by Frazer, *Golden Bough, passim.*

which have been struck by lightning, or knocked down by inundations, or which have fallen in the direction of the south, or which grew on a burning ground or consecrated site, or at the confluence of large rivers or by the roadside; those which have withered tops or an entanglement of heavy creepers upon them, or are the receptacles of many honey-combs or birds' nests, are reckoned unfit for the fabrication of bedsteads, as they are unauspicious and sure to bring on disease or death.[1] The step from such beliefs to the worship of any curious or remarkable tree as a fetish is easy

Connected with phallicism.

Though this branch of the theory has been pushed to quite an unreasonable length in some recent books,[2] there may be some association with phallic worship, such as is found in the Asherah or "groves" of the Hebrews, the European Maypole, and so on. This has been suggested as an explanation of the honour paid by the great gypsy class of Germany to the fir-tree, the birch and the hawthorn, and of the veneration paid by the Welsh gypsies to the fascinated vegetable growth known to them as the *broado koro.*[3] In the same way, possibly on this principle, the *bel* tree is connected with the Saiva worship of the *lingam* and the lotus with the *yoni.* But this part of the subject has been involved in so much crude speculation that any analogies of this kind, however tempting, must be accepted with the utmost caution.

Connected with totemism.

Further than this, it may be reasonably suspected that this cultus rests to some extent on a basis of totemism. Some of the evidence in support of this view will be discussed elsewhere: but it is on the analogy of the various modes in which the Bráhmanic pantheon has been created, not improbable that trees or plants like the *tulasi* or the *pípal* may have been originally tribal totems imported into Hinduism

---

[1] *Brihat Sanhita* quoted by Rajendra Lala Mitra: *Indo-Aryans*, I, 245. The Indian evidence does not seem to support Mr. Grant Allen's belief in his *Attis* that trees were revered because they spring from the ashes of the dead.

[2] Forlong, *Rivers of Life*: Westropp, *Primitive Symbolism*.

[3] Groome, *Encyclopædia Britannica*, 9th edition. sv. *Gipsies*.

from some foreign source. On the whole, it is tolerably certain that there is more in tree worship than can be accounted for either by Mr. Ferguson's theory that the worship sprang from a perception of the beauty or utility of trees, or by Mr. Spencer's theory of nicknames. It is sufficient to say that both fail to account for the worship of insignificant and comparatively useless shrubs, weeds or grasses.

Popular tree worship.

Tree worship holds an important part in the popular ritual and in folklore. This is, in the first place, shown by the prejudice against cutting trees and the belief that planting them is meritorious—both of which ideas prevail widely. The jungle tribes are very averse to cutting certain trees, particularly those which are regarded as sacred. If a Kharwár cuts his tribal tree, the *karama,* he loses wealth and life, and none of these tribes will cut the large *sál* trees which are fixed by the Baiga as the abode of the forest godling. This feeling prevails very strongly among the Maghs of Bengal. Nothing but positive orders and the presence of Europeans would make them trespass on many hilltops regarded by them as occupied by the tree demons. With the Europeans, however, they would advance fearlessly, and did not hesitate to fell the trees, the blame of such sacrilege being always laid on the strangers. On felling any large tree, one of the party was always ready prepared with a green sprig, which he ran and placed in the centre of the stump when the tree fell, as a propitiation to the spirit which had been displaced so roughly, pleading at the same time the orders of the strangers for the work. In clearing one spot an orderly had to take the dáh or cleaver and fell the first tree himself before a Magh would make a stroke, and was considered to bear all the odium of the work with the disturbed spirits, till the arrival of the Europeans relieved him of the burden.[1]

The tree in folklore.

So in folklore we have constantly recurring the Kalpataru or Kulpadruma, one of the trees of Swarga or Indra's paradise, which grants all desires.

[1] *Calcutta Review,* XXVI, 512.

The king Jímútaketu had one in his house which came down from his ancestors, and was known as "the giver of desires": the generous Induprabha craved a boon from Indra, and became a wishing tree in his own city: and the faithful minister of Yasaketu sees a wave rise out of the sea and then a wishing tree appear, "adorned with boughs glittering with gold, which were embellished with sprays of coral, and bore lovely fruits and flowers of jewels. And he beheld on its trunk a maiden, alluring on account of her wonderful beauty, reclining on a gem-bestudded couch."[1] So in the story of Devadatta, the tree is cloven and a heavenly nymph appears: in another we have a tree like that in the Odyssey which bears fruit and flowers at the same time: and in a third, a link of connection between tree and serpent worship, the great palace of the snake king is situated under a solitary *asoka* tree in the Vindhyan forest.[2] In the same collection of folktales we meet continually instances of tree worship. The Bráhman Somadatta worships a great *Asvattha* or fig-tree by walking round it so as to keep it on his right, bowing and making an oblation: Mrigánkadatta takes refuge in a tree sacred to Ganesa: and Naraváhanadatta comes to a sandal-tree surrounded with a platform made of precious jewels, up which he climbs by means of ladders and adores it.[3] In the more modern collections we have the tree or plant which talks. The mango tree shows the hero how the magic bird is to be cut out of it: the heroine is blessed and aided by a plantain, cotton tree and sweet basil; she is rewarded by a plum and fig-tree for services rendered to them.[4] We have besides a long series of legends by which certain famous trees are supposed to have been produced from the tooth twig of some saint. Such are those at Ludhiána attributed to Abdul Qádir Jiláni, the Buddha tree at Saketa and the great banyan at Broach, which was similarly produced by Kabír.[5]

---

[1] Tawney, *Katha Sarit Ságara*, I, 174: II, 181, 592, 286.
[2] *Ibid.*, I, 229, 480 (*Odyssey*, VII, 117): II, 149.
[3] *Ibid.*, I, 153: II, 387, 460.
[4] Temple, *Wideawake Stories*, 413.
[5] *North Indian Notes and Queries*, I, 4, 37: *Bombay Gazetteer*, II, 355.

Sacred groves.

Next come the numerous sacred groves scattered all over the country. These, as we have seen, are very often regarded as a survival from the primeval jungle, where the forest spirits have taken refuge. The idea is common to the Aryan as well as the aboriginal races, from the latter of whom it was almost certainly derived. Thus among the jungle races we find that there are many sacred groves known as *Sarna,* in which the Cheros and Kharwárs offer triennial sacrifices of a buffalo or other animal. The Kisáns, again, have sacred groves called *Sá.* The Mundári Kols keep "a fragment of the original forest, the trees in which have been for ages carefully protected, left when the clearance was first made, lest the sylvan gods of the place, disgusted at the wholesale felling of the trees which protected them, should abandon the locality. Even now if a tree is destroyed in the sacred grove, the gods evince their displeasure by withholding seasonable rain." Among the Kols, in these groves the tutelary deities of the village are supposed to sojourn when attending to the wants of their votaries.[1] In the Central Provinces the Badiyas worship the manes of their ancestors in a grove of sáj trees.[2] In Berár the wood of the Pathrot forests is believed to be dedicated to a neighbouring temple, and no one will cut or buy it: and in other places in the same province the sacred groves are so carefully preserved, that during the annual festivals held in them it is the custom to collect and burn solemnly all dead and fallen branches and trees.[3] The same feelings attach to the holy groves of Mathura, each of which has appropriated one of the legends of the Krishna Myth. Thus there is a particularly sacred grove at Bhadanwára, and it is believed that any one violating the sanctity of the place by telling a lie within its precincts will be stricken with leprosy. In another at Hasanpur Bara the trees are under the protection of the curse of a Faqír, and in many places people object to having toddy collected from the palm trees because it necessitates cutting their necks.[4] The

[1] Dalton, *Descriptive Ethnology*, 129, 132, 141, 186, 188.
[2] Hislop, *Papers*, 20.
[3] *Berar Gazetteer*, 28, 31.
[4] Growse, *Mathura*, 70, 76 *sqq.*: 83, 420, 470, 458.

maintenance and preservation of these little patches of the primeval jungle, with a view to conciliate the sylvan spirits of the place, are exactly analogous to what is known in Scotland as the "Gudeman's croft," "Cloutie's croft," or "Gudeman's field." Often in Northern India little patches are left uncultivated in the corners of fields as a refuge for the spirits, as in North Scotland many farmers leave a corner of the field untilled, and say it is for the "Aul man" or Devil.[1]

Trees connected with persons and places.

Some trees are, again, considered to be mystically connected with the fortunes of people and places. Thus the *chilbil* tree at Gonda, which, like others which have been already mentioned, sprouted from the tooth twig of a saint, was supposed to be mysteriously associated with the fate of the last of the Gonda Rájas. His kingdom was to last until the day a monkey sat on the tree, and this, it is said, happened on the morning when the Mutiny broke out which ended in the ruin of the dynasty.[2]

Tree sprites.

We have already referred to some of the regular tree sprites like the Churel, Rákshasa and Bansaptí Má. They are like Khiddo, the North British sprite, who can transform himself into a tree, small and delicate at first, but rapidly shooting into the clouds, while everything it overshadows is thrown into confusion.[3] An excellent instance is given from Bombay by Mr. Campbell. "In the Dakkhin, when a man is worried by a spirit he gives it a tree to live in. The patient, or one of his relations, goes to a seer and brings the seer to his house, frankincense is burnt, and the sick man's spirit comes into the seer's body. The people ask the spirit in the seer why the man is sick. He says, 'The ghost of the man you killed has come back, and is troubling you.' Then they say, 'What is to be done?' The spirit says, 'Put him in a place in his or in your own land.' The

[1] Conway, *Demonology*, I, 315 *sq.*: Farrer, *Primitive Manners*, 309: Scott, *Letters on Demonology*, 79: Gregor, *Folklore of N.E. Scotland*, 116, 179: Henderson, *Folklore of the Northern Counties*, 278.

[2] *Oudh Gazetteer*, I, 566.

[3] Henderson, *loc. cit.*, 273.

people say, 'How can we put him?' The spirit says, 'Take a cock, five cocoanuts, rice and red lead, and fill a bamboo basket with them next Sunday evening, and by waving the basket round the head of the patient, take the ghost out of the patient.' When Sunday afternoon comes they call the exorcist. If the ghost has not haunted the sick man for a week, it is held that the man was worried by that ghost, who is now content with the proposed arrangement. If the patient is still sick, it is held that it cannot be that ghost, but it must be another ghost, perhaps a god who troubles him. The seer is again called, and his familiar spirit comes into him. They set the sick man opposite him, and the seer throws rice on the sick man, and the ghost comes into the patient's body and begins to speak. The seer asks him, 'Are you going or not?' The ghost replies, 'I will go if you give me a cock, a fowl, a cocoanut, red lead and rice.' They then bring the articles and show them to the spirit. The spirit sees the articles and says, 'Where is the cocoanut?' or 'Where is the red lead?' They add what he says and ask, 'Is it right?' 'Yes; it is right,' replies the spirit. 'If we take you out of Bápu will you come out?' ask the people. 'I will come out,' replies the ghost. The people then say, 'Will you never come back?' 'I will never come back,' replies the ghost. 'If you ever come back,' says the seer's spirit, 'I will put you in a tanner's well, sink you and ruin you.' 'I will,' says the spirit, 'never come back, if you will take these things to the *pípal* tree in my field. You must never hurt the *pípal*. If you hurt the *pípal* I will come and worry you.' Then the friends of the patient make the cooked rice in a ball, and work a little hollow in the top of the ball. They sprinkle the ball with red powder, and in the hollow put a piece of a plantain leaf, and on the leaf put oil, and a wick which they light. Then the Gádi or flesh-eating priest brings the goat in front of the sick man, sprinkles the goat's head with red powder and flowers, and says to the spirit, 'This is for you: take it.' He then passes three fowls three times from the head to the feet of the sick man, and then from the head lowers all the other articles. The Gádi, a Mhár and some friends of the patient start for the place named by the spirit. When the party leave, the sick man is taken into the house and set close to the threshold. They put water on his eyes, and filling a pot with water, throw it outside where the articles were, and inside and outside scatter cowdung ashes, saying, 'If you come in you will have the curse of Ráma and Lakshmana.' When the Gádi and the party reach their destination, the Gádi tells the party to bring a stone the size of a cocoanut. When the stone is brought, the Gádi washes it and puts it to the root of the tree and sets about it small stones. On the tree and on the middle stone he puts red lead, red powder and frankincense. The people then tell the spirit to stay there, and promise to give him a cocoanut every year if he does them no harm. They then kill the goat and the fowls, and letting the blood fall in front of the stone, offer the heart and liver to the spirit, and then return home."[1] From ceremonies such as this, in which a malignant disease spirit is entombed in a tree, the transition to the general belief in tree sprites is easy. The use of the various articles to scare spirits will be understood from what has already been said on that subject.

The karam tree.

Passing on to trees which are considered specially sacred, we find a good example in the *karam* (*neuclea parvifolia*) which is revered by the Kharwárs, Mánjhís and some of the other allied Dravidian races of the Vindhyan and Kaimúr ranges. In Sháhabad their great national festival is the worship of the holy tree. "Commenced early in the bright portion of the month of Bhádon (August-September) it continues for fifteen days. It marks the gladness with which people wind up their agricultural operations all over the world. The festivities begin with a fast during the day. In the evening the young men of the village only proceed in a gay circle to the forest. A leafy branch of the *karam* is selected, cut and daubed with red lead and butter. Brought in due state, it is planted in the yard in front of the house, and is decorated with wreaths of wild flowers, such as autumn yields to the hillmen with a bountiful hand. The homely

[1] Campbell, *Notes*, 221, *sq*.

ritual of the Kharwár then follows, and is finished with the offering of corn and molasses. The worship over, the head of the village community serves the men with a suitable feast. But the great rejoicing of the season is reserved for a later hour. After dinner the men and women appear in their gala dress, and range themselves in two opposite rows. The *mándar*, or national drum of the aborigines, is then struck and the dance commences with a movement forward, until the men and women draw close. Once face to face, a gradual movement towards the right is commenced and the men and women advance in a slow but merry circle, which takes about an hour to describe. Under the influence of the example of the Hindus, the practice of a national dance in which women take a prominent part is already on the decline. When indulged in, it is done with an amount of privacy, closed to the public, but open to the members of the race only. It is difficult, however, to explain why the *karam* tree should be so greatly adored by the Kharwárs. It is an insignificant tree with small leaves, which hardly affords shelter or shade,[1] and possesses no title to be considered superior to others of its native forest. Nor in the religious belief of the Kharwárs have we been able to trace any classic tale connected with the growth of the *karam* grove, similar to that of the peaceful olive of old, or aromatic laurel. One important, though the last incident of the *karam* worship is the appearance of the demon to the Kharwár village men. Generally at the conclusion of the dance the demon takes possession of a Kharwár, who commences to talk, tremble and jump, and ultimately climbs up the branch of the *karam* and begins to eat the leaves. Consultation about the fortunes of the year then takes place, and when the demon has foretold them the festivities are concluded.[2]"

The karama in Mirzapur.

I have seen the *karama* several times danced by the Mánjhis, a Dravidian tribe in Mirzapur closely allied to the Kharwárs. The people there seem to affect no secrecy about it, and are quite ready to come and dance it

[1] This is hardly the case with the *karam* tree of the Mirzapur jungles. It is a decidedly pretty, though not large, tree, and has beautiful light green leaves.

[2] *Calcutta Review*, LXIX, 364 *sq*.

before Europeans for a small gratuity. The men expect to receive a little native liquor between the acts, but the ladies of the ballet will accept only a light supper of coarse sugar. The troupe consists of about a dozen men and the same number of women. The sexes stand in rows opposite to each other, the women clinging together each one with her arms clasped round her neighbour's waist. One man carrying the sacred *mándar* drum, beats it and leads the ballet, hopping about in a curious way on one leg alternately. The two lines advance and retreat, the women bowing low all the time with their heads bending towards the ground, and joining occasionally in the refrain. They sing all the time a series of verses in tune to the music, and occasionally clap their hands in a rythmical manner. Most of the songs are apparently modern, bearing on the adventures of Rama, Lakshmana and Síta: some are love songs, many of which are, as might have been expected, rude and indecent.[1] The whole scene is a curious picture of genuine aboriginal life. At the regular autumn festival the ceremony degenerates into regular saturnalia, and is, if common repute be trusted, accompanied by an absolute abandonment of decency and self-respect, which culminates in the most unrestrained debauchery. The modern explanation of the ceremony is embodied in a folktale which turns on the verbal confusion between the words *karam*, the name of the tree, and the Sanskrit *karam* meaning "good works." It is, of course, absolutely valueless as a means for ascertaining the real basis of the custom, which is probably of totemistic origin.

The fig: a sacred tree.

Among the sacred trees the various varieties of the fig hold a conspicuous place. Many ideas have probably united in securing reverence to them. Thus the banyan with its numerous stems may fitly be regarded as the abode of gods or spirits. Others are valued as a source of food or because they possess juices valued as drink or medicine. Such is the *umbar*, the *udumbara* of the Sanskrit writers, which is

[1] For a characteristic hunting *karama* song of the Korwas see *North Indian Notes and Queries*, I, 159.

known as *kshíra vriksha* or "milk tree" and *hemadugdha* or "golden juiced," the *ficus glomerata* of botanists, from the succulent roots of which water can be found in seasons of drought. The juice has, in popular belief, many valuable properties. A decoction of it is useful for bile, melancholy and fainting, it prevents abortion and increases the mother's milk.[1] So with the *pípal* (*ficus religiosa*), which is connected with old temples as it forces its roots into the crumbling masonry, grows to a great age and moves its leaves, like the poplar, at the slightest breath of wind. It is believed to be the abode of the sacred triad, Brahma, Vishnu and Siva. The *Nyagrodha* or *ficus indica* was, according to the ancient ritual, possessed of many virtues, and the king was directed to drink its juice instead of the soma.[2] The famous Allahabad fig tree is mentioned in the Rámáyana and in the Uttara Ráma Charitra; Ráma, Sítá and Lakshmana are said to have rested under it. The Buddhist pilgrim Hwen Thsang says that in his time before the principal room of the temple there was a tree with wide-spreading branches, which was said to be the dwelling of a man-eating demon. The tree was surrounded with human bones, the remains of pilgrims who had offered themselves at the temple, a custom which had been observed from time immemorial. General Cunningham identifies this tree with the Akshaya Vata or "the undecaying banyan tree," which is still an object of worship.[3] It corresponds with the well-known banyan tree of Ceylon.[4] The five sacred trees under which the Buddha used to sit were the Bodhi, the Nigrodho (*ficus indica*), the Machalindo (*stravadia*) and Rajatana (*buchania latifolia*). The famous Bodhi tree at Buddha Gaya, under which he obtained enlightenment, is well known.[5] The great sacred fig tree of the Himalaya is said to have reached from Badri Náth to Nand Prayág, a distance of eighty miles.[6]

---

1 Campbell, *Notes*, 237.
2 Haug, *Aitareya Bráhmanam*, II, 486 *sq.*
3 *Archæological Reports*, I, 297, *sq.*
4 Tennant, *Ceylon*, II, 613, *sqq.*: 632, *sqq.*
5 Cunningham, *Bhilsa Topes*, 24: *Archæological Reports*, I, 5, *sq.*: Ferguson, *Eastern Architecture*, 69.
6 Atkinson, *Himalayan Gazetteer*, II, 783.

Domestic worship of the fig tree.

The various fig trees hold an important part in the domestic ritual. In Rájputána the *pipal* and *bargad* are specially worshipped by women on the 29th of the month Baisákh (April-May) to preserve them from widowhood.[1] The *pipal* is invoked at the ceremony of the investiture with the sacred thread, at marriages and at the foundation-laying of houses: vows are made under its shade for male offspring. and pious women veil their faces when they pass it. It is worshipped by moving round it in the course of the sun, one hundred and eight times, and as they revolve a string of untwisted cotton is rolled round the trunk. The vessel of water for the comfort of the departing soul on its journey to the land of the dead is hung from its branches, and beneath it are placed the rough stones which constitute the shrine of the village gods. Its wood is used in part of the Araní or sacred fire drill, and for the spoons with which butter is poured on the sacred fire. When its branches are attacked by the lac insect, a branch on which they have settled is carried to the Ganges at Allahabad and consigned to the sacred waters. This, it is believed, saves the tree from further injury. It should be touched only on Sunday, when Lakshmi, the goddess of wealth, takes up her abode in it: on every other day in the week, poverty and misfortune take up their quarters in it. The son of a deceased parent should pour three hundred and sixty brass vessels of water at its root to ensure the repose of the dead man. Hindus on Sunday after bathing pour a vessel full of water round its root, and walk round it four times. Milk and sugar are sometimes mixed with the water to intensify the charm. When the new moon falls on Monday pious Hindus walk one hundred and eight times round it and wind cotton threads about the trunk. In rich Hindu families small silver models of the tree answer the same purpose. When a statement is made on oath the witness takes one of the leaves in his hand and invokes the gods who sit above him to crush him as he crushes the leaf if he is guilty of falsehood. The story of the Banyas who

[1] Tod, *Annals*, I, 611.

objected to *pípal* trees being planted in the bazár, as it would prevent them from roguery, appears now to be reserved for the confiding European tourist. It is needless to say that this regard for the *pípal* extends through Africa, New Zealand, Australia, Sumatra and Java.[1]

The sál.

The *sál* or *sákhu* (*shorea robusta*) is also a sacred tree. It is held in much respect by the jungle races, who consider it the abode of spirits and erect their shrines under its shade. Patches of this tree are often reserved as fragments of the primeval jungle, of which it must have constituted an important part.[2]

The jand.

In the Panjáb the *jand* tree (*prosopis spicigera*) is very generally reverenced, more especially in those parts where it forms a chief feature in the larger flora of the great arid grazing grounds. It is commonly selected to mark the abode or shelter the shrine of some deity: it is to it that, as a rule, rags are dedicated as offerings, and it is employed in the marriage ceremonies of many tribes. Most Khattris and Bráhmans perform ceremonies to it, especially at festivals connected with domestic occurrences. A custom prevails in some families of never putting home-made clothes upon the children, but of begging them from friends. This is, as we have already seen, done with the view of avoiding the Evil eye. The ceremony of putting on these clothes is usually performed when the child is three years of age. It is taken to the *jand* tree, from which a bough is cut with a sickle and planted at the root of the tree as a propitiation of the indwelling spirit. A *swástika* symbol is made before it with the rice, flour and sugar brought as an offering to the tree. Nine threads from the *mauli*, or string used by women to tie up their back hair, are then taken out and cut into lengths, one of which is tied round the tree with the knot characteristic of Siva or Krishna, and another round a piece of dry molasses, which is placed on the *swástika*. Spells

[1] See instances collected by Wake, *Serpent Worship*, 18.
[2] Dalton, *loc. cit.*, 234, 261, 198.

(*mantra*) are repeated, the sugar and rice are distributed among the women and children, for no male adult except the officiating Bráhman attends the ceremony. The Bráhman then dresses the child in its new clothes, on which he impresses the mark of his hand in saffron, and girds the child's loins with a hair string, on which is tied the bag or purse containing the Bráhman's fee. The hair string has in front a triangular piece of red silk, lined with red or yellow cotton cloth, which, as we have already noted, is one of the most familiar forms of amulet to repel the influence of evil spirits. Similarly, at marriages they perform the ceremony of cutting off and burying a small branch of the tree, and offerings are made to it by the relations of persons suffering from small-pox.[1]

The áonla.

The *áonla* (*emblica officinalis*) is another sacred tree. It is considered propitious and chaste and is worshipped in the month of Kárttik (December) by Bráhmans being fed under it, hair strings (*mauli*) being tied round it, and seven circumambulations made in the course of the sun. The eleventh of the month Phálgun (February) is sacred to it, and on this occasion libations are poured at the foot of the tree, a string of a red or yellow colour is bound round the trunk, prayers are offered to it for its fruitfulness, and the ceremony concludes with a reverential inclination to the sacred tree[2]

The mahua.

The *mahua* (*bassia latifolia*) which so admirably combines beauty with utility and is one of the main sources whence the jungle tribes derive their food and intoxicants, is held in the highest respect by the people of the Central Indian Highlands.[3] It is the sacred tree of some of the Dravidian races, such as the Bhuiyas, and a branch is placed in the hands of the bride and bridegroom during the marriage ceremony. They also revolve round a bough of the tree planted in the ground

---

[1] Ibbetson, *Panjáb Ethnography*, 118: *Panjáb Notes and Queries*, II, 55: O'Brien, *Multáni Glossary*, 82.

[2] *Panjáb Notes and Queries*, II, 74: Elliot, *Supplemental Glossary*, 26.

[3] On the respect paid to plants like the soma and the vine which yield intoxicants see Spencer, *Principles of Sociology*, I, 347, *sqq*.

by the Baiga, or aboriginal priest. Some of the semi-Hinduized Bengal Gonds have the remarkable custom of tying the corpses of adult males by a cord to the *mahua* tree in an upright position, previous to burial. It is also a rule with them that all adult males go to the forest and clear a space round an *ásan* tree (*terminalia alata tormentosa*), where they make an altar and present offerings to the local god, Bara Deo, after which they have a general picnic.[1]

The semal.

The *salmali* or *semal* (*bombax hephtaphyllum*), the cotton tree, is likewise sacred, an idea perhaps derived from its usefulness and weird appearance. A thorny rod from it appears in the older mythology as used for torturing the wicked in hell. In the folktales a hollow cotton tree is the refuge of the heroine.[2] The posts of the marriage pavilion and the stake round which the bride and bridegroom revolve are very commonly made of the wood of this tree among the Kols, as are also the parrot totem emblems used at marriages by the Kharwars and allied tribes. "Among the wild tribes it is considered the favourite seat of gods still more terrible than those of the *pípal*, because their superintendence is confined to the neighbourhood, and having their attentions less occupied, they can venture to make a more minute scrutiny into the conduct of the people immediately around them. The *pípal* is occupied by one or two of the Hindu triad—the gods of creation, preservation and destruction—who have the affairs of the universe to look after, but the cotton and other trees are occupied by some minor deities, who are vested with a local superintendence over the affairs of a district, or perhaps of a single village."[3]

The nim.

The *nimba* or *ním* (*azidirachta indica*) is also a sacred tree. We shall meet with it elsewhere in connection with snake worship. In this it resembles

[1] Dalton, *Descriptive Ethnology*, 148, 281, 283; Rousselet, *India and its Native Princes*, 369, *sq*.
[2] Tawney, *Katha Sarit Ságara*, I, 162.
[3] Sleeman, *Rambles and Recollections*, II, 112: Tylor, *Primitive Culture*, II, 225

the Yggdrassil of Europe, the roots of which were half destroyed by the serpents which nestled among them : the leaves and wood of the ash are still regarded throughout all Northern Europe as a powerful protective from all manner of snakes and evil worms.[1] *Ním* leaves are, it may be noted, useless as a snake scarer, unless they are fresh.[2] The leaves are also used throughout Northern India as a purification from the death pollution. After the funeral the mourners chew the bitter leaves, and water is sprinkled over them from a branch of this tree. "So great is the power of the *ním* over spirits and spirit diseases that in Bombay when a woman is delivered of a child *ním* leaves and cow's urine are, as a rule, kept at the entrance of the lying-in room, in order that the child and its mother may not be affected by an evil spirit, and on their New Year's Day it is considered essential for every Hindu to worship the *ním* tree and to eat its leaves mixed with pepper and sugar, that he may not suffer from any sickness or disease during the year. In practice very few worship the tree, but its leaves are generally eaten by most of them. Among the Chitpáwan Bráhmans a pot filled with cow's urine is set at the door of the lying-in room with a *ním* branch in it, and any one coming in must dip the branch in the urine and with it sprinkle his feet. Among the Govardhan Bráhmans of Púna, when a child is born, *ním* leaves are hung at the front and back doors of the house. In Ahmadnagar when a person is bitten by a snake he is taken to Bhairoba's temple, crushed *ním* leaves mixed with chillies are given to him to eat, and *ním* branches waved round his head. Among the Namdeo Shempis of Ahmadnagar each of the mourners carries from the pyre a twig of the *ním* tree, and the Kanphatas of Cutch get the cartilage of their ears slit, and in the slit a *ním* stick is stuck, the wound being cured by a dressing of *ním* oil."[3] We have already found this tree connected with sun worship in the case of the Nímbárak Vaishnavas as well as with that of Sítala, the goddess of small-pox.

---

[1] *Quarterly Review*, CXIV, 226.
[2] See the Legend of Newal Dái. Temple, *Legends of the Panjáb*, I, 473.
[3] Campbell, *Notes*, 234.

Among the wilder tribes it is also revered. The Jogis, a criminal tribe in Madras, reverence it and brand their dogs with a representation of the tree.[1] The Banjáras, or wandering grain-carriers, use a branch of the tree as a test of continence. The jealous husband throws it on the ground and says, "If thou be a true woman, lift that *ním* branch." The Doms or vagrant sweepers of the eastern districts of the North-Western Provinces, hold the *ním* tree sacred to Káli or Sítala, and the Kurmis dedicate it to Káli Bhawáni, and worship this tree and the pípal under which the image of Devi is placed.[2]

The cocoanut.

The cocoanut is considered one of the most sacred fruits: and is called Sriphala or the fruit of Srí, the goddess of prosperity. It is the symbol of fertility, and all through Upper India is kept on shrines and presented by the priests to women who desire children. The respect for it is probably based on its uses for food and as a source of intoxicating liquor. But it is not a native of Northern India, and is naturally more revered in its home along the western coast. In Gujarát and Kánara it represents the house spirit, and is worshipped as a family god. The Konkan Kunbis put up and worship a cocoanut for each of their relations who dies, and before beginning to cut the rice break a cocoanut and distribute it to the reapers. The Prabhus, at every place where three roads meet, wave a cocoanut round the face of the bridegroom and break it into pieces to avoid evil influences, and the Musalmáns of the Dakkhin cut a cocoanut and lime into pieces and throw them over the head of the bridegroom to scare malignant spirits. In Western India the cocoanut is the commonest of all offerings, and seems to have taken the place of the human victim.[3]

The khair.

The mimosa (*khair*) (*acacia catechu*) seems to owe most of the estimation in which is is held to its use in producing the sacred fire. It forms on account of its hardness the base of the *araní* or sacred fire-drill

[1] Mullaly, *Notes on Madras Criminal Tribes*, 20.
[2] *Panjáb Notes and Queries*, III, 38.
[3] Campbell, *Notes*, 226, *sq.*

and in it the wedge of the softer *pípal* wood works, and fire is produced by friction. It was also used to form the sacrificial post (*yúpa*) in the earlier ceremonies. Of the *khair* Bishop Heber writes in his journal:[1] "As I returned home I passed a fine tree of the mimosa with leaves at a little distance so much resembling those of the mountain ash, that I was for a moment deceived, and asked if it did not bear fruit. They answered,—"No; but it was a very noble tree, being called the 'Imperial tree' for its excellent properties. That it slept all night, and was alive all day, withdrawing its leaves if any one attempted to touch them. Above all, however, it was useful as a preservative against magic: a sprig worn in the turban, or suspended over the bed, was a perfect security against all spells, evil-eye, &c., insomuch that the most formidable wizard would not, if he could help it, approach its shade. One, indeed, they said, who was very renowned for his power (like Lorrinite of Kehama) of killing plants and drying up their sap with a look, had come to this very tree and gazed upon it intently: 'but,' said the old man who told me this with an air of triumph, 'look as he might, he could do the tree no harm,' a fact of which I make no question. I was amused and surprised to find the superstition which in England and Scotland attaches to the rowan tree here applied to a tree of nearly similar form." This idea attached to the rowan tree and the elder is familiar in European folklore. In Ireland the roots of the elder tree and the roots of an apple tree which bears red apples boiled together and drunk fasting expel evil spirits. In connection with this idea that the mimosa sleeps at night, pious Hindus prefer not to eat betel leaves after sunset, as catechu forms part of the ingredients with which they are prepared.

The plantain.

The plantain is also sacred, probably on account of the value of its fruit. The leaves are hung on the marriage booth. In Bengal in consecrating an image of Durgá, a plantain tree is brought in and bathed. It is then clothed as a woman with *bel* apples as breasts; nine sorts of

[1] I, 287. The coronation chair of Sivají was made of *khair* wood, *Bombay Gazetteer*, XI, 370.

leaves smeared with red paint are hung round the breast and it is worshipped.[1] In the folktales the deserted wife sweeps the ground round a plantain tree and it gives her a blessing.[2]

Pomegranate.

So with the pomegranate, which, among the Pársís of Bombay, is held in high respect. Its twigs were used to make the sacred broom, its seeds to scare spirits were thrown over the child when it was girt with the sacred thread, and its juice was squeezed into the mouth of the dying.[3] In its fruit the fairy of the folktales Princess Pomegranate (*Anár Sháhzádi*) commonly lies hidden. But it is in Upper India considered unlucky to have such a tree in the house, as it is envious and cannot bear that any one should be lovelier than itself.[4]

Tamarind.

The Oraons of Bengal revere the tamarind and bury their dead under its branches.[5]

Siras.

In the Panjáb the leaves of the *siras* (*acacia sirisa*) are a powerful charm. They are hung up in cases of disease of men or animals with a mystic inscription on an earthern platter in the centre.[6]

Mango.

The mango is also used in the same way. It is, as we shall see, used in making the aspersion at rural ceremonies. The leaves are hung up at marriages in garlands on the house door and on the shed in which the ceremony is performed, and after the wedding these are carefully consigned to running water by the bride and bridegroom. It is also used as a charm. Before you see a flower on a tree shut your eyes and make some one lead you to one in flower. Rub the flowers into your hands and you thus acquire the power of curing scorpion

[1] Ward, *Hindus*, II, 13, quoted by Campbell, *Notes*, 229.
[2] Lál Bihári De, *Folktales*, 280.
[3] Campbell, *loc. cit.*, 229.
[4] *North Indian Notes and Queries*, I, 207.
[5] Dalton, *Descriptive Ethnology*, 189.
[6] *Sirsa Settlement Report*, 154.

stings by moving your hand over the place. But this power lasts only for one year and must be renewed when the season of flowers again returns.

Tulasí.

The *tulasí* or holy basil is closely associated with the worship of Vishnu. The god, so runs the legend, was fascinated with the beauty of Vrindá, the wife of Jalandhara, to redeem him from which enthralment the gods applied to Lakshmí, Gaurí and Swadhá. Each gave them seed to sow where Vishnu was enchanted. Those given by Lakshmí, spring up as the Dhátri (*emblica myrobolan*), málatí, the jasmine and the tulasí, and appearing in female form they attracted the admiration of the deity, and saved him from the wiles of Vrindá.[1] The plant is specially worshipped by women after bathing, and more particularly at the full moon of Kárttik (November-December), if the bathing be in the Ganges. Most Vaishnava sects wear necklaces and carry rosaries made of this wood. Among the Amáts of Bengal, if a person die at a distance from the Ganges, the ashes are collected under a small platform on which a tulasí plant is grown.[2]

Palása.

The *palása* or *dhák* is sacred, partly on account of its use in producing the sacred fire, and partly because of its orange blossoms, which are used to dye the coloured dust and water thrown about at the Holí festival. The ancient ritual directed that the sacrificial post (*yúpa*) was to be made out of of the wood of the *khádira* (*acacia catechu*), the *bilva* or *bel* (*ægle marmelos*) or of that of the *palása*. The wood is by preference used in making the funeral pyre. It was a Vedic custom to drive the cows from their calves by striking them with a rod of the *palása* tree. In some parts of Scotland the milkmaid carries a switch of the magical rowan to expel the demon which sometimes enters the cow; and in Germany striking the cow with this magical wand is believed to render her fertile.[3]

---

[1] Wilson, *Works*, III, 68.
[2] Risley, *Tribes and Castes*, I, 18.
[3] Kelly, *Curiosities*, 159: Conway, *Demonology*, I, 126: Gubernatis, *Zoological Mythology*, I, 225.

Bel.

The *bel* (*ægle marmelos*) perhaps became sacred owing to the value of its fruit as medicine. We have already seen that it is one of the trees out of which the sacrificial post was made. But it is chiefly used in Saiva worship where the leaves laid on the *lingam* cool and refresh the heated deity.

The babúl.

To close this catalogue of sacred trees we may note that, unlike the other acacias, the *babúl* (*acacia arabica*) is an unlucky tree. If you throw water for thirteen days consecutively on a *babúl* tree you will get the evil-spirits which inhabit it into your power. The ghost of a man burnt with this wood will not rest quietly, and any one who sleeps on a bed made of it is afflicted with evil dreams. As an old servant once told me, such a bed should be reserved for the use of clergymen, who, by virtue of their office, are naturally protected against such uncanny visitations.

Tree marriages.

We now come to discuss the curious question of marriages to trees. The custom prevails throughout the Panjáb. In some parts of Kangra if a betrothed, but as yet unmarried girl, can succeed in performing the marriage ceremony with the object of her choice round a fire made in the jungle with certain wild plants, her betrothal is annulled and this informal marriage holds good.[1] So, in the Panjáb, a Hindu cannot be legally married a third time. If he wishes to take a third wife, he is married to a *babúl* tree (*acacia arabica*) or to the *ákh* plant (*asclepias gigantea*) first, so that the wife he subsequently marries is counted as his fourth, and the evil consequences of marrying three times are thus avoided.[2] Rich people who have no children marry a Bráhman to the *tulasi* plant. The pseudo-father of the bride treats the Bráhman ever afterwards as his son-in-law, which, it is needless to say, is a very good thing for the Bráhman.[3]

---

[1] Ibbetson, *Panjáb Ethnography*, 119.

[2] *Panjáb Notes and Queries*, II, 42. This marriage with the *ákh* is known as *arka viváh*, and the plant is believed to die soon after. *North Indian Notes and Queries*, II, 27.

[3] *Ibid.*, II, 151, *sq.*

If the birth of a child does not follow this ceremony, they have good reason for apprehending that a messenger from Yama, the god of death, will harass them on their way to the spirit world.[1] Among the Kadva Kunbis of Gujarát, when a girl is marriageable and a bridegroom cannot be found, the practice is to substitute a bunch of flowers, and the marriage ceremony proceeds. The next day, by which time the flowers have begun to fade, they are thrown into a well and the bride of yesterday is considered a widow. As a widow can marry at any time without social discredit, the parents find a husband for her at their leisure.[2] Many ordinary marriage customs appear to be based on some analogous principle. Thus among the Báwariyas, a vagrant tribe of Sirsa, the bride and bridegroom go outside the village to a *jand* tree, which, as we have seen already, is regarded as sacred, move round it seven times and then cut off a branch with an axe.[3] In a Bhíl marriage the pair walk round a *salyára* tree, which is placed in the middle of the marriage booth, twelve times.[4] In Bengal, again, the Rautiyas before the wedding go through the form of marriage to a mango tree.[5] Among the Mundári Kols "the bride and bridegroom are well anointed with turmeric and then taken and wedded, not to each other, but the bride to a *mahua* tree (*bassia latifolia*), and the groom to a mango, or both to mango trees. They are made to touch the tree with red lead, and then to clasp it, and they are tied to it"[6]: and among the Kurmis the bridegroom on the wedding morning is first married to a mango tree. He embraces the tree, is for a time tied to it in a particular manner with a thread, and he daubs it with red lead. Then the thread is removed from the tree and is used to attach some of the leaves to the bridegroom's wrist. The bride is similarly wedded to a *mahua* tree.[7] Similarly in the Lower Himalayas, if any one desires to marry a third time, whether his other wives are alive or not, he is married to the *akh* plant (*asclepias gigantea*). He

[1] *Ibid.*, III, 23.
[2] *Bombay Gazetteer*, VII, 61.
[3] *Settlement Report*, 167.
[4] *Bombay Gazetteer*, III, 221.
[5] Risley, *Tribes and Castes*, II, 201.
[6] Dalton, *Descriptive Ethnology*, 194.
[7] *Ibid.*, 319.

builds an altar near the plant, or brings a branch home and places it near the altar. The regular marriage ceremony is then performed, and a thread is wound ten times round the plant with the recitation of appropriate verses. Four days the plant remains where it was fixed, and on the fifth day the celebrant is entitled to commence the marriage ceremony with his third wife. Similarly, a person is married to an earthen jar, when from some conjunction of the planets the omens are unfavourable, or when, from some bodily or mental defect, no one will marry the boy or girl. The usual ceremonies are gone through, and the neck of the boy or girl is connected by a string with the neck of the vessel and water is sprinkled over them with a brush made of five leaves.[1] In Nepál every Newár girl is, while a child, married to a *bel* fruit, which after the ceremony is thrown into some sacred river. When she arrives at puberty a husband is selected for her, but should the marriage prove unpleasant, she can divorce herself by the simple process of placing a betel nut under her husband's pillow and walking off. Widows are allowed to remarry; in fact a Newár woman is never a widow, as the *bel* fruit to which she was first married is presumed to be always in existence.[2]

Origin of tree marriages.

The custom of tree marriages appears, then, to rest on two distinct sets of ideas. In the first place, by the fiction of marriage with a tree it is intended to obviate the condition of widowhood, which is always regarded with abhorrence by primitive races, or to remove the disgrace connected with the necessity of keeping a girl unmarried after she has reached puberty, a feeling widely prevalent among the Indian peoples. Secondly, it is difficult to separate the actual tree marriage as an adjunct to the ordinary ceremony from totemism.[3] Symbolism of the same kind is used even in the case of inanimate objects. No one can taste the fruit of a mango grove until one of the trees is married to another tree, usually to a tamarind standing

[1] Atkinson, *Himalayan Gazetteer*, II, 912, *sq.*
[2] Wright, *History of Nepál*, 33.
[3] See instances collected by Frazer, *Totemism*, 33, *sqq.*

near it in the garden. In the same way a grove is wedded to its well, and every Hindu who goes to the expense of making a tank does not drink of its waters until he has married the tank to a plantain tree planted on the bank for the purpose.[1]

Tree and serpent worship.

In the story of the king and his son told in the Baitál Pachísí the king supplicates a sacred tree to give him a son. This request is granted, and the king then implores the tree to make his people happy: the result was that poor wretches hitherto living in the woods came forth and concerted measures to seize his kingdom. Rather than shed blood, the old king, his queen and his son retired to a lofty mountain. There the son finds someting white lying under a mimosa tree. On enquiring he learns that it is a heap of serpents' bones left there by Garuda, who comes daily to feast on serpents. On hearing this the king goes towards a temple, but is arrested by the cry of a woman who says, "My son to-day will be eaten by Garuda." She and her people were, in fact, serpents in human shape. The king was moved to pity, and as in the famous legend of Buddha and the tigress, he offered to expose himself to Garuda in the room of her son. This is discovered: Garuda releases the king, and at his request re-animates the serpents to whom the bones belong.[2] Here we have an example of the combination of tree and serpent worship, and it would be easy to adduce other instances as has been done by Mr. Ferguson and other writers of his school. But in dealing with this phase of belief much caution is needed. As Dr. Tylor observes, "serpent worship unfortunately fell years ago into the hands of speculative writers, who mixed it up with occult philosophies, Druidical mysteries, and that portentous nonsense called the Arkite symbolism, till now sober students hear the very name of ophiolatry with a shudder."[3]

---

[1] See Sleeman, *Rambles and Recollections*, I, 42, *sq.*

[2] Manning, *Ancient Indias*, II, 330, *sq.*: Tawney, *Katha Sarit Ságara*, I, 185. For Garuda as the foe of serpents see *Folklore*, II, 94. Tawney, *Ibid.*, II, 312.

[3] *Primitive Culture*, II, 239.

Principles of serpent worship.

It does not appear difficult to disentangle the principles on which the worship is based. To begin with, the snake is dreaded and revered on account of the mysterious fear which is associated with it, its stealthy habits and the suddenness and deadliness of its attacks. It would soon be discovered that there were various harmless snakes which would come to be identified with the ancestral ghosts as the protectors of houses and goods. The power of controlling and taming the more venomous snakes would then be discovered, and the snake charmer would come to be regarded as the wisest of mankind, as a wizard and finally as a priest. We have thus three aspects under which the serpent is worshipped by many savage races—as a dreaded enemy, as the protector of home and treasure, as the accompaniment and attribute of wisdom. The village temple would be often in early times a store house of treasure, and the snake respected as its guardian would finally, as in Kashmír, be installed there as a god. Next we have the early connection between the serpent and the powers of nature, the cloud and the rain, as appears in the familiar myth of Indra and the Dragon Ahi, and Seshanága, the great world serpent, which appears in so many of the primitive mythologies. The serpent would, again, receive respect as an emblem of life: his form would be associated with the ring as a symbol of eternity: he is excessively long-lived and periodically renews his life. He has, further, as in the Saiva cultus, become associated with phallicism and with the sexual powers, as in the Adam legend.[1] Lastly the cultus may have a totemistic basis.

Totemism connected with serpent worship.

As Strabo describes the Ophiogeneis or serpent races of Phrygia actually retaining physical affinity with the snakes to whom they were popularly believed to be allied, the Cheros of the eastern districts of the North-Western Provinces and the Bais Rájputs of Oudh profess to be descended from the Great Serpent. Gautama Buddha himself is said to have been of serpent lineage. But the great

[1] This side of the matter has been developed, often on insufficient evidence, by Mr. Wake in his *Serpent Worship*, and Gen. Forlong in his *Rivers of Life*.

serpent race was that of the Nágas, to whom much ill-considered argument and crude speculation has been devoted. According to one theory, they were Skythic emigrants from Central Asia, but whether antecedent or subsequent to the so-called Aryan inroad is disputed. They seem to have been accustomed to use the serpent as a national symbol, and hence came to be identified with the snake. Some of the myths seem to imply that they suffered persecution at the hands of the Bráhmans, such the tale of the burning of the Khándava forest, the opening scenes of the Máhábharata and the exploits of the youthful Krishna. They are again associated with Buddhism on monuments like those of Ajanta, and another theory would make them out to be the Dasyus, or aboriginal races of Upper India who were the first to adopt Buddhism and were exterminated in the Bráhmanical revival. Little, in fact, is known of them, save that they may have been early worshippers of the snake, may have embraced Buddhism, and may have introduced the worship into India from some northern home.[1] But Mr. Ferguson's theory that snake worship was of purely Turanian origin is, to say the least, very doubtful: and his theory that Saivism is antagonistic to snake worship, while his assertion that Vaishnavisn, which he regards as a modification of Buddhism, encourages it, is opposed by the numerous instances of the connection of the serpent with the *lingam*.

Seshánaga.

Below the seven Pátálas, according to the Vishnu Purána, is Vishnu incarnated as Seshanága, and known by the name Ananta or "Endless." He has a thousand heads adorned with the mystical Swástika, and in each head a jewel to give light. He is accompanied by Váruni, the goddess of wine, supports the world on his head, holds in one hand a pestle and in the other a plough, which connects him, as we shall see later on, with agriculture.

[1] See Wheeler, *History of India*, I, 148: *Gazetteer, Central Provinces*, LXIII, LXXII: Campbell, *Notes*, 269: Ferguson, *Tree and Serpent Worship*, Appendix D: Elliot *Supplemental Glossory* sv. *Gaur Taga*: Tod, *Annals*, I, 38: Atkinson, *Himalayan Gazetteer*, II, 280 *sqq.*, 297: Temple, *Legends of the Panjáb*, I, 414, *sqq.*

Snake shrines.

In various places snakes are provided with special shrines. Thus in Garhwál, Sesha Nága is honoured at Pandukeswar: Bhekal Nág[1] at Ratgáon: Sangal Nág at Taror; Bánpa Nág at Margánw, and many others of the same kind.[2] In fact, all along the Himalaya the worship extensively prevails. Kailang Nág is the chief Himalayan snake god, and as the Vedik Ahi controls the clouds, so he gives fine weather. A victim is killed and one of his disciples after drinking the blood gets into a state of afflatus. Finally he gasps out that the sacrifice is accepted and falls down in a state of exhaustion. The old shrine to the serpent deity at Kangra, known as Baghsu Nág, has been converted into a Saiva temple under the name of Baghsunáth—another example of the adoption of unorthodox deities into official Hinduism. "The Nág is specially the guardian of cattle and water springs. According to the legend, the valleys of Kashmír and Nepál were in some remote period the abode of Nágs. The first milk of a cow is usually presented to a Nág, and goats and sheep are sacrificed to him as to other godlings. So far as I am aware, the only place in the Himalaya where the living snake is worshipped is at the foot of the Rotung pass."[3] The Gonds worship a snake every three years by leaving a vessel of milk for his use.[4] The Nepál Serpent King is Karkotaka, who dwelt in the lake Nága Vása. In one of the Nepál temples is a representation of a Nág Kanyá, a serpent maiden or mermaid, sitting on a tortoise.[5] This serpent maiden constantly appears in Indian folklore. Such is Vijayavatí, daughter of Gandamálin, one of the snake kings, who is of surpassing loveliness, who rescues and marries the hero. She is represented by Melusina in European legend.[6]

[1] Bhekal Nág is perhaps the Sanskrit *bheka*—frog. It has been suggested that the Gypsy *Beng* or devil is connected with Bheka and is thus allied to serpent worship (Groome, *Encyclopædia Britannica*, Art. *Gypsies*.) Sir G. Cox (*Introduction*, 87, note) makes out Bheki or "Squatting frog" to be an old name for the sun.

[2] For a full list of Himalayan Snake shrines see Atkinson, *Himalayan Gazetteer*, II, 374, *sq.*

[3] Oldham, *Contemporary Review*, April 1885.

[4] *Journal, Asiatic Society, Bengal*, 1890, p. 281.

[5] Oldfield, *Sketches*, II, 204: Wright, *History*, 85.

[6] Tawney, *Katha Sarit Ságara*, II, 173: II, 544.

Curious as it may appear, all the Kashmír temples were originally surrounded by artificial tanks constructed in order to propitiate the Nágas. Ancient stones covered with figures of snakes are still occasionally to be seen worked up into the walls of modern buildings. Abul Fazl says that in his time there were nearly seven hundred figures of snake gods existing in Kashmír. The snake, it is needless to say, is a common emblem in temples all over the country. An ancient temple at Biláspur in the Central Provinces has, as its only image, that of the Cobra.[1]

Snake worship in history and legend.

Snake worship appears constantly in history and legend. There is a passage in Plutarch from which it appears to have been the custom to sacrifice an old woman (previously condemned to death for some crime) to the serpent gods by burying her alive on the banks of the Indus. Ktesias also mentions the worship of snakes. In the Buddhist legends serpents are often mentioned as the guardian deities of certain towns.[2] In the folktales, Naraváhanadatta worships snakes in a grove sacred to them, and Bhímabhata goes to the temple of the chief of the snakes which he finds full of long wreaths of flowers in form like serpents and a great lake sacred to Vásuki, studded with red lotuses, which seemed like clouds of smoke from the fire of snake poison.[3]

The Sankisa snake.

The old Chinese Buddhist traveller thus describes the serpent deity in the temple at Sankisa in the Farukhabad district: "A white-eared dragon is the patron of this body of the priests. It is he who causes fertilizing and seasonable showers of rain to fall within their country, and preserves it from plagues and calamity, and so causes the priesthood to dwell in security. The priests in gratitude for these favours have erected a dragon chapel, and within it placed a seat for his accommodation: and moreover they make special contributions in the

[1] *Calcutta Review*, LI, 304, *sq.*; LIV, 25, *sq.*: Ferguson, *Eastern Architecture*, 289: *Central Provinces Gazetteer*, 86.
[2] See authorities quoted by Tawney, *loc. cit.*, I, 577.
[3] *Ibid.*, I, 312; II, 225.

shape of religious offerings to provide the dragon with food. Towards the end of each season of rest the dragon incontinently assumes the form of a little serpent both of whose ears are edged with white. The body of priests recognizing him, place in the midst for his use a copper vessel full of cream. The serpent then proceeds to come down from the highest part of the alcove, all the while moving as though he would pay his respects to all those around him. He then suddenly disappears. He makes his appearance once every year." According to General Cunningham, the only spot which can be identified with any certainty[1] at Sankisa is the Tank of the Nága, which still exists to the south-east of the ruins. The name of the Nága is Kárewar, which appears to mean "the black one," and that of the Tank Kandaiya Tal. Milk is offered still to him on every day of May, at the Nágpanchamí festival in August, and at any other time when rain is wanted.[2] We have already seen that the worship of the Nág is connected with the regulation of the weather. Numerous instances of this occur,[3] and the plan of propitiating the dragon with an offering of milk is found also in the case of the Durham legend of the Lambton Worm.[4]

Other sacred dragons.

There are many other sacred dragons of the same kind. That in the dragon tank at Rámagráma used to assume the form of a Bráhman.[5] Dr. Buchanan tells of another at Bhágalpur: "They showed me a hole in the rock opening into a hollow space close by the path leading up to their village. They said that this hole was the abode of a very large serpent which they considered a kind of god. In cold weather they never saw it, but in the hot season it was constantly observed lying in the hollow before its den. The people pass by it without apprehension, thinking that it understands their language and would on no account injure one of them, should even a child or a drunken person fall on it."[6]

[1] Beal, *Travels of Fah Hian*, 67 *sq.*
[2] *Archæological Reports*, I, 274.
[3] Wright, *History of Nepal*, 85, 141.
[4] Henderson, *Folklore of the Northern Counties*, 289.
[5] Beal, *loc. cit.*, 90.
[6] *Eastern India*, II, 149.

But all such snakes are not friendly. In the Hitopadesa the serpent is introduced into the oriental form of the tale of Bethgelert, where the Bráhman kills the faithful mungoose which had rescued his child from the snake. The same story is localized at a tank near the Asthbhuja Hill, close to Mirzapur, where the merchant under a mistake kills his faithful dog.[4] The origin of the tale is probably Buddhistic, with the tenets of which creed the self-sacrifice of an animal for the good of others is particularly cognate. The travels of this famous legend from the East to the West form one of the most instructive chapters in comparative folklore.[1] Aghásur, the serpent king, tried to devour the divine infant Krishna. When he and his foster-father were asleep together a huge boa constrictor laid hold of Nanda by the toe, and would speedily have devoured him, but Krishna, hearing his cries, ran to his side and lightly set his foot on the monster's head. At the very touch the serpent was transformed and assumed the figure of a lovely youth: "for years ago a Ganymede of Heaven's Court by name Sudarsan, in pride of beauty and exalted birth, had vexed the holy Sage Angiras when in deep contemplation by dancing backwards and forwards before him, and by his curses had been metamorphosed into a snake, in that vile shape to expiate his offence until the advent of the gracious Krishna."[2] Another famous Mathura snake is represented by an ancient image of a five-headed Nága carved in stone by the side of a small tank at Jait. His tail is supposed to reach under ground to Brindaban, seven miles away.[3] The curious dragon cave at Kausambhi near Allahabad was one of the last notable discoveries of the Archæological Survey

Malignant dragons.

Besides these sacred Nágas there are the regular snake gods. The serpent deity of Benares is Nágeswar, who is represented by a serpent twining

Snake gods.

---

[1] See Jacob's *Celtic Fairy Tales*, 259, *sq.*
[2] Growse, *Mathura*, 55, 58.
[3] *Ibid.*, 71.
[4] *Reports*, XXI, 2: *Academy*, 9, 23rd April 1887.

round the chief idol, and like his kindred rules the weather: the Nág Kuán or dragon well is one of the oldest shrines in the city.[1] Among these serpent gods we have actual deified snakes like Vásuki and Sesha Nága, as well as heroes raised to the heaven in connection with snakes. Vásuki or Básuk Nág has many temples, and in all of them, as in his shrine at Dáraganj near Allahabad, the priest in charge is always a man of low caste,—a fact pointing to the non-Aryan character of his worship. Vásuki often appears in the folk-tales. We find him resisting Garuda, the destroyer of his subjects. His brother's son Kírtisena is according to one legend a Bráhman and weds a mortal maiden by the Gándharva form: his eldest brother Vasunemi presents a benevolent Savara with a magic lute: Vásuki himself marries the princess Yasodhará, and their son is Priyadarsaná: Vásuki himself has a thousand eyes and a thousand ears. Once he served the gods by becoming the rope with which Mount Mandara was whirled round and the sea was churned and produced Srí or Lakshmí.[2] The foot of the celebrated iron pillar at Delhi was driven so deep in order that it might rest on the head of Vásuki. A Bráhman told the king that this would ensure the stability of his kingdom. The Rája doubted this and had the pillar dug up, when its base was found wet with the blood of the serpent king. Owing to the incredulity of the Rája it could never again be firmly fixed, and his want of faith led to the ultimate ruin of his dynasty.

The Sinhas: snake gods.

Next come the Sinhas or snake gods of the Panjáb and western part of the North-Western Provinces. "They are males, and though they cause fever they are not very malevolent, often taking away pain. They have got great power over milch cattle, and the milk of the eleventh day after calving is sacred to them, and libations of milk (as in the case of the Sankisa dragon) are always acceptable. They are generally distinguished by some colour, the most commonly

[1] Sherring, *Sacred City*, 75, 87, *sqq.*: and for weather snakes Tawney, *Katha Sarit Ságara*, I, 438.
[2] Tawney, *Katha Sarit Ságara*, I, 32, 55, 538; II, 568.

worshipped being Káli (black), Hari (green), Bhúra (grey) Sinh. But the diviner will often declare a fever to be caused by some Sinh no one has ever heard of before, but to whom a shrine must be built. And so they multiply in the most perplexing manner. Dead men also have a way of becoming snakes,—a fact which is revealed in a dream, when again a shrine must be built. If a peasant sees a snake he will salute it, and if it bite him, he or his heirs, as the case may be, will build a shrine on the spot to prevent the recurrence of the occurrence. They are the servants of Vásuki Nága, King of Pátála or Tartarus, and their worship is certainly connected with that of the Pitris or ancestors, though it is difficult to see exactly in what the connection lies."[1]

Connection between snakes and ancestor worship.

The connection is thus explained by Mr. H. Spencer—"the other self of the dead relative is supposed to come back occasionally to the old home: how else is it possible for the survivors sleeping there to see him in their dreams? Here are creatures which commonly, unlike wild animals, come into houses: come in, too, secretly at night. The implication is clear. That snakes which especially do this are the returned dead is inferred by people in Africa, Asia, and America: the haunting of houses being the common trait of the kinds of snakes revcrenced and worshipped.[2]" In this view of its relation to man the snake is friendly and we find him in the folktales assisting the hero.[3]

Deified snake heroes.

We have already mentioned the regular snake god Gúga. With him is often worshipped his father Jaur or Jewar Sinh, and Arjan and Sarjan, his twin half-brothers.[4] Pípa the Bráhman is another deity of the same class in Rájputána. He was in the habit of giving offerings of milk to a serpent whose retreat was on the banks of the Sampu or

[1] Ibbetson, *Panjáb Ethnography*, 114: Temple, *Legends of the Panjáb*, I, 426.

[2] *Principles of Sociology*, I, 345: and see Gubernates, *Zoological Mythology*, II, 407, *sq.*: Wake, *Serpent Worship*, 105: Tylor, *Primitive Culture*, II, 240: 8.

[3] *e.g.*, Temple, *Wideawake Stories*, 196, *sqq.*

[4] *Panjáb Notes and Queries*, I, 2.

Snake Lake. The serpent in return used to present him daily with two pieces of gold.[1] Being obliged to go away on business, he gave instructions to his son to continue the offering: but the youth deeming it a good opportunity of becoming master of the treasure took a stick with him, and when the serpent issued forth for his expected food he struck him violently. But the snake managed to retreat into his hole. On his return the young Bráhman related his adventures to his mother. She was horrified at the account and forthwith made arrangements for sending her son away out of danger: but in the morning when she went to call him she found to her horror a huge serpent coiled up in her son's bed. Pípa on his return was inconsolable, but stifling his revenge he propitiated the monster with copious libations of milk. The serpent was appeased and revealed to Pípa the treasures he guarded; commanding him to erect a monument which should transmit the knowledge of the event to future ages. Hence Pípa has become a sort of snake godling, and the town of Pípár and the Sampu Lake still by these names commemorate the legend.[2]

Snakes treasure guardians.

Snakes throughout folklore are the guardians of treasure.[3] It is a common belief that when a very rich man dies without an heir he cannot take away his thoughts from his treasure, and returns to guard it in the shape of a monstrous serpent. But after some time he becomes tired of this serpent life, and either in a dream or assuming the human voice, he asks the persons living near the treasure to take it and offer him one of their dearest relatives in return. When some avaricious person complies with the serpent's wishes, he gets possession of the wealth and the serpent then enters some other state of existence. Snake charmers are supposed to have the power of recognizing these serpent treasure guardians, follow them stealthily

---

[1] These animals which present the hero with gold commonly appear in the folktales. In India it is generally a goat which does this. In Europe it is very usually an ass. Jacob's *English Fairy Tales*, 207, 251.

[2] Tod, *Annals*, I, 777, *sq.*: there is a very similar story in the Panchatantra: Manning, *Ancient India*, II, 284.

[3] Gubernatis, *Zoological Mythology*, II, 407.

to their holes and ask them to point out the deposit. This they will do in consideration of the offering of a drop of blood from the little finger of a first born son,[1] an obvious survival of human sacrifice which is constantly found connected with the serpent cultus. Various suggestions have been made to account for the idea of snakes guarding treasure. By one theory there is some connection between the serpent and primitive metallurgy; by another, that the snake may have been the totem of the early jewellers; by a third, that the jewelled head of the snake is at the root of the matter.[2] But it seems more probable that the idea is based on the conception of the snake as a haunter of houses and temples and a divine protector of the inmates. Indian folklore is full of such stories. In the Dakkhin tale Seventee Bái gets possession of the enormous diamond which the cobra used to take about in his mouth: and in the Bengal story Faqír Chand obtains the serpent's crest jewel.[3] Mr. Forbes tells rather a ghastly tale in connection with this idea. He personally investigated a mysterious chamber supposed to contain treasure. Viewed from above it was a gloomy dungeon of great depth. He desired his men to enter it, but they positively refused, alleging that "wherever money was concealed there existed one of the Genii in the mortal form of a snake to guard it." He at last prevailed on them to descend by means of ropes. They had not been at the bottom many seconds when they called out vehemently that they were encircled by a large snake. Finally he observed something like billets of wood or rather more resembling a ship's cable coiled up in a dark hole. Then he saw the monster raise his head over an immense length of body, coiled in volumes on the ground. A large snake was subsequently destroyed by fire, but no treasure was found, "the proprietor having doubtless already removed it."[4]

Powers of snakes in folklore.

Manifold are the powers of the snake in folklore. He has the power of spitting fire from his mouth which destroys his enemies and consumes forests.

[1] *Panjáb Notes and Querries*, II, 91.
[2] Conway, *Demonology*, I, 353 *sq*.
[3] Miss Frero, *Old Deccan Days*, 33: Lál Bihári De, ***Folktales***, 19.
[4] *Oriental Memoirs*, II, 19: II, 385.

In the legends of Rája Rasálu, Gúga, and Newal Dáí the snake has power to kill and restore to life; it has the faculty of metamorphosis and of flying through the air. There are snake women who go about at night and then resume their hateful form; she is the Lamiá or Vasudeva, the mystic serpent. The humanity of the serpent race very clearly comes out in the legend of Safidon, which attributes the leprosy still found in the Panjáb to the sacreligious acts of Rája Vásuki, the king of the serpents.[1]

Modern snake worship.

In the present day snake worship prevails widely. The great snake festival is the Nágpanchamí or "dragon's fifth," held on the fifth day of the month Bhádon. In the Hills it is called the Rikhí or Birurí Panchamí. Rikhesvara has now become a title of Siva as lord of the Nágas, a form in which he is represented as surrounded by serpents and crowned with a chaplet of hooded snakes. On the day of the feast the people paint figures of serpents and birds on the walls of their houses, and seven days before the festival they steep a mixture of wheat, gram, and pulse in water. On the morning of the feast they take a wisp of grass, tie it up in the form of a snake, dip it in the water in which the grain has been steeped and offer it with money and sweetmeats to the serpents.[2] In Udaypur on this day they strew particular plants about the thresholds of houses to prevent the entrance of venomous reptiles, and in Nepál the day is observed as the anniversary of a great struggle between a famous Nág and Garuda, the foe of the serpent race.[3] In the eastern districts of the North Western Provinces on this day milk and dried rice are poured into a snake's hole; while doing this they merely call out 'Snake! Snake!" and in Behár low caste women go about singing songs to propitiate snakes.[4] In Bombay during the feast snakes are fed in a curious way described by M. Rousselet.[5] After

[1] Tawney, *Katha Sarit Ságara*, II, 99: Temple, *Legends of the Panjáb*, I, Intro., XV: *Widewake Stories*, 193, 331.
[2] Atkinson, *Himalayan Gazetteer*, II, 851.
[3] Tod, *Annals*, I, 614: Wright, *History*, 37.
[4] *Panjáb Notes and Queries*, III, 38: Grierson, *Maithili Chrestomathy*, 23, *sqq.* where examples of the songs are given.
[5] *India and its Native Princes*. 28.

the Diwáli in Kangra a festival is held to say good-bye to snakes, at which an image of the Nág made of cowdung is worshipped. If a snake is seen after that it is called "ungrateful" and immediately killed.[1] In the North-Western Provinces the usual custom is for the head of the family to bathe on the morning of the feast, to paint on the wall of his sleeping room two rude representations of serpents, and to make offerings to Bráhmans. The women also make a snake-like line of flour all round the dwelling house as a sort of magic circle through which no snake can pass. On this day many people pray to what Dr. Buchanan[2] calls "the chief eight dragons of the pit": girls throw some playthings into the water, and labourers take a holiday and worship the tools of their craft. In Behár during the month of Sáwan (August) crowds of women calling themselves Nágin or wives of the snake, go about begging for two and a half days, during which period they neither sleep under a roof nor eat salt. Half the proceeds of the begging are given to Bráhmans and the other half invested in salt and sweetmeats, which are eaten by all the people of the village.[3] In Garhwál the ground is freely smeared with cowdung and mud, and figures of five, seven, or nine serpents are rudely drawn with sandal wood powder or turmeric: rice, beans, or gram are parched: lamps are lighted and waived before them: incense is burnt and food and fruit offered. These observances take place both morning and evening, and the night is spent in listening to stories in praise of the Nág.[4]

Cure of snake bite.

In Hoshangabad there were once two brothers, Rájwa and Soral: the ghost of the former cures snake bite and that of the latter cattle murrain. The moment a man is bitten he must tie a string or a strip of his dress in five knots and fasten it round his neck crying "Mercy, O god Rájwa!" To call on Ghori Bádsháh, the Delhi Emperor, who conquered the country, or Rámjí Dás Bába will do as well. At the same time he makes a vow to give so much to the god if he recovers.

[1] *Panjáb Notes and Queries*, III, 75.
[2] *Eastern India*, II, 481.
[3] Grierson, *Bihár Peasant Life*, 405.
[4] Atkinson, *Himalayan Gazetteer*, II, 836.

When he gets home they use various tests to ascertain if the poison is in him still. They take him in and out over the threshold and light a lamp before him, acts which have the effect of developing latent poison They then give him salt and leaves of the bitter *ním* tree. If he can take them he is safe. These are all, as we have already seen, scarers of evil spirits, in this case the snake demon. If he cannot take them, the whole village goes out and cries to Rájwa Deo until he recovers. No one (Sir C. A. Elliott's informant told him) had ever been known to die of a snake bite after this treatment, but the god has no power over the dreaded biscobra.[1] The bitten man must not tie the string round his neck till the day when he goes to offer what he vowed, which should be, at latest, on the next Dasahra: but if he attempts to cheat the god by offering ever so little less than he promised, he will die on the spot in agonies.[2] All through Upper India the stock remedy for snake bite is the exorcism of the Ojha or sorcerer—a performance known as *jhár phúnk*, consisting of a series of passes and incantations which is supposed to disperse the venom.

The snake in Folklore and popular belief.

The references to the snake in folklore and popular belief are so numerous that only a few instances can be given. The *dháman* (*ptyas mucosus*), a quite harmless snake, is said in Bombay to give a fatal bite on Sundays and to kill cattle by crawling under them or putting its tail up their nostrils. Its shadow is also considered malignant. Of the *ghonas* snake it is believed that it bites only at night, and at whatever hour of the night the victim is bitten he dies just before daybreak.[3] One special power snakes possess is that of identifying the heirs of kingdoms who have been unjustly deprived of their inheritance, and in the folktales it is usually the disguised Sanyási or ascetic who destroys the deadly serpent.[4] In the mythology

1 The biscobra is the Hindi Biskhapra, Sanskrit Vishakharpara or "poison headed," which is said to be so deadly that its very breath is venomous. This is almost certainly a delusion. See Yule and Burnell, *Hobson Jobson*, *sv.*

2 *Settlement Report*, 120 *sq.*

3 *Gazetteer*, XI, 36.

4 Tod, *Annals*, II; 282: 384: Lál Bihári De, *Folktales*, 134 148.

the Nága King Machalinda spreads his hood over the Buddha to protect him from the rain and flies.[1] The fight between Indra and Ahi is analogous to the Scotch tale describing how Froach killed the great serpent at the Ross of Mull.[2] Some of these Nágs are however friendly, as in the case of the Banjára, who in order to avoid octroi duty declared his valuable goods to be Glauber's salts, and Glauber's salts they became until they were restored to their original condition by the intercession of the kindly Nág of the Gundwa tank.[3]

Snakes should, of course, be addressed euphemistically as "Maternal uncle," "Tiger," or "Rope," and if a snake bites you, you should never mention its name, but say "a rope has touched me." The Mirzapur Kharwárs tell a tale of a man who once came upon a Nágin laying her eggs: when she saw him she fell at his feet and asked him to throw the eggs into a water-hole. So he took up the eggs on a bamboo litter and went with her to the brink. The Nágin plunged in and said "Come on, do not be afraid." He followed her, the waters dried up and he came to the palace of the Nág, who entertained him royally, and offered to give him anything he wished. The boor asked only for a pan, pot and spoon, which the Nág gave him, and he came home to find his relations doing the death ceremonies in his honour, believing he had been carried off by a tiger. He said nothing of his adventures till the day of his death when he told the story. If the shadow of a pregnant woman falls on a snake it becomes blind.[4]

The snake jewel.

The snake like the "toad ugly and venomous" wears on his head the precious jewel or *maní* which is a stock subject in the Indian folktales.[5] It is sometimes metamorphosed into a beautiful youth: it equals the treasure of seven kings: it can be hidden or secured only by cowdung

---

[1] Hardy, *Manual of Buddhism*, 146.
[2] Miss Gordon Cumming *From the Hebrides to the Himalayas*, I, 144.
[3] *Oudh Gazetteer*, I, 597.
[4] *Panjáb Notes and Queries*, I, 15.
[5] Tawney, *Katha Sarit Ságara*, I, 561; II, 315, quoting Benfey, *Panchatantra* I, 214.

or horsedung being thrown over it: and if it is acquired the serpent dies. It lights the hero on his way to the palace under the sea where is the silver jewelled tree: or it is possessed by the sleeping beauty who cannot return to her home beneath the waters and loses the hero until it is recovered. Its presence acts as an amulet against evil, and secures the attainment of every wish. It protects the owner from drowning—the waters parting on each side of him and allowing him to pass over rivers dryshod.[1]

Rainbow and snake.

So the rainbow is connected with the snake, being the fume of a gigantic serpent blown up from underground. In Persia it was called the "celestial serpent," and it is possibly under the influence of the connection between snakes and treasure that English children believe that a crock of gold is buried at its base.[2]

Household snake.

In the Panjáb hills, every householder keeps an image of the Nág or harmless snake, as contrasted with the Sámp, which is venomous. This snake is given charge of the householder's homestead, and is held responsible that no cobra or dangerous serpent enters it. They are supposed to have the power to order all cobras out of the place Should rain drive the house snake out of his hole, he is worshipped. No image of a cobra or other dangerous snake is ever made for purposes of worship. Anthills are supposed to be the home of snakes, and there the people offer sugar, rice and millet for forty days.[3] These correspond to the benevolent domestic snakes, of whom Aubrey says that "the Bramens have them in great veneration: they keep their corne. I think it is Tavernier mentions it."[4] They are, in fact, as we have already seen, the representatives of the benevolent ancestral ghosts. Hence the deep-rooted prejudice against killing the snake, who is both guardian and god. "If," says Mr. Lang,

---

[1] Temple, *Wideawake Stories*, 304; 424: *Panjáb Notes and Queries*, I, 15, 76.
[2] Sleeman, *Rambles*, I, 46: Conway, *Demonology*, I, 354.
[3] *Panjáb Notes and Queries*, III, 92, *sq*.
[4] *Remainnes*, 39.

"the serpent were the deity of an earlier race, we could understand the prejudice against killing it, as shown in the Apollo legend."[1] The evidence accumulated in this chapter will perhaps go some way to settle this question as far as India is concerned.

[1] *Custom and Myth*, II, 197.

CHAPTER VIII.

TOTEMISM AND FETISHISM.

Olim truncus eram ficulnus, inutile lignum,
Cum faber incertus scamnum faceretne Priapum,
Maluit esse deum.

HORACE, SAT., I, viii, 1—3.

Totemism defined.

"A totem is a class of material objects which a savage regards with superstitious respect, believing that there exists between them and every member of the class an intimate and altogether special relation."[1] As distinguished from a fetish a totem is never an isolated individual, but always a class of objects, generally a species of animals or plants, rarely a class of inanimate objects, very rarely a class of artificial objects.

Origin of totemism.

As regards the origin of totemism great diversity of opinion exists. Mr. Herbert Spencer considers that it arose from "a misinterpretation of nick-names: savages first took their names from natural objects, and then confusing these objects with their ancestors of the same name, paid the same respect to the material totem as they were in the habit of doing to their own ancestors."[2] The objection to this is, as Mr. Frazer shows, that it attributes to verbal misunderstandings far more influence than, in spite of the so-called comparative mythologists, they ever seem to have exercised. Sir J. Lubbock derives the idea from the practice of naming persons and families after animals, but "in dropping the intermediate links of ancestor worship and verbal misunderstanding, he has stripped the theory of all that lent it even an air of plausibility."[3] Recent enquiries in the course of the

---

[1] Frazer, *Totemism*, 1, and his article on *Totemism* in *Encyclopædia Britannica*, 9th ed.

[2] *Principles of Sociology*, I, 367.

[3] *Origin of Civilisation*, 260: and Mr. Frazer's criticism, *loc. cit.*

Ethnographical Survey of Bengal and the North-Western Provinces enable us perhaps to approach a solution of the problem. To begin with, at a certain stage of culture the idea of the connection between men and animals and plants is exceedingly vivid and reacts powerfully on current beliefs. The animal or plant is supposed to have a soul or spirit like that of a human being, and this soul or spirit is capable of transfer from the man to the animal and *vice versá*. This feeling comes out strongly in popular folklore, much of which is made up of instances of metamorphoses such as this. The witch or sorcerer is always changing into a tiger, a monkey or a fish: the princess is always appearing out of the aubergine or pomegranate. This principle, which is thoroughly congenial to the belief of all primitive races, naturally suggests a much closer union between man and other forms of the animal or vegetable world than people at a higher stage of development accept or admit. With people, then, at this stage, the theory that the ancestor of a clan may have been a bear or tortoise would present no features of improbability. In the next place the result of the Indian evidence, so far as it has been collected, goes to show that it is only in connection with the rules of exogamy that totemism at the present day displays any considerable degree of vitality.

Totemism and exogamy.

The rule of exogamy is widespread, but its origin cannot be said as yet to have been ascertained with any degree of certainty: and it is possible that this stage of the marital relations may have been reached by different races by diverging routes. There is much to be said in favour of the theory advocated by Mr. Westermarck that the horror of incest among the members of the large house communities so constantly found among primitive races may have suggested a rule of local or intertribal exogamy and have led ultimately to intratribal exogamy and thus to marriage by capture; or, on the other hand, the reverse process may have led to the same result, as is suggested by the fact that intratribal exogamy was probably in India antecedent to the intertribal form. Further, in Northern India at least, the small groups of foreign emigrants unable to intermarry with the repulsive, dark faced woman of the Dasyus or aboriginal races would be compelled by the force of circumstances to adopt some rule of the kind. Once established, such a rule would be likely to gain strength among races with whom the struggle for existence was unusually severe, and the excess of health and vigour among peoples who enforced marriage outside the local group would give them such a decided advantage as compared with an endogamous race, that by the rule of selection they would rapidly attain the mastery. Some form of exogamy would, in other words, be a necessary condition precedent to the successful development of a clan, and the advantages resulting from it would lead to its compulsory extension. This extension would probably be to a large degree unconscious. From what we know of savage races we may be almost certain that the evils of interbreeding as leading to the production of weakly children would not at the outset force themselves into notice. Of all the feelings of the savage his erotic instincts are those which are least under control, and to suppose that partially civilised races like the Korwas or Dhángars were from the outset influenced by any direct regard for sanitary regulations is most improbable. But this does not render it impossible that the spread of such principles may have been unconscious or instinctive. However this may be, once arrived at, the rule of exogamy would require regulation, and in particular some formula determining the prohibited degrees would become a pressing necessity. Now, as Mr. Risley has shown, different races have arrived at this result in different ways. Among some of the Mongoloid tribes the groups are based on nicknames, among Bráhmans they are mostly eponymous, among Rájputs they are local or territorial. And it is more than probable that the Dravidians, among whom alone totemism at the present day retains any degree of vitality, may have selected the totemistic system of defining the exogamous groups as the most simple and convenient. The marriage taboo would readily ally itself with the animistic conception of the close relation between man and the animal or plant, the supposed kindred with which would be the first tangible link between the elements constituting the exogamous group. But it would, it is almost certain, be incorrect to say that while totemism is at present most active among the Dravidians in connection with marriage, it was peculiar to them. It is more reasonable to infer that it continues to flourish among these peoples because of their isolation from Brahmanical influence. As among the inferior races of the Gangetic valley, the primitive family customs connected with marriage, birth and death, have undergone a process of denudation from their association with their more advanced Hindu neighbours, so to a large degree in Northern India, the totemistic sept names have been shed off and have been replaced by an eponymous, local or territorial nomenclature. In short, under the pressure of higher culture the kindred of the swan, turtle or parrot have preferred to call themselves *Kanaujiya* or men of Kanauj, *Sarwariyas* or residents beyond the river Sarju or *Raghuvansa* or *Bhriguvansa*, the descendants of Raghu or Bhrigu, some ancient king or sage. We find then among such races, as might have been expected, that at the present day the totemistic sept system exists only in obscure and not easily recognizable forms. Folk etymology has also exercised considerable influence, and a sept ashamed of its totemistic title readily adopts some eponymous or local cognomen of a sage or king or country sounding something like the name of the primitive totem. It is perhaps too much to expect that a careful exploration of the sept titles or tribal customs of Northern India will lead to any extensive discoveries of the primitive totemistic organization. The process of trituration which has affected the caste nomenclature for such a lengthened period and the obscuration of primitive belief by association with more cultured tribes have been so continuous as to leave only a few fragments and isolated survivals: but it is by such a course of enquiry that the totemistic basis of the current caste system can alone be reached.

Tests of totemism.

For the purposes of such an investigation it is convenient to have some sort of a working classification of the tests of, and the forms in which, totemism usually appears. These have been laid down by Professor Robertson Smith as follows :—

(*a*) The existence of stocks named after plants, animals or similar totems.

(*b*) The prevalence of a conception that the members of the stock are of the blood of the eponym, or are sprung from a plant, &c., of the species chosen as the totem.

(*c*) The ascription of a sacred character to the totem.

These will be discussed as far as the scanty evidence at present available renders it possible to do so.

Stocks named from animals, plants, &c.

First, then, as to stocks named from animals, plants, &c. There are two divisions of the Púra Bráhmans of the Dakkhin known as Bakriyár and Chherviyár, founded on the names of the male and female goat.[1] In Upper India the Káchhis or market gardeners and the Kachhwáha sept of Rájputs allege that they take their name from the *kachchhapa* or tortoise, as the Kurmis refer their name to the *kúrma* turtle. The Ahban Rájputs and the Ahiwásis of Mathura connect their names with Ahi, the dragon. The Kalhans Rájputs derive their name from the *Kála hans* or black goose. Among Bráhmans and other high castes *Bháradvaja,* the lark, "the bringer of food," has given its name to many septs. The Chandrabansi and Súrajbansi Rájputs are said to take their name from *Chandra* the moon, and *Súraj* the sun, from which, like the Dravidian Birhors and Kharwárs, they claim descent. Mr. Risley thinks that the fact of there being a Kásyapa division of Kumhárs, who venerate the tortoise, points to the name being a corruption of *Kachchhapa,* in which case their name would have the same origin as the Káchhis already mentioned. According to Capt. J. Montgomerie,[3] round Kashmír and among the aboriginal hill tribes of the Himalayan slopes men are usually named after animals, as the Bakhtiyáris, one

[1] *Kinship and Marriage in Early Arabia,* 188.
[2] Wilson, *Indian Castes,* II, 194.
[3] Quoted by McLennan, *Fortnightly Review,* 1869, p. 419.

of the nomad tribes of Persia, name their children usually not after the prophet, but after wild animals such as the wolf, lion, tiger and the like, adding some descriptive epithet.[1] In the same way a tribe of Lodi Patháns in the Panjáb are known as Nahar or "wolf." This is said to be due to their rapacity, but may really be the survival of some totemistic title.[2]

Totem names among Davidians.

The evidence on this point is, as has been already said, much more distinct among the Dravidians than among the more Hinduised races. Thus to take the Dhángars, a caste in Mirzapur allied to the Oráons of Bengal, we find that they have eight exogamous septs, all or most of which are of totemistic origin. Thus *Ilha* is said to mean a kind of fish which members of this sept do not eat: *Kujur* is the name of a jungle herb which this sept does not use: *Tirik* is probably the *Tirki* or bull sept of the Oráons. In Chota Nágpur members of this sept cannot touch any cattle after their eyes are open. It illustrates the uncertainty of these usages that in other places they say that the word *Tírki* means young mice which they are prohibited from eating.[3] Again, the Mirzapur sept of the Dhángars known as *Lakara* is apparently identical with that called *Lakrar* among the Bengal Oráons, who must not eat tiger's flesh as they are named after the tiger: in Mirzapur they derive their name from the hyæna (*lakar bagha*), which they will not hunt or kill. The *Bara* sept is evidently the same as the *Barar* of the Oráons, who will not eat the leaves of the *bar* tree or *ficus Indica*. In Mirzapur they will not cut this tree. The *Ekka* sept in Mirzapur say that this name means leopard, an animal which they will not kill, but in Chota Nagpur the same word is said to mean tortoise and to be a totemistic sept of the Oráons. So the Mirzapur Dhángars have a *Tiga* sept, which they say takes its name from a jungle root which is prohibited to them: but the Oraons of Bhágalpur have a *Tig* sept, which according to them means monkey. The last of the Mirzapur septs

[1] Benjamin, *Persia*.
[2] O'Brien, *Multáni Glossary*. 260, *sq*.
[3] Dalton, *Descriptive Ethnology*, 254: Risley, *Tribes and Castes*, II, 327.

is the *Kháka* which, like the *Khakhar* sept of Oráons, means crow, and neither will eat this bird. Similar instances might be almost indefinitely repeated from usages of allied tribes in Mirzapur and the adjoining Bengal districts.

The Panjáb snake tribe.

In the Panjáb there is a special snake tribe. They observe every Monday and Thursday in the snake's honour, cooking rice and milk, setting a portion by for the snake, and never eating or making butter on those days. If they find a dead snake they put clothes on it and give it a regular funeral. They will not kill a snake, and assert that its bite is harmless to them. This snake, they say, changes its form every hundred years, and then becomes a man or a bull.[1]

Totemism in proper names.

The subject of Indian proper names has not as yet received the attention it deserves. The only attempt made, so far, is that of Major Temple. In his copious lists there is ample evidence that names are freely adopted from those of animals, plants, etc.[2] Thus we have *Bágha*, "Tiger": *Bheriya*, "Wolf": *Billa*, "Cat": *Chuha*, "Rat": and so on from animals: *Bagla*, "Heron": *Mor*, "Peacock": *Tota*, "Parrot": and so on from birds: *Ajgar*, "Python": *Mendak*, "Frog": *Kachhwa*, "Tortoise": *Bhaunra*, "Bumble bee": *Ghun*, "Weevil": *Dimak*, "White Ant," etc. From plants come *Buta*, "Tree": *Harabansa*, "Green bamboo": *Níma*, "Ním tree": *Pípal*, "Fig tree": *Gulába*, "Rose": *Imliya*, "Tamarind": *Sewa*, "Apple": *Ilácha*, "Cardamum": *Mirchi*, "Pepper": *Bhutta*, "Maize." The evidence of nomenclature must of course be received with caution. Many of these may be nicknames, or titles of opprobrium selected, as we have already shown, to baffle the evil eye or the influence of demons. Besides, as has been pointed out, it does not necessarily follow because an Englishman lives in "Acacia Villa" or "Laburnum Cottage," and calls his daughters "Rose" or "Violet," that he is in the totemistic

---

[1] *Panjáb Notes and Queries*, II, 91.
[2] *Dissertation on the proper names of Panjábis*, 155, *sqq.*

stage. But the prevailing habit of savages of using totem titles of this kind cannot be ignored.

Descent from the totem.

We next come to Professor Robertson Smith's second test—the belief in descent from the totem. This branch of the subject has been very fully illustrated by Mr. Frazer.[1] In old times in Georgiana, according to Marco Polo, all the King's sons were born with an eagle on the right shoulder marking their royal origin.[2] Chandragupta, King of Ujjain, was the son of a scorpion. "His mother accidentally imbibed the scorpion's emission, by means of which she conceived."[3] The Jaitwas of Rajputána trace their descent from the monkey god Hanumán, and confirm it by alleging that the spine of their princes is elongated like a tail.[4] In the fortieth canto of the Rámáyana one of the wives of King Ságara give birth to a son who continues the race: the other wife produced an *ikshváku,* a gourd or cane containing sixty thousand sons. The famous Chandragupta was miraculously preserved by the founder of his race, the bull Chando.[5] The wolf is in the same way traditionally connected with the settlement of the Janwár Rájputs in Oudh, and they believe that the animal never preys on their children. The Cheros of the Vindhyan plateau claim descent from the Nág or dragon. Similar examples are numerous among the allied Dravidian tribes. The Rája and chief members of the Chota Nágpur family wear turbans so arranged as to make the head dress resemble a serpent coiled round the skull with its head projecting over the wearer's brow. The seal of the Mahárája and arms of his family show as a crest a cobra with a human face under its expanded hood surrounded with all the insgnia of royalty, The Santál legend ascribes the origin of the tribe to the wild goose, and similar stories are told by the family of the Rája of Singhbhúm, the Hos, the Malers and the Kúrs.[6]

---

[1] *Totemism*, 3, *sqq.*
[2] Yule, *Marco Polo*, I, 52.
[3] Spence Hardy, *Manual of Buddhism*, 251.
[4] Tod, *Annals*, I, 123.
[5] Max Müller, *Ancient Sanskrit Literature*, 290.
[6] Dalton, *Descriptive Ethnology*, 126, 162, 165, *sq.*: 179, 185, 209, 231, 265.

Next come instances of special respect paid to the totem.

Special respect to the totem.

Some idea of the kind may be partly the origin of the worship of the cow and the serpent. Dr. Ball describes how some Khánds refused to carry the skin of a leopard because it was their totem.[1] The Parihár Rájputs of Rájputána will not eat the wild boar probably for the same reason, but they have now invented a legend that one of their princes went into a river while pursuing a boar and was cured of a loathsome disease.[2] The Bengal Báwariyas take the heron as their emblem and must not eat it.[3] The Orissa Kumhárs abstain from eating and even worship the *sál* fish because the rings on its scales resemble the wheel which is the symbol of the craft.[4] The peacock is a totem of the Játs and of the Khánds, as the Yizidis worship the Taous, a half mythical peacock which has been connected with the Phœnix whose picture Herodotus saw in Egypt.[5] The Parhaiyas have a tradition that their tribe used to hold sheep and deer sacred and used the dung of these animals instead of cowdung to plaster their floors. So the Keriyas do not eat the flesh of sheep and may not even use a woollen rug.[6]

One of the best illustrations of this form of totemism is the

The Devak.

Devak or guardian gods of Berár and Bombay. Before concluding an alliance, the Kunbi and other Berár tribes look to the Devak which literally means the deity worshipped at marriage ceremonies: the fact being that certain families hold in honour particular trees and plants, and at the marriage ceremony branches of these trees are set up in the house. It is said that a betrothal, in every other respect irreproachable, will be broken off if the two houses are discovered to pay honour to the same tree,[7] in other words, if they worship the same family totem. The same custom prevails widely in Bombay.

---

[1] *Jungle Life in India*, 600.
[2] *Rájputána Gazetteer*, I, 223.
[3] Dalton, *loc. cit.*, 327.
[4] Risley, *Tribes and Castes*, Intro., XLVII.
[5] Conway, *Demonology*, I, 27: Herodotus, II, 73.
[6] Dalton, *loc. cit*,. 131 note: Ball, *loc. cit.*, 89.
[7] *Berar Gazetteer*, 187.

"The usual Devaks are some animals like the elephant, stag, deer, or cock, or some tree as the mango, *jambul* (*Calyptranthes jambolana*), *ber* (*Zizyphus jujuba*) or banyan. The Devak is the ancestor or head of the house, and so families which have the same guardian cannot intermarry. If the Devak be an animal, its flesh is not eaten: but if it be a fruit tree the use of the fruit generally is not forbidden, though some families abstain from eating the fruit of the tree which forms their Dewak or badge."[1] Mr. Campbell gives numerous examples of these family totems, such as wheat bread, a shell, an earthen pot, an axe, a banyan tree, an elephant. Oilmakers have as their totem an iron bar or an oil mill: scent makers use five piles, each of five earthen pots, with a lighted lamp in the middle. One clan of Vakkals do not eat the stag, another the deer, a third the woodcock. The Bangars' Devak is a conch shell, that of the Pardesi Rájputs an earthen pot filled with wheat, and so on. Many of these are really tribal or occupational fetishes of which instances will be given in another place.

The Váhanas and Avatáras.

There is a series of indications in the mythology which have been taken to point to totemism, but this is far from certain. Thus, it has been suggested that the Váhanas or "Vehicles" of the gods may represent tribal totem deities adopted into Hinduism. Bráhma rides on the Hansa or goose: Vishnu on Garuda, half eagle and half man, which is the crest of the Chandrabansi Rájputs: Siva on his bull Nandi: Yama on the buffalo: Karttikeya on a peacock: Kamadeva on the marine monster Makara or on a parrot: Agni on a ram: Varuna on a fish. Ganesa is accompanied by his rat, which an ingenious comparative mythologist makes out to be a symbol of "the pagan Sun God crushing under his feet the mouse of night."[2] Váyu rides on an antelope, Sani or Saturn on a vulture and Durgá on a tiger. The same is the case with the Avatáras or incarnations of the deities. Vishnu appears in the form of Varáha, the boar: Kúrma, the tortoise: Matsya, the fish: Nara Sinha, the man lion: Kalki,

---

[1] Campbell, *Notes*, 8, *sqq*.
[2] Gubernatis, *Zoological Mythology*, II, 68; and see Lang, *Custom and Myth*, 113.

the white horse. Rudra and Indra are also represented in the form of the boar. How the boar came to be associated with Vishnu has been much disputed. One explanation suggested is that the boar is a destroyer of snakes.[1] This is more than doubtful. We know that in Rájputána there was a regular spring festival at which the boar was killed because he was regarded as the special enemy of Gaurí, the Rájput tribal goddess.[2] The comparative mythologists account for the spring boar hunt by connecting it with the ceremonial eating of the boar's head at Christmas in Europe, as a symbol of the gloomy monster of winter killed at the winter solstice, after which the days grow longer and brighter.[3] But it is much simpler to believe with Sir A. Lyall that "when the Bráhmans convert a tribe of pig-worshipping aborigines they tell their proselytes that the pig was an *avatára* of Vishnu.[4] The Mínas in one part of Rájputána used to worship the pig. When they took a turn towards Islám they changed their pig into a Saint called Father Adam and worshipped him as such." It is quite possible that the worship of Varáha is an illustration of the same principle. We know that among the Dravidian races and many of the menial tribes of Hindustán the pig is the favourite offering to the local gods. Swine's teeth are still worn by Hindu ascetics, and among the Kolarian races women are forbidden to eat the flesh. It was possibly from the usages of tribes like these that the Varáha incarnation was adopted. Garuda, another of these vehicles, is the wonder-working bird common to many mythologies, the Rukh of the Arabian Nights, the Eorosh of the Zend, the Simurgh of the Persians, the Kimi of Japan, the Dragon of China and the Griffin of Chivalry and Temple Bar.

Food totems.

From totemism we get a clue to many curious usages, especially in the matter of food. From this idea probably arose the unclean beasts of the Hebrew ritual. Many Hindu tribes will not eat the onion or the

[1] Conway, *Demonology*, I, 144.
[2] Tod, *Annals*, I, 599.
[3] De Gubernatis, *loc. cit.*, II, 13.
[4] *Asiatic Studies*, 264.

turnip. Bráhmans and Bachgoti Rájputs object to potatoes. The Rájputs put a special value on the wood of the *ním* tree: one clan alone, the Raikwárs, are forbidden to use it as a tooth stick. Some Kolarian tribes, as we have already seen, refuse to use the flesh or wool of the sheep. The Murmu or Santáls of the blue bull sept will not eat the flesh of that animal. And the system of the Oráons is more elaborate still, for no sub-tribe can eat the plant or animal after which it is named. So the Bansetti Binjhiyas, who take their name from the bamboo, do not touch the tree at a wedding: the Harbans Chamárs cannot wear bones in any shape: the Rikhiasan Chiks do not eat beef or pork: the Sanuani Dhenuárs cannot wear gold: the Dhanuar Khariyas cannot eat rice gruel. Numerous instances of this kind are given by Mr. Risley.[1] The transition from such cases to the elaborate food regulations of the modern castes is not difficult. We have already noticed the customs of caste marks and tattooing as possibly pointing in the same direction.

Fetishism defined.

Fetishism is "the straightforward, objective admiration of visible substances fancied to possess some mysterious influence or faculty............... The original downright adoration of queer-looking objects is modified by passing into the higher order of imaginative superstition. First, the stone is the abode of some spirit, its curious shape or position betraying possession. Next, the strange form or aspect argues some design or handiwork of supernatural beings, or is the vestige of their presence upon earth, and one step further leads us to the regions of mythology and heroic legend."[2] The unusual appearance of the object is thus supposed to imply an indwelling ghost, an agent without which deviation from the ordinary type would be inexplicable. It thus depends on the theory of animism and the ghost theory to which in order of time it must have succeeded.

[1] *Tribes and Castes*, Vol. II, App.: Dalton, *loc. cit.*, 162, Note: 213, 254.
[2] Lyall, *Asiatic Studies*, 9, *sq.*

Fetishism illustrated: in Afghánistán.

The process by which the worship of such a fetish grows is well illustrated by Ferrier: "It is sufficient for an Afghán devotee to see a small heap of stones, a few rags or some ruined tomb, something, in short, upon which a tale can be invented, to imagine at once that some saint is buried there. The idea conceived, he throws some more stones upon the heap and sticks up a pole and flag: those who come after follow the leader: more stones and more rags are added: at last its dimensions are so considerable that it becomes the vogue: a mullah is always at hand with a legend which he makes or had revealed to him in a dream: all the village believe it: a few pilgrims come: crowds follow: miracles are wrought and the game goes on much to the satisfaction of the holy speculator who drives a good trade by it, till some other mullah more cunning than himself starts a saint of more recent date, and greater miraculous powers, when the traffic changes hands."[1]

The Lorik legend.

The same process is daily going on before our eyes in Northern India, and it would be hard to suggest anything curious or abnormal which the Hindu villager will not adopt as a fetish. The legend of Lorik is very popular among the Ahír tribe and has been localised in the Mirzapur district in a curious way which admirably illustrates the principles which we are considering. The story is related at wearisome length, but the main features of it according to the Shahabad version are as follows. Shiudhar, an Ahír, marries Chandaní and is cursed by Párvatí with the loss of all passion. Chandaní forms an attachment for her neighbour Lorik and elopes with him. The husband pursues, fails to induce her to return, fights Lorik and is beaten. The pair go on and meet Mahápatiya, a Dusádh, the chief of the gamblers. He and Lorik play until the latter loses everything, including the girl. She urges that her jewels did not form part of the stake, and induces them to gamble again. She stands opposite Mahápatiya and distracts his attention by giving him a

[1] *Caravan Journey*, 186.

glimpse of her pretty ankles. Finally Lorik wins everything back.[1] The girl then tells Lorik how she has been insulted, and Lorik with his sword weighing two maunds cuts off the gambler's head,[2] when it and the body were turned into stone. Lorik had been betrothed to a girl named Satmanain, who was not of age and had not joined her husband. She had a sister named Lurki. Lorik had an adopted brother named Semru. Lorik and Chandani, after killing the gambler, went on to Hardoi near Mongir, where Lorik defeated a Rája and conquered his country. Lorik was finally seized and put into a dungeon, whence he was released by the intercession of the goddess Durgá. He again conquered the Rája, recovered Chandani, had a son born to him and gained considerable wealth. So they determined to return to their native land Meanwhile Semru, Lorik's brother by adoption, had been killed by the Kols and all his cattle and property plundered. Lorik's real wife, Satmanain, hád grown into a handsome woman, but still remained in her father's house. Lorik was anxious to test her fidelity, so when she came to sell milk in his camp, not knowing her husband, he stretched a loin cloth across the entrance. All the other women stepped over it, but the delicacy of Satmanain was so excessive that she would not put her foot across it.[3] Lorik was pleased and filling her basket with jewels covered them with rice. When she returned, her sister saw the jewellery and charged her with obtaining them as the price of her dishonour. She indignantly denied the accusation, and her nephew, Semru's son, prepared to fight Lorik to avenge the dishonour of his aunt. Next day the matter was cleared up to the satisfaction of all parties. Lorik then reigned with justice and Indra determined to destroy him, so the goddess Durgá took the form of his mistress Chandani and tempted him. He succumbed to her wiles and she struck him so that his

[1] This gambling match forms a stock incident in Indian folklore. The plot of the Mahábhárata chiefly turns on it. See Muir, *Ancient Sanskrit Texts*, V, 425, *sqq* : Lál Bihari De, *Folktales of Bengal*, 193, *sq.* : 277, *Legends of the Panjáb*, 48, *sqq.* : Temple, *Wideawake Stories*, 277, *sqq.*

[2] The magic sword also constantly appears: see Tawney, *Katha Sarit Ságara*, I, 69; II, 172, 270; 521. etc.

[3] These fidelity tests constantly appear in folklore: *cf.*. Grimm, *Household Tales*, I, 453.

face turned completely round. Overcome by grief and shame he went to Benares and there he and his friends were turned into stone and sleep the sleep of magic at Manikarnika Ghat.[1]

The Mirzapur version.

The Mirzapur form of the story is interesting from its association with fetishism. As you descend the Markundi pass into the valley of the Son you observe a large isolated boulder split into two parts with a narrow fissure between them. Further on in the bed of the Son is a curious water-worn rock, which, to the eye of faith, suggests a rude resemblance to a headless elephant. On this foundation has been localised the legend of Lorik which takes us back to the time when the Aryan and the aboriginal Dasyu contended for mastery in the wild borderland. There was once, so the tale runs, a barbarian king who ruled at the fort of Agori, the frontier fortress on the Son. Among his dependents was a cowherd maiden named Manjaní who was loved by her clansman Lorik. He with his brother Sánwán came to claim her as his bride. The Rája insisted on enforcing the *Jus primæ noctis*. The heroic brothers, in order to escape this infamy, carried off the maiden. The Rája pursued on his famous mad elephant, which Lorik decapitated with a single blow. When they reached in their flight the Markundi pass, the wise Manjaní advised Lorik to use her father's sword which, with admirable forethought, she had brought with her. He preferred his own weapon, but she warned him to test both. His own sword broke in pieces against the huge boulder of the pass, but Manjaní's weapon clave it in twain. So Lorik and his brother with the aid of the magic brand defeated the infidel hosts with enormous slaughter and carried off the maiden in triumph. If you doubt the story, there are the cloven boulder and the petrified elephant to witness to its truth, and both are worshipped to this day in the name of Lorik and his bride with oblations of milk and grain.[2]

[1] A fairly full abstract of this famous legend is given in *Archæological Reports*, VIII, 79. The analogy to the Paris-Helen legend and the tale of Arthur is obvious

[2] For instances of conversion of living creatures into stones see Tylor, *Primitive Culture*, I, 352, note, and for instances in Indian folklore, Temple, *Wideawake Stories*, 419, *sqq*.

Of a similar type is the Jiráyá Bhaváni, who is worshipped at Jungaii, south of the Son. In her place of worship, a cave on the hillside, the only representative of the goddess is an ancient rust-eaten coat of mail. This gives her name, which is a corruption of the Persian *zirah*, meaning a coat of armour. Close by is a little stream known as the Suaráya, the meaning of which is, of course, assumed to be "Hog river," from the Hindi *Súar*, a pig. Here we have all the elements of a myth. In one of the early fights between Hindu and Musalmán a wounded hero of Islám came staggering to the bank of the stream and was about to drink when he heard that its name was connected with what is an abomination to the true believer. So he preferred to die of thirst, and no one sees any incongruity in the fact that the armour of a martyr of the faith has become a form of the Hindu goddess. The shrine is now on its promotion and Jiráyá Bhaváni will be provided with a Sanskrit etymology and develop before long into a genuine manifestation of Káli.

Jiráyá Bhaváni.

There is hardly a village in Northern India without a fetish of this kind which is usually not appropriated to any special deity but represents the *gánwdevata* or *deohár*, the collective local divine cabinet which has the affairs of the community under its charge. Why spirits should live in stones has been debated. Mr. Campbell suggests that the fact is that stones were found to contain fire; and that heated stones being found useful in disease, cooking, etc., may have strengthened the idea. "The earliest theory was perhaps that as the life of the millet was in the millet seed and the life of the mango tree was in the mango stone, a human spirit could live in a rock or pebble. The belief that the soul or part of the soul of a man lives in his bones seems closely connected with the belief in the stone as a spirit house. Probably it was an early belief that the bones should be kept so that if the spirit comes back and worries the survivors he may have a place to go to."[1] But it is probable that other considerations

Village fetish stones.

---

[1] *Notes*, 163.

also influenced the spread of the idea. In a stoneless land like the alluvial plains of Northern India the stone would be regarded as a curiosity and inspire reverence. The curious appearance of some stones, like the *Sálagráma*, would excite wonder and respect. Others like prehistoric stone weapons often found on shrines of Mahádeva would be regarded as the work of superhuman artizans. The form of some, again, would be associated with phallicism. Bored or perforated stones such as the Sálagráma would be specially respected. This perhaps is one reason why the family grindstone is so commonly worshipped at marriages. The Kunbis of Kolába place a grindstone in the lying-in-room and on it set a rice-flour image of a woman which is worshipped as a goddess and the baby is laid before it. Such a stone readily passes into a fetish, as at Ahmadnagar, where there is a stone with two holes which any two fingers of any person's hand can fill and the mosque where it stands is, in consequence, much respected.[1] But much of the stone worship appears to be the result of the respect paid to the tombstone or cairn, which, as we have already seen, keeps down the spirit of the dead man and is often a place in which his ghost chooses to reside.

Fetish stones and human sacrifice.

These rude stones are very often smeared with ruddle or red ochre. We have here a survival of the blood sacrifice of a human being or animal which was once universal.[2] Such sacrifices rest on the principle that it is necessary to supply attendants to the dead or to the tribal gods in the other world: and the commutation of human sacrifices, first, into those of animals and then into a mere scarlet stain on the fetish stone is a constantly recurring fact in the history of custom.[3] It may be worth while to discuss this transition from the Indian evidence.

---

[1] *Bombay Gazetteer*, XI, 56; XVII, 698.

[2] On this see Robertson Smith, *Kinship and Marriage*, 49: Lubbock, *Origin of Civilisation*, 306: Tylor, *Primitive Culture*, II, 164: Conway, *Demonology*, II, 284.

[3] Spencer, *Principles of Sociology*, I, 268: Lang, *Custom and Myth*, I, 270.

Human sacrifice among Indian Aryans.

That human sacrifice prevailed among the early Aryans in India is on all sides admitted. The whole question has been treated in detail by the eminent Hindu scholar Rájendra Lála Mitra.[1] He arrives at the conclusion that looking to the history of ancient civilisation and the ritual of the Hindus, there is nothing to justify the belief that the Hindus were incapable of sacrificing human beings to their gods: that the Sunahsepha hymns of the Rig Veda Sanhitá most probably refer to a human sacrifice : that the Aitareya Bráhmana refers to an actual, and not a typical, human sacrifice : that the Purushamedha originally required the actual sacrifice of men : that the Taittiríya Bráhmana enjoins the sacrifice of a man at the horse sacrifice : that the Satapatha Bráhmana sanctions human sacrifices in some cases, but makes the Parushamedha emblematic : that the Puránas recognize human sacrifices to Chandiká, but prohibit the Parushamedha rite : and that the Tantras enjoin human sacrifices to Chandiká, and require that when human victims are not available, an effigy of a human being should be sacrificed to her.

Evidence from folktales.

The proof of the existence of human sacrifices in early times is also derived from the folktales. We have in Somadeva constant references to human sacrifices made to Chandiká or Chamundá. We find one Muravára a Turushka or Indo-Skythian, who proposes to make a human sacrifice to his dead father: we have expiatory sacrifices to Chandiká to save the life of a king. In one of the Panjáb tales a ship will not leave port till a human victim is offered.[2]

Human sacrifices in modern times.

Up to quite modern times the same was the case, and there is some evidence to show that the custom has not quite ceased. Until the beginning of the present century the custom of offering a first born child to the

[1] *Indo-Aryans*, II, 70, *sqq.* : *Journal, Asiatic Society of Bengal*, 1876, and compare Max Müller, *Ancient Sanskrit Literature*, 408, *sq.* : Muir, *Ancient Sanskrit Texts*, Vols. I, II, *passim* : Wilson, *Rig Veda*, I, 59, 63 : *Essays*, II, 247 *sqq.* : Atkinson, *Himalayan Gazetteer*, II, 800, 867.

[2] Tawney, *Katha Sarit Ságara*, I, 336 : II, 253, 338 : Temple, *Wideawake Stories* 147 : Lál Bihari De, *Folktales*, 194 : Miss Frere, *Old Deccan Days*, 6, etc.

Ganges was common.[1] Akin to this is the Gangá Játra, or murder of sick relatives on the bank of the sacred river, of which a case occurred quite recently at Calcutta.[2] The modern instances of human sacrifice among the Khándhs of Bengal and the Mers of Rájputána are notorious.[3] It also prevailed among the races of Chutia Nágpur up to quite recent times. The Kharwárs, since adopting Hinduism, performed human sacrifices to Kálí in the form of Chándí: some of our people who fell into their hands in 1857 were so dealt with. The same was the case with the Bhuiyas, Khánds and Mundas. Some of the Gonds of Sirguja used to offer human sacrifices to Burha deo, and still go through a form of doing so.[4] There is a recent instance quoted among the Tiyars, a class of boatmen in Benares; and one Tonurám sacrificed four Bengalis in the hope of recovering the treasures of seven Rájas: another man was killed in order to propitiate a Rákshasa who guarded a treasure supposed to be concealed in the house where the deed was committed.[5] The Kurháda Bráhmans of Bombay were accused of offering human victims to their goddess Mahálakshmi.[6] There seems reason to suspect that even in the present day such sacrifices are occasionally committed at remote shrines of Kálí or Deví. Within the last two years a significant case of the kind occurred in Benares. There are numerous instances from Nepál.[7] At Jaipur near Vizagapatam the Rája is said at his installation in 1861 to have sacrificed a girl to Durgá.[8] A recent case of such sacrifice to recover hidden treasure occurred in Berár: a second at Muzaffarnagar connected with witchcraft.[9] At Chánda and Lánji in the province of Nágpur there are shrines to Kálí at which human victims have been offered to Kálí almost within the memory of the

[1] Rájendra Lála Mitra, *op. cit.*, II, 76.
[2] Chevers, *Indian Medical Jurisprudence*, 625.
[3] Campbell, *Thirteen Years' Service Among the Wild Tribes of Khondistán: passim*: Frazer, *Golden Bough*, I, 384, *sqq.*: *Rájputána Gazetteer*, II, 47.
[4] Dalton, *Descriptive Ethnology*, 130, 147, 176; 285, *sq.*, 281.
[5] Chevers, *loc. cit.*, 406, 411.
[6] Wilson, *Indian Caste*, II, 22, *sq.*: Campbell, *Notes*, 339: *Bombay Gazetteer*, X, 114.
[7] Wright, *History*, 11, *Note*.
[8] Ball, *Jungle Life*, 580.
[9] *North Indian Notes and Queries*, I, 112, 148.

present generation. In 1870 a Musalmán butcher losing his child was told by a Hindu conjurer that if he washed his wife in the blood of a boy, his next infant would be healthy. To ensure this result a child was murdered. A similar case occurred in Muzaffarnagar where a child was killed and the blood drunk by a childless woman.[1] It would be easy to add largely to instances of this kind.

Survivals of human sacrifice.

There are in addition numerous customs which appear to be survivals of human sacrifice. Among the lower castes in Northern India the parting of the bride's hair is marked with red, a survival of the original blood covenant by which she was introduced into the sept of her husband. Among the Kewats of Bengal a tiny scratch is made on the little finger of the bridegroom's right hand and of the bride's left, and the drops of blood drawn from these are mixed with the food. Each then eats the food with which the other's blood has been mingled. Among the Santáls blood is drawn in the same way from the little finger of the bride and bridegroom, and with it marks are made on both above the clavicle.[2]

Human sacrifice and buildings.

One standing difficulty at each decennial Census has been the rumour which spread in remote tracts that the Government required victims to be sacrificed at some bridge or other building or that a toll of the pretty girls was to be taken to reward the soldiery after some war. This idea that great public works require a victim before they can be completed prevails widely among the rural population. The rumour spread quite recently in connection with the Hooghly Bridge at Calcutta and the Benares Water-works. The Narbadá, it was believed, would never allow herself to be bridged until she carried away part of the superstructure and caused the loss of lives as a sacrifice. At Ahmadábád, by the advice of a Bráhman, a childless Ványa was induced to dig a tank to appease the goddess Sítalá.

[1] *Report, Inspector-General of Police*, N.-W. P., 1870, p. 93: *Panjáb Notes and Queries*, II, 205, *sq.*: III, 74, *sq.*: 162: Chevers, *op. cit.*, 842, *sq.*, 396, *sq.*, and for other instances Campbell, *Notes*, 338, *sqq.*

[2] Risley, *Tribes and Castes*, I, 456: Dalton, *Descriptive Ethnology*, 220.

The water refused to enter it without the sacrifice of a man. As soon as the victim's blood fell on the ground the tank filled, and the goddess came down from heaven and rescued the victim. The Vadála lake in Bombay refused to hold water till the local spirit was appeased by the sacrifice of the daughter of the village headman. When the Shorkot Fort was being built one side repeatedly fell down. A faqır advised the Rája to put a first born son under the rampart. This was done and the wall stood. The child's mother went to Mecca and returned with an army of Muhammadans; but they could not take the fort. Then a faqír transformed himself into a cock and flew on the roof of the palace where he set up a loud crow. The Rája was frightened and abandoned the place. As he was leaving it he shouted "Shame on thee, O Fort, to remain standing," and the walls at once fell down.[1]

Modification of human sacrifices.

There are also many instances of the transition from human sacrifices to those of a milder form. Thus when Ahmadábád was building, Manik Báwa, a saint, every day made a cushion and every night picked it to pieces. As he did so the day's work fell down. The Sultán refrained from sacrificing him, but got him into a small jar and kept him there till the work was over.[2] Formerly in Hoshangabad men used to swing themselves from a pole, as in the famous Bengal Charakh Púja. In our territories this is now uncommon, as the village headmen being afraid of responsibility for an accident, generally, instead of a man, fasten up a white pumpkin, which they swing about.[3] At the installation of a Bhuiya Rája a man comes forward whom the Rája touches on the neck, as if about to cut off his head. The victim disappears for three days: then he presents himself before the Rája, as if miraculously restored to life. Similarly the Gonds, instead of a human sacrifice, now make an image of straw which they find answer the purpose; the Bhuiyas of

---

[1] *Bombay Gazetteer*, II, 349: XIV, 49: *Archæological Reports*, V, 98: and for other instances see *ibid.*, XX, 124: *Folklore Record*, III, Pt. II, 182: *Oudh Gazetteer*, III, 253: *Indian Antiquary*, XI, 117: *Calcutta Review*, LXXVII, 166: Lál Bihári De, *Folktales of Bengal*, 130.

[2] *Bombay Gazetteer*, IV, 276.

[3] *Settlement Report*, 126.

Keonjhar used to offer the head of their prime minister to Thakuráni Mái. She is now transformed into the Hindu Durgá and accepts a sacrifice of goats and sheep.[1] In Nepál after the Sithi Játra feast the people divide into two parties and have a match at stone throwing: formerly this used to be a serious matter, and any one who was knocked down and fell into the hands of the opposite side was sacrificed to the goddess Kankeswarí. The actual killing of the victim, as in the case of the sacrifices to the goddess Bachhlá Deví, has now been discontinued under the influence of British officers.[2]

Momiái.

In connection with human sacrifice may be mentioned the curious superstition about *Momiái* or mummy. The virtues of fat as a magical ointment appear all through folklore. Indian witches are believed to use this mystic application to enable them to fly through the air, as their European sisters are supposed to use the fat of a toad.[3] Human fat is believed to be particularly efficacious for such purposes. In one of Somadeva's stories the Bráhman searches for treasure with a candle made of human fat in his hand.[4] One of the Mongol Generals, Marco Polo tells us, was accused of boiling down human beings and using their fat to grease his mangonels: and Carpini says that when the Tartars cast Greek fire into a town, they used to shoot human fat with it in order to cause the fire to burn more fiercely.[5] So in Europe a candle of human fat is said to have been used by robbers with the Hand of Glory to prevent the inmates waking, and on the Scottish border the torch used in the mystic ceremony of "saining" was made from the fat of a slaughtered enemy.[6] In India the popular idea about *Momiái* is that a boy, the fatter and blacker the better, is caught, a small hole is bored in the top of his head, and he is hung up by the heels over a slow fire. The juice or essence of his body is in this way distilled into seven drops of the

---

[1] Dalton, *Descriptive Ethnology*, 146, 281: Risley, *Tribes and Castes*, I, 115.
[2] Wright, *History*, 35, *sq.*: 156 note: 205, 265, 126.
[3] Tawney, *Katha Sarit Ságara*, II, 594.
[4] *Ibid.*, I, 306.
[5] Yule, *Marco Polo*, II, 165.
[6] Henderson, *Folklore of the Northern Counties*, 54, 200, *sqq.*

potent medicine known as *Momiái.* This substance possesses healing properties of a supernatural kind. Sword cuts, spear thrusts, wounds from arrows and other weapons of warfare are instantly cured by its use, and he who possesses it is practically invulnerable. It is further believed that a European gentleman, known as the *Momiái wála Sáhib*, has a contract from Government of the right of enticing away suitable boys for this purpose. He makes them smell a stick or wand which obliges them to follow him and he then packs them off to some hill station where he carries on this most nefarious manufacture. "A very black servant of a friend of mine states that he had a very narrow escape from this Sáhib at the Nauchandi fair at Meerut, where Government allows him to walk about for one day and make as many suitable victims as he can by means of his stick. The Sáhib had just put his hand in his pocket and taken out the stick, which was dry and shrivelled and a span long, when the servant with great presence of mind held out his hands and said *bas! bas!* 'enough! enough!' Thus intimidated, the Sáhib went away into the crowd. In connection with *Momiái* a lady here narrowly escaped a very uncanny reputation. Some of her servants gave out that she possessed a *Momiái* stick for which she had paid a hundred rupees; and on hearing this an enquiry was made which brought out that the lady had missed a pod of vanilla about seven inches long, of a very special quality, that she kept rolled up in a piece of paper among some of her trinkets. The ayah who mislaid it was scolded for her carelessness, and told that it was worth more than she thought. She promptly put two and two together. The shrivelled appearance (which is supposed to be peculiar to mysterious sticks such as snake charmers produce), the fuss made about it, and the value attached to it, convinced her that her mistress owned a *Momiái* stick."[1] Every native boy, particularly those who are black and fat, believes himself to be a possible victim to the wiles of this dreaded Sáhib, who frequents hill stations because he is thus enabled to carry on his villainous practices with impunity and less danger of detection. Even to whisper the

[1] *North Indian Notes and Queries*, I, 190.

word *Momiái* is enough to make the crowd of urchins who dog the steps of a European officer in a town disperse in dismay. Surgeons are naturally exposed to the suspicion of being engaged in this awful business, and some years ago most of the coolies deserted one of the hill stations because an enthusiastic anatomist set up a private dissecting room of his own. Freemasons, who are looked on by the general native-public as a kind of sorcerers or magicians, are also not free from this suspicion. That such ideas should prevail among the rural population is not to be wondered at when even in our modern England it is generally believed that luminous paint is made out of human fat.[1]

Dánapurwála Sáhib.

Another of these dreaded Sáhibs is the Dánapurwála Sáhib, or gentleman from Dinapur. Why this personage should be connected with Dinapur, a respectable cantonment, no one can make out. At any rate, it is generally believed that he has a contract from Government for procuring heads for some of our Museums, and he too has a magic stick with which he entices unfortunate travellers on dark nights and chops off their heads with a pair of shears. The wand which both these worthies use is clearly the analogue of the mystic rod which appears throughout folklore.[2] Its influence through smelling may be associated with the fact that the nose is a spirit entry as we have seen in the case of sneezing.

Fetish stones.

To return after this digression to fetish stones. Of this form of belief we have well-known instances in the Coronation stone in Westminster Abbey which is associated with the dream of Jacob and the Hajuru'l Aswad of Mecca which Sir R. Burton believed to be an aërolite. No one will bring a stone from the sacred hill at Gobardhan near Mathura, because it is supposed to be endowed with life. The Yádavas, who are connected with the same part of the country had a stone fetish,

---

[1] *Folklore Record*, III, Pt. II, 283. For an account of the commonplace *Momiái* see Watts' Dictionary of Economic Products, II, 115. This *Momiái* is used as application for women at parturition.

[2] Lál Bihári De, *Folktales*, 121; Jacob's *English Fairy Tales*, 201, 209, 223.

described in the Vishnu Purána, which brought rain and plenty. The stalactites in the Behár hills are regarded as images of the gods.[1] The pestle and mortar in which a noted Darvesh of Oudh used to grind his drugs are now worshipped, and a leading family in the Lucknow district keep before their residence a large square stone which they reverence. They say that their ancestors brought it from Dehli, and that it is the symbol of their title to the estates which were granted to one of them by the Emperor. He enjoined them to take it as the foundation of their settlement, and since that time each new Rája on his accession presents flowers, sweetmeats and money to it.[2] A great rock in the river above Badrináth, the famous shrine in the hills, is worshipped as Brahm Kapál or the skull of Brahma, and Nanda Deví, the mountain goddess of the Himalaya, is reverenced in the form of two great stones glittering with mica, and reflecting the rays of the sun.[3] At Amosi in the Lucknow district they worship at marriages and births of boys the door-post of the house of an old Rájput leader, named Bináik, who is honoured with the title of Baba or father.[4] At Deodhúra in the hills the grey granite boulders near the crest of the ridge are said to have been thrown there in sport by the Pándavas. Close to the temple of Deví at the same place are two large boulders, the uppermost of which called Ransila, or "stone of battle," is cleft through the centre by a deep, fresh-looking fissure, at right angles to which is a similar rift in the lower rock. A small boulder on the top is said to have been the weapon with which Bhímsen produced these fissures, and the point of his five fingers is still to be seen upon it. Ransila itself is marked with the lines for playing the gambling game of Pachísí, which though it led to their misfortunes, the Pandavas could not even in their exile abandon. Similarly at Bhímghora about Haridwár the priests show on the rocks the imprint of the hoofs of Bhímsen's horse.[5]

---

[1] Buchanan, *Eastern India*, I, 526.
[2] *Oudh Gazetteer*, I, 303; II, 415.
[3] Atkinson, *Himalayan Gazetteer*, II, 311 note; II, 792, *sq.*
[4] *Oudh Gazetteer*, I, 61.
[5] Atkinson, *Himalayan Gazetteer*, II, 282.

Fetishes among the Dravidians.

The Santáls, like all uncivilised races, have a whole army of fetishes. A round piece of wood, nearly a foot length, the top of which is painted red, is called Banhí, or the goddess of the jungle. Another stands for Lugú, the protectress of the earth, who is sometimes represented by a mountain. An oblong piece of wood, painted red, stands for Mahámáyá, the great mother, Deví's daughter: a small piece of white stone daubed with red is Burhiyá Mái, or the "old mother," her grand-daughter: an arrow head stands for Dudhá Mái "the milk mother," the daughter of Burhiyá: a trident painted red represents the monkey god Hanumán, who executes all the orders of Deví. "Sets of these symbols are placed, one on the east and one on the west of their huts to protect them from evil spirits, snakes, tigers and all sorts of misfortunes."[1] On the same principle in the Mirzapur jungles the Ahírs, who, though possibly of different origin, have closely assimilated their customs to those of the Dravidian races who surround them, erect wooden fetishes to represent Bírnáth, one of their deified ghosts who protects their animals from tigers and their families from fever. These statues are very commonly in pairs to represent the male and female principle, and on the side facing east a rude face is carved before which offerings are made in times of danger and trouble.

Fetish stones which cure disease.

Many of these stones have the power of curing disease: and water with which they have been bathed is used as a medicine. This is the case with a number of sacred lingams of Mahádeva all over the country. We have already noticed the fetish bowl, the washings of which are administered by midwives to secure easy parturition. We find the same custom in Java, where a decoction of the lichen which grows on fetish stones is used as a remedy in disease, and in the Isle of Lewis cattle disease is attributed to the bite of serpents and the suffering animals are made to drink water into which charm stones are put.[2]

---

[1] Dalton, *Descriptive Ethnology*, 220.
[2] Forbes, *Wanderings of a Naturalist*, 103: Henderson, *Folklore of the Northern Counties*, 165.

The virtue of all these fetish stones rests on the spirits of gods or deified men which they are supposed to embody. This is a common idea in folklore. In one of Miss Stokes's fairy tales,—"The man who went to seek his fate," the fate is found in stones, some standing up and some lying down. The man beats the stone which embodies his fate, because he is miserably poor. Mr. H. Spenser thinks that the idea of persons being turned into stones may have arisen from instances of actual petrifaction of trees, &c., but this is not very probable, and it is much simpler to believe with Dr. Tylor that it depends on the principle of animism.[1]

Fetish stones the abode of spirits.

Some fetishes are special to a particular family. Such is the case with the Thárus, an aboriginal tribe in the sub-Himalayan Tarái. Each member of the tribe constructs a hollow mound opposite his door, and thereon erects a stake of *palása* wood (*butea frondosa*) which is regarded as the family fetish and periodically worshipped.

Family fetishes.

Next comes the worship of the tool fetish, which according to Sir. A. Lyall is "the earliest phase or type of the tendency which later on leads those of one guild or one walk in life to support and cultivate one god who is elected in lieu of the individual trade fetishes melted down to preside over their craft or trade interests."[2] A good example of this is the pickaxe fetish of the Thags. When Kálí refused to help them in the burial of their victims she gave them one of her teeth for a pickaxe, a rib for a knife and the hem of her lower garment for a noose. Hence the pickaxe was venerated by the Thags. Its fabrication was superintended with the greatest care, and it was consecrated with many ceremonies. A lucky day was selected, and a smith was appointed to forge it with the most profound secresy. The door was closed against all intruders: the leader never left the forge while the manufacture was going on; and the smith was

Tool fetishes.

[1] Spencer, *Principles of Sociology*, I, 109, *sq.*: 310: Tylor, *Primitive Culture*, I, 353.
[2] *Asiatic Studies*, 16.

allowed to engage in no other work until this was completed. Next came the consecration. This was done on Monday, Tuesday, Wednesday or Friday, and care was taken that the shadow of no living thing fell upon the axe. The consecrator sat with his face to the west and received the implement in a brass dish. It was then washed in water which was allowed to fall into a pit made for the purpose. Then further ablutions followed, the first in sugar and water, the second in sour milk and the third in spirits. The axe was then marked from the head to the point with seven spots of red lead, and replaced on the brass dish with a cocoanut, some cloves, white sandal wood and other articles. A fire was next made of cowdung and the wood of the mango and *ber* or plum tree. All the articles deposited on the brass plate, with the exception of the cocoanut, were thrown into the fire, and when the flame rose the Thag priest passed the pickaxe with both hands seven times through the fire. The cocoanut was then stripped of its husk and placed on the ground. The officiant holding the axe by the point asked,—"Shall I strike?" The bystanders assented, and he then broke the cocoanut with the butt end of the weapon, exclaiming,—"All hail, mighty Deví! great mother of us all!" The spectators responded,—"All hail Deví! and prosper the Thags!" If the cocoanut was not broken at one blow all the labour was lost: the goddess was considered unpropitious, and the entire ceremony had to be repeated. The broken shell and cocoanut were then thrown into the fire, the pickaxe wrapped in white cloth was placed on the ground towards the west, and all present prostrated themselves before it.[1] We have here another example of magic in its sympathetic form, and the various classes of spirit scarers employed have been already discussed.

Weapon and implement fetishes.

In the same way soldiers and warlike tribes worship their weapons. Thus the sword was worshipped by the Rájputs.[2] The Nepalese worship their weapons and regimental colours at the Dasahra festival. At the Diwálí or feast of lamps, on the first day they worship dogs; on the

[1] *Illustrations of the History and Practices of the Thags*, 46, *sqq.*
[2] Tod, *Annals*, I, 615.

second day, cows and bulls; on the third day, capitalists worship their treasure under the name of Lakshmi, the goddess of wealth; on the fourth day every householder worships as deities the members of his family, and on the fifth day sisters worship their brothers.[1] So in Upper India the hair scraper of the tanner is worshipped by curriers and the potter's wheel, regarded as a type of productiveness, is reverenced at marriages by many of the lower castes. In Bengal the Alakhiya sect of Saiva ascetics profess profound respect for their alms-bag: the carpenters worship their adze, chisel and saw: and the barbers their razors, scissors and mirror.[2] At the Srípanchamí, or the morning of the fifth lunar day of the month of Mágh, the writer class worship their books, pens and inkstands. The writing implements are cleaned and the books, wrapped in white cloth, are strewn over with flowers and the leaves of young barley.[3] The same is the case in Bombay. A mill is the *devak* or guardian of oil makers: dancing girls worship a musical instrument: jewellers worship their pincers and blowpipe: curriers worship an axe, and market gardeners a pair of scales.[4] In the Panjáb, farmers worship their oxen in August, their plough at the Dasahra festival, and they have a ceremony at the end of October to drive away ticks from their cattle: shepherds worship their sheep at the full moon of July; bankers and clerks worship their books at the Diwálí festival; grain sellers worship their weights at the Dasahra, Diwálí and Holí, and, in a way, every morning as well: oilmen worship their presses at odd times: artisans salute their tools daily when they bathe; and, generally speaking, the means of livelihood, whatever they may be, are worshipped with honour at the Diwálí, Dasahra and Holí.[5] So the Pokharna Bráhmans, who are said to have been originally the navvies who excavated the sacred lake of Pushkar, worship in memory of this the *kudála* or mattock.[6] All these customs are as old as the time of the Chaldæans, "who sacrifice into their

[1] Oldfield, *Sketches*, 344, 352.
[2] Risley, *Tribes and Castes*, I, 16, 67, 93.
[3] Wilson, *Essays*, II, 188: Risley, *loc. cit.*, I, 451, *sq.*
[4] Campbell, *Notes*, 9.
[5] *Panjáb Notes and Queries*, II, 20, *sq.*, 93.
[6] Tod, *Annals*, II, 320.

net and burn incense unto their drag, because by them their portion is fat and their meat plenteous."[1]

The corn sieve fetish.

Among these tool fetishes there are two of special importance, the corn sieve and the plough. The corn sieve or winnowing basket, Virgil's *Mystica Vannus Iacchi*, has always enjoyed reputation as an emblem of increase and prosperity and as possessing magical powers. Divination was performed with a pair of shears and a sieve. Aubrey describes how "the sheaves are stuck in a sieve, and the maydens hold up ye sieve with the top of their fingers by the handle of the shiers: then say 'By St. Peter and St. Paule such a one hath stolen such a thing': the others say 'By St. Peter and St. Paule he hath not stolen it.' After many adjurations the sieve will turn at the name of the thief."[2] In India the sieve is the first cradle of the baby, and when a mother has lost a child she puts the next in a sieve and drags it about calling it Kadheran or Ghasítan "the dragged one," so as to baffle the Evil eye by a pretence of contempt. All through Upper India at low caste marriages the bride's brother accompanies the pair as they revolve in the marriage shed and sprinkles parched grain on the ground out of a sieve as a spell for good luck and fertility. So Irish brides in old times used to be followed by two attendants bearing high over the heads of the young couple a sieve filled with meal, a sign of the plenty that would be in their house and an omen of good luck and the blessing of children.[3] At the Diwálí festival a woman takes a sieve and a house broom, which is also a scarer of evil spirits, and beats them in every corner of the house, exclaiming "God abide and poverty depart. !" The fan is then carried outside the village generally to the east or north, and being thrown away is supposed, like the scapegoat, to bear away with it the poverty and distress of the household. Among the Kols when a vacancy occurs in the office of the village priest the winnowing fan with some rice is used, and by its magical power it drags the person who

[1] *Habakkuk*, I, 16: *Isaiah*, XXI, 5.
[2] *Remaines*, 25.
[3] Lady Wilde, *Legends*, 116.

holds it towards the individual on whom the sacred mantle has fallen. The same custom prevails among the Oraons.[1] So the Greeks had a special name, *koskinomantis*, for the man who divined in this way with the sieve, and the practice is mentioned by Theocritus.[2] The sieve is also very commonly used in India as a rude form of the planchette. Through the wicker work of the raised side or back a strong T-shaped twig is fixed, one end of which rests on the finger. A question is asked and according as the sieve turns to the right or left the answer is "Yes" or "No." This is exactly what is known as "cauff riddling" in Yorkshire and Scotland.[3] In the eastern districts of the North-Western Provinces when the Ojha or "cunning man" is called in to cure disease or possession by evil spirits, he puts some sesamum into a sieve, shakes it about and then proceeds to identify the ghost concerned by counting the number of grains which remain stuck between the reeds. At a Santál cremation a man takes his seat near the ashes and tosses rice on them with a winnowing fan till a frenzy appears to seize him and he becomes inspired and says wonderful things.[4] It is one of the curiosities of comparative folklore that the instrument should be credited with magical powers all over two continents.[5]

The plough fetish.

Next comes the plough as a fetish. The carrying about of the plough and the prohibition common in Europe against moving it on Shrove Tuesday and other days have, like many other usages of the same class, been connected with Phallicism.[6] But, looking at the respect which an agricultural people would naturally pay to the chief implement used in cultivation, it is simpler to class it with other tool fetishes of a similar kind. In India, as in Europe, on Plough Monday[7] there is a regular worship of the plough at the end of the sowing season,

[1] Dalton, *Descriptive Ethnology*, 187, Note: 247.
[2] *Idyils*, III, 31.
[3] Henderson, *Folklore of the Northern Counties*, 52: Gregor, *Folklore of N.E. Scotland*, 43, 92.
[4] Dalton, *loc. cit*, 218.
[5] See *Academy* 23rd July 1887: *Gentlemen's Magazine*, July 1887: Henderson, *loc. cit.*, 233: Brand, *Observations*, 233: Lady Wilde, *Legends*, 207.
[6] Cox, *Mythology of the Aryan Nations*, II, 119, note.
[7] For which see Chambers' *Book of Days*, I, 94, *sq.*

when the beam is coloured with turmeric, adorned with garlands and brought home from the field in triumph. After that day it is considered unlucky to use it or lend it. The beam is put up in the village cattle track when rinderpest is about as a charm to drive away the disease. Among some castes the polished share is fixed up in the marriage shed during the ceremony. Among the Orâons the bride and bridegroom are made to stand on a currystone, under which is placed a sheaf of corn resting on the plough yoke, and among the same people their god Darha is represented by a ploughshare set upon an alter dedicated to him.[1] Here we have the mystic influence of iron combined with the agricultural implement fetish.

The fire fetish.

Fire is undoubtedly a very ancient Hindu protective fetish, and its virtue as a scarer of evil demons is very generally recognized. One of the earliest legends of the Hindu race is that recorded in the Rig Veda where Agni, the god of fire, concealed himself in heaven, was brought down to earth by Mátarisvan and made over to the priestly tribe of Bhrigu, in which we have the oriental version of the myth of Prometheus.[2] As no sacrifice could be performed without fire, Agni was called "the mother of the gods," Yavishtha or "younger," and Pramantha, because on each occasion when he was required, he was produced by friction of the Araní or fire drill made of the wood of the sacred fig tree. This word Pramantha is possibly equivalent to the Prometheus of the Greeks.

Origin of fire worship.

According to Dr. Tylor "the real and absolute worship of fire falls into two great divisions—the first belonging rather to fetishism, the second to polytheism proper, and the two apparently representing an earlier and later stage of theological ideas. The first is the rude barbarous adoration of the actual flame which he watches writhing, devouring, roaring like a wild animal: the second belongs to an advanced

[1] Dalton, *loc. cit.*, 252, 258.

[2] *Rig Veda*, III, 9, 5: X, 46, 2: I, 164, 46: Max Müller, *Early Sanskrit Literature*, 567: Cox, *Mythology of the Aryan Nations*, II, 201, *sq*.

generalisation that any individual fire is a manifestation of one general elemental being, the fire god."[1] In a tropical country it would naturally be associated with the worship of the sun, and with the worship of the sainted dead as the medium by which the spirit wings its way to the other world. Among many races, fire is provided for the ghost after interment to enable it to warm itself and cook its food.[2] And as Mr. Spencer points out, the grave fire would tend to develop into kindred religious rites.

The sacred fire.

But it is almost certainly erroneous to class the sacred fire as an institution peculiar to the so-called Aryan races. The *Homa* is, of course, one of the most important elements of the modern Hindu ritual; but at the same time it prevails extensively as a means of propitiating the local or village gods among various of the Dravidian races, who are quite as likely to have discovered for themselves the mystical art of fire production by mechanical means as to have adopted it by a process of conscious or unconscious imitation from the usages of their Hindu neighbours. The production of fire by means of friction is a discovery which would naturally occur to jungle races who must have seen it constantly occur by the ignition of the bamboo stalks rubbed together by the blasts of summer. From this would easily be developed the very primitive fire drill or *asgara* used to this day by the Cheros, Korwas, Bhuiyas and other Dravidian forest tribes of Mirzapur. These people, even at the present day, habitually produce fire in this way. A small round cavity is made in a dry piece of bamboo in which two men alternately with their open hands revolve a second pointed piece of the same tree. Smoke and finally fire are rapidly produced in this way and the sparks are received on a dry leaf or other suitable tinder. The use of the flint and steel is also common and was possibly an early and independent invention of the same people. Even at the present day in some of their more secret worship of the village godlings of disease, fire is produced for the fire sacrifice by this primitive method.

---

[1] *Primitive Culture*, II, 277.

[2] See Spencer, *Principles of Sociology*, I, 158, 273.

The fire drill.

What has been called the Aryan fire drill—the Araní, which in one sense means "foreign" or "strange" and in another "moving," "entering," "being inserted—" is not apparently now-a-days used in the ordinary ritual for the production of fire for the *homa* sacrifice. In Northern India, at least, it seems to have become a speciality of one branch of Bráhmans—the Gujaráti, who are employed to conduct certain special services occasionally performed at large cost by wealthy devotees and known as *Jag,* Sanskrit *Yaksha* or worship. The Araní in its modern form consists of five pieces. The *adharárani* is the lower bed of the implement and is usually made of the hard wood of the *khadira* or *khair* (*acacia catechu*). In this are bored two shallow holes—one, the *garta,* a small shallow round cavity in which the plunger or revolving drill works and produces fire by friction. Close to this is a shallow oblong cavity known as the *yoni* or matrix in which combustible tinder, generally the husk of the cocoanut, is placed and in which the sparks and heated ashes are received and ignited. The upper or revolving portion of the drill is known as *uttarárani* or *pramantha.* This consists of two parts, the upper portion a piece of hard, round wood which one priest revolves with a rope or cord known as *netra.* This part of the implement is known as the *mantha* or "churner." It has a socket at the base in which the *sanku,* spike or dart, is fixed. This *sanku* is made of a softer wood (generally that of the *pípal* or sacred fig tree) than the *adharárani* or base: and each *araní* is provided with several spare pieces of fig wood for the purpose of replacing the *sanku* as it becomes gradually charred away by friction. The last piece is the *upamantha* or "upper churner," which is a flat board with a socket. This is pressed down by one priest so as to force the *sanku* deep and hard into the *garta* or lower cavity so as to increase the resistance. The working of the implement thus requiries the labour of two priests, one of whom presses down the plunger and the other who revolves the drill rapidly by means of the rope. It is not easy to obtain specimens of the implement which is regarded as possessing mystical properties, and the production of the sacred fire is always conducted in secret. We have in the folktales at least one reference to this production of the sacred fire—"Then the Bráhman blessed the King and said to him, I am a Bráhman named Nága Sarman, and bear the fruit I hope from my sacrifice. When the god of fire is pleased with this *vilva* sacrifice, then *vilva* fruits of gold will come out of the fire cavity. Then the god of fire will appear in bodily form and grant me a boon, and so I have spent much time in offering *vilva* fruits." Then "the seven-rayed god appeared from the sacrificial cavity, bringing the King a golden *vilva* fruit of his tree of valour."[1] The *agnikunda*, the hole or enclosed space for the sacred fire, out of which according to the popular legend various Rájput tribes were produced, is thus probably derived from the *garta* or pit out of which the sparks fly in the *araní* or fire drill. The germ of the sacred fire is still carefully preserved, as at the Roman temple of Vesta, in charge of special guardians at certain shrines, such as those of Sambhunáth and Kharg Jogini in Nepál.[2]

The Muhammadan sacred fire.

But it is not only in the Hindu ritual that the sacred fire holds a prominent place. Thus in ancient Ireland the sacred fire was obtained by the friction of wood and the striking of stones, and it was "supposed that the spirits of fire dwelt in these objects, and when the priests invoked them to appear they brought good luck to the household for the coming year, but if invoked by other hands on that special day their influence was malific."[3] So among the Muhammadans in the time of Akbar "at noon of the day when the sun enters the 19th degree of Aries, the whole world being surrounded by the light, they expose a round piece of a white shining stone called in Hindi *Súrajkránt*.[4] A piece of cotton is then held near it, which catches fire from the heat of the stone.

[1] Tawney, *Katha Sarit Ságara*, I, 322.

[2] Oldfield, *Sketches*, II, 242: Wright, *History of Nepál*, 35: and see Prescott, *Peru*, I, chapter 3: Lubbock, *Origin of Civilization*, 312.

[3] Lady Wilde, *Legends*, 126.

[4] Abul Fazl seems to have confused Súraj Sankrántí or the sun's entry into a new sign of the zodiac with Súrya Kánta or "sun beloved," the sun crystal or lens which gives out heat when exposed to the sun's rays.

This celestial fire is committed to the care of proper persons."[1] Perhaps the best example of the Muhammadan sacred fire is that at the Imámbára in Gorakhpur. There it was first started by a renowned Shiah Faqír, named Roshan Ali, and has been maintained unquenched for more than a hundred years, a special body of attendants and supplies of wood being maintained for it. It is respected by Hindus as well as Muhammadans, and as in the case of the fires kept up by many noted Jogis, the ashes have a reputation for the cure of fever. A modern Muhammadan of the advanced school has endeavoured to rationalize it by the suggestion that it is the potash in it which works the cure: but probably the element of mystic faith has much more to do with it.[2]

Volcanic fire Will-o-the-wisp.

Fire of a volcanic nature is, as might have been expected, regarded with veneration. Such is the fire which in some places in Kashmír rises out of the ground.[3] The meteoric light or Shahába is also respected. In Hoshangábád there is a local godling known as Khapra Bába, who lives on the edge of a tank, and is said to appear in the darkness with a procession of lights. These are probably *ignes fatui*. There appears to be in Northern India no trace of the idea which so wildly prevails in Europe that such lights are the souls of unbaptised children.[4]

The tomb fetish.

Next comes the respect paid to the cairn which covers the remains of the dead or commemorates a death. We have already seen instances of this in the pile of stones which marks the place where a tiger has killed a man and in the cairns in honour of the jungle deities or the spirits which reside in dangerous passes. The rationale of these sepulchral cairns is to keep down the soul of the dead man and prevent it from injuring others. We see the same idea in the rule of the old ritual, that on the departure of the last mourner after the conclusion of the funeral ceremony,

---

[1] Blochmann, *Aín-i-Akbari*, I, 48.
[2] *North Indian Notes and Queries*, I, 199.
[3] Hugel, *Travels*, 42, quoted by Jarrett, *Ain-i-Akbari*, II, 314.
[4] *Settlement Report*, 121; Conway, *Demonology*, I, 225.

the Adhvarya or officiating priest should place a circle ot stones behind him to prevent death overtaking those who have gone forward.[1]

The primitive grave heap grows into the cairn and the cairn into the tope or stupa.[2] In the way of a tomb Hindus will worship almost anything. The tomb of an English lady is worshipped at Bhandára in the Central Provinces; the tomb of an English officer near the fort of Bijaygarh, in the Aligarh district, was, when I visited it some years ago, revered as the shrine of the local village God; there is a similar case at Rawalpindi.[3]

Miscellaneous fetishes.

We have already referred to the Sálagráma fetish. Akin to this is the Vishnupada, the supposed footmark of Vishnu, which is very like the footmark of Hercules of which Herodotus speaks.[4] It was probably derived from the footmark of Buddha, which is a favourite subject in the early Buddhistic sculptures. Dr. Tylor, curiously enough, thinks that it may have some connection with the footmarks of extinct birds or animals imprinted on the strata of alluvial rocks.[5] Even among Muhammadans we have the same idea, and the Qadam-i-Rasúl, or mosque of the footmark of the prophet at Lucknow, used to contain a stone marked with his footmark which was said to have been brought by some pilgrim from Arabia. It disappeared during the Mutiny.[6] There is another in the town of Chunar. The same respect is paid to the footmark of Rámananda in his monastery at Benares, and the pin of Bráhma's slipper is now fixed up in the steps of the bathing place at Bithúr, known as the residence of the infamous Nána Sáhib, where it is worshipped at an annual feast.

---

1 Rajendra Lálá Mitra, *Indo-Aryans*, I, 146.

2 Ferguson, *Tree and Serpent Worship*, 88: *History of Indian Architecture*, 60: Cunningham, *Bhilsa Topes* 9; Spencer, *Principles of Sociology*, I, 254, *sq.*

3 *Central Provinces Gazetteer*, 63; *Panjáb Notes and Queries*, III, 8;

4 IV, 82.

5 Tennent, *Ceylon*, II, 132; Ferguson, *Indian Architecture*, 184, *with engraving*: Tylor, *Early History*, 116.

6 *Oudh Gazetteer*, II, 370.

CHAPTER IX.

ANIMAL WORSHIP.

Τῶ δὲ καὶ Αὐτομέδων ὕπαγε ζυγὸν ὠκέας ἵππους
Ξάνθον καὶ Βαλίον τὼ ἅμα πνοίῃσι πετέσθην
Τοὺς ἔτεκε Ζεφύρῳ παρὰ ῥόον Ὠκεανοῖο.

ILIAD, xvi, 148—51.

Origin of animal worship.

WE now come to the special worship of certain animals. The origin of this form of belief may probably be traced to many different sources. In the first place, no savage fixes the boundary line between man and the lower forms of animal life so definitely as more civilised races are wont to do. The animal, in their belief, has very much the same soul, much the same feelings and passions as men have—a theory exemplified in the way the Indian ploughman speaks to his ox or the shepherd calls his flock. To him the belief is familiar that the spirits of his ancestors appear in the form of animals, as among the Dravidian races they come in the shape of a tiger which attacks the surviving relatives, or as a chicken which marks its footsteps in the ashes when it revisits its former home. And all these people firmly believe that a witch can take the form of a tiger or a bear or fly through the air like a bird. This idea of metamorphosis is common throughout the whole range of folklore. Thus in one of Somadeva's tales, his mistress turns a man into an ox: in another his wife transforms him into a buffalo: in a third the angry hermit turns the king into an elephant. [1] Animals constantly assume other shapes. In one of the Bengal stories the mouse becomes a cat. [2] In fact, a large part of the incidents of Indian stories turns on various forms of metamorphosis: and every English child knows how the lover of Earl Mar's daughter took the shape of a dove [3]

---

1 Tawney, *Katha Sarit Sâgara*, I, 342, II, 135: 230.
2 Lál Bihári De, *Folktales*, 139.
3 Jacobs, *English Fairy Tales*, 159, and numerous examples carefully classified by Temple *Wideawake Stories*, 419, sqq.

We have again the very common incident in folktales of animals understanding the speech of human beings and *vice versâ.* Thus in Somadeva the Vaisya Bháshájna knows the language of all beasts and birds, a faculty which in Germany is gained by eating a white snake.[1] So animals constantly warn the hero or heroine of approaching danger as in the story of Bopolúchi.[2] This idea of grateful animals assisting their benefactors, runs through the whole range of folklore.[3]

Another series of cognate ideas has been very carefully analysed by Mr. Campbell.[4] The spirits of the dead haunt two places, the house and the tomb : those who haunt the house are friendly ; those who haunt the tomb are unfriendly. Two classes of animals correspond to these two classes of spirits—an at-home, fearless class, as the snake, the rat, flies, and ants, and perhaps bees, into which the home haunting or friendly spirits would go : and a wild, unsociable class, bats, owls—and to some extent dogs, jackals, and vultures—into which the unfriendly or tomb-haunting spirits would go. In the case of some of these tomb-haunting animals—the dog, jackal, and vulture—the feeling towards them as tomb haunters, seems to have given place to the belief that as the spirit lives in the tomb where the body is laid, so, if the body is eaten by an animal, the spirit lives in the animal as in a living tomb.

Other animals again are invested with particular qualities, fierceness and courage, strength or agility, and eating part of their flesh or wearing a portion of them as an amulet, conveys to the possessor the qualities of the animal. A familiar instance of this is the belief in the claws and flesh of the tiger as amulets or charms against disease.

Lastly, certain animals are respected for their use to man or as scarers of evil influences, as the cow, as possessors of wisdom

[1] Tawney, *loc. cit.*, I, 499 : II, 276 ; Grimm, *Household Tales*, No. 33, I, 357.

[2] Temple, *loc. cit.*, 74, 412 : Lál Bihári De, *loc. cit.*, 40, 106, 134, 138, 155, 210, 223.

[3] See for example the fourth story in Campbell's *Tales of the West Highlands* ; XII XXII, of Miss Stokes's *Indian Fairy Tales* ; De Gubernatis, *Zoological Mythology* II, 129.

[4] *Notes*, 259.

like the elephant or snake, as semi-human in origin or character as the ape. But it is perhaps dangerous to attempt, as Mr. Campbell has done, to push the classification much farther, because the respect paid to any particular animal is possibly based on varied and diverging lines of belief.

Horse worship in folklore.

To illustrate some of these principles from the worship of certain special animals, we may begin with the horse. War-horses were so highly prized by the early Aryans in their battles with the Aborigines, that the horse under the name of Dadhikra soon became an object of worship, and in the Veda we have a spirited account of the honour paid to this godlike being.[1] Another famous horse of the early legends was Uchaihsravas, or horse of Indra, of whom there is a special legend in Nepál. In the folktales he consorts with mares of mortal race and begets steeds of unrivalled speed like the divine Homeric coursers of Æneas[2]. So in Somadeva, we find the king addressing his faithful horse and praying his aid in danger as Achilles speaks to his steeds Xanthos and Balios, and in the Karling legend of Bayard[3]: and the horse of Manidatta which was "white as the moon; the sound of its neighing was as musical as that of a clear conch or other sweet-sounding instrument; it looked like the waves of the sea of milk surging on high; it was marked with curls on the neck, and adorned with the crest-jewel, the bracelet and other signs which it seemed as if it had acquired by being born in the race of the Gandharvas": and the horse Uchaisravas restores the dead Asuras to life by smelling them.[4] The flying horse of the Arabian Nights has been transferred into many of the current folktales. There are numerous other horses famous in Hindu legend. The Saint Alam Sayyid of Baroda was known as the horse saint (*ghorá-ká-pír*). His horse was buried near him, and Hindus hang images of the animal on trees round his tomb.[5] We have already

[1] *Rig Veda*, IV, 33; Dutt, *History of Civilisation*, I, 72, *sq.*, 79.
[2] Wright, *History*, 165: *Iliad*, V, 265, *sqq.*; Tawney, *Katha Sarit Ságara*, II, 593.
[3] Tawney, *ibid.*, I, 130, 574, quoting Grimm, *Teutonic Mythology*, I, 392.
[4] Tawney, *ibid.*, II, 218, I, 444.
[5] Rousselet, *India and its Native Princes*, 116.

spoken of Gúga and his mare Javádiyá. The horse of the king of Bhilsa or Bhadrávati was of dazzling brightness and was regarded as the palladium of the kingdom, but in spite of the care taken of it, it was carried off by the Pándavas. There is a stock horse-miracle story told in connection with Lál Beg, the patron saint of sweepers. The king of Delhi lost a valuable horse and the sweepers were ordered to bury it, but as the animal was very fat, they proceeded to eat it themselves, giving one leg to the king's priest. They took it home and began to cook it, but being short of salt, they sent an old woman to buy some. She went to the merchant's house and pressed him to give her the salt at once. "If you do not hurry," said she, "a thousand rupees' worth of meat will be ruined." He informed the king, who, suspecting the state of the case, ordered the sweepers to produce the carcass. On this they placed the bones on a mound sacred to Lál Beg, and prayed to him to save them, whereupon the horse stood up, but only on three legs. So they went to the king and confessed how they had disposed of the fourth leg. The unlucky priest was executed and the horse soon after died also.[1]

The horse is considered a lucky animal, and the entry of a man on horseback into a sugarcane field during sowing time, is believed auspicious. In the Dakkhin, the foam of the horse is believed to scare spirits who are more afraid of a horse than of any other animal.[2] But there does not appear to be in India any trace of the idea prevalent in England that the animal has the power of seeing ghosts, or that it can cure diseases such as the whooping cough.[3] It is popularly believed that the horse originally had wings, and that the chestnuts or scars on his legs are the places where the wings originally grew. Eating horse flesh is supposed to bring on cramp, and when a sepoy at rifle practice misses the target, his comrades taunt him with having eaten the unlucky meat.[4]

---

[1] *Indian Antiquary*, XI, 325, *sq.*; *Panjáb Notes and Queries*, II, 2.
[2] Campbell's *Notes*, 292.
[3] Henderson, *Folklore of the Northern Counties*, 142.
[4] *Panjáb Notes and Queries*, I, 113.

Modern horse-worship.

Of modern horse-worship there are many examples. The Palliwál Bráhmans of Jesalmer worship the bridle of a horse, which Colonel Tod takes to prove the Skythic origin of the early colonists who were equestrian as well as nomadic.[1] Horse-worship is still mixed up with the creed of the Buddhists of Yunan, who, of course, derived it from India.[2] In Western India this form of worship is common. It is the chief object of reverence at the Dasahra festival. Some Rájput Bhíls worship a deity called Ghoradev or a stone horse: the Bhátiyas worship a clay horse at the Dasahra, and the Ojha Kumbhárs make a clay horse on the sixth day after birth, and get the child to worship it. Rag horses are offered to saints' tombs in Gujarát. The Kunbis wash their horses on the day of the Dasahra, decorate them with flowers, sacrifice a sheep to them, and sprinkle blood on them.[3] The custom among the Dravidian races of offering clay images of horses to the local gods, has been already noticed. The Gonds have a horse god in Kodapen. At the opening of the rainy season they worship a stone in his honour outside the village. A Gond priest offers a pottery image of the animal and a heifer, saying, "Thou art our guardian: protect our oxen and cows; let us live in safety." The heifer is then sacrificed, and the meat eaten by the worshippers.[4] The Asvamedha or horse-sacrifice extends back to early Vedik times. Its efficacy was so highly considered that one hundred such sacrifices were held to entitle the sacrificer to displace Indra from his paradise of Swarga.[5]

The Ass.

The worship of the ass is found only in connection with the cult of Sítalá. But the contempt for the animal seems to have arisen in post-Vedik times. Indra had a swiftfooted ass, and one of the epithets of Vikramáditya was Gardabha rúpa or, "He in the form of an ass." In the

---

1 *Annals*, II, 319.
2 Lubbock, *Origin of Civilisation*, 275.
3 Campbell, *loc. cit.*
4 Hislop, *Papers*, Appendix I, III.
5 Wilson, *Rig Veda.* II, Intro XII: Tod, *Annals*, I, 81: Monier Williams, *Sanskrit Dictionary*, S. V.

early ritual a student convicted of incontinency was obliged to offer an ass to the Rákshasas.[1] The story of the ass in the lion's skin has spread from India through the whole range of western folklore.[2]

The Lion.

The lion, from his comparative rarity in Northern India, appears little in popular belief. It is one of the vehicle of Párvatí, and rude images of the animal are sometimes placed near shrines dedicated to Devi. There is a current idea that only one pair of lions exists in the world at the same time. They have two cubs, a male and a female, which, when they arrive at maturity, devour their parents. In the folktales the childless king is instructed that he will find in the forest a boy riding on a lion which shall be his son. The lovely maiden in the legend of Jímút a váhana, is met riding on a lion. We have the lion Pingalaka, King of beasts, with the jackal as his minister, and in one of the cycle of tales in which the weak animal overcomes the more powerful, the hare by his wisdom causes the lion to drown himself. The basis of the tale of Androclus is probably Buddhistic, but only a faint reference to it occurs in Somadeva.[3]

The Tiger.

The tiger naturally takes the place of the lion. According to the comparative mythologists "the tiger, panther, and leopard possess several of the mythical characteristics of the lion as the hidden sun. Thus Dionysos and Siva, the phallical God *par excellence*, have these animals as their emblems."[4] Siva, it is true, is represented as sitting in his ascetic form on a tiger skin, but it is his consort, Durga, who uses the animal as her vehicle. Quite apart from the solar myth theory, the belief that witches are changed into tigers and the terror inspired by him, are quite sufficient to account for the honour bestowed on him. Much also of the worship of the tiger is probably

[1] Gubernatis, *Zoological Mythology*, I, 372; Vasishtha, *Books of the East*, XIV, 117.

[2] Tawney, *Katha Sarit Ságara*, II, 65.

[3] Tawney, *loc. cit.*, I, 37, 78; II, 28, 32: Grimm, *Household Tales*, II, 404; Tawney, II, 107.

[4] Gubernatis, *loc. cit.*, II, 160.

of totemistic origin. Thus, the Baghel Rájputs claim descent from him and from him (*bágh, vyághra,* "the striped one") derive their name. This tribe will not in Central India destroy the animal. The Bhíls, the Bajráwat Rájputs of Rajputána, and the Santáls, also claim tiger origin. [1] Another idea appearing in tiger worship is that he eats human flesh, and thus obtains possession of the souls of the victims whom he devours. For this reason a man-eating tiger is supposed to walk along with his head bent, because the ghosts of his victims sit on it and weigh it down. [2] He is, again, often the disguise of a sorcerer of evil temper, an idea similar to that which was the basis of the European legend of lycanthropy and the were-wolf. [3] Hence the jungle people who are in the way of meeting him will not pronounce his name, but speak of him as "the jackal" (*gidar*), "the beast" (*jánwar*), or use some other euphemistic term. They do the same in many places with the wolf and bear, and though they sometimes hesitate to kill the animal themselves, they will readily assist sportsmen to destroy him, and make great rejoicings when he is killed. A shikári on the road will break off a branch as he goes along and say "as thy life has departed, so may the tiger die," and when he is killed, they will bring forward some spirits and pour it on the head of the animal, addressing him "Mahárája! During your life you confined yourself to cattle and never injured your human subjects. Now that you are dead, spare us and bless us!" In Akola, the gardeners are unwilling to inform sportsmen of the whereabouts of a tiger or panther, which may have taken up its quarters in their plantation, for they have a superstition that a garden plot loses its fertility from the moment one of these animals is killed there. In Nepál they have a regular festival in honour of the tiger known as the Bágh Játra, in which the worshippers dance in the disguise of tigers. [4]

[1] Forsyth, *Highlands of Central India*, 278; Tod, *Annals*, II, 660; Rowney *Wild Tribes*, 139; Dalton, *Descriptive Ethnology*, 214.

[2] Trumbull, *Blood Covenant*, 312; Tylor, *Primitive Culture*, I, 309; Sleeman, *Rambles*, I, 161, *sqq*.

[3] Lyall, *Asiatic Studies*, 13; Spencer, *Principles of Sociology*, I, 323; Conway, *Demonology*, I, 313, *sq.*; Scott, *Letters on Demonology*, 174.

[4] *Berar Gazetteer*, 62; Wright, *History of Nepál*, 38.

Tiger worship among jungle races.

But, as is natural, the worship of the tiger prevails with most vigour among the jungle tribes. We have already met with Bágheswar, the tiger deity of the Mirzapur forest races. The Santáls also worship him, and the Kisáns honour him as Banrája, or "Lord of the jungle." They will not kill him, and believe that in return for their devotion he will spare them. Another branch of the tribe does not worship him, but all swear by him. The Bhuihárs, on the contrary, have no veneration for him and think it their interest to slay him whenever they have an opportunity. The Juángs take their oaths on earth from an ant hill and on a tiger skin : the ant hill is a sacred object with the Kharrias, and the tiger skin is brought in when the Hos and Santáls are sworn. Among the eastern Santáls the tiger is worshipped, but in Rámgarh only those who have suffered from the animal's ferocity, condescend to adore him. If a man is carried off by a tiger the Bágh Bhút or "Tiger ghost" is worshipped, and an oath on a tiger's skin is considered most solemn. [1]

Bágh deo, the tiger godling.

Further west the Kurkus of Hoshangábád worship the tiger godling Bágh deo who is the Wághdeo of Berár. At Petri in Berár is a sort of altar to Waghái Deví, the tiger goddess, founded on a spot where a Gond woman was once seized by a tiger. She is said to have vanished, as if rescued by some supernatural agency, and the Gonds who desire protection from wild beasts, present to her altar gifts of every kind of animal from a cow downwards. A Gond presides over the shrine and receives the votive offerings. In Hoshangábád the Bhomka is the priest of Bágh deo. "On him devolves the dangerous duty of keeping tigers out of the boundaries. When a tiger visits a village, the Bhomka repairs to Bágh deo, and makes his offerings to the God, and promises to repeat them for so many years on condition that the tiger does not appear for that time. The tiger, on his part, never fails to fulfil the compact thus silently made by his lord : for he is pre-eminently an upright and honourable beast, 'pious withal' as Mandeville says, not faithless or treacherous like the

[1] Dalton, *loc. cit.*, 132, 133, 158, 214.

leopard, whom no compact can bind. Some Bhomkas, however, masters of more powerful spell, are not obliged to rely on the traditional honour of the tiger, but compel his attendance before Bágh deo: and such a Bhomka has been seen, a very Daniel among tigers, muttering his incantations over two or three at a time as they crouched before him. Still more mysterious was the power of Kalibhit Bhomka (now, alas! no more): he died the victim of misplaced confidence in a Louis Napoleon of tigers, the basest and most blood-thirsty of his race: he had a fine large *Sáj* tree into which when he uttered his spells he would drive a nail. On this the tiger came and ratified his compact with his enormous paw, with which he deeply scored the bark. Much such a sign manual was that of Timur the Lame, when he dipped his mighty hand in blood and stamped its impression on a parchment grant."[1] In the same way in other parts of the Central Provinces the village sorcerers profess to be able to call tigers from the jungles, to seize them by the ears and control their voracity by whispering to them a command not to come near their villages, or they pretend to know a particular kind of root by burying which they can prevent the beasts of the forest from devouring men or cattle. With the same view they lay on the pathway small models of bedsteads and other things which are supposed to act as charms and stop their advance.

Magical powers of dead tigers.

All sorts of magical powers are ascribed to the tiger after death: the fangs, the claws, the whiskers, are potent charms, valuable for love phyltres and prophylactics against demoniacal influence, the Evil eye, disease and death. The milk of a tigress is valuable medicine, and this is one of the stock impossible tasks or tests imposed on the hero to find and fetch it, as he is sent to get the feathers of the eagle, water from the well of death or the mystical cow guarded by Dános or Rákshasas. The fat is considered a valuable remedy for rheumatism and similar maladies. The heart and flesh are tonics, stimulants and aphrodisiacs, and give strength and courage to those who use

[1] *Berár Gazetteer*, 191, *sq.*; *Hoshangabad Settlement Report*, 255, *sq.*,

[2] Hislop, *Papers*, 19.

them. This depends, as we have already seen, on the theory that the powers of a conquered antagonist are supposed to be gained by devouring him. The whiskers are believed, among other qualities, to be a slow poison when taken with food, and the curious rudimentary clavicles, known as *Santokh* or "happiness," are highly valued as amulets. There is a general belief that a tiger gets a new lobe to his liver every year. A favourite amulet for demoniacal possession consists of the whiskers of the tiger or leopard mixed with nail parings, some sacred root or grass and red lead, and hung on the throat or upper arm. This treatment is particularly valuable in the case of young children immediately after birth. Tiger's flesh is also a potent medicine and charm: it is burnt in the cowstall when cattle disease prevails. The flesh of the tiger, or if that be not procurable, the flesh of a jackal is burnt in the fields to keep off blight from the crops. The flesh of the wild dog is used for the same purpose.[1]

Tigers, propitiation of.

Some tigers are supposed to be amenable to courtesy. Colonel Tod describes how a tiger attacked a boy near his camp and was supposed to have, like the fierce Rákshasa of the Nepál legend, released the child when he addressed him as "uncle."[2]

"This Lord of the Black Rock, for such is the designation of the tiger, is one of the most ancient *bourgeois* of Morwan: his freehold is Kalá Pahár, between this and Magarwár: and his reign during a long series of years has been unmolested, notwithstanding numerous acts of aggression on his bovine subjects: indeed only two nights before he was disturbed gorging on a buffalo belonging to a poor oilman of Morwan. Whether the tiger was an incarnation of one of the Mori Lords of Morwan, tradition does not say, but neither gun, bow, or spear, had ever been raised against him. In return for this forbearance, it is said, he never preyed on man: or if he seized one would, on being entreated with the endearing epithet of "uncle," let go his hold."[3]

---

1 Forbes, *Wanderings of a Naturalist*, 116.
2 Wright, *History of Nepal*, 169.
3 Tod, *Annals*, *II*, 669.

Tiger worship among Gonds.

Among the Gonds tiger worship assumes a particularly disgusting form. At marriages among them a terrible apparition appears of two demoniacs possessed by Bagheswar, the tiger God: they fall ravenously on a bleating kid and gnaw it with their teeth till it expires. "The manner," says Captain Samuells, who witnessed the performance, "in which the two men seized the kid with their teeth and killed it was a sight which could only be equalled on a feeding day in the Zoölogical gardens or a menagerie." [1]

Men metamorphosed into tigers.

The only visible difference between the ordinary and a man metamorphosed into a tiger was explained to Colonel Sleeman to consist in the fact that the latter has no tail. In the jungles about Deori, there is said to be a root, which if a man eats, he is converted into a tiger on the spot; and if, when in this state, he eats another species of root he is turned back into a man again. "A melancholy instance of this", said Colonel Sleeman's informant, "occurred in my own father's family when I was an infant. His washerman, Raghu, was, like all washermen, a great drunkard. Being seized with a viloent desire to ascertain what a man felt like in the state of a tiger, he went one day to the jungle and brought back two of these roots and desired his wife to stand by with one of them, and the instant she saw him assume the tiger's shape to thrust the root she held into his mouth. She consented, and the washerman ate his root and instantly became a tiger, whereupon she was so terrified that she ran off with the antidote in her hand. Poor old Raghu took to the woods and there ate a good many of his friends from the neighbouring villages: but he was at last shot and recognized from his having no tail. You may be quite sure when you hear of a tiger having no tail, that it is some unfortunate man who has eaten of that root, and of all the tigers he will be found to be the most mischievous."[2] This is a curious reversal of the ordinary theory regarding the tail of the tiger to which a murderous strength is attributed. A Hindu proverb says that the hair of a

[1] Dalton, *Descriptive Ethnology*, 280.
[2] *Rambles and Recollections, I*, 163, *sqq.*

tiger's tail may be the means of losing one's life, which has been compared by Prof De Gubernatis with the tiger Mantikora, spoken of by Ktesias, which has on its tail hairs which are darts thrown by it for the purpose of defence.[1] A Nepál legend describes how some children made a clay image of a tiger, and thinking the figure incomplete without a tongue, went to fetch a leaf to supply the defect. On their return they found that Bhairava had entered the image and had begun to devour their sheep.[2] We have the same legend in the Panchatantra and Somadeva, where four Bráhmáns resuscitate a tiger and are devoured by it.[3]

Dog worship.

Here we have Bhairava associated with the tiger, but his prototype the local godling Bhairon has the dog as his sacred animal, and this is the only Benares temple into which the dog is admitted.[4] Two conflicting lines of thought seem to meet in the case of dog worship. As Mr. Campbell says—"There is a good house-guarding dog, and an evil, scavenging, and tomb-haunting dog. Some of the products of the dog are so much valued in driving off spirits that they seem to be a distinct element in the feeling of respect shown to the dog. Still it seems better to consider the dog as a man eater, and to hold that, like the tiger, this was the original reason why the dog was considered a guardian."[5] It is perhaps, in the connection that the dog is associated with Yama, the God of death. The most touching episode of the Mahabhárata is where Yudhishthira refuses to enter Indra's heaven without his favourite dog, which is really Yama, in disguise. These dogs of Yama probably correspond to the Orthros and Kerberos of the Greeks, and Kerberos is connected etymologically with Sarvari which is an epithet of the night, meaning originally "dark" or "pale[6] The same idea shows itself in the Pársi respect for the dog, which may be traced to the belief of the early Persians. The dog's muzzle is placed near

---

[1] *Zoological Mythology*, *I*, 160, *sq*.
[2] Wright, *History of Nepal*, 30.
[3] Tawney, *Katha Sarit Ságara*, *II*, 348, *sqq*.
[4] Sherring, *Sacred City*, 63-65.
[5] *Notes*, 276.
[6] Cox, *Mythology of the Aryan Nations*, *II*, 336.

the mouth of the dying Pársi in order that it may receive his parting breath and bear it to the waiting angel, and the destruction of the corpse by dogs is looked on with no feeling of abhorrence. The same idea is found in Buddhism, where, on the early coins "the figure of a dog in connection with a Buddhist Stúpa recalls to mind the use to which the animal was put in the bleak highlands of Asia, in the preferential form of sepulchre over exposure to birds and wild beasts in the case of deceased monks or persons of position in Thibet. Strange and horrible as it may seem to us to be devoured by domestic dogs, trained and bred for the purpose, it was the most honourable form of burial among Thibetans."[1]

Modern dog worship..

In modern times dog worship appears chiefly in connection with the cultus of Bhairava, the Bhairoba of Western India. No Marátha will lift his hand against a dog. In Western India many Hindus worship the dog of Kála Bhairava, though the animal is considered unclean by them. In Púna, Dattatreya is guarded by four dogs which stand for the four Vedas : and at Jejuri and Nágpur, children are dedicated to the dogs of Khanderáo. The Ghisádis on the seventh day after birth go and worship water, and on coming back rub their feet on a dog. At Dharwár, on the fair day of the Dasahra at Malhári's temple, the Vaggayya ministrants dress in blue woollen coats and meet with bells and skins tied round their middle, the pilgrims barking and howling like dogs. Each Vaggayya has a wooden bowl into which the pilgrims put milk and plantains. Then the Vaggayyas lay down the bowls, fight with each other like dogs, and putting their mouths into the bowl eat the contents.[2] In Nepál there is a festival known as the Khicha Pújá, in which worship is done to dogs, and garlands of flowers are placed round the neck of every dog in the country.[3] Among the Gonds, if a dog dies or is born, the family has to undergo purification.[4]

[1] *Journal Asiatic Society of Bengal, LIX,* 212. The horror with which the Homeric Greeks regarded the eating of a corpse by dogs comes out very strongly in the Iliad.

[2] Campbell, *Notes*, 276, *sq.*

[3] Wright, *History*, 39. *sq.*

[4] Hislop, *Papers*, 6.

Dogs in folklore.

Throu hout folklore dogs are associated with the spirits of the dead,[1] and are regarded as guardians of the household which they protect from evil spirits. According to Aubrey "all over England a spayed bitch is accounted wholesome in a house: that is to say they have a strong belief that it keeps away evil spirits from haunting of a house"[2] As in the Odyssey, the two swift hounds of Telemachus bear him company and recognize Athene when she is invisible to others, and the dogs of Virgil howl as the goddess approaches, so in Northern India it is believed that dogs have the power of seeing spirits, and when they see one they howl. Hence the howling of dogs in the vicinity of a house is a sign of approaching misfortune. In the Panjáb the grave of a dog at Laháru is respected. This dog belonged to the chief of the victorious Thákurs, and is credited with having done noble service in battle, springing up and seizing the wounded warriors' throats, many of whom it slew. Finally it was killed and buried on the spot with beat of drum. This is like the Sagparast of Naishapur in Khusru's Darvesh tales.[3] So the Banris of Bengal will on no account kill a dog or touch its body, and the water of a tank in which a dog has been drowned cannot be used until an entire rainy season has washed the impurity away. They allege, that as they kill cows and most other animals they deem it right to fix on some beast which should be as sacred to them as the cow to the Bráhman and they selected the dog because it was a useful animal when alive and not very nice to eat when dead—"a neat reconciliation of the twinges of conscience and the cravings of appetite."[4] Various omens are in the Panjáb drawn from dogs. When out hunting, if they lie on their backs and roll, as they generally do when they find a tuft of grass or soft ground, it shows that plenty of game will be found. If a dog lies quietly on his back in the house, it is a bad omen, for the

---

[1] Conway, *Demonology*, I, 134; Gregor, *Folklore* of *N.-E. Scotland*, 126, *sq.;* Burton, *Arabia*, I, 290.

[2] *Remaines*, 53.

[3] Cunningham, *Archæological Reports*, XXIII, 26.

[4] Risley, *Tribes and Castes*, I, 79, *sq.*

superstition runs that the dog is addressing heaven for support, and that some calamity is bound to happen.[1] The wild dogs in the hills are known as "God's hounds" and no native sportsman will kill them.[2] A black dog is universally respected in villages and is fed as a sort of propitiation, especially when small-pox prevails. It is curious that this veneration for a black dog appears also in English folklore.[3] Another sacred dog in Indian tales is that of the hunter, Shambuka. His master threw him into the sacred pool of Uradh in the Himalaya. Coming out dripping he shook some of the water on his master, and such was the virtue of even this partial ablution that, on their death, both hunter and dog were summoned to Siva's heaven.[4] Among Muhammadans the dog is impure. If it drinks from a vessel it must be washed seven times and scrubbed with earth. The Qurán directs that before a dog is slipped in chase of game, the sportsman should call out "In the name of God, the great God!" Then all game seized by him becomes lawful food.

The goat.

The goat is another animal to which mystic powers are attributed. It is the favourite animal for sacrifice, and if of a black colour it is preferred. Mr. Conway asks whether this is due to the smell of the animal, its butting and injury to plants, or was it demonized merely because of its uncanny and shaggy appearance?[5] Probably the chief reason is because it has a curious habit of occasionally shivering, which is regarded as caused by some indwelling spirit. The Thags in their sacrifice used to select two goats, black and perfect in all their parts. They were bathed and made to face the west, and if they shook themselves and flung the water from their hair, they were regarded as a sacrifice acceptable to Deví. Hence in India a goat is led along a contested boundary, and the place where it shivers is regarded as the proper line. Plutarch says that the Greeks would not sacrifice a goat if it did not

[1] *Panjáb Notes and Queries*, I, 88.
[2] *Asiatic Society Bengal, Journal*, 1847, p. 234.
[3] Brand, *Observations*, 175, 599, 709: Gregor, *loc. cit.*, 127.
[4] Atkinson, *Himalayan Gazetteer*, II, 329.
[5] *Demonology*, I, 122.

shiver when water was thrown over it. In the Panjáb it is believed that when a goat kills a snake it eats it and then ruminates. after which it spits out a *manka* or bead which, when applied to a snake-bite, absorbs the poison and swells. If it is then put into milk and squeezed, the poison drips out of it like blood, and the patient is cured. If it is not put into milk, it will burst in pieces.[1] So if a person suffers from spleen they take the spleen of a he-goat, if the patient be a male, or of a she-goat, if the patient be a female. It is rubbed on the region of the spleen seven times on a Sunday or Tuesday, pierced with acacia thorns and hung on a tree. As the goat's spleen dries up, the spleen of the patient reduces. In the Panjáb goats are supposed to have a special power of finding old wells concealed in the jungle. The herd is driven about, and finally they all sit down in the place where a well can be discovered by excavation.[2] Martial describes how in his time the Roman shrines were covered with horns.

Dissimulatque deum cornibus ora frequens.[3]

So the local shrines in the Himalaya are decorated with horns of the wild sheep, ibex and goat: and it was perhaps on the same principle that Akbar covered his milestones or *kos minars* with the horns of the deer he had killed.[4]

Goats and totemism.

We get a glimpse of totemism in connection with the goat in some of the early Hindu legends. When Parusha, the primeval man, when divided into his male and female parts, produced all the animals, the goat was first formed out of his mouth. There is again mystical connection between Agni, the fire-god, Bráhmans and goats, as between Indra, the Kshatriyas and sheep, Vaiysas and kine, Súdras and the horse. These may possibly have been tribal totems of the races by whom these animals were venerated.[5] The sheep. as we have already seen, is a totem of the Keriyas.

---

1 *North Indian Notes and Queries*, I, 15.

2 *Panjáb Notes and Queries*, I, 3, 15, 39.

3 *Epigrams*, I, 6.

4 Moorcroft, *Travels*, I, 22: *Journal Asiatic Society of Bengal*, 1840, p. 572: *Ain-i-Akbari*, I, 289.

5 Muir, *Ancient Sanskrit Texts*, I, 24, *sq.*; 16: III, 166, 310, *sq*: McLennan, *Fortnightly Review*, 1870, p. 198, *sq*.

But the most famous of these animal totems or fetishes is the cow or bull. According to the mythologists the bull which bore Europé away from Kadmos, is the same from which the dawn flies in the Vedic hymn. He, according to this theory, is the bull Indra, which, like the sun, traverses the heavens, bearing the Dawn from the east to the west: "but the Cretan bull, like his fellow in the Gnossian labyrinth who devours the tribute children from the city of the dawn goddess, is a dark and malignant monster, akin to the throttling snake, who represents the powers of night and darkness."[1] This may be so, but it is open to the obvious objections that it limits the ideas of the early Aryans to the weather, and their dairies, and antedates the regard for the cow to a period when the animal was held in much less reverence than it is at present.

Cow and bull worship.

That the respect for the cow is of comparatively modern date, is best established on the authority of a writer, himself a Hindu. "Animal food was in use in the Epic period, and the cow and bull were often laid under requisition. In the Aitareya Bráhmana, we learn that an ox, or a cow which suffers miscarriage, is killed when a king or honoured guest is received. In the Bráhmana of the Black Yajur Veda the kind and character of the cattle which should be slaughtered in minor sacrifices for the gratification of particular divinities are laid down in detail. Thus a dwarf one is to be sacrificed to Vishnu, a drooping-horned bull to Indra, a thick-legged cow to Váyu, a barren cow to Vishnu and Varuna, a black cow to Púshan, a cow having two colours to Mitra and Varuna, a red cow to Indra, etc., etc. In a larger and more important ceremonial, like the Aswamedba, no less than one hundred and eighty domestic animals, including horses, bulls, cows, goats, deer, etc., were sacrificed. The same Bráhmana lays down instructions for carving, and the Gopatha Bráhmana tells us who received the portions. The priests got the tongue, the neck, the shoulder, the rump, the legs, etc., while the master of the house wisely appropriated to himself the sirloin,

Respect for cow—Modern.

[1] Cox, *Mythology of the Aryan Nations*, I, 107, 437, *sq*: II, 49, *sq*.

and his wife had to be satisfied with the pelvis. Plentiful libations of the *soma* beer were allowed to wash down the meat. In the Satapatha Bráhmana we have a detailed account of the slaughter of a barren cow and its cooking. In the same Bráhmana there is an amusing discussion as to the propriety of eating the meat of an ox or cow. The conclusion is not very definite. 'Let him (the priest), not eat the flesh of the cow and the ox.' Nevertheless Yajnavalkya said (taking apparently a very practical view of the matter), 'I, for one, eat it, provided it is tender.'"[1] The evidence to prove that cows were freely slaughtered in early times could be largely extended. It is laid down in the early laws that the meat of milch cows and oxen may be eaten; and a guest is called "a cow-killer" (*goghna*), because a cow was killed for his entertainment.[2] In another ancient ritual the sacrifice of a cow is very similar to that of the Satí, and according to an early legend kine were created from Parusha, the primal male, and are to be eaten as they were formed from the receptacle of food.[3] It need hardly be said that the worship of the cow is not peculiar to India.[4]

Origin of cow worship.

The explanation of the origin of cow worship has been a subject of much controversy. The modern Hindu, if he has formed any ideas at all on the subject, bases his respect for the cow on her value in supplying milk and for general agricultural purposes. Besides this the *pancha-gávya*, —or five products of the cow—milk, curds, butter, urine and dung, are efficacious as scarers of demons, are used as remedies, and play a very important part in the current ritual. *Gaurochana*, a bright yellow pigment prepared from the urine or bile of the cow, or, as is said by some, vomited by her or found in her head, is used for making the sectarial mark, and as a sedative, tonic and anthelmintic. In Bombay it is specially used as a remedy for measles, which

[1] Romesh Chander Dutt, *History of Indian Civilisation*, I, 253, *sq.*
[2] Buhler, *Sacred Laws*, Pt. I, I, 64, 119, note.
[3] Rajendra Lála Mittra, *Indo-Aryans*, II, 134: Muir, *Ancient Sanskrit Texts*, I, 24, *sqq.*
[4] See the authorities collected by Schliemann, *Ilios*, 112: Rawlinson, *Herodotus*, II, 27, *sq.*; 41: Ewald, *History of Israel*, II, 4.

is considered to be a spirit disease.[1] All this is sufficient to explain the respect for the cow without regarding the cow and bull as types of the sun and moon, or attributing the worship to phallicism, or to the practice of nicknames.[2] At the same time there is something to be said for the theory which finds in these animals tribal totems or fetishes.[3] We have a parallel case among the Jews where the bull was probably the ancient symbol of the Hyksos, which the Israelites having succeeded them could adopt, especially as it may have been retained in use by their confederates the Midianites; and it appears in the earliest annals of Israel as a token of the former supremacy of Joseph and his tribe, and was subsequently adopted as an image of Jahveh himself.[4] There is some evidence that the same process may have occurred in India. It is at least significant that the earlier legends represent Indra as created from a cow: and we know that Indra was the *kuladevata* or family godling of the race of the Kusikas, as Krishna was probably the clan deity of some powerful confederacy of Rájput clans.[5] Cow-worship is thus closely connected with Indra and with Krishna in his forms as the "herdsman god"—Govinda or Gopála: and it is at least plausible to conjecture that the worship of the cow may have been due to the absorption of the animal as a tribal totem of the races who venerated these two divinities.

Connected with phallicism and transmigration.

Further, the phallic significance of the worship, in its modern form at least, cannot be altogether ignored. This is particularly shown in the close connection between Siva's bull Nandi and the *Lingam* worship: and there seems some reason to suspect that the bull is intended to intercept the evil influences, which in the popular belief, are continually emitted from the female principle through

---

[1] Campbell, *Notes*, 285.

[2] Gubernatis, *Zoological Mythology*, I, 3, *sqq*: Cox, *Introduction to Mythology and Folklore*, 151, *sqq*: Kuenen, *Religion of Israel*, I, 236, *sq*: Goldziher, *Mythology among the Hebrews*, 226, 343: Wake, *Serpent worship*, 35: Spencer, *Principles of Sociology*, I, 340.

[3] McLennan, *Fortnightly Review*, 1870, p. 199.

[4] Ewald, *loc. cit.*, II, 183, note: *Antiquities of Israel*, 225, *sqq*.

[5] *Rigveda*, IV, 18-1: Muir, *Ancient Sanskrit Texts*, I, 348: Lang, *Custom and Myth*, II, 126.

the *Yoni*. The dread of this form of pollution is universal.[1] Hence when the *lingam* is set up in a new village the people are particular in turning the spout of the *yoni* towards the jungle and not in the direction of the roads and houses, lest its evil influence should be communicated to them; and in order still further to secure this object the bull Nandi is placed sitting as a guardian between the *yoni* and the inhabited site.[2] Cow-worship assumes another form in connection with the theory of transmigration. It has become part of the theory that the soul migrates into the cow immediately preceding its assumption of the human form, and she escorts the spirit across the dreaded river Vaitarani, which bounds the lower world.

Cow-worship; its later developement.

Though cow-worship was little known in the Vedic period, by the time of the compilation of the Institutes of Manu it had become part of the popular belief. He classes the slaughter of a cow or bull among the deadly sins: "the preserver of a cow or a Bráhman atones for the crime of killing a priest[3]" and we find constant references in mediæval folklore to the impiety of the Savaras and other Dravidian races who killed and ate the sacred animal. Saktideva one day, "as he was standing upon the roof of his palace, saw a Chandála coming along with a load of cow's flesh and said to his beloved Vindumatí, 'Look, slender one! How can this evildoer eat the flesh of cows, those animals that are the object of veneration to the three worlds?' Then Vindumatí hearing that, said to her husband, 'The wickedness of this act is inconceivable, what can we say in palliation of it? I have been born in this race of fishermen for a very small offence owing to the might of cows. But what can atone for this man's sin?'"[4]

Re-birth through the cow.

When the horoscope forbodes some crime or special calamity the child is clothed in scarlet, a colour which repells evil influences, and tied on

---

[1] Fraser, *Golden Bough*, I, 185, *sqq*.
[2] See Sellon, *Memoirs Anthropological Society of London*, I, 328.
[3] *Institutes* XI, 60-80.
[4] Tawney, *Katha Sarit Sâgara*, I, 227.

a new sieve, which is, as we have seen, a powerful fetish. This is passed through the hind legs of a cow forwards, through the forelegs towards the mouth and again in the reverse direction, signifying the new birth from the sacred animal. The usual worship and aspersion take place and the father smells his child as the cow smells her calf. The same idea is illustrated in the legend of the Pushkar Lake, which probably represents a case of that fusion of races which undoubtedly occurred in ancient times. The story runs that Bráhma proposed to do worship there, but was perplexed where he should perform the sacrifice, as he had no temple on earth like the other gods. So he collected all the gods, but the sacrifice could not proceed, as Sávitrí alone was absent: and she refused to come without Lakshmí, Párvatí and Indrání. On hearing of her refusal Bráhma was enraged and said to Indra, "Search me out a girl that I may marry her and commence the sacrifice, for the jar of ambrosia weighs heavy on my head." Indra accordingly went and found none except a Gújar's daughter, whom he purified, and passing her through the body of a cow, brought her to Bráhma, telling him what he had done. Vishnu said "Bráhmans and cows are really identical: you have taken her from the womb of a cow, and this may be considered a second birth." Siva said, "As she has passed through a cow she shall be called Gayatrí." The Bráhmans agreed that the sacrifice might now proceed: and Bráhma, having married Gayatrí, and having enjoined silence upon her, placed on her head the jar of ambrosia and the sacrifice was performed.[1]

Respect paid to the cow.

The respect paid to the cow appears everywhere in folklore. When a disputed boundary is under settlement, a cowskin is placed over the head and shoulders of the arbitrator, who is thus imbued with the divine influence and gives a just decision. It is curious that until quite recently there was a custom in the Hebrides of sewing up a man in the hide of a bull, and leaving him for the night on a hilltop, that he might become a spirit medium.[2] The pious Hindu touches

---

[1] Atkinson, *Himalayan Gazetteer*, II, 914: *Rájputána Gazetteer*, II, 67.
[2] Miss Gordon Cumming, *From the Hebrides to the Himalayas*, I, 141.

the cow's tail at the moment of dissolution, and by its aid he is carried across the river of death which appears in all the mythologies. I have more than once seen a criminal ascend the scaffold with the utmost composure if he is only allowed to grasp a cow's tail before the hangman does his office. The tail of the cow is also used in the marriage ritual, and the tail of the wild ox or yak, though now-a-days used only by grooms, was once the symbol of power, and waved over the ruler to protect him from evil spirits. The Hill legend tells how Siva once manifested himself in his fiery form, and Vishnu and Bráhma went in various directions to see how far the light extended. On their return, Vishnu declared he had been unable to find out how far the light prevailed: but Bráhma said that he had gone beyond its limits. Vishnu then called on Kámadhenu, the celestial cow, to bear testimony, and she corroborated Bráhma with her tongue, but shook her tail by way of denying the statement. So Vishnu cursed her that her mouth should be impure, but her tail considered sacred for ever.[1]

Modern cow-worship.

There are numerous instances of modern cow-worship. The cattle are decorated and supplied with special food on the Gopashtamí or Gokulashtamí festival, a practice which goes back to an early legend embodied in the old ritual. In Nepál there is a Newárí festival known as the Gáe Játra or "cow feast," when all persons who have lost relations during the year ought to disguise themselves as cows and dance round the palace of the king.[2] In many of the Central Indian States about the time of the Diwáli the Maun Charaun, or silent tending of cattle, is celebrated. The celebrants rise at daybreak, wash and bathe, anoint their bodies with oil, and hang garlands of flowers round their necks. All this time they remain silent and communicate their wants by signs. When all is ready they go to the pasture in procession in perfect silence. Each of them holds a peacock's feather over his shoulder to scare demons.

[1] Atkinson, *loc. cit.*, II, 771: Wright, *History of Nepál*, 82.
[2] *Panjáb Notes and Queries*, III, 109: Wright, *loc. cit.*, 37, *sq.*, Haug, *Aitareya Bráhmanam*, II, 287.

They remain in silence with the cattle for an hour or two and then return home. This is followed by an entertainment of wrestling among the Ahírs or cowherds. When night has come a gun is fired, and the Mahárája breaks his fast and speaks.[1] During an eclipse the cow, if in calf, is rubbed on the horns and belly with red ochre to secure an unblemished calf. Cattle are not worked on the Amáwas or Ides of the month. Many people keep a cow in the house as a guardian and place her so that the first glance of the house master falls on her as he wakes. Cow hair is regarded as an amulet against disease and danger, in the same way as the hair of the yak was valued by the people of Central Asia in the time of Marco Polo.[2] An ox with a fleshy excrescence on his eye is sacred, and is known as Nádiya or Nandi, the title of the bull of Siva. He is not used in agriculture, but given to a Jogi, who covers him with cowry shells and takes him about on begging excursions. The Gonds kill a cow at a funeral and hang the tail on the grave as a sign that the ceremonies have been duly performed.[3] Among Hindus on the eleventh day of mourning a bull is branded with the trident mark of Siva, and let loose in the name of the deceased. Some excitement was caused not long ago by a legal decision that such animals are in the grade of *feræ naturæ*, and that it is no offence to steal or appropriate them.

Feeling against cow-killing.

The feeling against cow-killing prevails to a certain extent. To the orthodox Hindu, killing a cow, even accidentally, is a serious matter, and involves the feeding of Bráhmans and performance of pilgrimages. It is very interesting to watch how rapidly this feeling is spreading among the Dravidian races of Central India, as they are gradually being converted to Bráhmanism. In the hills a special ritual is prescribed in the event of a plough ox being killed by accident.[4] The idea that misfortunes follow the killing of a cow is common. It

---

[1] *North Indian Notes and Queries*, I, 154.
[2] Yule's *Marco Polo*, II, 341.
[3] Dalton, *Descriptive Ethnology*, 283.
[4] Atkinson, *Himalayan Gazetteer*, II, 913.

used to be said that storms arôse on the Pír Panjál pass in Kashmír if a cow was killed.[1] Colonel Sleeman gives a case at Ságar where an epidemic was attributed to the practice of cattle slaughter, and a popular movement arose for its suppression.[2] Sindhia offered Sir John Malcolm in 1802 an additional cession of territory if he would introduce an article into the Treaty with the British Government prohibiting the slaughter of cows within the territory he had been already compelled to abandon. Akbar had ordered that cattle should not be killed during the twelve sacred days (*Pachúsar*) observed by the Jainas: Sir John Malcolm gives a copy of the original Firmán.[3] Cow-killing is to this day rigidly prohibited in orthodox Hindu States like Nepál.

Bull-worship among Banjáras.

There is a good example of bull-worship among the wandering tribe of Banjáras. "When sickness occurs they lead the sick man to the feet of the bullock called Hatádiya: for though they say that they pay reverence to images and that their religion is that of the Sikhs, the object of their worship is this Hatádiya, a bullock devoted to the god Bálájí. On this animal no burden is ever laid, but he is decorated with streamers of red-dyed silk and tinkling bells, with many brass chains and rings on neck and feet, and strings of cowry shells and silken tassels hanging in all directions: he moves steadily at the head of the convoy, and the place he lies down on when tired, that they make their halting place for the day. At his feet they make their vows when difficulties overtake them, and in illness, whether of themselves or cattle, they trust to his worship for a cure." The respect paid by Banjáras to cattle seems, however, to be diminishing. Once upon a time they would never sell cattle to a butcher, but now it is an everyday occurrence.[4]

---

1 Jarrett, *Aín-i-Akbari*, II, 348: quoting Erskine, *Babar, Intro*, page 47.
2 *Rambles and Recollections*, I, 259, *sqq*: 99.
3 *Central India*, I, 329; Note, II, 164.
4 Balfour, *Migratory Tribes of Central India: Journal Asiatic Society of Bengal*, XIII, N. S.: Gunthorpe, *Notes on Criminal Tribes of Berár*, 36.

Prejudice against use of cow's milk.

Here may be noticed the curious prejudice against the use of cow's milk which prevails among some tribes, such as the Hos and the aborigines of Assam. The latter use a species of wild cattle known as *mithun* for milking purposes.[1]

The buffalo.

The respect paid to the cow does not fully extend to the buffalo. The male buffalo is the vehicle of Yama, the god of death. The female buffalo is in Western India regarded as the incarnation of Savitrí, wife of Bráhma, the Creator.[2] Buffalo-sacrifice is specially made to Durgá, one of whose titles is Mahishásura ghátiní, or destroyer of the buffalo-formed Asura Mahisha. The Toda worship of the buffalo is familiar to all students of Indian ethnology

The black buck.

The black buck was in all probability the tribal totem of some of the races inhabiting the tract of country anciently known as Aryavarta. Mr. Campbell bases the respect for the animal on the use of hartshorn as a remedy for faintness, swoons, and nervous disorders.[3] But this hardly accounts for the special regard paid to it: and the use of its dung by the Bengal Parhaiyas instead of cowdung to smear their floors, looks as if it were based on totemism.[4] According to the old ritual, its skin was the prescribed dress for the student of theology, and it is still the seat of the ascetic.[5] In the folktales the skin is a charm against bees, and the deer often acts as a *deus ex machiná* which leads away the hero in the chase, and Pándu is cursed because he shoots a hermit who takes the shape of a deer.[6] There is a Nepálese legend of the appearance of the three gods—Vishnu, Bráhma and Siva in the form of deer, whence the place where they were seen is known as Mrigasthali.[7]

---

1 Ball, *Jungle Life*, 165: *North Indian Notes and Queries*, I, 60.
2 Campbell, *Notes*, 284.
3 *Ibid*, 287.
4 Dalton, *Descriptive Ethnology*, 131.
5 Manu, *Institutes*, II, 41.
6 Tawney, *Katha Sarit Ságara* II, 201: I, 166, quoting the xviiith tale of the *Gesta Romanorum*.
7 Wright, *History*, 81.

The elephant.

The elephant is revered as the representative of Ganesa. According to the old mythology there are eight guardian elephants of the world—Airávata of of the East, Pundaríka of the South-East, Vámana of the South, Kumuda of the South-West, Anjana of the West, Pushpadanta of the North-West, Sárvabhauma of the North and Supatríka of the North-East. Modern elephants have their descent from these. "When occasion arises people read incantations in their names and address them in worship. They also think that every elephant in the world is the offspring of one of them. Thus, elephants of a white skin and white hairs are related to the first. Elephants with a large head and long ears, of a fierce and bold temper, and eyelids far apart, belong to the second. Such as are good looking, black and high in the back, are the offspring of the third. If tall, ungovernable, quick in understanding, short-haired and with red and black eyes, they come from the fourth. If bright black, with one tusk longer than the other, with a white breast and belly and long and thick forefeet, from the fifth. If fearful, with prominent veins, with a short hump and ears, and a long trunk, from the sixth. If thin-bellied, red-eyed and a long trunk, from the seventh. And if of a combination of the preceding seven qualities from the eighth.[1]" The elephant appears constantly in the folk-tales. The wooden horse of Troy is represented by an artificial elephant filled with soldiers: other elephants have the power of flying through the air: in another story an elephant, as in one of La Fontaine's Fables, selects a king by raising him up with his trunk: the elephant Kuvalyapída is the guardian of a kingdom. We have also numerous instances of the metamorphosis of human beings into elephants.[2] The hair of the elephant's tail is in high repute as an amulet, and little village children, when an elephant passes, pat the dust where its feet have rested and sing a song. In the Fatehpur district there is an elephant turned into stone. The famous Jay Chand of Kanauj offered, as in the Carthage legend, to Parásura Rishi as

---

[1] Blochmann, *Ain-i-Akbari*, I, 121.

[2] Tawney, *Katha Sarit Ságara*, I, 73, 328: II, 102, 215, 500, 540.

many villages as an elephant could walk round. Finally it halted at Irádatpur where it was turned into stone, and once a year an enormous fair is held in its honour.

The crow.

Passing on to birds, the crow is a famous fetish or totem.[1] It personifies in Hindu tradition the soul of the dead man; to give food to the crows, known in Northern India as Kágaur, is equivalent to offering food to the manes. Ráma in the Rámayana orders Sítá to make this offering, and Yama, in reward for its services, conceded to the crow the right of eating the funeral meats, for which reason the shades of the dead, when this food is given to the crows, are enabled to pass into a better world.[2] Hence the bird is known as *Balipushta* or "nourished by offerings" and *Balibhuj* or "devourer of oblations." In the Mahábhárata, the son of Drona, one of the few survivors of the Kauravas, sees an owl killing the crows on a sacred fig-tree, and this suggests to him the idea of attacking the camp of the Pándavas. This contest of the owl and the crow forms the subject of one of the tales of Somadeva.[3] The Bhátus of Central India, a class of migratory athletes, worship Náráyana and the bamboo with which all their feats are performed. When they bury their dead they place rice and oil at the head of the grave, and stand near to worship whatever animal comes to eat the offerings. They draw the happiest omen of the state of the departed from crows visiting the spot.[4] The Hill legend describes how Karma Sarma was killed in the forest by a tiger. A crow took up one of his bones and carried it to the shrine at Tungkshetra, and such is the virtue of the soil there, that Karma Sarma was forthwith removed to the heaven of Indra.[5] Bhusundi is the legendary crow of the battlefield, who drinks the blood of the slain. He had more blood than he could drink in the wars of the two Asuras, Sumbha and Nisumbha who contended with the gods. He just quenched his thirst in the

---

[1] For the crow in English folklore see Henderson, *Folklore of the Northern Counties*, 126: Gregor, *Folklore of N. E. Scotland*, 135, sq.
[2] Gubernatis, *Zoological Mythology*, II, 253, sq: *Panjáb Notes and Queries*, I, 27.
[3] Tawney, *ibid*, II, 64, 73.
[4] Balfour, *Journal Asiatic Society of Bengal*, N. S., XIII.
[5] Atkinson, *Himalayan Gazetteer*, II, 329.

wars of Ráma, but broke his beak against the hard, dry ground, which had soaked in the small amount of blood shed by the comparatively degenerate heroes of the Mahábhárata. The brains of a crow are a specific against old age, but the cawing of a crow at the commencement of a journey is an evil omen.

The Hand of Glory.

It is a common belief in Europe that the Hand of Glory, or the dried-up hand of a criminal who has been executed, is a most powerful spell for thieves. In Ireland "if a candle is placed in a dead hand, neither wind nor water can extinguish it, and if carried into a house the inmates will sleep the sleep of the dead so long as it remains under the roof, and no power on earth can wake them while the dead hand holds the candle." The hand of a dead man is also used to stir the milk when butter will not form.[1] This according to Sir G. Cox is "the light flashing from the dim and dusky storm cloud:"[2] but this can hardly, with the utmost ingenuity be invoked to explain the similar usage of Indian burglars, who carry about with them the stick out of a crow's nest, the *gad-ki-lakri*, which opens locks and holds the household spell-bound. The Indian thief, like his English brother, by the way, often carries about a piece of charcoal as a charm in his operations.

The fowl.

Among some of the Indian races the value set on the fowl may possibly, as Mr. Campbell suggests, depend on the feeling that the spirits of the dead wandering near their ancient homes find an asylum in the domestic fowls.[3] Many of the hill tribes in Mirzapur after a death lay out ashes on the floor and recognise the visit of the ghost from the mark of a fowl's foot upon it.

Dove and pigeon.

Another bird regarded with respect is the dove or pigeon. The Kheshgi Patháns of Qasûr will not kill them, they are similarly protected at Bhartpur, and among Muhammadans they rank as the Sayyid of birds.[4]

---

[1] Lady Wilde, *Legends*, 81 *sq*; 172: *Panjáb Notes and Queries*, III, 24: Brand, *Observations*, 732: Henderson, *loc. cit.*, 239, *sq*: Aubrey, *Remaines*, 197.
[2] *Mythology of the Aryan Nations*, II, 219, *sq.*
[3] *Notes* 264.
[4] *North Indian Notes and Queries*, I, 12, 42, 60.

The goose.

The goose is a good illustration of what is probably a tribal totem. "It is said in the Bhágavata Purána that one time there existed but one Veda, one god Agni, and one caste. This, we learn from the commentator, was in the Krita age, and the one caste he tells us of was named Hansa, or "the swan" The Hansas are again, in the Vishnu Purána, said to be one of four castes or tribes existing in a district exterior to India: and finally we learn from the Linga Purána that Hansa was a name of Bráhma himself. It is reasonable to suppose that we have a Swan tribe in the Indian Hansas."[1] The goose, it may be added, was a favourite Buddhist emblem: a flock of them is depicted upon the Lion Pillar at Bettiah in Tirhut.[2] In the story of Nala and Damayanti, a flock of these birds arranges the interviews between the lovers. According to the comparative mythologists, it is needless to say that the Hansa is the sun.[3] But as an argument in favour of the theory that the Hansa was a tribal totem, we find that the Kalhans Rájputs of Oudh are said to take their name from the Black Swan (*Kála Hansa ;*) that Rájputs now-a-days will not eat it, and that the same respect is shown to a bird of allied type, the Bráhmani duck and its mate, the *Chakwa-Chakwi* of our rivers. They were once two lovers who were separated by Fate, changed into ducks, and all through the night they call sadly to each other across the broad stream of the Ganges which keeps them apart.

Sundry sacred birds.

Mention has been already made of the respect paid to the peacock and to the eagle, Garuda. A bird known as the *malahári*, or "filth destroyer," is a sort of totem of the Kanjar gypsies. If they see it sitting and singing on a green branch to the front or right, it is an auspicious omen, and they start at once on the prowl. So with the *Khanjarít*, or wagtail, to which every pious Hindu bows when he sees it for the first time in the morning. In Ireland "beware of killing the water wagtail, though it is an omen of death, for it has three drops of the

[1] McLennan, *Fortnightly Review*, VI, 582.
[2] Ferguson, *History of Indian Architecture*, 54: Tennent, *Ceylon*, I, 484.
[3] Gubernatis, *Zoological Mythology*, II, 307, *sqq*.

devil's blood in its little body, and ill-luck ever goes with it and follows it."[1] The Ojhyals or wizards of the Central Provinces sell the skins of a species of Buceros, called *Dhanchirya*, which are used to hang up in the house to secure wealth (*dhan*), whence its name: and thigh bones of the same bird are hung round the wrists of children as a charm against evil spirits.[2] The parrot is also a sacred bird. The wife of the Sage Kasyapa was, according to the Vishnu Purána, the mother of parrots. In the folktales we have a parrot who knew the four Vedas, who is like the falcon in the Squire's tale of Chaucer.[3] So he warns the hero of fortune, befriends the heroine, and is the companion of Rájá Rasálu.[4] The talking parrot constantly warns the deceived husband. The bird seems to have been a sort of marriage totem of the Dravidian races, for images of it made of the wood of the cotton tree or of clay are hung up in the marriage shed among the Kols and minor castes in the North-Western Provinces.

The alligator.

The alligator is a sacred animal. Makara, a sort of marine monster half crocodile and half shark, is the vehicle of Kámadeva, the god of love. Suicide to the alligators at Gangaságara was once common. They are sometimes put into tanks and worshipped: and they are supposed, incorrectly of course, never to touch fishermen.[5]

Fish.

Fish are in many places considered sacred. The sacred speckled trout are found in many Irish wells,[6] and the same idea prevails in many parts of Europe. Colonel Tod describes the sacred fish at Kotah and in the Mahánadi river, and M. Rousselet those in the Betwa near Bhilsa.[7] They are protected at various sacred places, such as Hardwár, Mathura, Mirzapur and Benares. In the Saráswata pool in the Himalaya live the sacred fish called Mrikunda: they are fed on the fourteenth of the light half of each month and

[1] Lady Wilde, *Legends*, 177.
[2] Hislop, *Papers*, 6.
[3] Tawney, *Katha Sarit Ságara*, II, 18.
[4] Temple, *Wideawake Stories*, 139, 205, 255, *sq*.
[5] *North Indian Notes and Queries*, I, 4, 138.
[6] Lady Wilde, *Legends*, 238, *sq*.
[7] *India and its Native Princes*, 402.

oblations are offered for the repose of the manes of deceased ancestors.[1] The fish is the vehicle of Khwája Khizr, the water god, and hence has become a sort of totem of Shiah Muhammadans and the crest of the late royal family of Oudh. Pictures of fish are commonly drawn on houses as a charm against demoniacal influence.

The fish in folklore.

The fish constantly appears in the folktales. We have in Somadeva the fish that laughed when it was dead; the fish that swallows the hero or heroine or a boat,[2] and in many of the modern stories it takes the form of the life index. The King Bhartari, the brother of the celebrated Rája Vikramaditya, who is now a godling and spends part of the day at Benares and part in the Chunár fort, had a fish "the digestion of which gave him knowledge of all that occurred in the three worlds." By a divine curse the nymph Adhriká was transformed into a fish which lives in the Jumna. Here she conceived by the King Uparichara, was caught by a fisherman, taken to the king and opened, when she regained her heavenly form and from her were produced Matsya the male and Matsyá the female fish, the progenitors of the fishy race. A great sea fish in the Ramáyana swallows Hanumán as the whale swallowed Jonah. The fish incarnation of Vishnu possibly represents the adoption of a tribal fish totem into Bráhmanism. It is needless to say that this fish of legend has been identified with the sun by comparative mythologists.[3]

Insects.

Even insects are regarded with veneration. The ant is fed by Hindus and Jainas on certain days with flour and sugar. Some of the Dravidian races swear on a white anthill.[4] The souls of the dead are believed to enter bees and flies; hence in parts of Great Britain news of a death in the family is whispered into the beehive. A fly falling into an inkstand is a lucky omen. One of the Panjáb saints was kind enough to clear the town of Pánipat of flies; but the people

[1] Atkinson, *Himalayan Gazetteer*, II, 380, 775.
[2] Tawney, *Katha Sarit Ságara*, I, 24, 207; II, 599, 605.
[3] Cox, *Mythology of the Aryan Nations*, I, 292: Note, II, 25, *sq.*
[4] Dalton, *Descriptive Ethnology*, 158, 223.

could not get on without them, and now they are more numerous the ever. In the folktales metamorphosis into bees or flies is common.[1] In another the skin of a black antelope is an antidote to bees.[2] Lastly comes the tasar silkworm. Those who collect the silk have "established certain rules of purity, as they call it, which they allege are absolutely necessary, and they assert that any infringement of them would totally destroy the insect. Women, who are best fitted for such work, are absolutely excluded from it as totally impure: nor are they permitted to approach the place. And, while employed in this work, the men totally abstain from the company of their wives. Again, most of the low, vile castes are excluded by their appetites, abandoned to the gross impurity of animal food. The breeders eat sparingly once a day of rice cleaned without boiling, and seasoned only with vegetables. They are considered also to preserve their purity by never employing the washerman or barber."[3] The exclusion of women is probably based on the prevalent idea of female impurity, to which reference has been made elsewhere.[4]

---

[1] Tawney, *loc. cit.*, I, 120: Miss Stokes, *Indian Fairy Tales*, XXI.
[2] Tawney, *ibid*, II, 201.
[3] Buchanan, *Eastern India*, II, 157.
[4] See Fraser, *Golden Bough*, I, 185, 187.

CHAPTER X.

THE BLACK ART.

Simulacraque cerea figit

Et miserum tenues in jecur urget acus.

OVID, HEROIDES, vi, 91—92.

FROM the Baiga or Ojha, who by means of his grain sieve fetish identifies the particular evil spirit by which his patient is afflicted, we come to the regular witch or wizard. He works by means and appliances which can be readily paralleled by the procedure of his brethren in Western countries. [1]

The witch.

The position of the witch has been so clearly stated by Sir A. Lyall, that his remarks deserve quotation. "The peculiarity of the witch is that he does everything without the help of the gods. It begins when a savage stumbles on a few natural effects out of the common run of things, which he finds himself able to work by unvarying rule of thumb. He becomes a fetish to himself. Fetishism is the adoration of a visible object supposed to possess active power. A witch is one who professes to work marvels, not through the aid or council of the supernatural beings in whom he believes as much as the rest, but by certain occult faculties which he conceives himself to possess. There is a real distinction even in fetishism between the witch and the brother practitioner on a fetish, or between the witch and the Sháman who rolls about the ground and screams out his oracles: and this line, between adoration and inspiration, vows and oracles on the one side, and thaumaturgy by occult, incomprehensible arts on the other side, divides the two professions from bottom to top. Hence the witch, and not the man who works through

---

[1] For the European witch consult, among other authorities, Scott, *Letters on Demonology and witchcraft, passim*: Chambers, *Book of Days*, I, 356, *sq*: Gregor, *Folklore of N.-E. Scotland*, 69, *sq*: Conway, *Demonology*, II 317, 327: Lubbock, *Origin of Civilisation*, 245, *sq*.

the fetish, is proscribed. Hence any disappointment in the aid which the aboriginal tribes are entitled to expect from their gods to avoid a verting disease or famine, throws the people on the scent of witchcraft." Again, "the most primitive witchcraft looks very like medicine in the embryonic state; but as no one will give the aboriginal physician any credit for cures or chemical effects produced by simple human knowledge, he is soon forced back into occult and mystic devices, which belong neither to religion nor to destiny, but are a ridiculous mixture of both; whence the ordinary kind of witchcraft is generated." And he goes on to show how "the great plagues, cholera and the small-pox, belong to the gods; but a man cannot expect a great incarnation of Vishnu to cure his cow, or find his lost purse; nor will public opinion tolerate his going to any respectable shrine with a petition that his neighbour's wife, his ox or his ass, may be smitten with some sore disease."[1] This, however, must be taken with the correction that, as we have seen already, the deities which rule disease are of a much lower grade than the divine cabinet which rules the world. The main difference, then, between the hedge priest and the witch is, as Sir A. Lyall shows, that the former serves his god or devil, whereas the latter makes the familiar demon, if one is kept, serve him.

Witchcraft how developed.

The belief in witchcraft is general among the lower and less advanced Indian races. Colonel Dalton's assertion that the Juángs, who were quite recently in the stage of wearing leaf aprons, do not believe in witchcraft or sorcery, must be accepted with great caution.[2] It is quite certain that all the allied Dravidian races, even those at a somewhat higher stage of culture than the Juángs, such as Kols, Kharwárs and Cheros, firmly believe in witchcraft. But all these people observe the most extreme reticence on the subject. If you ask a Mirzapur hillman if there are any witches in his neighbourhood, he will look round furtively and suspiciously,

[1] *Asiatic Studies*, 79, *sqq*; 89, *sqq*.
[2] *Descriptive Ethnology*, 157.

and even if he admits that he has heard of such people, he will be very reluctant to give much information about them. A belief in witchcraft is then primarily the heritage of the more isolated and least advanced races, like Kols and Bhíls, Santáls and Thárús. In fact, whatever may be the ethnical origin of the theory, it is at present in Northern India the special heritage of the Dravidian or aboriginal peoples. The belief that a certain person is a witch is probably generated in various ways. Many a one becomes reputed as a witch from the realisation of some unlucky prophecy or the fulfilment of some casual, passionate curse or imprecation upon an enemy or rival. The old Scottish lines exactly express this feeling—

> "There dwelt a weaver in Moffat toun,
> That said the minister would die sune;
> The minister died and the foulk o' the toun,
> They brant the weaver wi' the wadd of the lune.
> And ca'd it weel-waned on the warloch loon." [1]

With this is untimately connected the belief in the Evil-eye, and that certain persons have the power of calling down on their enemies the influence of evil spirits; and, as in Western lands, such a power is often attached to persons afflicted with ugliness, deformity, crankiness of temper, liability to sudden fits of passion, epilepsy and the like. Disease or death, accident or famine, or any form of trouble never, in popular belief, comes naturally. There is always behind calamity some malignant power which selects the victim, and the attribution of this faculty to any one naturally regarded as uncanny, or who practises rites or worship strange to the orthodox belief, is only reasonable.

The Jigar Khor.

One particularly dreaded form of witch is the *Jigar Khor*, or liver-eater, of whom Abul Fazl gives a description. "One of this class can steal away the liver of another by looks and incantations. Other accounts say that by looking at a person he deprives him of his senses, and then steals from him something resembling the seed of a

[1] Chambers, *Popular Rhymes of Scotland*, 23.

pomogranate, which he hides in the calf of his leg : after being swelled by the fire, he distributes it among his fellows to be eaten, which ceremony concludes the life of the fascinated person. A *Jigar Khor* is able to communicate his art to another by teaching him incantations, and by making him eat a bit of the liver cake. These *Jigar Khors* are mostly women. It is said they can bring intelligence from a great distance in a short space of time, and if they are thrown into a river with a stone tied to them, they nevertheless will not sink. In order to deprive any one of this wicked power they brand his temples and every joint of his body, cram his eyes with salt, suspend him for forty days in a subterraneous chamber, and repeat over him certain incantations."

The witch in folklore.

We have already learnt to look to the folktales for the most trustworthy indications of popular belief, and here the dark shadow of witchcraft overclouds much of their delicate fancy. Here we find the witch taking many forms—of an old woman in trouble, of a white hind with golden horns, of a queen. Others, like the archwitch Kálarátri or "black night," are of repulsive appearance; she has dull eyes, a depressed flat nose; her eyebrows, like those of the werewolves or vampires of Slavonia,[1] meet together : she has large cheeks, widely-parted lips, projecting teeth, a long neck, pendulous breasts, a large belly, and broad expanded feet. "She appeared as if the Creator had made a specimen of his skill in producing ugliness." Like the *Jigar Khor*, she obtains her powers by eating human flesh, or like modern witches who claim to possess the *dáyan ká mantra* or Dákini's spell, by which she can tear out the heart of her victim. The powers of such witches are innumerable. They can find anything on earth, can open or patch up the sky, possess second sight, can restore the dead to life, can set fire to water or turn stone into wax, can separate lovers, can metamorphose the hero into any animal they please. They carry on their unholy revels in cemeteries and cremation grounds. They meet under the leadership of the dreaded Bhirava, as German witches assem-

[1] Tylor, *Primitive Culture*, II, 176.

ble on the Blocksberg. They obtain control over the imp of the fever demon. They can fasten a string round the hero's neck, and by a spell turn him into an ape. She extracts her husband's entrails, sucks them, and replaces them as before : and the heroine, like Genoveva, is often falsely accused of killing her own child and is expelled from her home until the plot is discovered and she is restored to her husband's love.[1] Lastly, we have the conflict between the powers of good and evil, the benevolent and malignant witch, which forms one of the stock incidents of European folktales.[2] The malignant, liver-eating witch is in modern belief naturally associated with the tomb-hunting badger. One of these appeared quite recently at Ahmadábád, and being supposed to carry off children in the disguise of a badger, was called *Adam Khor*, or devourer of the sons of men.[3]

Instruction in witchcraft.

Witchcraft is an art which can be learnt. Among the Agariyas of Bengal there are old women, professors of witchcraft, who stealthily instruct the young girls. "The latter are all eager to be taught, and are not considered to be proficient till a fine forest tree selected to be experimented on is destroyed by the potency of their charms : so that the wife a man takes to his bosom has probably *done* her tree, and is confident in the belief that she can, if she pleases, dispose of her husband in the same manner if he makes himself obnoxious."[4] So in Bombay, "when a *guru* or teacher wishes to initiate a candidate into the mysteries of the black art, he directs the candidate to watch a favourable opportunity for the commencement of the study, the opportunity being the death of a woman in childbirth. As soon as this event takes place, the candidate is instructed what to do. He watches the procession as the dead is being carried to the burning or burial ground, and takes care to see who the bearers are. He then takes a small tin box in his hand, and

---

[1] Temple, *Wideawake Stories*, 395 : Tawney, *Katha Sarit Ságara*, I, 157, 159, 289, 340 ; II, 164, 240, etc.

[2] Tawney, *ibid*, I, 313.

[3] *Bombay Gazetteer*, IV, 27 : and see Temple, *Legends of the Panjáb*, III, 13.

[4] Dalton, *Descriptive Ethnology*, 323.

picking up a pinch of earth out of the hind footprints of the two rear bearers, he keeps the earth in the tin box. Then he watches where the dead body is being burnt, and goes home. Next day he goes to the spot, and taking a little of the ashes of the corpse, puts it in the tin box. Subsequently, on a suitable day, that is, on a new moon or on an eclipse day, he goes to the burning ground at midnight, and, taking off his clothes, he sits on the ground, and, placing the tin box in front of him, lights a little incense and repeats the incantations taught to him by his *guru* or teacher. When he has practised the repetition of the incantations, the spirit Hadal becomes subject to his control, and by her help he becomes able to annoy any one he pleases. Among the troubles which the witch or magician brings on his enemies, the following are said to be the most frequent in the Dakkhin as well as the Konkan. The witch causes star-shaped or cross-like marks of marking nuts on the body of the person whom she has a grudge against. The peculiarity of these marks is that they appear in numbers in different parts of the body, and as suddenly disappear. The other troubles are the drying up of the milk of milch cattle, or turning the milk into blood: stopping or retarding the growth of the fœtus in cattle, and turning them into moles, stealing grain or other field produce from the farmyards of the victim: letting loose wolves, jackals or rats into the victim's field, so as to destroy his cattle, sheep, and crops: pricking needles or thorns into the victim's eyes or body: applying turmeric to the body of a female victim, or putting lamp-black into her eyes: or tearing the open end of her robe: and causing death to the enemy by means of a method of the black art called *múth*, literally "a handful." The *múth* generally consists of a handful of rice or *urad* pulse (*phaseolus radiatus*) charmed and sent by the witch against her enemy though the agency of the familiar spirit. It is likened to a shock of electricity sudden and sharp, which strikes in the centre of the heart, causes vomiting and spitting of blood, and may, if not warded off, end in the death of the victim. Practised experts pretend to see the *múth* rolling through the air like a red hot ball, and say that they can avert its evil consequences in two ways—either by satiating it, which is done by cutting the little finger so as to cause a little bleeding, and allowing the blood to drop on a charmed lemon, which is afterwards cut and thrown into a river; or by reversing its motion and sending it back to the person who issued it, which is done by charging a lemon and throwing it in the direction whence the *múth* has been seen to come. The operation of a *múth* is most dreaded in many parts of Bombay and particularly in the Konkan. Cases of sudden sickness, blood vomiting or sudden death, are frequently attributed to the agency of a *múth* or charmed handful of rice or pulse sent by an enemy."[1] With this may be compared the theory of the Churel and nudity charms already discussed.

Central Indian witches.

So in Central India, witches are supposed by the aid of their familiars who are known as Bír or "hero" to inflict pain, disease and death upon human beings. Their power of witchcraft, like that of all Indian witches, exists on the 14th, 15th and 29th of each month, and in particular at the Diwáli or feast of lamps, and the Naurátri, or nine days devoted to the worship of Durgá. In the same way the Irish fairies flit on November Eve, and "on that night mortal people should keep at home, or they will suffer for it: for souls of the dead have power over all things on that one night of the year, and they hold a festival with the fairies, and drink red wine from the fairy cups and dance to fairy music till the moon goes down."[2] At other times the Indian witches appear, dress, talk and eat like other women, but "when the fit is on them they are sometimes seen with their eyes glaring red, their hair dishevelled and bristled, while their heads are often turned round in a strange, convulsive manner. On the nights of those days, they are believed to go abroad, and, after casting off their garments, to ride about on tigers and other wild animals: and if they desire

[1] Campbell, *Notes*, 203, *sq*.
[2] Lady Wilde, *Legends*, 78.

to go on the water, alligators come like the beasts of the forest at their call, and they disport in rivers and lakes upon their backs till dawn of day, about which period they always return home and resume their usual forms and occupations." [1]

Witches taking the form of tigers.

The idea that witches take the form of tigers is widespread. Colonel Dalton describes how a Kol, tried for the murder of a wizard, stated in his defence that his wife having been killed by a tiger in his presence, he stealthily followed the animal as it glided away after gratifying its appetite, and saw that it entered the house of one Pusa, a Kol, whom he knew. He called out Pusa's relations, and when they heard the story, they not only credited it, but declared that they had long suspected Pusa of possessing such power: on entering they found him, and not a tiger: they delivered him bound into the hands of his accuser who at once killed him. In explanation of their proceedings, they deposed that Pusa had one night devoured an entire goat, and roared like a tiger while he was eating it: and on another occasion he had informed his friends that he had a longing for a particular bullock, and that night that very bullock was carried off by a tiger [2] Mr. Campbell gives a very similar story from Bombay, where a man-eating tiger was supposed to be a witch in disguise.[3] All these stories very closely resemble those of the European were-wolf and similar legends. [4] In Mirzapur they tell a story of one of the aboriginal Bhuiyárs, whose wife went recently on the Pura Mamuár hill, when an evil spirit in the form of a tiger attacked and killed her. This was after her death ascertained to be the case by the enquiries of the village Baiga, who now does an annual sacrifice near the place. For such witch tigers the favourite remedy is to knock out their teeth to prevent

[1] Malcolm, *Central India*, II, 212, *sq*.
[2] *Descriptive Ethnology*, 29,089.
[3] *Notes*, 257, *sq*.
[4] Tylor, *Primitive Culture*, I, 312 sqq: Henderson, ***Folklore of the Northern Counties***, 201, *sq*.

them doing any further mischief and becoming the Indian equivalent of the loupgarou.[1]

Extracting of substances from victims by witches.

Another remedy is thus described by Abul Fazl. "The sorceress casts something out of her mouth like the grain of a pomegranate, which is believed to be part of the heart which she has eaten. The patient picks it up as part of his own intestine and greedily swallows it. By this means, as if his heart was replaced in his body, he recovers his health by degrees." The idea that witches extract substances out of a sick person's body is very common.[2] Colonel Sleeman gives a case of a trooper who had taken some milk from an old woman without payment and was seized with severe internal pains which he attributed to her witchcraft. She was sent for, but denied having bewitched him. She admitted, however, that "the house gods may have punished him for his wickedness." She was ordered to cure him, and set about collecting materials for the purpose, but meanwhile the pains left him. Another man took a cock from an old Gond woman, and was similarly affected. "The old cock was actually heard crowing in his belly." In spite of all the usual remedies he died, and the cock never ceased crowing at intervals till his death. He tells of another witch who was known to be such by the juice of the sugarcane she was eating turning into blood.. A man saw her staring at him and left the district at once. "It is well known that these spells and curses can only reach a distance of ten or twelve miles, and if you offend one of these witches, the sooner you put that distance between you and them, the better." Another witch was bargaining with a man for some sugarcane. She seized one end of the stalk and the purchaser the other. A scuffle ensued, and a soldier came up and cut the cane in two with a sword. Immediately a quantity of blood flowed from the cane on the ground, which the witch had been drawing through it from the man's body. "It is the general belief that there is not a village or a single family without its witch

[1] Balfour, *Cyclopædia*, I, 961: Lyall, *Asiatic Studies*, 85: *Panjáb Notes and Queries*, 111, 7.

[2] Tylor, *Early History*, 276.]

in this part of the country. Indeed, no one will give his daughter in marriage to a family without one, saying, 'If my daughter has children, what will become of them without a witch to protect them from witches of other families in the neighbourhood?'"[1] Sir John Malcolm notices the same fact. "In some places men will not marry into a family where there is not a witch (*Dákiní*) to save them from the malice of others: but this name, which is odious, is not given to those persons by their relations and friends. They are termed *Rákhwálí* or guardians."[2]

Witch ordeals: cats.

There are various forms of ordeals used for the discovery of witches.[3] One sign of a witch is, that she is generally accompanied by a cat. This is an idea common all over the world. Thus in Ireland, cats are believed to be connected with demons. On entering a house the usual salutation is "God save all here except the cat." Even the cake on the griddle may be blessed, but no one says "God bless the cat."[4] The Oráons of Chota Nágpur believe that Chordeva or the birth fiend, comes in the form of a cat and worries the mother.[5] The Thags used to call the caterwauling of cats *Kálí-kí-mauj* or the roaring wave of *Kálí*, and it was of evil omen. The omen could be obviated only by gargling the mouth in the morning with sour milk and spitting it out. To kill a cat is hence very dangerous, and in Bombay any one who commits this sin has to do penance and give a golden cat to a Bráhman.[6] Everywhere in Western folklore the cat is the witch's attendant.[7] In the folk-tales the cunning, malignancy and hypocrisy of the cat are often referred to. The famous cat of Rája Rasálu saves him from ruin when he gambles with Rája Sarkap.[8] It was for this reason that Zálim Sinh, the famous Regent of Kotah, on one occasion when

---

1 *Rambles and Recollections*, I, 90, 92, 94, 95.
2 *Central India*, II, 216.
3 For savage ordeals generally see Farrer, *Primitive Manners*, 173, *sq.*
4 Lady Wilde, *Legends*, 151.
5 Dalton, *Descriptive Ethnology*, 252.
6 *North Indian Notes and Queries*, I, 34: Campbell, *Notes*, 296.
7 Gubernatis, *Zoological Mythology*, II, 62, *sqq*: Conway, *Demonology*, II, 301, *sq*: Henderson, *Folklore of the Northern Counties*, 206.
8 Temple, *Wideawake Stories*, 276, *sqq*: *Legends of the Panjáb*, I, 48; Tawney, *Katha Sarit Ságara*, II, 67, 636.

he believed himself exposed to enchantment, ordered that every cat should be expelled from his cantonment.[1]

Zálim Sinh, however, generally used the water ordeal.[2] This variety of test is known all over the world. Even Pliny knew that Indian witches could not sink in water.[3] We have already seen that water is a well-known means of dispelling evil spirits. Manu prescribes it as a form of oath, and to this day it is a common form of oath ordeal for a man to stand in water when he is challenged to swear.[4] Zálim Sinh used to say that handling balls of hot iron was too slight a punishment for such sinners as witches, for it was well known they have substances by means of which they are enabled to do this with impunity: so he used to throw them into a pond of water: if they sank they were innocent: if they, unhappily, came to the surface, their league with the powers of darkness was apparent. A bag of cayenne pepper tied over the head, if it failed to suffocate, afforded another test. "The most humane method employed was rubbing the eyes with a well-dried capsicum: and certainly if they could furnish the demonstration of their innocence by withholding tears, they might justly be deemed witches."[5] Akin to this is the folktale ordeal by which the calumniated heroine bathes in boiling oil to prove her chastity.[6]

Ordeal by water.

Forbes[7] gives the tests in vogue in his day among the Santáls whom he calls Soontaar. Branches of the *Sál* tree (*Shorea robusta*), marked with the names of all the females of the village, whether married or unmarried, who had attained the age of twelve years, were planted in the morning in water for the space of four and a-half hours: and the withering of any of these branches was proof of witchcraft against the person

Santál witch ordeals.

[1] Malcolm, *Central India*, II, 214, Note.
[2] Tod, *Annals*, II, 106.
[3] *Natural History*, VII, 2.
[4] *Institutes*, VIII, 114, *sq.*
[5] Tod, *Annals*, II, 638: Malcolm, *loc. cit.*, II, 212, *sq.*
[6] Temple, *Legends of the Panjáb*, I, Intro., XXI: *Wideawake Stories*, 429.
[7] *Oriental Memoirs*, II, 374, *sq.*

whose name was attached to it. Small portions of rice enveloped in pieces of cloth marked as before, were placed in a nest of white ants: the consumption of the rice in any of the bags was proof of witchcraft against the woman whose name it bore. Lamps were lighted at night: water was placed in cups made of leaves, and mustard oil was poured drop by drop into the water, while the name of each woman in the village was pronounced. The appearance of the shadow of any woman in the water during the ceremony proved her to be a witch.

Witch tests, Biláspur.

One of the most noted witch-finders in the Biláspur district of the Central Provinces had two most effectual means of checkmating the witches. "His first effort was to get the villagers to describe the marked eccentricities of the old women of the community, and when these had been detailed his experience soon enabled him to size on some ugly or unlucky idiosyncracy which indicated in unmistakeable clearness the unhappy offender. If no conclusion could be arrived at in this way, he lighted an ordinary earthen lamp, and repeating consecutively each woman's name in the village, he fixed on the witch or witches by the flicker of the wick when the name or names were mentioned. The discovery of the witch soon led to her being grossly maltreated, and under the Native Government, almost invariably in her death. Since the introduction of the British rule these cases are becoming year by year rarer: but the belief itself remains strong and universal, and the same class of superstitions pervades every-day life."[1]

Witch tests, Bastar.

In Bastar "a fisherman's net is wound round the head of the suspected witch to prevent her escaping or bewitching her guards. Two leaves of the *pípal* or sacred fig tree, one representing her and the other her accusers, are thrown upon her outstretched hands. If the leaf in her name fall uppermost she is supposed to be a suspicious character: if the leaf fall with the lower parts upwards, it is possible that she

[1] *Central Provinces Gazetteer*, 110, *sq.*

may be innocent, and popular opinion is in her favour." The final test is the usual water ordeal.[1]

Miscellaneous tests.

Several persons, natives of the Khasiya hills, were convicted of beating to death a man whom they believed to be a wizard. They confessed freely, saying that he destroyed their wives and daughters by witchcraft. One of the accused was the brother of the wife of the deceased. It appeared that they discovered he was a sorcerer by the appearance of an egg when broken.[2] A similar case is reported among the Banjáras of Berár.[3] Numerous instances of the use of eggs to scare evil spirits are collected by Mr. Campbell. In the Konkan Kunbis give a mixture of eggs and turmeric to a man who spits blood: and to remove the effect of the Evil Eye, they wave bread and an egg round the sick person. The Velális of Púna offer eggs on the fifth day after childbirth to the knife which cuts the umbilical cord. The Sultánkárs when their wives are possessed with evil spirits offer rice, a fowl and an egg, and the spirit goes away. The Beni Israels to avert evil, break a hen's egg under the forefoot of the bridegroom's horse. All this is probably based on the same idea as the use of Easter eggs in England.[4] In Chhattisgarh a pole of a particular wood is erected on the banks of a stream, and each suspected person after bathing is required to touch the pole: it is supposed that when this is done the hand of the witch will swell.

The Rowan tree.

According to British folklore the proper antidote for witches is a twig of the rowan tree bound with scarlet thread, or a stalk of clover with four leaves laid in the byre, or a bough of the whitty or "way-faring tree."[5] In India the substitute for these magic trees is a branch of the tamarind, or a stalk of the castor-oil plant (*palma Christi*). If after receiving in silence an ordinary scourging by the usual

---

1 *Central Province, Gazetteer*, 39.
2 *Reports, Nizámat Adalat*, 11th December 1854.
3 *Berár Gazetteer*, 197.
4 Campbell, *Notes*, 83.
5 Gregor, *Folklore of N.-E. Scotland*, 188: Henderson, *Folklore of the Northern Counties*, 201, 218, *sqq.*; 224: Aubrey, *Remaines*, 247: Farrer, *Primitive Manners*, 290, *sq.*

methods, the suspected person cries out at a blow with the magic branch, he is certainly guilty.[1] These plants everywhere enjoy a powerful influence over witches: and even in places like the North-Western Provinces, where witch-hunting is happily a thing of the past, a Currier or Chamár, a class which enjoy an uncanny reputation, are exceedingly afraid of even a slight blow with a castor-oil switch.

Witch-finding among Kols.

The Kolavian witch-finder's test is to put a large wooden grain measure under a flat stone as a pivot on which the stone can revolve. A boy is then seated on the stone supporting himself with his hands and "the names of all the people in the neighbourhood are slowly pronounced. As each name is uttered a few grains of rice are thrown at the boy. When they come to the name of the witch or wizard, the stone turns and the boy rolls off. This, no doubt, is the effect of the boy's falling into a state of coma, and losing the power of supporting himself with his hands."[2]

Marks of witches.

Some witches are believed to learn the secrets of their craft by eating filth. We have already seen that this is believed also to be the case with evil spirits. Such a woman, in popular belief, is always very lovely and scrupulously neat in her personal appearance, and she always has a clear line of red lead applied to the parting of her hair. Witches have a special power of casting evil glances on children, and after a child is buried they are believed to exhume the corpse, anoint it with oil and bring it to life to serve some occult purpose of their own. On the same principle the Kafirs believe that dead bodies are restored to life and made hobgoblins to aid their owners in mischief.[3] Indian witches, moreover, are believed to keep a light burning during the ceremony of child burial, and if the father or mother has the

---

[1] *Central Provinces Gazetteer*, 157.
[2] Dalton, *Descriptive Ethnology*, 199.
[3] Spencer, *Principles of Sociology*, I, 240.

courage to run and snatch away the child just as it is revived before the witch can blow out the light, the child will be restored to them safe and sound.[1]

On the principle that—

"He who'd read her aright must say her
Backwards, like a witch's prayer"—

Indian witches are supposed to repeat two letters and a-half from a verse in the Qurán, known only to themselves, backwards. This backward reciting is a common belief.[2] We have it in the folktales of Somadeva—where Bhímabhata prays in his extremity to Mother Ganges and she says,—"Now receive from me this charm called 'forwards and backwards.' If a man repeats it forwards he will become invisible to his neighbour: but if he repeats it backwards he will assume whatever shape he desires."[3] The use of this charm enables the witch to take the liver out of a living child and eat it. But in order to do this effectively she must first catch some particular kind of wild animal not larger than a dog, feed it with cakes of sugar and butter, ride on it and repeat the charm one hundred times. When dying the breath will not leave the body of the witch until she has taught the two and a-half letters to another woman, or failing a woman until she has repeated it to a tree.[4]

Charms recited backwards.

An idea is common to all folklore that a witch can acquire power over her victim by getting possession of a lock of his hair, the parings of his nails, or some other part of his body. In Ireland nail parings are an ingredient in many charms, and hair cuttings should not be placed where birds can find them, for they take them to build their nests and then you will have headaches all the year after.[5] On the same principle English mothers hide away the first tooth of a child.[6]

Witchcraft by means of hair, nail parings, etc.

[1] *Panjáb Notes and Queries*, II, 6.
[2] Henderson, *Folklore of the Northern Counties*, 32: Gregor, *Folklore of N.-E. Scotland*, 183.
[3] Tawney, *Katha Sarit Ságara*, II, 221.
[4] *Panjáb Notes and Queries*, III, 7.
[5] Lady Wilde, *Legends*, 197, 206.
[6] Aubrey, *Remaines*, 11: and for other instances of similar practices see Sir W. Scott, *Letters on Demonology*, 273: Spencer, *Principles of Sociology*, I, 243: Tylor, *Primitive Culture*, I, 116; II, 149: Lubbock, *Origin of Civilisation*, 241, 244: Henderson, *Folklore of the Northern Counties*, 148: Farrer, *Primitive Manners*, 287.

Hence natives of India are very careful about the disposal of hair cuttings and nail parings: and it is only at shrines and sacred places of pilgrimage, where shaving is a religious duty, that such things are left lying on the ground. The sanctity of the place is regarded as a protective against sorcery: but some extra careful people take precautions to consign their hair clippings to running water.

Witchcraft by images.

Another means which witches are supposed to employ to injure those whom they dislike, is to make an image of wax or flour and torture it with the idea that the pain will be communicated to the person whom they desire to annoy. Among Muhammadans when the death of an enemy is desired, a doll is made of earth taken from a grave or a place where bodies are cremated, and various sentences of the Qurán are read backwards over twenty one small wooden pegs. The officiant is to repeat the spell three times over each peg, and is then to strike them so as to pierce various parts of the body of the image. The image is then to be shrouded like a corpse, conveyed to a cemetery and buried in the name of the enemy whom it is intended to injure. He will, it is believed, certainly die after the ceremony. There are various other methods of the same kind which are detailed by Dr. Herklots.[1] It is needless to say that the same idea prevails in Europe. Examples of such images may be seen in the Pitt-River's collection at Oxford. Sir W. Scott describes how under the threshold of a house in Dalkeith was found the withered heart of some animal, full of many scores of pins, which had been placed there as a charm; and Aubrey tells us of one Hammond of Westminster who was hanged or tried for his life about 1641, for killing a person by means of an image of wax.[2] In Bengal "a person sometimes takes a bamboo which has been used to keep down a corpse during its cremation, and making a bow and arrow with it, repeats incantations over them. He then makes an image of his enemy in clay, and lets fly an arrow into this image. The person whose image is thus pierced is said to be immediately seized with a pain in his breast."[3] In the folktales

[1] *Qánún-i-Islám*, 229, *sq.*
[2] *Letters on Demonology*, 273: *Remaines*, 61, 228.
[3] Ward, *Hindus*, I, 100.

restoration to life is usually effected by collecting the ashes or bones of the deceased and making an image of them into which life is breathed.[1]

Punishment of witches.

The methods by which witches are punished display a diabolical ingenuity. The Indian newspapers last year recorded that six out of nine murders in the Sambalpur district were due to "the superstition, which is so general, that the spread of cholera is due to the sorcery of some individual whose evil influence can be nullified if he is beaten with rods of the castor-oil plant. The people who are thus suspected are so cruelly beaten that in the majority of cases they die under the infliction." A milder form of treatment is to make the witch drink the filthy water of a washerman's tank which is believed to destroy her skill.[2] The punishment in vogue in Central India was to make witches drink the water used by curriers—leather being, as we have seen, a scarer of evil spirits, and drinking such water involves degradation from caste. In more serious cases the witch's nose was cut off, or she was put to death.[3] In Bastar, if a man is adjudged guilty of witchcraft, he is beaten by the crowd, his head is shaved, the hair being supposed to constitute his power of mischief: his front teeth are knocked out, in order, it is said, to prevent him from muttering incantations, but more probably, as we have already seen, to prevent him from becoming a loup garou. All descriptions of filth are thrown at him: if he be of good caste, hog's flesh is thrust into his mouth, and lastly, he is driven out of the country followed by the abuse and execrations of his enlightened fellowmen. Women suspected of sorcery have to undergo the same ordeal: if found guilty, the same punishment is awarded, and after being shaved, their hair is attached to a tree in some public place. In Chhattísgarh a witch has her head shaved with a blunt knife, her two front teeth are knocked out, she is branded in the

---

[1] Temple, *Legends of the Panjáb*, I: Intro. XVII: and compare Tawney, *Katha Sarit Ságara*, II, 242 *sq.*
[2] *Hoshangabád Settlement Report*, 287.
[3] Malcolm, *Central India*, II, 212 *sq.*

hinder parts, has a ploughshare, which is a strong fetish, tied to her legs, and she is made to drink the water of a tannery.[1]

In former times among the Dravidian races persons denounced as witches were put to death in the belief that witches breed witches and sorcerers. A terrible raid was made upon these unfortunate people when British authority was relaxed in the Mutiny, and most atrocious murders were committed. "Accusations of witchcraft are still sometimes made, and persons denounced are subjected to much ill-usage, if they escape with their lives."[2] Among the Bhils suspected persons used to be suspended from a tree head downwards, pounded chillies being first put into the witch's eyes to see if the smarting would draw tears from her. Sometimes after suspension she was swung violently from side to side. She was finally compelled to drink the blood of a goat, slaughtered for the purpose, which is regarded as a substitute for the sick man's life, and to satisfy the witch's craving for blood. She was then brought to the patient's bedside, and required to make passes over his head with a *nim* branch: a lock of hair was also cut from the head of the witch and buried in the ground, that the last link between her and her former powers of mischief might be broken.[3]

Witchcraft punishments among Dravidians.

Dr. Chevers has collected a number of instances in which the punishment of death or mutilation was inflicted on supposed witches. He quotes a case in 1802, in which several of the witnesses declared that they remembered numerous instances of persons being put to death for sorcery: one of them, in particular, proved that her mother had been tried and executed as a witch. In another case a Kol, thinking that some old women had bewitched him, placed them in a line and cut off all their heads except that of the last who, objecting to this drastic form of ordeal, run away and escaped. In another, the nose-ring of a suspected witch was torn out with such violence

Other witchcraft punishments.

[1] *Central Provinces Gazetteer*, 39, 157.
[2] Dalton, *Descriptive Ethnology*, 199.
[3] Chevers, *Indian Medical Jurisprudence*, 540, sq

as to cause extensive laceration. There are recorded instances of even more brutal forms of mutilation.[1] A case occurred at Dakka in which some people went to the house of a reputed witch, intending, they said, to make her discontinue her enchantments, and ill-treated her in such a shameful way as to leave her in a dying state. She appears to have been in the habit of prescribing medicines for children, and this seems to have been the only basis for the reports that she practiced magic.[2] At the present day in Mirzapur when a woman is marked down as a witch, the Baiga or Ojha pricks her tongue with a needle and the blood thus extracted is received on some rice which she is compelled to eat. In other cases she is pricked on the breast, tongue and thighs and given the blood to drink. This ceremony is most efficacious if performed on the banks of a running stream. This is evidently a survival of the ancient blood sacrifice of a witch.

Witch haunts.

"In any country an isolated or outlying race, the lingering survivors of an older nationality, is liable to the imputation of sorcery."[3] This is exactly true of Asia. Marco Polo makes the same assertion about Pachai in Badakhshán. He says that the people of Kashmír "have extraordinary acquaintance with the devilries of enchantment, insomuch, that they can make their idols to speak. They can also by their sorceries bring on changes of weather, and produce darkness, and do a number of things so extraordinary, that without seeing them no one would believe them. Indeed, this country is the very original source from which idolatry has spread abroad." In Tibet, he says, "are the best enchanters and astrologers that exist in that part of the world: they perform such extraordinary marvels and sorceries by diabolical art, that it astounds one to see or even hear of them."[4] The same is the case with the Konkan in Bombay.[5] The semi-aboriginal Thárus of the Himalayan Tarái are sup-

[1] Chevers, Indian Medical Jurisprudence, 12, Note 14; Note: 393, 488, 492; Note, 493.
[2] *Ibid*, 514, Note: also see Ball, *Jungle Life*, 115 *sq*: *Calcutta Review*, V, 52.
[3] Tylor, *Primitive Culture*, I, 113.
[4] Yule, *Marco Polo*, I, 172, 175 with Note; II, 41.
[5] Campbell, *Notes*, 141.

posed to possess special powers of this kind, and Tharuhat or "the land of the Thárus" is a synonym for "witches' country," as was the North of Europe in early days.[1] At Bhágalpur, Dr. Buchanan was told that twenty-five children died annually through the malevolence of witches. These reputed witches used to drive a roaring trade, as women would conceal their children on their approach and bribe them to go away. In Gorakhpur he says that until lately the Tonahis or witches were very numerous, "but some Judge sent an order that no one should presume to injure another by enchantment. It is supposed that the order has been obeyed, and no one has since imagined himself injured—a sign of the people being remarkably easy to govern."[2] The wandering half-gypsy Banjáras or grain-carriers, are notoriously witch-ridden.

Nona Chamárin, The witch.

Now-a-days the half-deified witch most dreaded in the eastern districts of the North-Western Provinces is Loná or Noná, a Chamárin or woman of the currier caste. Her legend is in this wise. The great physician Dhanwantara, who corresponds to Luqmán Hakím of the Muhammadans, was on his way to cure King Parikshit, and was deceived and bitten by the snake king Takshaka. He, therefore, desired his sons to roast him and eat his flesh and thus succeed to his magical powers. The snake king dissuaded them from eating the unholy meal, and they let the cauldron containing it float down the Ganges. A currier woman named Loná found it and ate the contents, and thus succeeded to the mystic powers of Dhanwantara. She became skilful in cures, particularly of snake bite. Finally she was discovered to be a witch by the extraordinary rapidity with which she could plant out rice seedlings. One day the people watched her and saw that when she believed herself unobserved, she stripped herself naked, and taking the bundle of plants in her hands threw them into the air, reciting certain spells. When the seedlings forthwith arranged themselves in their proper places, the spectators called out in astonishment, and

1 Sir W. Scott, *Letters on Demonology*, 86, *sq.*
2 *Eastern India*, II, 108, 445.

finding herself discovered Noná rushed along over the country, and the channel which she made in her course is the Loni river to this day. So a saint at Broach formed a new course for a river by dragging his clothes behind him. In Noná's case we have the nudity charm of which instances have been already given.

Pútaná. The witch.

Another terrible witch whose legend is told at Mathura is Pútaná. She found the infant Krishna asleep and began to suckle him with her devil's milk. The first drop would have poisoned a mortal child, but Krishna drew her breast with such strength that he drained her lifeblood and the fiend terrifying the whole country of Braj with her groans of agony, fell lifeless to the ground. European witches suck the blood of children; here the divine Krishna turns the table on the witch.[1]

The witch of the Palwárs.

The Palwár Rájputs of Oudh have a witch ancestress. Soon after the birth of her son she was engaged in baking cakes. Her infant began to cry, and she was obliged to perform a double duty. At this juncture her husband arrived just in time to see his demon wife assume gigantic and supernatural proportions, so as to allow both the baking and the nursing to go on at the same time. But finding her secret discovered the witch disappeared, leaving her son as a legacy to her astonished husband.[2] Here, though the story is incomplete, we have almost certainly, as in the case of Noná Chamarin, one of the Melusina type of legend where the supernatural wife leaves her husband and children, because he violates some taboo by which he is forbidden to see her in a state of nudity or the like.[3]

The history of witchcraft in India is, as in Europe, one of the saddest pages in the annals of the people. Now-a-days the power of British law has almost entirely suppressed the horrible outrages which under the native administration were habitually practised. But

---

[1] Gubernatis, *Zoological Mythology*, II, 202 : Growse, *Mathura*, 53.
[2] *Oudh Gazeteer*, III, 480.
[3] Hartland, *Science of Fairy Tales*, 270, *sqq*.

particularly in the more remote and uncivilised portions of the country this superstition still lies heavy on the minds of the people, and occasional indications of it, which appear in our criminal records, are quite sufficient to show that any relaxation of the activity of our Magistrates and Police would undoubtedly lead to its revival in some of its more shocking forms.

CHAPTER XI.

SOME RURAL FESTIVALS AND CEREMONIES.

> Ἐν δ' ἐτίθει νειὸν μαλακὴν πίειραν ἄρουραν,
> Εὐρεῖαν τρίπολον: πολλοὶ δ' ἀροτῆρες ἐν αὐτῇ
> Ζεύγεα δινεύοντες ἐλάστρεον ἔνθα καὶ ἔνθα.
>
> ILIAD, xviii, 541—43.

THE subject of rural festivals is much too extensive for treatment in a limited space. Here reference will be made only to a few of those ceremonies which illustrate the principles recently elucidated by Messrs. Frazer, Gomme and Mannhardt.[1]

The Akhtíj.

The agricultural year in Northern India begins with the ceremony of the Akhtíj, "the undecaying third," which is celebrated on the third day of the light fortnight of the month of Baisákh (May). In the North-Western Provinces the cultivator first fees his Pandit to select an auspicious hour on that day for the commencement of ploughing. In most places he does not begin till 3 p. m; in Mirzapur the time fixed is during the night, as secrecy is in most of these rural observances an important element in the ritual. In Rohilkhand the cultivator goes at daybreak to one of his fields, which must be of a square or oblong shape. He takes with him a brass drinking vessel of water, a branch of the mango tree, all of which are, as we have seen, efficacious in scaring evil spirits, and a spade. The object of the ceremony is to propitiate Prithiví, "the broad world," as contrasted with Dharti Má, or "the mother soil," and Sesha Nága, the great snake, which supports the world. The Pandit first makes certain observations by which he is able to determine in which direction the snake happens to be lying, because in order to ease himself of his burden, he moves about beneath the world and lies sometimes North and South, North-West and South-West, and

[1] Frazer, *Golden Bough*: Gomme, *Ethnology in Folklore*: Mannhardt, *Wald and Feld Kulte*.

so on. This imaginary line having been marked off, the peasant digs up five clods of earth with his spade. This a lucky number, as it is a quarter more than four. Hence Sawáí or one and a quarter has been taken as one of the titles of the Mahárája of Jaypur. He then sprinkles water five times with the branch of the sacred mango into the trench. The object of this is by a form of sympathetic magic to ensure the productiveness of his crop. During all these proceedings he watches the omens most carefully, and if anything inauspicious happens, the ceremony must be discontinued and recommenced at a luckier hour later on in the day. When he gets home some women of his family, not a widow, who is of course unlucky, presents him with curds and silver for good luck. He then stays all day in the house, rests and does no work and does not even go to sleep. He avoids quarrels and disputes of all kinds, and on that day will give neither grain nor money nor fire to any one. Next day he eats sweet food and balls of wheaten flour toasted with curds and sugar, but carefully abstains from salt. This rule against giving fire on the sowing day prevailed in Rome, and is still observed in the rural parts of England.[1] In Ireland it is believed that fire and salt are the most sacred things given to man, and if you give them away on May day, you give away your luck for the year: no one will give fire from a house whilst an unbaptised baby is in it.[2]

The custom in Rájputána and Mirzapur.

In Rájputána the ceremony is less elaborate. The first day of ploughing after the rains begin, is known as the *halṣotiya* festival. Omens being favourable, the villagers proceed to the fields, each householder carrying a new earthen pot coloured with turmeric, the virtues of which have been already explained, and full of *bájra* millet. Looking to the north, the home of the gods, they make an obeisance to the earth, and then a selected man ploughs five furrows. The ploughman's hands and the bullock's hoofs are rubbed with henna, and the former receives a dinner of delicacies.[3] In Mirzapur only

[1] Henderson, *Folklore of the Northern Counties*, 74.
[2] Lady Wilde, *Legends*, 103, 106, 203.
[3] *Gazetteer*, III, 237.

the northern part of the field, that facing the Himálaya, is dug up in five places with a piece of mango wood. The peasant, when he comes home, eats rich food and abstains from quarrels. All over the country the people seem to be becoming less careful about these observances. Some, without consulting a Pandit at all, go early to the field on the morning after the Holí fire is lighted, scratch the ground with a ploughshare, and on their return eat cakes and sweetmeats. Others on the first day after the Holi, when they hear the voice of the *Koil* or Indian cuckoo at twilight, go in silence to the field and make a few scratches. Among the Dravidian hill tribes of Mirzapur, the ceremony seems to be merely a formal propitiation of the village godlings. Among the Korwas before ploughing commences, the Baiga makes a burnt offering of butter and molasses in his own field. Then he sacrifices in the same way at the village shrine. After this ploughing commences. The Kharwárs, before sowing, take five handfuls of grain from the sowing basket and pray to Dhartí Mátá, the earth goddess, to be propitious. They keep the grain, grind it and offer it at her annual festival in Sáwan or August. The Pankas only do a burnt sacrifice through the Baiga and offer up some cakes and other food, known as *neuj*. Before the spring sowings a general offering of five cocks is made to the village gods by the Baiga, who consumes the sacrifice himself. All these people do not commence agricultural work till the Baiga starts work in his own field, and they prefer to do this on Monday.

Ceremony in Hoshangábad.

In Hoshangábád the ceremony is somewhat different. The ploughing is usually begun by the landlord, and all the cultivators collect and assist at the ceremony in his field before they go on to their own. "It is the custom for him to take a rupee and fasten it up in a leaf of the *Palása* tree with a thorn. He also folds up several empty leaves in the same way, and covers them all with a heap of leaves. When he has done worship to the plough and bullocks, he yokes them and drives them through the heap, and all the cultivators then scramble for the leaf which contains the rupee. They then each plough their fields a little, and returning in a body, they are met by the daughter or sister of the landlord, who comes out to meet them with a brass vessel full of water, a light in one hand and two wheaten cakes in the other. The landlord and each of the cultivators of his caste put a rupee into her water vessel, and take a bit of the cake which they put on her head. On the same day an earthern jar full of water is taken by each cultivator to his threshing-floor and placed to stand on four lumps of earth, each of which bears the name of one of the four months in the rainy reason. Next morning, as many lumps as are wetted by the leaking of the water jar (which is very porous and always leaks), so many months of rain will there be, and the cultivator makes his preparations for sowing accordingly.[1]

Ceremony in the Himalaya.

In the Himalaya again there is a different ritual. "On the day fixed for the commencement of ploughing the ceremony known as Kudkhyo and Halkhyo take place. The Kudkhyo takes place in the morning or evening, and begins by lighting a lamp before the household deity, and offering rice, flowers, and balls made of turmeric, borax and lemon juice. The conch is then sounded, and the owner of the field or relative, whose lucky day it is, takes three or four pounds of seed grain from a basin and carries it to the edge of the field prepared for its reception. He then scrapes a portion of the earth with a mattock and sows a part of the seed. One to five lamps are placed on the ground and the surplus seed is given away. At the Halkhyo ceremony the balls as above described are placed on the ploughman, plough and plough-cattle: four or five furrows are ploughed and sown, and the farm servants are fed."[2] This custom of giving away what remains of the seed grain to labourers and beggars prevails generally throughout Northern India.

Ceremony among the Dravidians.

Going on to the Dravidian races, the Mundas have a feast in May at the time of sowing for the first rice crop. "It is held in honour of the ancestral shades and other spirits, who, if unpropitiated would prevent the seed from germinating. A he-goat and a cock are

[1] *Settlement Report*, 123, *sq.*
[2] Atkinson, *Himalayan Gazetteer*, II, 856.

sacrificed." Again in June they have a festival to propitiate the local gods, that they may bless the crops. "In the Mundári villages every one plants a branch of the *bel* tree in his field, and contributes to the general offering, which is made by the priest in the sacred grove—a fowl, a pitcher of beer and a handful of rice." In July, again, each cultivator sacrifices a fowl, and after some mysterious rites, a wing is stripped off and inserted in a cleft of a bamboo, and stuck up in the rice field or dung heap. If this is omitted, the rice crop, it is supposed, will not come to maturity. It appears more like a charm than a sacrifice. Among the Kols of Chota Nágpur there is a special dance—"the women follow the men and change their attitudes and positions in obedience to signals from them." In one special figure "the women all kneel and pat the ground with their hands, in tune to music, as if coaxing the earth to be fertile."[1]

Prohibition of ploughing.

There are certain days on which ploughing is unlawful—the Nágpanchamí or snake feast held on the 5th of the light half of Sáwan, and the 15th of the month Kártik. But Mother Earth is supposed to sleep on six days in every month—the 5th, 7th, 9th, 11th, 21st and 24th, or, as others say—the 1st, 2nd, 5th, 7th, 10th, 21st and 24th. On such days it is advisable not to plough if it can possibly be avoided. The fifteen days in the month of Kuár, which are devoted to the worship of the Pitri or sainted dead, are also an inauspicious time for agricultural work. All these ceremonies at the commencement of the agricultural season remind us in many features of the observance of the festivals of "Plough Monday" and similar customs in the English Western Counties.[2]

Rakshabandhan and Javi festivals.

We have already noticed the use of the knotted cord or string as an amulet. On the full moon of Sáwan is held the Salono or Rakshabandhan festival. when women tie these amulets round the wrists of their friends. Connected with this is what is known as the barley feast (*Jayí* or

[1] Dalton, *Descriptive Ethnology*, 198.
[2] Chambers, *Book of Days*, I, 94, *sqq* : Aubrey, *Remaines*, 40, *sq*.

Jawára) in Upper India, and Bhujariya in the Central Provinces. It is supposed to be in some way connected with the famous story of Alha and Udal, which forms the subject of a very popular local epic. They were Rájputs of the Banáphar clan and led the Chandels in their famous campaign against the Rahtors of Kanauj, which immediately preceded, and in fact led up to, the Muhammadan conquest of Upper India.[1] In connection with this simple rural feast a most elaborate ritual has been prescribed under Bráhmanical influence,[2] but all that is usually done is that on the 7th day of the light half of Sáwan, grains of barley are sown in a pot of manure, and spring up so rapidly, that by the end of the month the vessel is full of long yellowish-green stalks. On the first day of the next month, Bhádon, the women and girls take these out, throw the earth and manure into water, and distribute the plants to their male friends, who bind them in their turbans and about their dress. This reminds us of the English rural custom of "Wearing the Rose." It is merely emblematical of the healthy growth of the seedlings at the approaching sowing of the winter crops.[3]

The Diwali or feast of lamps.

The regular Diwáli or feast of lamps, which is performed on the last day of the dark fortnight in the month of Kártik, is more a city than a rural festival. The feast has of course been provided with an appropriate legend. Once upon a time, an astrologer foretold to a Rája that on the new moon of Kártik his fate (*Kál*) would appear at midnight in the form of a snake; that the way to avoid this was that he should order all his subjects, on that night, to keep their houses, streets and lanes clean; that there should be a general illumination; that the king, too, should place a lamp at his door and at the four corners of his couch, and sprinkle rice and sweetmeats everywhere. If the door lamp went out it was foretold that he would become insensible, and that he was to tell his Rání to sing the praises of the snake when it arrived.

---

[1] See Cunningham, ***Archæological Reports***, II, 455.
[2] For details see Atkinson, ***Himalayan Gazetteer***, II, 886.
[3] See ***Hoshangábád Settlement Report***, 124 : Crooke, ***Rural Glossary***, svv : ***Salono, Rakhí, Jayi, Jurai*** : Atkinson, ***Himalayan Gazetteer***, II, 870 : ***Panjáb Notes and Queries***, IV, 197.

These instructions were faithfully carried out, and the snake was so pleased with his reception, that he told the Ráni to ask any boon she pleased. She asked for long life for her husband. The snake replied that it was out of his power to gran this, but that he would make arrangements with Yama Rája, the lord of the dead, for the escape of the king: and that she was to continue to watch his body. Then the snake carried off the spirit of the king to Yama Rája. When the papers of the king's life were produced before Yama, his age was denoted by a cypher, but the kindly snake put a seven before it and thus varied his age to 70 years. Then Yama Rája said: "This person, I find, has still 70 years to live. Take him back at once." So the snake brought back the soul of the king, and he revived and lived 70 years more, and established this feast in honour of the event.[1] The original basis of the feast seems to have been the belief that on this night the spirits of the dead revisit their homes which are cleaned and lighted for their reception. Now it is chiefly in honour of Lakshmi, the goddess of wealth, who is propitiated by gambling. On this night the women make what is known as "the new moon lamp black" (*amáwas ká kájal*) which is used throughout the following year as a charm against the Evil Eye, and as we have already seen, the symbolical expulsion of poverty goes on. Immediately following it is the Bhaiya Dúj or "Brother's second," when sisters make a mark on the foreheads of their brothers and make them eat five grains of gram. These must be swallowed whole, not chewed, and bring length of days. She then makes her brother sit facing the east and feeds him with sweetmeats, in return for which he gives her a present. The idea that the souls of the dead return at this time is exactly the same as that of the "All Souls' Day" in Germany.[2]

The Gobardhan.

Following the Diwálí comes what is known as the Gobardhan or Godhan, which is a purely rural feast. In parts of the North-Western Provinces the women on a platform outside the house make a little hut of

[1] This is something like a story in Grimm, *Household Tales*, No. 176.
[2] See Spencer, *Principles of Sociology*, I, 297, Note. The emphatic denial of this theory by Job (VII, 9-10) is noteworthy.

mud and images of Gauri and Ganesa : there they place the parched grain which the girls offered on the night of the Diwálí; near it they place some thorny grass, wave a rice pounder round the hut, and invoke blessings on their relations and friends. This is also a cattle feast, and cowherds come round half drunk and collect presents from their employers. They sing "May this house grow as the sugarcane grows, as Gangá increases at the sacred confluence at Prayág!" In the Panjáb "the women make a Gobardhan of cowdung, which consists of Krishna lying on his back surrounded by little cottage loaves of dung to represent mountains, in which are stuck stems of grass with tufts of cotton or rag on the top for trees, and by little dung balls for cattle, watched by dung men dressed in bits of rag. Another opinion is that the cottage loaves are cattle, and the dung balls calves. On this they put the churn staff, five white sugarcanes, some parched rice, and a lighted lamp in the middle. The cowherds are then called in, and they salute the whole, and are fed with rice and sweets. The Bráhman then takes the sugarcane and eats a bit, and till then no one must eat, press, or cut cane. Rice-milk is then given to the Bráhmans, and the bullocks have their horns dyed and are extra well fed."[1] Akbar used to join in this festival.[2] The custom in Cawnpur, known as the Dáng or "Club" Diwálí, is very similar. The cowherds worship Gobardhan in the form of a little heap of cowdung decorated with cotton, and go round to the houses of the persons whose cattle they graze, dance to the music of two sticks struck together, and a drum beaten by a Hindu weaver, and get presents of grain, cloth or money.[3]

Cattle festivals.

There are a number of similar usages in various parts of the country solemnised with the object of protecting the herds. Thus in Hoshangábád, they have a curious custom of frightening the cattle. "Every one keeps awake all night, and the herdsmen go about begging in a body, singing, and keeping the cattle from sleeping. In the

[1] Ibbetson, *Pánjab Ethnography*, 120.
[2] Blochmann, *Áín-i-Akbarí*, 1, 217.
[3] Wright, *Cawnpur Memo.*, 105 ; Buchanan, *Eastern India*, I, 194.

morning they are all stamped with the hand dipped in yellow paint for the white ones, and white paint for the red ones, and strings of cowries or peacocks' feathers are tied to their horns. Then they are driven out with wild whoops or yells, and the herdsman standing at the doorway smashes an earthen water jar on the last. The neck of this is placed on the gateway leading to the cattle sheds, and preserves them from the Evil-eye. In the afternoon the cattle are all collected together, and the Parihár priest sprinkles them with water, after which they are secure from all possible evil."[1] This reminds us of the custom of Manx cattle dealers, who drive their herd through fire on May-day, so as to singe them a little and preserve them from harm.[2]

So in Bengal, on the last day of Kártik (October, November) a pig is turned loose among a herd of buffaloes who are encouraged to gore it to death. The carcase is given to the Dosádh village menials to eat. The Ahírs, who practise this strange rite, aver that it has no religious significance, and is merely a sort of popular amusement. They do not themselves partake of any portion of the pig.[3] It is plainly a survival of a regular sacrifice.

Similar customs prevail in other parts of the country. Thus, in Mirzapur, at the Diwálí, a little earthen bell is procured from the village potter, and hung round the necks of the cattle as a protective. In Berár, at the Pola festival, the bullocks of the whole village pass in procession under a sacred rope made of twisted grass and covered with mango leaves. The sacred pole of the headman is then borne aloft to the front. He gives the order to advance, and all the bullocks (his own leading the way) file under the rope according to the respective rank of their owners. The villagers vie with each other in having the best painted and decorated bullocks, and large sums are often expended in this way.[4] This rope is supposed to have the magic power of protecting the cattle from disease or accident. In Northern India

[1] *Settlement Report*, 17.
[2] *Folklore*, II, 303.
[3] Risley, *Tribes and Castes*, I, 290.
[4] *Berar Gazetteer*, 207.

it is a common charm in cattle disease to hang a rope of straw on which mango leaves are suspended over the roadway by which the cattle enter or leave the village on their way to pasture. Among the Dravidians of South Mirzapur, two poles and a cross bar are fixed up at the entrance of the village with the same object. The charm is rendered more powerful if a plough beam is sunk in the ground close by.

The custom of silent tending of cattle has been already referred to. At the cattle festival in Rájputáná, in the evening the cow is worshipped, the herd having been previously tended. "From this ceremony no rank is excepted; on the preceding day dedicated to Krishna, prince and peasant all become pastoral attendants of the cow in the form of Prithiví or the Earth."[1] In some places the flowers or other ornaments of the cattle which they lose in their wild flight are eagerly picked up and treated as relics bringing good fortune. The ceremony in its various forms is plainly only a rustic expression of the affection and respect paid by the peasant to his cattle as essential to agriculture: and the same idea is seen in the blessing of cattle which prevails in Italy.[2] This also is probably the origin of the observance described by Aubrey when "in Somersetshire, where they wassaile (which is on, I think, Twelfe Eve) the ploughmen have their Twelfe cake, and they go into the ox-house to the cattle, and drink to the ox with the crumpled horne that treads out the corne."[3]

The sleep of Vishnu

According to the rural belief, Vishnu sleeps for four months in the year, from the 11th of the bright half of the month Asárh, the Deosoní Ekádashí, "the reposing of the god," until the 11th of the bright half of Kártik, the Deothán or "god's awakening." On the day he retires to rest women mark their houses with lines of cow-dung, fast during the day, and eat sweetmeats in the evening. During the four months of the god's rest it is considered unlucky to marry, repair the thatch of a hut, or make the house cots. His rising at the Deothán marks

[1] Tod, *Annals*, I, 631.
[2] Gubernatis, *Zoological Mythology*, I, 51.
[3] *Remaines*, 40: and see Brand, *Observations*, 17.

the commencement of the sugarcane harvest, when the cane-mill is marked with red lead and lamps are lighted upon it. The owner of the crop then does worship in his field, and breaks off some stalks of sugarcane which he puts upon the boundary. He distributes five canes each to the village Bráhman, blacksmith, carpenter, washerman, and water-carrier, and takes five home. Then, on a wooden board about one and a half feet long, two figures of Vishnu and his wife, Párvatí, are drawn with butter and cow-dung. On the board are placed some cotton, lentils, water-nuts, and sweets: a fire sacrifice is offered, and the five canes are placed round the board and tied together at the top. The Sálagráma, or stone emblematical of Vishnu is lifted up, and all sing a rude melody, calling on the god to wake and join the assembly. "Then all move reverently round the emblems, the tops of the canes are broken off and hung on the roof till the Holí, when they are burnt. When the worship has been duly performed and the officiating Bráhman has declared that the fortunate moment has arrived, the cutting may commence. The whole village is a scene of festivity, and dancing and singing go on frantically. Till this day no Hindu will eat or touch the crop. They believe that even jackals will not eat the cane till then. The real fact is that till then the juice has not properly come up, and the cane is not worth eating. On the first day the cane is cut the owner eats none of it: it would bring him bad luck."[1]

Ceremonies to avert blight, etc.

There are various ceremonies intended to save certain crops from the ravages of blight and insects. Blight is very generally attributed to the constant measurement of the soil which goes on during settlement operations, or to the irreligious custom of eating beef, or to a demon of the east wind, who can be appeased by prayers and ceremonies.[2] When sugarcane germinates, the owner of the crop does worship on the next Saturday before noon. On one of the days of the Naurátri in the month of Kuár the cultivator himself or

---

[1] *Bareilly Settlement Report*, 93, *sq.*: Elliot, *Supplementary Glossary sv. Dithwan*; Crooke, *Rural Glossary*, Svv *Deosoni*, *Deothan*.
[2] Sleeman, *Rambles and Recollections*, I, 248, *sq.*: II, 250.

through his family priest burns a fire sacrifice in the field and offers prayer. In the month of Kártik he has a special ceremony to avert a particularly dangerous grub known as the *Súndí*. For this purpose he takes from his house butter, cakes, sweets and five or six lumps of dough pressed into the shape of a pear, with some clean water. He goes to the field, offers a fire sacrifice, and presents some of the cakes. He then buries one of the lumps of dough at each corner of his field and having eaten the rest of the cakes goes home happy.[1]

General Sleeman gives a case of a cowherd who saw in a vision that the water of the Biyás river should be taken up in pitchers and conveyed to the fields attached with blight, but that none of it should be allowed to fall on the ground in the way. On reaching the field a small hole should be made in the bottom of the pitcher so as to keep up a small, but steady stream, as the bearer carried it round the border of the field, so that the water might fall in a complete ring, except at a small opening which was to be kept dry; so that the demon of the blight might make his escape through it. Crowds of people came to fetch the water which was not supposed to have any particular virtue except that arising from this revelation.[2]

Locusts scaring.

Locusts are scared by shouting, lighting of fires, beating of brass pots, and in particular, by ringing the temple bell. In South Mirzapur when a flight comes the people catch one, decorate his head with a spot of red lead, salaam to him, and let him go, when he immediately departs with his companions.

Betel planting.

When cultivators in the North-West Provinces sow betel they cook rice-milk near the plants and offer it to the local god. They divide the offering, and a little coarse sugar is dedicated to Mahábír, the monkey god, which is taken home and divided among the children. This is known as the *Jeonár pújá*. In Bengal the Barnis or betel planters worship

[1] *Bareilly Settlement Report*, 93.
[2] *Rambles and Recollections*, 1, 263.

their patron goddess on the 4th of Baisákh with offerings of flowers, rice, sweetmeats, and sandal-wood paste. Some do the *Navamí pújá* without a Bráhman in honour of Ushas or Aurora on the 9th of the waning moon in Ásin. Plantains, rice, sugar, and sweetmeats are placed in the centre of the garden, from which the worshippers retire, but after a little return, and carrying out the offerings, distribute them to the village children. In Bikrampur Sungai a form of Bhagávatí is worshipped. They do not employ Bráhmans in the worship, because, they say, a Bráhman was the first cultivator of the betel. Through neglect the plant grew so high that he used his sacred thread to fasten up its tendrils, but as it still shot up faster than he could supply thread, its charge was given to a Káyasth or writer. Hence it is that a Bráhman cannot enter a betel garden without defilement.[1] All over Northern India the betel is regarded as being very susceptible to demoniacal influence, and a woman or a person in a condition of ceremonial pollution is excluded from the nursery.

All these customs are rather like the English rule of the young men and girls walking round the corn to bless it on Palm Sunday, an observance which Aubrey drily remarks in his time "gave many a conception."[2]

Sugarcane sowing.

When sugarcane is being planted the sower is decorated with silver ornaments, a necklace, flowers, and a red mark is made on his forehead. It is considered a favourable omen if a man on horseback come into the field while work is going on. After the sowing is completed, all the men employed come home to the farmer's house and have a good dinner.[3] All surplus seed is carefully destroyed by fire, as it is believed that the plants grown from it would be worthless and produce only flowers and seed. In the Panjáb on the first day of sowing sweetened rice is brought to the field, the women smear the outside of the vessel with it, and it is then distributed to the labourers. Next morning a woman puts on a necklace and walks round

---

[1] Risley, *Tribes and Castes*, I, 72.
[2] *Remaines*, 9.
[3] *Bareilly Settlement Report*, 93.

the field, winding thread on to a spindle. These forms of sympathetic magic are now falling into disuse.[1]

Cotton planting.

When the cotton has sprung up the owner of the field goes there on Sunday forenoon with some butter, sweetmeats, and cakes. He burns a fire sacrifice, offers up some of the food, and eats the remainder in silence. Here we have another instance of the taboo against speaking, which is so common in these rural ceremonies.[2] When the cotton comes into flower, some parched rice is taken into the field on a Wednesday or Friday: some is thrown broadcast over the plants, and the rest given to children—the object assigned being that the bolls may swell, as the rice does when parched. Here we have another excellent example of symbolic or sympathetic magic. When the cotton is ripe and ready for picking, the women pickers go to the north or east quarters of the field with parched rice and sweetmeats. These directions are of course selected with reference to the Himálaya, the home of the gods, and the rising sun. They pick two or three large pods, and then sit down and pull out the cotton in as long a string as possible, without breaking it. They hang these threads on the largest cotton plant in the field round which they sit, and fill their mouths as full as possible with the parched rice, which they blow out again as far as possible in every direction, the idea being of course the same as in the ceremony when the plant flowers. A fire offering is made and picking commences. The custom in Karnál is very similar. When the pods open and the cotton is ready for picking, the women go round the field eating rice-milk, the first mouthful of which they spit on the field towards the west. The first cotton picked is exchanged for its weight in salt, which is prayed over and kept in the house till the picking is over.[3]

The last sheaf.

In Hoshangábád when the reaping is nearly over, a small patch of corn is left standing in the last field, and the reapers rest a little. Then they rush at

[1] *Karnál Settlement Report*, 151.
[2] *Bareilly Settlement Report*, 93, and compare Tylor, *Primitive Culture*, II, 40: Lady Wilde, *Legends*, 199.
[3] *Bareilly Settlement Report*, 87, *sq.*: *Karnál Settlement Report*, 183.

this piece, tear it up and cast it into the air, shouting victory to their deities—Omkár Maháráj, Jhamají, Ramjídás, or other local gods, according to their persuasions. A sheaf is made of this corn, which is tied to a bamboo, stuck up on the last harvest cart, carried home in triumph, and fastened up in the threshing floor or to a tree or on the cattle shed, where its services are essential in averting the Evil eye. The same custom prevails in the Eastern districts of the North-Western Provinces. Sometimes a little patch in the corner of the field is left untilled as a refuge for the field spirit, sometimes it is sown and the corn reaped with a rush and shout and given to the Baiga as an offering to the local gods, or bestowed as above to a beggar. This is a most interesting analogue of a branch of European folklore which has been copiously illustrated by Mr. Fraser. It is the Devon custom of "Crying the neck." The last sheaf is the impersonation of the Corn Mother, and is worshipped accordingly. We have met already with the same idea in the reservation of small patches of the original forest for the accommodation of the spirits of the jungle.[1]

Other harvest observances.

The first pressing of the sugarcane is attended with special observances. When the work of pressing commences the first piece is distributed to friends and some is offered in the Western districts of the North-Western Provinces in the name of the Saint Shekh Faríd, who from this probably gains his name of Shakkarganj or "Treasury of sugar." The Santáls have a harvest home feast in December, at which the Jag Mánjhi or headman of the village entertains the people: the cattle are anointed with oil and daubed with vermilion, and a share of rice-beer is given to each animal.[2] Everywhere in treading out the grain the rule that the cattle move round the stake in the course of the sun is rigidly observed.

Ceremonies at winnowing.

Winnowing is a very serious and solemn operation, not lightly to be commenced without due consultation of the stars. In Hoshangábád, when the

[1] *Hoshangábád Settlement Report*, 78: Fraser, *Golden Bough*, I, 333, *sqq.*: Brand, *Observations*, 311: Henderson, *Folklore of the Northern Counties*, 87.
[2] Dalton, *Descriptive Ethnology*, 213.

village priest has fixed the favourable time, the cultivator, his whole family and his labourers, go to the threshing floor, taking with them the prescribed articles of worship, such as milk, butter, turmeric, boiled wheat, several kinds of grain, etc. The threshing floor stake is washed in the water, and these things are offered to it and to the heap of threshed grain. The boiled wheat is scattered about in the hope that the spirits (*Bhút*) may content themselves with it, and not take any of the harvested corn. Then the master stands on a three-legged stool, and taking five baskets from the threshed heap winnows them. After winnowing, the grain and chaff are collected again and measured: if the five baskets are turned out full, or anything remains over, it is a good omen. If they cannot fill the baskets, the place where they began winnowing is thought unlucky, and it is removed a few yards to another part of the threshing floor. The five basketsful are presented to a Bráhman or distributed in the village, not mixed with the rest of the harvest. Winnowing can then go on as convenient, but one precaution must be taken. As long as winnowing goes on, the basket must never be set down on its bottom, but always upside down. If this were not done the spirits would use the baskets to carry off the grain. The day's results are measured generally in the evening. This is done in perfect silence, the measurer sitting with his back to the unlucky quarter of the sky, and tying knots to keep count of the number of the baskets. The spirits rob the grain until it is measured, but when once it has been measured they are afraid of detection. [1]

In the Eastern Panjáb the clean grain is collected into a heap. Preparatory to measuring, the greatest care has to be observed in the preparation of this heap, or evil spirits will diminish the yield. One man sits facing the north and places two round balls of cow-dung on the ground. Between them he sticks in a plough coulter. This symbol is called Shaod or "the goddess of fertility." A piece of the *Ákh* tree or swallow-wort and some *dúb* grass are added, and they salute it, saying, "O Mother Shaod Give the increase, and make our bankers and rulers contented." The man then carefully

---

[1] *Settlement Report*, 78, *sq.*

hides the image of Shaod from all observers while he covers it up with grain, which the others throw over his head from behind. When it is well covered, they pile the grain upon it, but three times during the process the ceremony of *cháng* is performed. The man stands to the south of the heap and goes round it towards the west the first and third times, and the reverse way the second time. As he goes round he has the hand furthest from the heap full of grain, and in the other a winnowing fan with which he taps the heap. When the heap is finished they sprinkle it with Ganges water, salute it, and put a cloth over it till it is time to measure the grain. A line is then drawn on the ground all round the heap inside which none but the measurer must go. All these operations must be performed in profound silence.[1]

In Bareilly when the whole of the grain and chaff has been winnowed, all the dressed grain is collected into a heap. "The winnower with his basket in his right hand goes from the south towards the west, and then towards the north till he reaches the pole to which the treading out cattle have been fastened. He then returns the same way, goes to the east till he reaches the pole, and back again to the south: then he places his basket on the ground and utters some pious ejaculation. Then an iron sickle, a stick of the sacred *Kusa* grass and a bit of swallow-wort, with a cake of cow-dung in a cleft stick are placed on the heap, and four cakes of cow-dung at the four corners: and a line is traced round it with cow-dung. A fire offering is then made, and some butter and coarse sugar are offered as sacrifice. Water is next thrown round the piled grain and the remainder of the sugar distributed to those present."[2]

In the Etah district the owner of the field places to the north of the pile of grain a threshing floor rake, a bullock's muzzle, and a rope at a distance of three spans from the piled grain: and between these things and the pile he lays a little offering consisting of a few ears of grain, some leaves of the swallow-wort, and a few

[1] *Karnál Settlement Report*, 173.
[2] *Settlement Report*, 78.

flowers. These things are laid on a piece of cow-dung. He then covers the pile of grain with a cloth to protect it from thieving Bhúts, and puts in a basket three handfuls of grain as the perquisite of the village priest, who lights the Holí fire. Something is also laid by for the village beggars. Then he sprinkles a little grain on the cloth and fills a basket full of grain which he pours back over the pile. He then bows to the north, the home of the gods, and mutters a prayer: it is only on this occasion that he breaks the silence with which the whole ceremony is performed. The cloth is then removed and the worship is considered complete.

Measurement of grain.

All these precautions are based on principles which have been already discussed, and we find in them the familiar fetishes and demon scarers, of which we have already quoted instances—the iron implements, the sacred grasses and plants, water and milk, cow-dung, the winnowing fan, etc. All over Upper India a piece of cow-dung known as *barháwan,* "that which gives the increase" is laid on the piled grain and a sacred circle is made with fire or water round it. Silence, as we have already seen, is a special element in the worship. All this rests on the idea that until the grain is measured, vagrant Bhúts will steal or destroy it. This is something like the principle of travellers who keep a cowry or two in their purses so that thieves may not be able to divine the contents. So in a Talmudic legend we read "It is very difficult for devils to obtain money, because men are careful to keep it locked or tied up: and we have no power to take anything that is measured or counted: we are permitted to take only what is free and common."[1] In the Eastern Panjáb grain must not be measured on the day of the new or full moon, and Saturday is a bad day for it. It must be begun at dawn, or midday, or sunset, or midnight when the Bhúts are otherwise engaged. Four men go inside the enclosure line with a wooden measuring vessel, and no one must come near them till they have finished. They sit facing the north and spread a cloth on the ground. One fills the measure from the heap with the winnowing

[1] Conway, *Demonology,* II. 117.

fan, another empties it on the cloth, and the two others carry off the full cloth and empty it out, substituting an empty one for it. The man who has the measure puts down for each measure filled a small heap of corn by which the account is kept. Perfect silence must be observed until the whole operation is finished, and especially all counting aloud of the number of measures must be avoided. But when once the grain is measured it is safe from the Evil eye and the people are at liberty to quarrel for it. [1]

Secresy in rural ceremonies.

The element of secresy in these harvest ceremonies can be further illustrated from the customs of the Gaiti Gonds. [2] Their great festival is held after the in-gathering of the rice harvest, when they proceed to a dense part of the jungle, which no woman is permitted to enter and where, to represent the great god, a copper coin has been hung up, enclosed in a joint of bamboo. Arriving at the spot, they take down the copper god in his case, and selecting a small area about a foot square, they lay on it the copper coin, before which they arrange as many small heaps of uncooked rice as there are deities worshipped by them. The chickens brought for sacrifice are loosed and permitted to feed on the rice: after which they are killed and their blood sprinkled between the copper coin and the rice. Goats are also offered and their blood presented in the same manner. Until prohibited by the Hindus, sacrifices of cows were also common. On the blood country spirits are poured as a libation to their deities. The copper coin is now lifted, replaced in its bamboo case, which is shut up with leaves, wrapped up in grass, and returned to its place in the tree to remain there till it is required on the following year.

The Holí: its origin

The most famous and interesting of the village festivals is the Holí, which is held in the early spring at the full moon of *Phálgun*. One account of its origin describes it as founded in honour of a female demon or Rákshasí called Dundhás "she who would otherwise destroy many." Another account connects the observance with the well-known

[1] *Karnál Settlement Report*, 174.
[2] Hislop, *Papers*, 22.

legend of Hiranya Kasipu and his son Prahláda. Harnákas, as the father is called in the modern version of the story, was an ascetic who claimed that the devotion of the world was to be paid to him alone. His son Prahláda became a devotee of Vishnu, and performed various miracles such as saving a cat and her kittens out of a blazing potter's kiln. His father was enraged at what he considered his son's apostacy, and with the help of his sister Holí or Holiká commenced to torture Prahláda. Many attempts on his life failed, and finally Vishnu himself entered a pillar of hot iron, which had been prepared for the destruction of Prahláda, and tore Harnákas to pieces. Finally, Holí tried to burn herself and Prahláda together, but the fire left him unscathed and she was consumed. The fire is now supposed to be burned in commemoration of this tragedy. Another legend identifies Holí with the witch Pútaná, who attempted to destroy the infant Krishna by giving him her poisoned nipples to suck.[1]

Propitiation of sunshine.

There seems to be little doubt that the custom of burning the Holí fire rests on the same basis as similar observances in Europe. The whole subject has recently been copiously illustrated by Mr. J. G. Frazer.[2] His conclusion is that "they are sun charms or magical ceremonies intended to ensure a proper supply of sunshine for men, animals and plants. We have seen that savages resort to charms for making sunshine, and we need not wonder that primitive man in Europe has done the same. Indeed, considering the cold and cloudy climate of Europe during a considerable portion of the year, it is natural that sun charms should have played a much more prominent part among the superstitious practices of European peoples than among those of savages who live near the equator. This view of the festival in question is supported by various considerations drawn partly from the rites themselves, partly from the influences they are

[1] Buchanan, *Eastern India*, II, 480: Wilson, *Essays*, II, 233: Atkinson, *Himalyan Gazetteer*, II, 867, *sq*: *Panjáb Notes and Queries*, III, 127: Growse, *Mathura*, 56.

[2] *Golden Bough*, II, 246, *sqq*., also see Conway, *Demonology*, I, 65, *sqq*.: Henderson, *Folklore of the Northern Counties*, 72, *sqq*.: Gregor, *Folklore of N.-E. Scotland*, 167 *sq*: Brand, *Observations*, 165, *sqq*.

believed to exert on the weather and on vegetation. For example, the custom of rolling a burning wheel down a hill side, which is often observed on these occasions, seems a very natural imitation of the sun's course in the sky, and the imitation is particularly appropriate on midsummer day, when the sun's annual declension begins. Not less graphic is the imitation of his apparent revolution by swinging a burning tar-barrel round a pole. The custom of throwing blazing discs, shaped like suns, into the air, is probably also a piece of imitative magic. In these, as in so many cases, the magic force is supposed to take effect through mimicry or sympathy."[1]

It is true that the climatic conditions of Northern India do not, as a rule, necessitate the use of incantations to produce sunshine. But it must be remembered that the native of the country does not look on the fierceness of the summer sun with the same dread as is felt by Europeans. It is to them about the pleasantest and healthiest season of the year, and people who are sometimes underfed and nearly always insufficiently dressed have more reason to fear the chills of December and January than the warmth of May and June. It is also usually recognized in popular belief that seasonable and sufficient rainfall depends on a due supply of sunshine.

The Holí observances.

The Holí, while generally observed in Upper India, is performed with special care by the cowherd classes of what is known as the land of Braj, and it is here that we meet with curious incidents which are undoubtedly survivals of the most primitive usages. The ceremonies in vogue at Mathura have been made carefully recorded by Mr. Growse.[2] He notes "the cheeriness of the holiday-makers as they throng the narrow, winding streets on their way to and from the central square of the town of Barsána, where they break into groups of bright and ever varying combinations of colour, with the buffooneries of the village clowns, and the grotesque dances of the lusty swains, who with castinets in hand, caricature in their movements the

[1] *Golden Bough*, II, 268.
[2] *Mathura*, 84, *sq.*

conventional graces of the Indian ballet girl. Then follows a mock fight between the men of the adjoining village of Nandgánw and the women of Barsána. The women have their mantles drawn down over their faces, and are armed with long, heavy bamboos with which they deal their opponents many shrewd blows on the head and shoulders. The latter defend themselves as best they can with round leather shields and staghorns as they dodge in and out amongst the crowd, and now and again have their flight cut off, and are driven back upon the crowd of excited viragos. Many laughable incidents occur. Not unfrequently blood is drawn; but an accident of this kind is regarded rather as an omen of good fortune, and has never been known to give rise to any ill-feeling. Whenever the fury of their female assailants appears to be subsiding, it is again excited by the men shouting at them snatches of ribald rhymes."

The lighting of the Holi fire.

Next day the Holí fire is lit. By immemorial custom, the boys are allowed to appropriate fuel of any kind for the fire, the wood-work of deserted houses, fences, and the like, and the owner never dares to complain. Mr. Growse goes on to describe how a large bonfire had been stacked between the pond and temple of Prahláda (who as we have already seen is connected with the legend) inside which the local village priest, the Kherapat or Panda, who was to take the chief part in the performances of the day, was sitting, telling his beads. At 6 p.m. the pile was lit, and being composed of the most inflammable materials, at once burnt into a tremendous blaze. The lads of the village kept running close round it, jumping and dancing, and brandishing their bludgeons, while the Panda went round and dipped in the pond, and then with his dripping turban and loin-cloth on, ran back and made a feint of passing through the fire. In reality he only jumped over the outermost verge of the smouldering ashes, and then dashed into his cell again, much to the dissatisfaction of the spectators, who say that the former incumbent used to do it much more thoroughly. If on the next recurrence of the festival, the Panda shows himself equally timid, the village proprietors threaten to eject him as an impostor from the land which he holds rent free, simply on the score of his being fire-proof.

The throwing of the powder.

Next followed a series of performances characterised by rude horse-play and ribald singing. Next day comes the throwing of the powder. "Handfuls of red powder mixed with glistening talc were thrown about, up to the balconies above and down on the heads of the people below: and seen through this atmosphere of coloured cloud, the frantic gestures of the throng, their white clothes and faces all stained with red and yellow patches and the great timbrels with bunches of peacock's feathers, artificial flowers and tinsel stars stuck in their rims, borne above the players' heads, and now and then tossed up in the air, combined to form a curious and picturesque spectacle." Then followed another mock fight between men and women, conducted with perfect good humour on both sides, and when it was all over many of the spectators ran into the arena, and rolled over and over in the dust, or streaked themselves with it on the forehead, taking it as the dust hallowed by the feet of Krishna and the Gopis.

The Holí at Márwár.

Colonel Tod gives an interesting account of the festival as performed in Márwár. He describes the people as lighting large fires into which various substances, as well as the common powder, were thrown; and around which groups of children dance and scream in the streets, "like so many infernals; until three hours after sunrise of the new moon of the month of Chait, these orgies are continued with increased vigour: when the natives bathe, change their garments, worship and return to the ranks of sober citizens, and princes and chiefs receive gifts from their domestics."[1] The belief in the efficacy of the Holí fire in preventing blight, and in the ashes as a cure for disease has been already noticed.

Basis of the Holí ceremony.

We have seen that the primary basis of these ceremonies is probably the propitiation of the sunshine. But other ideas have probably been combined in

---

[1] *Annals*, I. 599, *sq.*

the present form of the observance. We seem to reach a more primitive cultus in Nepál, where a wooden post adorned with flags is erected in front of the palace and this is burned at night, representing the burning of the body of the old year.[1] So among the Dravidian hill tribes of Mirzapur, they do not perform the Holí ceremony like their Hindu neighbours: but on the same date the Baiga burns a stake—a ceremony which is known as *Sambat jalána*, or "the burning of the old year." From this date the new year begins. This combined with the fact that among Hindus, the person who lights the fire is not a Bráhman, but a Kherapat or local village priest, often a man selected from one of the lower castes, seems to show that in all probability the ceremony may be of non-Aryan origin: and that the legends connecting it with Prahláda and Krishna are of subsequent growth. The fire would be then possibly an emblematical representation of the burning of the old year, and the revival through the purifying influence of fire of the new year, more propitious than the last to the families, cattle, and crops of the worshippers. The observance seems also to include certain ceremonies intended to scare evil spirits. The compulsory entry of the local priest into the fire cannot well be anything but a modified survival of human sacrifice performed with the same object; and the dancing, singing, waving of flags, screaming and throwing of red powder, a colour as we have seen supposed to be obnoxious to evil spirits, are probably based on the same train of ideas. Finally comes the indecency which is a distinct element in the observance. There seems reason to believe that in the worship of certain deities in spring, promiscuous intercourse was regarded as a necessary part of the rite.[2] We have already noticed the practice of indecency as a rain charm: and it seems at least a plausible hypothesis that the unchecked profligacy which prevails among the Hindus at the Holi in Spring and the Kajalí in Autumn may be intended as a mode of repelling the evil influence of spirits at the two annual harvests. The same idea also probably underlies the licentious observance of the Karama among the Dravidian races. The same theory explains similar usages

[1] Wright, *History*, 41.
[2] *Folklore*, II, 178: and for indecency in Egypt see Herodotus, II, 58.

in Europe, such as the Lupercalia, Festum Stultorum, Matronalia Festa, Liberalia, and our All Fools' Day, where the indecent part of the performance has disappeared under the influence of a purer faith and a higher morality, and a little kindly merriment is its only survival. We have already seen that the custom of a mock fight is regarded as a rain charm, and this possibly explains its connection with the Holí.

Saturnalia of the Dravidians.

Some of the Dravidian races enjoy the Saturnalia in other forms. The Gond women have the curious festival known as the *Gurtutná* or "breaking of sugar." "A stout pole about twelve or fifteen feet high is set up, and a lump of course sugar with a rupee in it, placed on the top: round it the Gond women take their stand, each with a little green tamarind rod in her hands. The men collect outside, and each has a kind of shield made of two parallel sticks joined by a cross piece, held in the hand to protect themselves from the blows. They make a rush together, and one of them swarms up the pole; the women all the time plying these rods vigorously: and it is no child's play, as the men's backs attest next day. When the man gets to the top, he takes the piece of sugar, and slips down, and gets off as rapidly as he can This is done five or six times over with the greatest good humour, and generally ends with an attack of the women *en masse* upon the men. It is the regular Saturnalia for the women, who lose all respect even for a Settlement Officer; and on one occasion when he was looking on, he only escaped by the most abject submission and presentation of rupees."[1] The Bhíls of Gujrat plant a small tree or branch firmly in the ground. The women stand near it, and the men outside. One man rushing in tries to uproot the tree, and the men and women fall on him and beat him so soundly that he has to retire. He is succeeded by another, who is belaboured in the same way, and this goes on until one man succeeds in bearing off the tree, but seldom without a load of blows which cripples him for days.[2]

---

[1] *Hoshangábád Settlement Report*, 126, *sq.*
[2] *Bombay Gazetteer*, VI, 29.

The Desaulí of the Hos.

The Hos of Chutia Nágpur have a similar festival—the Desaulí held in January, "when the granaries are full of grain, and the people, to use their own expression, 'full of devilry.' They have a strange notion that at this period men and women are so overcharged with vicious propensities that it is absolutely necessary for the safety of the person to let off steam, by allowing for the time full vent to the passions. The festival, therefore, becomes a Saturnalia, during which servants forget their duty to their masters, children their reverence for their parents, men their respect for women, and women all notions of modesty, gentleness, and delicacy : they become raging Bacchantes. It opens with a sacrifice to Desaulí of three fowls. A cock and two hens, one of which must be black, and offered with some flowers of the *Palása* tree (*Butea frondosa*), bread made from rice flour, and sesamum seeds. The sacrifice and offering are made by the village priest, if there be one, or if not by any elder of the village, who possesses the necessary legendary lore: and he prays that during the year they are going to enter on, they and their children may be preserved from all misfortune and sickness and that they may have seasonable rain and good crops. Prayer is also made in some places for the souls of the departed. At this period an evil spirit is supposed to infest the locality, and to get rid of it, men, women, and children go in procession round and through every part of the village with sticks in their hands, as if beating for game, singing a wild chant and vociferating loudly till they feel assured that the bad spirit must have fled, and they make noise enough to frighten a legion. These religious ceremonies over, the people give themselves up to feasting, drinking immoderately of rice beer, till they are in a state of wild ebriety most suitable for the purpose of letting off steam."[1]

With these survivals of perhaps the most primitive observances of the races of Northern India, we may close this survey of their religion and folklore. To use Dr. Tylor's words in speaking of savage religions generally, "Far from its beliefs and practices

[1] Dalton, *Descriptive Ethnology*, 196, *sq.*

being a rubbish heap of miscellaneous folly, they are consistent and logical in so high a degree as to begin as soon as even roughly classified to display the principles of their formation and development: and these principles prove to be essentially rational, though working in a mental condition of intense and inveterate ignorance."[1]

[1] *Primitive Culture*, I, 22, *sq.*

BIBLIOGRAPHY.

Academy The, London, v. d.

Ain-i-Akbari. Translation by Professor Blockmann : Calcutta, v. d.

Asiatic Quarterly Review. London, v. d.

Asiatic Researches: Calcutta, v. d.

Athenœum. The, London, v. d.

Atkinson (E. T.) *Himalayan Gazetteer,* 2 vols. : Allahabad, 1882—84.

Aubrey (J.) *Remaines of Gentilisme and Judaisme,* edited by J. Britten : Folklore Society, London, 1881.

Ball (V.) *Jungle Life in India :* London, 1880.

Barth (A.) *Religions of India :* London, 1882.

Beal (S.) *Travels of Fah Hian and Sungyun :* London, 1869.

Benjamin (S. G. W.) *Persia and the Persians :* London, 1887.

Bernier (F.) *Travels in the Moghul Empire,* translated by Irving Birch, 2 vols. : London, 1826.

Bholanath Chunder. *Travels of a Hindu,* edited by J T Wheeler, 2 vols. : London, 1869.

Black (G. B.) *Folk Medicine :* Folklore Society, London, 1883.

Brand (J.) *Observations on Popular Antiquities* : London, 1877.

Briggs (Lt.-Col. J.) *History of the Rise and Fall of the Muhammadan Power in India, till the year* 1612, by Muhammad Qásim Farishta, 4 vols.: London, 1829.

Buchanan (F. H.) *Eastern India,* 3 vols. : London, 1833.

Burton (R.) *Anatomy of Melancholy :* London, 1883.

Burton (Sir R.) *Narrative of Pilgrimage to El Medinah and Mecca,* 3 vols.: London, 1855.

Calcutta Review : Calcutta, v. d.

Campbell (Major-Genl. J.) *A Personal Narrative of thirteen years' service among the wild tribes of Khondistán :* London, 1864.

Campbell (J. S.) *Notes on the Spirit Basis of Belief and Custom :* Bombay, 1885.

Carnegy (P.) *Notes on the Races, Tribes and Castes inhabiting the Province of Oudh :* Lucknow, 1868.

Chambers (R.) *Book of Days,* 2 vols. : London, v. d.

Chevers (Dr. N.) *A Manual of Medical Jurisprudence for India :* Calcutta, 1870.

Colebrooke (H. P.) *Miscellaneous Essays :* London, 1837.

Contemporary Review. The, London, v. d.

Conway (M. D.) *Demonology and Devil lore :* London, 1879.

Cooper (W. M.) *Flagellation and the Flagellants :* London, 1887

Cox (Sir. G. W.) *Introduction to the Science of Comparative Mythology and Folklore :* London, 1881.

Cox (**Sir G. W.**) *Mythology of the Aryan Nations*, 2 vols.: London, 1878.

Crooke (**W.**) *A Rural and Agricultural Glossary of the North-Western Provinces and Oudh*: Calcutta, 1888.

Cunningham (**Major-Genl. A.**) *Archæological Survey Reports*: Calcutta, v. D.

Cunningham (**Major-Genl. A.**) *The Bhilsa Topes; a Buddhist Monument in Central India*: London, 1854.

Dabistan. Translation by D. Shea and A. Troyer: Paris, 1843.

Dalton (**Col. E. T.**) *Descriptive Ethnology of India*: Calcutta, 1872.

Dey (**Lal Behari.**) *Folktales of Bengal*: London, 1879.

,, *Govinda Samanta*: London, 1874.

De Gubernatis (**A.**) *Zoological Mythology, or the Legends of Animals*, 2 vols.: London, 1872.

Dowson (**Prof. J.**) *A Classical Dictionary of Hindu Mythology and Religion, Biography, History and Literature*: London, 1879.

Duncker (**Max**) *The History of Antiquity*. Translation by E. Abbott, 5 vols.: London, 1877—81.

Dutt (**R. C**) *History of Civilisation in Ancient India*, 3 vols.: Calcutta, 1889.

Elliot (**Sir H. M.**) *Supplement to the Glossary of Indian terms*: Roorkee, 1860.

,, *History of India, as told by its own historians*, edited by Professor J. Dowson, 8 vols.: London 1867—77.

Elliott (**Sir C. A.**) *Settlement Report of Hoshangabad*: Allahabad, 1867.

Encyclopædia Britannica, 9th edition: Edinburgh, 1875.

Ewald (**H.**) *Antiquities of Israel*. Translation by H. Solly: London, 1876.

Ewald (**H.**) *The History of Israelt*. Translation by R. Martineau, 4th edition: London, 1883.

Farrer (**J. A.**) *Primitive Manners and Customs*: London, 1879.

Fausboll (**V.**) *The Buddhist Jatakas*: Copenhagen, 1861.

Ferguson (**J.**) *History of Indian Architecture*: London, 1876.

,, *Tree and Serpent Worship*: London, 1868.

Ferrier (**J. P.**) *Caravan Journeys and Wanderings in Persia, Afghanistan, Turkistan and Beluchistan*: London, 1856.

Folklore: London, v. D.

Folklore Record: Folklore Society, London, v. D.

Forbes (**H. O.**) *A Naturalist's Wanderings in the Eastern Archepelago*: London, 1885.

Forbes (**J.**) *Oriental Memoirs*: London, 1813.

Forlong (**I. G. R.**) *Rivers of Life*, 2 vols.: London, 1883.

Forsyth (**Capt. J.**) *Highlands of Central India*, 2nd edition: London, 1889.

Fortnightly Review: London, v. D.

Frazer (I. G.) *The Golden Bough*, 2 vols. : London, 1890. *Totemism*:
„ London, 1887.
Frere (Miss M.) *Old Deccan Days*: London, 1870.
Gazetteer of Berar. Bombay: 1870.
„ *Bombay* „ v. D.
„ *Central Provinces.* Nagpur: 1870.
„ *Himalayan Districts of the North-Western Provinces*, by E. T. Atkinson, 2 vols.: Allahabad, 1882—84.
„ *Oudh*, 3 vols. : Allahabad, 1870.
„ *Rajputana*, 3 vols. : Calcutta, v. D.
Goldziher (J.) *Mythology among the Hebrews.* Translation by R. Martineau: London, 1877.
Gordon-Cumming (Miss C. F.) *From the Hebrides to the Himalayas*, 2 vols. : London, 1876.
Gregor (Revd. W.) *Notes on the Folklore of the North-East of Scotland*: Folklore Society, London, 1881.
Grierson (G.) *Bihár Peasant Life*: Calcutta, 1885.
Grimm, *Teutonic Mythology.* Translation by J. S. Stallybrass, 4 vols. : London, 1880—88.
„ *Household Tales.* Translated by Margaret Hunt: London, 1884.
Grote (G.) *History of Greece*, 12 vols. : London, 1869.
Growse, *Mathura*, a District Memoir : Allahabad, 1880.
„ *Rámáyana of Tulsi Dás*: 1877—80.
Gunthorpe (Major E. J.) *Notes on the Criminal Tribes of Bombay, Berár and the Central Provinces*: Bombay, 1882.
Hardy (R. S.) *Manual of Buddhism* : London, 1880.
Hartland (E. S.) *Science of Fairy Tales*: London, 1891.
Haug (M.) *Aitareya Bráhmanam of the Rigveda*, 2 vols. Bombay, 1863.
Hearn (W. E.) *The Aryan Household*: London, 1879.
Heber (Bishop R.) *Narrative of a Journey through the Upper Provinces of India*, 2 vols. : London, 1861.
Henderson (W.) *Notes on the Folklore of the Northern Counties of England and the Border*: Folklore Society, London, 1879.
Herklots (G. A.) *Qánún-i-Islám*: Madras, 1863.
Herodotus. Translated by G. Rawlinson, 4 vols. : 3rd edition, 1875.
Hislop (Revd. S.) *Papers relating to the Aboriginal Tribes of the Central Provinces*: *Nagpur*, 1866.
Hughes (T. P.) *Dictionary of Islám*: London, 1885.
Ibbetson (D. C. J.) *Panjab Ethnography*: Calcutta, 1883.
Indian Antiquary. The, Bombay, v. D.
Jacobs (J.) *Celtic Fairy Tales*: London.
„ *English Fairy Tales*: London, 1890.
„ *Indian Fairy Tales*: London, 1891.

Jones (W.) *Finger Ring Lore*: London, 1877.
Lang (A.) *Custom and Myth*: London, 1885.
" *Myth, Ritual and Religion*: London, 1887.
Letourneau (C.) *Sociology based on Ethnography*: London, 1881.
Lubbock (Sir J.) *Origin of Civilisation and Primitive Condition of man*: London, 1882.
Lyall (Sir A. C.) *Asiatic Studies*: London, 1882.
Malcolm (Sir J.) *Memoir of Central India*, 2 vols.: London, 1823.
Manning (Mrs.) *Ancient and Mediæval India*, 2 vols.: London, 1869.
Manu, *Institutes of*. Translation by Sir W. Jones and G. C. Haughton: London, 1869.
Memoirs of the Anthropological Society of London, 3 vols.: London, 1865--70.
Mir Hasan Ali (Mrs.) *Observations on the Musalmans of India*, 2 vols.: London, 1832.
Moens (S. M.) *Bareilly Settlement Report*: Allahabad, 1874.
Muir (J.) *Original Sanskrit Texts*: 5 vols., London, 1868-70.
Muller (F. Max) *Chips from a German workshop*, 4 vols.: London, 1867.
Muller (F. Mah) *History of Ancient Sanskrit Literature*: London, 1859.
North Indian Notes and Queries: Allahabad, v. d.
O'Brien (E.) *Glossary of the Multáni language*: Lahore, 1881.
Oldfield (H. A.) *Sketches from Nepál*, 2 vols.: London, 1880.
Oldham (W.) *Memoirs of the Gházipur District*, 2 vols.: Allahabad, 1870—76.
Panjáb Notes and Queries, 4 vols.: Allahabad, 1883—87.
Proceedings Asiatic Society of Bengal: Calcutta, v. d.
" *Royal Asiatic Society*: London, v. d.
Rajendra (Lala Mitra) *Indo-Aryans*, 2 vols.: London and Calcutta, 1881.
Reid (J. R.) *Azamgarh Settlement Report*: Allahabad, 1881.
Risley (H. H.) *Tribes and castes of Bengal*, 2 vols.: Calcutta, 1891.
Robertson-Smith (W.) *Kinship and Marriage in early Arabia*: Cambridge, 1883.
Rousselet (L.) *India and its Native Princes*: London, 1890.
Rowney (H. B.) (Shoshee Chunder Dutt) *Wild Tribes of India*: London, 1882.
Schrader (O.) *Prehistoric Antiquities*: London, 1890.
Schlieman (H.) *Ilios*: London, 1880.
Scott (Sir W.) *Letters on Demonology and Witchcraft*: London, 1884.

Sherring (**M. A.**) *The sacred city of the Hindus*: London, 1868
" *Hindu tribes and castes*: Calcutta, 1872-81.
Sleeman (**Major-Genl. W. H.**) *Journey through the Kingdom of Oudh*, 2 vols.: London, 1858.
" " *Rambles and recollections of an Indian official*, 2 vols.: London, 1844.
Spencer (**H.**) *Principles of Sociology*, 3rd edition, 2 vols.: London, 1885.
Starcke (**C. N.**) *The Primitive Family*: London, 1889.
Stokes (**Miss M.**) *Indian Fairy Tales*: London, 1880.
Tawney. (**C. H.**) *Katha Sarit Sagara*: Calcutta, 1880.
Temple (**Major R. C.**) *Legends of the Panjab*: Bombay, v. d.
" " *Proper names of Panjabis*: Bombay, 1883.
" " *Wideawake stories*: Bombay, 1884.
Tennent (**Sir J. E.**) *Ceylon*, 2nd edition, 2 vols.: London, 1859.
Thomas (E.) *Chronicles of the Pathán Kings of Delhi*: London, 1871.
Thugs. *Illustrations of the History and Practices of the*, London, 1837.
Tod (**Lt.-Col. J.**) *Annals and Antiquities of Rajasthan*, 2 vols.: Calcutta, 1884.
Trumbull (**H. C.**) *The Blood Covenant*: London, 1887.
Tylor (**E. B.**) *Researches into the Early History of Mankind*: London, 1865.
" *Primitive culture*, 2nd edition, 2 vols.: London, 1873.
Wake (**C. S.**) *Serpent Worship*: London, 1888.
Ward (**W.**) *View of the History, Literature and Religion of the Hindus*: Madras, 1863.
Westropp (**H. M.**) *Primitive Symbolism*: London, 1885.
Wheeler (**J. T.**) *History of India*, 3 vols.: London, 1867—74.
Whitney (**W. D.**) *Oriental and Linguistic Studies*: New York, 1873.
Wilde (**Lady.**) *Ancient Legends, Mystic Charms and Superstitions of Ireland*: London, 1888.
Williams (**Sir M.**) *Sanskrit-English Dictionary*: Oxford, 1872.
Wilson (**Dr. J.**) *Indian Caste*, 2 vols.: Bombay, 1877.
" (Profesor H. H). *Works*, 12 vols.: London, 1862—71.
" *Vishnu Purána*: London, 1840.
" (J) *Karnál Settlement Report*: Lahore, 1886.
Wright (**D.**) *History of Nepál*: Cambridge, 1877.
Wright (**F. N.**) *Memorandum on the Agriculture of Cawnpore*: Allahabad, 1877.
Yule (**Col. H.**) *The book of Ser Marco Polo*, 2 vols.: London, 1871.

INDEX.

A.

C.

D.

E.

F.

G.

H.

K.

N.

O.

P.

Q.

R.